The Films of Laura Mulvey   Wollen

In memory of Peter Wollen (1938–2019)

The Films of Laura Mulvey and Peter Wollen

SCRIPTS, WORKING DOCUMENTS, INTERPRETATION

Edited by Oliver Fuke

THE BRITISH FILM INSTITUTE
Bloomsbury Publishing Plc
50 Bedford Square, London, WC1B 3DP, UK
1385 Broadway, New York, NY 10018, USA
29 Earlsfort Terrace, Dublin 2, Ireland

BLOOMSBURY is a trademark of Bloomsbury Publishing Plc

First published in Great Britain 2023 by Bloomsbury
on behalf of the
British Film Institute
21 Stephen Street, London W1T 1LN
www.bfi.org.uk

The BFI is the lead organisation for film in the UK and the distributor of Lottery funds for film. Our mission is to ensure that film is central to our cultural life, in particular by supporting and nurturing the next generation of filmmakers and audiences. We serve a public role which covers the cultural, creative and economic aspects of film in the UK.

ISBN: HB: 978-1-8390-2524-2
       PB: 978-1-8390-2525-9
       ePDF: 978-1-8390-2527-3
       eBook: 978-1-8390-2526-6

Design and layout by Ketchup/Tom Cabot
Printed and bound in India

To find out more about our authors and books visit www.bloomsbury.com and sign up for our newsletters.

Contents

Section 2 - Peter Wollen's *Friendship's Death*

Section 3 - Laura Mulvey's Later Collaborative Films

Section 4 - Outlines for Unmade Collaborative Films

Section 5 - Working Documents

Acknowledgements

Peter Wollen's 'Friendship's Death' was published in the Spring 1976 edition of Bananas. This text was reprinted in *Bananas*, ed. Emma Tennant (London and Tiptree: Blond & Briggs in association with Quartet, 1977), 146–158 and *Readings and Writings: Semiotic Counter-Strategies* (London: Verso, 1982), 140–152.

Laura Mulvey and Peter Wollen's '*Riddles of the Sphinx*: Script' was published in *Screen* 18(2) (Summer 1977), 61–78. This text was reprinted in *Screen Writings: Texts and Scripts from Independent Films*, ed. Scott MacDonald (Berkeley and Los Angeles, CA: University of California Press, 1995), 96–114.

Laura Mulvey and Peter Wollen's '*AMY!*' was published in *Framework* 14 (Spring 1981), 37–41.

Peter Wollen's '*Friendship's Death* (complete script)' was published in *Close Encounters: Film, Feminism, and Science Fiction*, ed. Constance Penley, Elisabeth Lyon, Lynn Spigel and Janet Bergstrom (Minneapolis, MN and Oxford: University of Minnesota Press, 1991), 237–281.

Laura Mulvey and Mark Lewis's 'SCRIPT: *Disgraced Monuments*' was published in *PIX* 2 (January 1997), 102–111.

There are many people we would like to thank for their involvement with this book. Most importantly, we thank the writers who have contributed essays to this volume: Nora M. Alter, Kodwo Eshun, Nicolas Helm-Grovas, Esther Leslie, Volker Pantenburg, Griselda Pollock, B. Ruby Rich and Sukhdev Sandhu.

We also thank Mark Lewis for permission to include the script for *Disgraced Monuments* (1994), and Lewis and Faysal Abdullah for permission to include the script for *23rd August 2008* (2013).

We thank everyone at BFI/Bloomsbury Publishing, particularly Rebecca Barden.

We thank Julian Rothenstein for designing the front cover.

We thank Wendy Russell, Claire Smith and Nigel Good at the British Film Institute, both for their help with research and for giving permission to reproduce material in this volume.

In many senses, this book developed from a film retrospective in 2016, *Laura Mulvey and Peter Wollen: Beyond the Scorched Earth of Counter-Cinema*, which started at the Whitechapel Gallery, London, and travelled to HOME, Manchester, and New

York University, New York. It has also been informed by an exhibition co-curated by Oliver Fuke and Nicolas Helm-Grovas, *Art at the Frontier of Film Theory*, first staged at Peltz Gallery, London, and reconfigured for Cooper Gallery, Dundee, and Camera Austria, Graz. We thank everyone involved in making those projects happen, including Peter Amoore, Matthew Barrington, Regina Barunke, Reinhard Braun, Sophia Hao, Angelika Maierhofer, Sukhdev Sandhu, Michael Temple and Jason Wood.

We would especially like to thank Gareth Evans for his crucial support and enthusiasm.

We would like to extend special thanks to Leslie Dick, Nicolas Helm-Grovas and Chad Wollen.

Oliver Fuke and Laura Mulvey

List of Contributors

Nora M. Alter is Professor of Film and Media Arts at Temple University in Philadelphia. She is author of several books including *Vietnam Protest Theatre: The Television War on Stage* (1996), *Sound Matters* (2004), *Chris Marker* (2006), *Essays on the Essay Film* (2017) and *The Essay Film after Fact and Fiction.* (2018). She has written on filmmaker/artists including John Akomfrah, Maria Eichhorn, Stan Douglas, Dan Eisenberg, Renée Green, Hans Haacke, Mathias Poledna, Martha Rosler, Hito Steyerl, and others. Future publications include a monograph on Harun Farocki.

Kodwo Eshun is Lecturer in Contemporary Art Theory at Goldsmiths, University of London, Professor of Visual Arts, Haut Ecole d'Art et Design, Genève and co-founder of The Otolith Group and author of *More Brilliant than the Sun: Adventures in Sonic Fiction* 2nd Ed. Verso, (2021) and *Dan Graham: Rock My Religion*, Afterall (2012) and co-editor of *Post Punk Then and Now* (2013), *The Militant Image: A Cine-Geography: Third Text* Vol 25 Issue 1 (2011), *Harun Farocki Against What? Against Whom* (2010) and *The Ghosts of Songs: The Film Art of the Black Audio Film Collective 1982–1998* (2007).

Oliver Fuke is an independent researcher. His projects include: *Laura Mulvey and Peter Wollen: Beyond the Scorched Earth of Counter-Cinema* (Whitechapel Gallery, London; HOME, Manchester and NYU, New York) and *Yvonne Rainer: The Choreography of Film* (Siobhan Davies Dance, London, 2018). With Nicolas Helm-Grovas, he has curated a series of exhibitions related to Mulvey and Wollen's work, at Peltz Gallery (London, 2019), Cooper Gallery (Dundee, 2020) and Camera Austria (Graz, forthcoming 2022). Fuke has also developed many exhibitions and projects with artists.

Nicolas Helm-Grovas is Lecturer in Film Studies Education at King's College London. He has written on topics such as semiotics and the history of the British journal *Afterimage* for publications including *Moving Image Review & Art Journal* and *Radical Philosophy*, and was Jerwood Arts Writer in Residence in 2018. With Oliver Fuke he has curated a series of exhibitions related to Mulvey and Wollen's work, at Peltz Gallery (London, 2019), Cooper Gallery (Dundee, 2020) and Camera Austria (Graz, forthcoming 2022).

Esther Leslie is Professor of Political Aesthetics at Birkbeck, University of London. Her books include various studies and translations of Walter Benjamin, as well as *Hollywood Flatlands: Animation, Critical Theory and the Avant Garde* (Verso, 2002); *Synthetic Worlds: Nature, Art and the Chemical Industry* (Reaktion, 2005); *Derelicts: Thought Worms from the Wreckage* (Unkant, 2014); *Liquid Crystals: The Science and Art of a Fluid Form* (Reaktion, 2016), *Deeper in the Pyramid* (with Melanie Jackson: Banner Repeater, 2018) and *The Inextinguishable* (with Melanie Jackson) (EVA, 2020).

Laura Mulvey is Professor of Film and Media Studies at Birkbeck College, University of London. She was Director of Birkbeck Institute for the Moving Image (BIMI) from 2012 to 2015. She is the author of *Visual and Other Pleasures* (1989); *Citizen Kane* (1992); *Fetishism and Curiosity* (1996); *Death 24x a Second: Stillness and the Moving Image* (2006); and *Afterimages: On Cinema, Women and Changing Times* (2019). She has co-edited *British Experimental Television* (2007); *Feminisms* (2015); and *Other Cinemas: Politics, Culture and British Experimental Film in the 1970s* (2017). Mulvey made six films in collaboration with Peter Wollen, including *Riddles of the Sphinx* (1977), and two films with artist and filmmaker Mark Lewis.

Volker Pantenburg is Professor of Film Studies at Freie Universität Berlin. He has published widely on essayistic film and video practices, experimental cinema, and contemporary moving image installations. Book publications in English include *Farocki/Godard. Film as Theory* (Amsterdam: Amsterdam UP 2015), *Cinematographic Objects. Things and Operations* (Berlin: August 2015, Editor) and *Screen Dynamics. Mapping the Borders of Cinema* (Vienna: Austrian Film Museum 2012; Co-Editor). In 2015, he co-founded the "Harun Farocki Institut," a platform for researching Farocki's visual and discursive practice and supporting new projects that engage with the past, present and future of image cultures.

Griselda Pollock is Professor of Social and Critical Histories of Art and Director of the Centre for Cultural Analysis, Theory and History at the University of Leeds. She has worked to produce feminist, postcolonial, queer and international art histories and cultural analyses, writing on the visual arts, film, and cultural theory. Her most recent publications include *Charlotte Salomon in the Theatre of Memory* (Yale 2018) and an edition of the papers of artist and theorist: Bracha L Ettinger, Matrixial Subjectivity, Aesthetics, Ethics edited and introduced by Griselda Pollock (Palgrave Macmillan, 2020). Forthcoming are *Monroe's Mov(i)es: Gender, Nation, Agency* and *Is Feminism a Bad Memory?*

B. Ruby Rich is the Editor of *Film Quarterly* and Professor Emerita of Film and Digital Media, University of California, Santa Cruz, where she taught in the Social Documentation MFA Program. She is the author of *New Queer Cinema: The Director's Cut* (2013) and *Chick Flicks: Theories and Memories of the Feminist Film Movement* (1998), both Duke UP. She has been active as a curator, film festival programmer and juror, journalist, radio and television commentator, prior program director for the NY State Council on the Arts, and a member of the Academy and SAG-AFTRA. She lives in San Francisco and Paris.

Sukhdev Sandhu writes for *Frieze, The Wire* and *Film Comment*. His books include *Night Haunts* and *Other Musics*. He directs the Colloquium for Unpopular Culture at New York University and runs the Texte und Töne publishing imprint.

Peter Wollen (1938–2019) was a filmmaker, film theorist, and screenwriter, whose crucial book, *Signs and Meaning in the Cinema* (1969), continues to challenge and provoke. His other books include: *Readings and Writings: Semiotic Counter-Strategies* (1982), *Raiding the Icebox: Reflections on Twentieth Century Culture* (1993), *Paris/Hollywood: Writings on Film* (2002), and *Paris/Manhattan: Writings on Art* (2004), all published by Verso, as well as the BFI Film Classic, *Singin' in the Rain* (1992). He taught film at a number of universities, including Brown University, New York University, and University of California, Los Angeles. With Mark Peploe, Wollen co-wrote the screenplay for Michelangelo Antonioni's *The Passenger* (1975) and subsequently wrote and directed six films in collaboration with Laura Mulvey. His final feature film was a solo project, *Friendship's Death* (1987), starring Tilda Swinton as an alien who lands in Amman, Jordan, during Black September, 1970. His expansive interests included organizing paradigm-shifting art exhibitions, such as *Frida Kahlo and Tina Modotti* (with Laura Mulvey, 1982) and *On the Passage of a Few People Through a Rather Brief Moment in Time: The Situationist International* (with Mark Francis, 1989). He also wrote on politics and culture for *New Left Review* and the *London Review of Books*, among many other journals.

Introduction

Oliver Fuke

During the course of an intense decade of critical and creative activity, the influential film theorists Laura Mulvey and Peter Wollen wrote and directed six films together: *Penthesilea: Queen of the Amazons* (1974), *Riddles of the Sphinx* (1977), *AMY!* (1980), *Crystal Gazing* (1982), *Frida Kahlo & Tina Modotti* (1983) and *The Bad Sister* (1983). After their collaboration came to an end, Mulvey and Wollen made films independently of one another. Wollen wrote and directed a solo feature film, *Friendship's Death* (1987), based on his short story published in *Bananas* in 1976. He also made documentaries on art and artists – including *Tatlin's Tower* (1983), *Full Cycle: The Art of Komar and Melamid* (1991) and *Images of Atlantis: The Photography of Milton Rogovin* (1992) – as well as various experimental works, such as *Peter Wollen Reads the U.S. Press* (1985). Mulvey co-directed *Disgraced Monuments* (1994) with Mark Lewis and *23rd August 2008* (2013) with Lewis and Faysal Abdullah. She also collaborated with Em Hedditch on one video work, *Visual Pleasure and Narrative Cinema* (2006), and made others independently.

The scripts for nine of the works mentioned above are collected in this volume – Mulvey and Wollen's six collaborative films, plus *Friendship's Death*, *Disgraced Monuments* and *23rd August 2008* – as well as essays by leading writers, which offer new interpretations of each film. The book also presents Wollen's short story *Friendship's Death*, the outlines for two unmade collaborative films – *Possible Worlds* (1978) and *Chess Fever* (1984) – and a number of working documents, including diagrams, drawings and early plans for films. This gathering of two filmmakers' scripts combined with a multi-authored collection of essays on their films places equal emphasis on the writing and interpretation of these works. The new essays in this volume have been written by some of the most critical and engaging writers on different forms of oppositional cinema and art, whose wide-ranging expertise and research illuminates the heterogeneous concerns and strategies in Mulvey and Wollen's collaborative and independent films. The volume has multiple aims: to make these fascinating scripts and outlines available, and thereby draw attention to their value as written texts; to encourage further study of Mulvey and Wollen's contribution to the theory and practice of avant-garde film; and to prompt further reflection on the script as a form within avant-garde film practice.

Section 1 focuses on Mulvey and Wollen's collaborative films, Section 2 on Wollen's *Friendship's Death* and Section 3 on two of Mulvey's later collaborations. In these sections, the script and essay for each film are presented one after the other. They are arranged chronologically, according to the date each film was completed. Wollen's short story is also included in Section 2. In Section 4, the two outlines for unmade films are presented.[1] Section 5 presents scans of working documents. In the second Introduction to this book, Laura Mulvey discusses the composition of her and Wollen's collaborative films and underscores how they were the result of a shared commitment to pursuing a project of feminist counter-cinema through rapidly changing economic and political conditions. In this introductory essay, I aim to give a sense of the documents gathered in this volume and the scriptwriting practices that produced them.

Scriptwriting

Peter Wollen's experiences of scriptwriting were various and reflect the wide range of his engagements with film at different moments in his life. First of all, in the early 1960s, he was commissioned by his cinephile friend Eugene Archer to write a script based on William Faulkner's novel *The Wild Palms* (1939).[2] They stayed in a chalet in Switzerland and, while the other guests went skiing, Wollen laboured away on the script. He then co-wrote a number of scripts with his friend Mark Peploe. The first, *The Other Side of the River*, was based on a novella by Heinrich von Kleist, *Michael Kohlhaas* (1810), which they transformed into a Western. Later, after Michelangelo Antonioni had asked Peploe to put in a proposal to Carlo Ponti, the influential film producer, to write and direct a film, Peploe and Wollen collaborated on other projects. The first was based on 'The Memorandum and Report on Victor de l'Aveyron' (1806) by the French physician Jean Itard. They began working on this script only to discover that François Truffaut was already shooting a film based on the same text. Following this false start, Peploe developed an original idea, partly informed by his experience as a documentary filmmaker and his dissatisfactions with it, and after some preliminary work he and Wollen went to Spain in early 1970 to develop a script around various locations, particularly in Barcelona. When another of Antonioni's projects was cancelled a few years later, Ponti suggested that he direct Peploe and Wollen's script instead. Thus, Antonioni came to direct *The Passenger*, starring Jack Nicholson and Maria Schneider, released in 1975.[3]

The main focus of this book, however, is Mulvey and Wollen's collaborative project, beginning in the early 1970s, of writing and directing feminist avant-garde films. By this time they had each made significant contributions as theorists; Mulvey had published important texts such as 'You Don't Know What is Happening Do You, Mr Jones?' (1973), and was working on her manifesto, 'Visual Pleasure and Narrative Cinema' (1975), while Wollen had published *Signs and Meaning in the Cinema* (1969/1972)[4] and numerous essays, including 'Counter Cinema: *Vent d'Est*' (1972).[5] According to Mulvey, the extension from theorising film to making films was a logical step. She cites two reasons for this move: first, the women's movement and the collective conviction that images of women were political and therefore sites of struggle and, second, the growth of radical film in the United Kingdom.[6]

The immediate cinematic influences for Mulvey and Wollen's early collaborations are numerous and from both avant-garde 'traditions' that Wollen outlined in his polemical 1975 essay 'The Two Avant-Gardes'. Hollis Frampton is probably the most significant influence from the first avant-garde, especially his work *Zorns Lemma* (1970), and Jean-Luc Godard and Jean-Marie Straub and Danièle Huillet from the second. In addition to North American and European avant-garde filmmakers, Mulvey and Wollen were also interested in the theory and practice of Third Cinema, a term first formulated by Fernando Solanas and Octavio Getino in 'Towards a Third Cinema: Notes and Experiences for the Development of a Cinema of Liberation in the Third World' (1969).[7][8] However, with the growth of women's liberation in the early 1970s, it was the experimental work of new women directors, including Jackie Raynal, Chantal Akerman and Yvonne Rainer, that was most influential on Mulvey and Wollen's project of constructing a feminist counter-cinema. If Raynal's film *Deux Fois* (1969) 'fell somewhere in between' the two avant-garde traditions Wollen schematically outlined, Akerman and Rainer showed how they could be combined, producing a third option.[9] More precisely, they showed how critical formal strategies could be combined with narrative and used to address complex issues thrown up by the women's movement, working on both form and content, signifier and signified. In 1974, Rainer, Akerman and Mulvey and Wollen all released key works (*Film About a Woman Who...*, *Je tu il elle* and *Penthesilea* respectively); Akerman's *Jeanne Dielman, 23 quai du Commerce, 1080 Bruxelles* and the Berwick Street Collective's *Nightcleaners* followed the year after. These crucial films make up a body of work that might be understood as a feminist avant-garde.

Mulvey and Wollen's collaborative films were produced at the intersection of different theoretical discourses – such as psychoanalysis, semiotics and Marxism – and were underpinned by feminist theory and activism.[10] The early 1970s witnessed the publication of many key feminist theoretical interventions, such as Claire Johnston's

'Women's Cinema as Counter-Cinema' (1973) and Juliet Mitchell's *Psychoanalysis and Feminism* (1974).[11] Griselda Pollock has suggested that this decade can be understood as an avant-garde moment, that differed from others because it was 'a specifically *feminist* avant-garde moment occurring at the singular conjunction, around 1970, of independent cinema and emergent video art practices, conceptual art, feminist engagement with contemporary psychoanalytical theories, and a renewed and politicized theorization of, and activism around, gender and sexuality.'[12] For Pollock, this conjunction is symbolised by Mary Kelly's *Post-Partum Document* (1973–1979), Julia Kristeva's 'Stabat Mater' (translated into English in 1977) and Mulvey and Wollen's *Riddles of the Sphinx* (1977). The feminist artists, theorists, films and artworks mentioned above suggest an intricate web of mutual influence, social connection and shared artistic and political projects.

As conventionally conceived, one of the many major differences between mainstream cinema and avant-garde cinema concerns the status of the script and synchronised sound. According to Scott MacDonald, the North American avant-garde's rejection of sound, most of all the spoken word and thus scripts, that had been determined at first by underlying economic constraints, mutated by the 1960s into both an ascetic refusal of one of mainstream cinema's central features and an insistence on the specificity of the medium. This position began to shift. 'As [16 mm] synch sound equipment became increasingly available to independents in the late sixties and the seventies, new avenues for critique opened up. Filmmakers could now develop screenplays for films that demonstrated the limitations of conventional industry screenplays from positions generically much closer to the problematic industry product than had been possible before. ... To choose silence when sound was economically feasible came to seem an implicit maintenance of the status quo, rather than a meaningful critique of it.'[13] The use of scripts and verbal language in avant-garde films – or in the 'New Talkies', as a small group of films came to be known – challenged their use in mainstream cinema and facilitated ideology critique more generally.[14] Mulvey and Wollen's collaborative filmmaking practice, in which they explored narrative and the relation of different types of writing to film, made an important contribution to these developments. As Wollen made clear in his article 'The Field of Language in Film' (1981), their project involved careful articulation, neither a refusal of verbal language, nor an uncritical reproduction of its use in dominant narrative cinema.[15] How might different instances of theoretical writing be extended into film? Could these instances be combined with narrative sections and dialogue, or even incorporated into them? How might experimental or constrained writing disrupt the conventional cinematic experience further? Mulvey and Wollen explored all these possibilities across their work in film.

Documents

In their first three collaborative films, Mulvey and Wollen worked with and across a number of different written documents, each of which might be understood as an individual script, or instance of scripting.[16] As a result, the project of publishing these texts here encountered archival and conceptual problems. Their first film, *Penthesilea*, illustrates the problem most vividly. In a 1974 interview, published in *Screen*, they described how it was written. For the second sequence, a performance-lecture delivered by Wollen to camera, he explained, 'the text was written and the camera movements were choreographed on paper for the camera man'.[17] Mulvey further explains that the script for the fourth sequence was compiled from letters that the feminist Jessie Ashley had published in the journal *Headquarters* and that the third and fifth were largely a matter of timing. However, she notes that in the final sequence, in which video monitors play back the previous four, a fifth video tape is introduced, adding footage of a 'carefully scripted' performance.[18] How, then, could and should the script for this film be reconstructed? There was no single document, *the* script, to turn to. The document presented in this volume, which has been carefully constructed in collaboration with Mulvey, has therefore been produced from the different texts and working documents referred to above – from the index cards that were written for Wollen's lecture, the camera movements that were written on a piece of paper for cameraperson Louis Castelli, the edited selection of Jessie Ashley's letters (on typed pages) and so on. It gathers these instances of scripting and supplements them with others: titles used in the film and brief descriptions at the start of each chapter, which, as with some of their other published scripts, describe how each of the film's five sequences function. The script for *Penthesilea* is thus a compilation of documents. The advantage of constructing the script in this way is that these material traces, despite their inherent fragility, clarify the precise nature of particular cinematic strategies used in the film, which are otherwise unclear.

Riddles and *AMY!* were also written across different working documents. Regardless of how these scripts were produced for previous publication (whether they were transcribed from film or reconstructed from working documents), they too combine different instances of scripting. In this volume, the script for *Riddles* is largely identical to its original publication in *Screen* (1977), except that some of the titles have been made consistent with the film and the names of various participants (in the film and credits) have been added. With *AMY!*, items omitted from the previous publication (small sections of voice-over, conversation in interview and song lyrics) in *Framework* (1980) have been reinserted here and some descriptions of camera movement have been amended. The script of *Frida Kahlo & Tina Modotti* has been constructed from an outline and typewritten pages of text. Meanwhile, Mulvey and

Wollen's fourth film, *Crystal Gazing*, required a slightly more conventional script. Nevertheless, the filmmaking process left openings for improvisation and experimentation, which were crucial for the film's overarching attempt to cross over with other independent cultural forms. The script that is in this volume includes these improvisational gaps, amends a few deviations from Mulvey and Wollen's written script, and adds references for some of the quotations. The script for Wollen's solo feature *Friendship's Death* was published in a book called *Close Encounters: Film, Feminism, and Science Fiction* (1991) and it is presented here largely unedited; however, a few key phrases, which were omitted, have been inserted.

The script that Mulvey and Wollen wrote for *The Bad Sister* was very different to their previous scripts – it was a much more unified, technical document. This was largely due to the different material conditions of the film's production. *Penthesilea* was a small-scale and self-funded project, outside industry constraints and without the requirements of funding bodies, using equipment and support made available by the university environment where it was made. These conditions allowed for the film to be written and produced in the informal way described above. Despite the fact that *Riddles*, *AMY!* and *Frida Kahlo & Tina Modotti* all received state funding (from the British Film Institute Production Board, Southern Arts and the Arts Council respectively), they were each written in a similarly informal way. *Crystal Gazing* received approximately £70,000 in funding from the BFI Production Board in association with Channel 4, and required a slightly more conventional script – though, as we have seen, an element of improvisation was maintained. *The Bad Sister*, however, was largely funded by Channel 4. Working in television involved a much bigger budget and required 'a more professionalized, less casual, way of working' that had an impact on all aspects of the film's production.[19] The script included in this volume has been derived from Mulvey and Wollen's original shooting script, which, in terms of *mise-en-scène*, costume and dialogue, is remarkably similar to the final film.

The text for Mulvey's first collaboration with Lewis, *Disgraced Monuments*, could not have been generated in the same way as the other films described above as this political documentary had no script, understood in either a conventional or an expanded sense. The document previously published in the journal *PIX* (1997) – which included the transcription of arranged interviews, the details of voice-over, titles, captions, commentary and music, together with a few visual descriptions – could therefore only have been produced from the documentary itself. That text has been slightly edited for this volume, so that the different examples of visual text (titles and captions) are clearly specified for the reader, and some spelling and transliteration have been amended. The text for Mulvey's collaboration with Lewis and Abdullah, *23rd August 2008*, presented here for the first time, is similar in status. It consists of Abdullah's twenty-one-minute monologue, details of the brief opening shot and titles. The texts for both *Disgraced Monuments* and *23ʳᵈ August 2008* are therefore transcripts of the films. They provide an entirely retrospective view of the films to which they correspond and include, or constitute, written traces of the audio testimonies within them.

The scripts gathered in this volume have different relations to their corresponding films, and the interest to be found in these texts shifts from one moment to the next. At times, they illuminate the films. For example, they clarify various aspects, such as the specific details for camera movement and camera position, and help unpack dense and layered sequences for the reader. They also allow for compositional rules – such as the symmetry and patterned arrangements of sections, which are often features of Mulvey and Wollen's collaborative films – to be easily discerned and verified. At other times, these texts can be read as creative and critical texts in their own right. In a discussion event, Griselda Pollock proposed to Mulvey that the 'script [Mulvey and Wollen] wrote for the *Riddles of the Sphinx* … makes *Riddles of the Sphinx* not just a cinematic text but a major piece of feminist poetry. It is a conjunction of feminist poetics and feminist philosophy'.[20] The availability of *Riddles* as a script – that is, as printed text, independent of images and sounds – allows for this poetic aspect of the work to emerge more clearly, and for the diverse modes of writing therein to be appreciated independently. To this end, in the remainder of this essay I would like to draw attention to some of the strategies employed by Mulvey and Wollen in writing their independent and collaborative films, and examine certain textual approaches that can be seen to cut across them.

Starting Points and Strategies

Mulvey and Wollen often began writing their collaborative films with a critical encounter with a particular story or set of artworks. The first three films all include feminist investigations of the way various stories have been previously narrated. Here, certain figures – the Amazon, the Sphinx and the heroine – function as emblems for reflections on patriarchal culture. The starting point for their first film, for example, was Kleist's 1808 play *Penthesilea*. In an interview, Mulvey commented on the interconnected reasons for her and Wollen's interest in this play, namely: Mulvey's work on male fantasies of women;[21] the question of whether the Amazon myth was politically useful for the women's movement; and the transformation of the myth itself over time through its retellings in art and literature.[22] These concerns are explored in various ways across the film, including a performance-lecture delivered by Wollen. The text he reads is maze-like, palimpsestic and contains a number of layered stories and digressions within it. This interest in myth was carried over into *Riddles*. In the second section of that film, Mulvey introduces a feminist perspective on the Oedipus myth, and in particular the forgotten figure of the Sphinx, direct to camera. Here, she describes the Sphinx as the film's 'imaginary narrator', and suggests that it is a suppressed figure, associated with motherhood and resistance to patriarchy. Hence the investigation of myth in *Riddles* is metaphorically tied to another story, which, in the film's central section, is told through a series of thirteen 360-degree pans and concerns a mother, Louise (Dinah Stabb), and her daughter, Anna (Rhiannon Tise).[23] (See Mulvey's Introduction for an account of the story's composition.) In order to investigate the figure of the heroine, *AMY!* takes Amy Johnson's 1930 solo flight from Croydon to Darwin as its starting point. The film, which includes theoretical texts read by both Mulvey and Wollen on the soundtrack, reflects on how Johnson's flight was rewritten into the form of legend.

The feature-length films that follow have a different relation to their source texts. Here the writing process is more akin to critical reworking or adaptation. *Crystal Gazing* is set in London during the early 1980s, but bases its four characters and aspects of its plot on Erich Kästner's 1931 novel *Fabian: The Story of a Moralist*.[24] The novel's depiction of mass unemployment and businesses going bankrupt no doubt resonated with the gloomy historical present of the film's writing and production: the Thatcher recession of the early 1980s, cuts to the arts and, as a newspaper headline incorporated into the film signals, 'three million jobless'. The central section of *Crystal Gazing* revolves around the radical interpretation of another story, Charles Perrault's 'Puss in Boots', which is the subject of the PhD thesis of one of the central characters. While the earlier three films all include a theoretical discussion of certain stories and their transformation over time, this film and some of the other feature-length films that would follow incorporate elements of theoretical discourse within the dialogues of the stories themselves.

Mulvey and Wollen's final collaborative film, *The Bad Sister*, is an adaptation of Emma Tennant's 1978 novel of the same name, itself a reworking of James Hogg's Gothic tale *The Private Memoirs and Confessions of a Justified Sinner* (1824).[25] Significantly, Tennant switched the genders of Hogg's protagonists. Mulvey and Wollen were interested in this gesture, just as they had been in Kleist's decision to make Penthesilea kill Achilles, rather than the reverse as in the original Greek myth. Here, Mulvey and Wollen's consistent interest in multi-layered or palimpsestic texts is apparent. However, as Mulvey explained in an interview, they were also drawn to Tennant's novel because it is full of 'invisible transitions between different worlds, and different kinds of consciousness'.[26] Furthermore, *The Bad Sister* 'is a story of a double, in which it's never quite clear whether there is an actual "doppelgänger" or double or whether the central character, is in a sense, splitting herself into two. There are a number of unresolved questions of dualism, dualities, fusions, hybridities'.[27] These fantastic aspects of the novel also lent themselves to the new production context of Channel 4, suggesting a way that Mulvey and Wollen's feminist engagement with concepts from psychoanalysis could be carried over into television and taken in new directions via experimentation with special effects.

Wollen's solo feature film *Friendship's Death* also involved the transformation of a pre-existing text: his own short story, which was first published in *Bananas*, the literary magazine that Tennant edited, in 1976. Wollen wrote about an experience he had had in Amman, Jordan, during the early days of September 1970, transforming it into a science fiction story set in the recent past. In this text, an unnamed reporter narrates his memories of meeting an extraterrestrial called Friendship during the events leading to Black September. In rewriting the short story for the screen, various aspects changed: Friendship is now a woman (Tilda Swinton) and the extraterrestrial's gift for the reporter, now named Sullivan (Bill Paterson), is different. In the story it is a 'translation'[28] of Stéphane Mallarmé's *L'Après-midi d'un faune*, but in the film it takes the form of a brightly coloured object, which Friendship refers to as an 'image unit', a 'kind of sketch-pad with a language facility', containing a collage of moving images.[29] In the film, as Kodwo Eshun has recently observed, the journalist and the extraterrestrial have a 'dialogue, this duet, this dance of ideas ... they are both personifications of Wollen's thinking, of Wollen's theoretical thought and of Wollen's fictional thought.' Eshun argues that science fiction suited Wollen because it is a 'cinema of ideas' and that the figure of the robot allowed him 'to enact, and to dramatise and to perform ideas that he held for many years.'[30]

In Mulvey and Wollen's collaborative films, the project of working critically with narrative is often accompanied by instances of poetic, speculative and constrained writing. In *Riddles*, for example, the voice-off moves through different modes of speech. In the first three sections of 'Louise's story', the central section of the film, it speaks in small sentences, and reads a poetic text that relates to domestic space and the experience of motherhood. In the ninth section, it enumerates a number of questions that open on to one another. Beginning with strategic questions about working conditions for mothers and the efficacy and focus of campaigns, it leads to a consideration of domestic labour, which, in turn, opens to broader questions about the politics of the unconscious: 'Does the oppression of women work on the unconscious as well as on the conscious? What would the politics of the unconscious be like?'[31] In this passage, the voice-off moves from the concrete to the highly theoretical and back again, raising a number of feminist questions related to the oppression of women, which, according to Mulvey, were just beginning to be formulated by the women's movement.[32] Then, in the final section of 'Louise's story', the voice-off employs the third-person female pronoun, 'she', and associates it with various memories. While in the ninth section the use of this 'shifter' appears to refer to Louise, the recollections described in the final pan seem to belong to her daughter, Anna. Paradoxically, however, the voice-off describes Anna's act of remembering from a later moment in her life. Here, unlike in previous sections, it is as if the voice-off is referring back to events in the diegesis from an undetermined point in the future, offering a complex account of the formation of her subjectivity.

While the poetic texts in the first three pans of *Riddles* were collaboratively worked on, Mulvey often credits Wollen with writing other sections alone. For example, in the twelfth pan of *Riddles*, Louise reads a transcript of a dream to another character, her friend, possible lover and, in Catherine Grant's words, 'guide to finding a more feminist life', Maxine (Merdelle Jordine).[33] Here, Wollen used a writing method adapted from the French writer Raymond Roussel, a precursor of Surrealism and Oulipo.[34] 'I took words from a French dictionary, according to an arbitrary system I had devised,' Wollen explained, 'and then incorporated them in sequence into a narrative... I also used some words from H.D.'[35] Mulvey noted that 'it was not so much that Peter intended to emulate dream language or the language of the unconscious, but rather to generate words, and images from words, that foregrounded a linguistic materiality in the same sense that avant-garde film had always foregrounded the materiality of its medium'.[36] In some autobiographical notes, Wollen states that 'Roussel pervades *Crystal Gazing* too'.[37] As working documents presented in this book show, Wollen generated lists of words that began and ended with the same letter, some of which were incorporated into the film. These quasi-palindromic words, scattered through the dialogue and passages of voice-over, mirror on a small scale the shape of the entire film, setting up a formal device that is almost imperceptible to the cinema viewer but undoubtedly generative for the writer.

As in much of the avant-garde art and literature that interested Mulvey and Wollen, as well as in many of their cinematic precursors and fellow travellers, the writing of Mulvey and Wollen's films utilised quotation as one of their central strategies. That this is the case should come as no surprise, for Wollen discusses Jean-Luc Godard's radical use of quotation in his 1972 essay on counter-cinema. There, he contrasts the closure of classic Hollywood films with the open-endedness and intertextuality of Godard's counter-cinema, arguing that a film that utilises such strategies 'can only be understood as an arena, a meeting place where different discourses encounter each other and struggle for supremacy'.[38] Mulvey and Wollen often deploy direct quotations from theoretical or literary sources. Each of the five sequences in *Penthesilea* contains an epigraph, while *Riddles* begins with a quote from Gertrude Stein. This use of quotation underscores the sense in which these films were not designed as self-sufficient works, but were structured in relation to other writers and discourses.

In many of their films, artworks, movies and 'found footage' are included on the image track and whole passages of text, including letters and poetry, are read aloud, either by characters in the films or voice-over on the soundtrack. For example, in *Crystal Gazing*, a character reads a passage from Antonin Artaud; *Friendship's Death* includes a recitation of Samih al-Qasim's poem 'Travel Tickets'; and Mary Kelly reads from the diaries she compiled for *Post-Partum Document*, introducing the idea of 'weaning from the dyad' and entry into 'the Oedipal triad', in *Riddles*.

Mulvey and Wollen also used quotation in a more radical way. This is most apparent in *AMY!*, which Wollen described as a 'collage portrait'. In this film, alongside titles, performed tableaux and shots of particular locations related to Johnson's life, different media and textual sources are used to evoke the historical figure of Amy Johnson, her flight from London to Australia, and its entanglement with the political realities of the 1930s. In section seven of the film, titles alert the viewer to the financial backer of Johnson's endeavor, Lord Wakefield, and his nefarious oil interests which, as Esther Leslie has noted, 'do not easily give up their underpinning, their enmeshment in colonial oppression, capitalist business practices and military adventures.'[39] This critical register is extended in the following section, in which Johnson's journey is tracked across a map and accompanied by a voice over that reads news headlines from *The Times*, May 1930. Here, Johnson's flight becomes part of a news cycle that makes reference to the rise of fascism, colonial subjugation, and racist atrocities, thereby presenting both the reportage of Imperial violence, and the casual violence of Imperial reportage.

In sections fourteen and fifteen of the film, Yvonne Rainer reads a text on the soundtrack that is composed of undifferentiated and unidentified snippets of quotation which, according to the film's credits, are taken from Bryher, Amelia Earhart, Lola Montez, Gertrude Stein and others.[40] Here quotation functions for Mulvey and Wollen as a method for writing a text, but one that is very different to the writing techniques employed in *Riddles* or *Crystal Gazing*. In other sections, two songs by Poly Styrene and X-Ray Spex are used on the soundtrack to directly comment on issues of celebrity and identity raised by the film. The inclusion of lyrics in the script (as opposed to a simple notation of the song name) marks the sense in which Mulvey and Wollen deployed them as text within the writing of their film. This also emphasises the sense in which this film itself is very much a textual and musical collage, one that interweaves many different types of writing and media which, as the quote from Wollen about Godard suggested, comment on, counteract and critique one another.

Mulvey and Wollen's filmmaking project also involved paying attention to the way words appear on the image track, in the form of epigraphs, superimpositions, titles and intertitles. Just as dialogue and voice-over provided codes and signifying practices to be explored and intervened with during the writing process, so too did intertitles and visual text. For example, in the performance-lecture that Wollen delivers in the second sequence of *Penthesilea*, the camera discovers a set of index cards written in felt-tip. These, in a sense, add another layer of meaning to the section; at times they reinforce what is being said, and at others – the instances where the text is different to that which is read – they undermine it. The viewer is thus presented with a series of problems to negotiate and questions to think through regarding the significance of the mismatch between what is being said and what is written on the cards, and, to make matters more complex, whether to read the cue cards presented on the image track or listen to the speaker on the soundtrack.

The exploration of the way that word becomes image continues in later films. In the central section of *Riddles*, Mulvey and Wollen also use an intertitle before each of the thirteen tableaux in 'Louise's story'. As the film unfolds, it becomes clear that the majority of these fragmentary texts present aspects of the story and the psychoanalytic and political issues with which it is concerned. The text in each intertitle is in a blue font and framed by a blue square, contrasting their visuality and their supportive, narrative function. Aside from the first and last intertitle, they all start and end in the middle of the sentence. This presentation of text on the image track suggests that these intertitles are – like the depiction of motherhood in the scenes in 'Louise's story' – sections of a larger whole. Furthermore, this sense of incompleteness relates to ongoing and repetitive acts of domestic labour.

The scripts gathered in this volume offer an opportunity to consider Mulvey and Wollen's collaborative and independent writing for film. These texts function as representations of the films in their absence, and as creative and critical texts in their own right. In the former sense, they provide a notation of the majority of verbal speech in their films, as well as details regarding how cinematography and structure were conceived and designed. In the latter sense, they are sites where different modes of writing are folded into one another in singular and novel ways. As such, in addition to facilitating the study of these films, these texts represent an important aspect of Mulvey and Wollen's broader practices. By comparison to the writing of theory, writing for film – whether collaborative or separate – allowed them to do three significant things: first, to proceed in an even more speculative and experimental manner; second, to engage with many of the textual conventions of cinema, to subvert them in the writing process and to open them up to new possibilities; finally, to juxtapose different sources and modes of writing, and in so doing approach the political subjects with which they were concerned from multiple standpoints. The meaning of each text is not one that is given but, like the documents themselves, has to be constructed. Thus the pleasure to be found in these texts may lie less in following an argument or story through to conclusion than in deciphering how these different instances and modes of writing merge and collide.

Notes

1. Wollen also wrote the outlines and treatments for many other projects that, often due to institutional limitations, did not reach production. After his collaborations with Mulvey, he co-wrote with film theorist Anne Friedberg the treatment for a film called *Extravagance* (1984). Around three years later, he co-wrote a proposal for a film on the Scratch Orchestra (c. 1987) with writer and later editor of the film publication *PIX* Ilona Halberstadt. Other unmade solo projects include *Dream Thief* (1984), *Eisenstein in Mexico* (c. 1985), *Expedition to the North Pole* (1985), *Grottoes* (1986) and *The de Man/Heidegger Affair* (1987). Wollen also wrote the treatment for a film called *Necessary Love*. The latter was written for Bandung Productions and published by *New Left Review* in 2006. See: Peter Wollen, 'Necessary Love', *New Left Review* 38 (May/April, 2006), 95–112.

2. Wollen alludes to this in his essay 'Who the Hell is Howards Hawks?' See: Peter Wollen, 'Who the Hell is Howards Hawks?', in *Paris Hollywood: Writings on Film* (London: Verso, 2002), 65.

3. The script for *The Passenger* was published by Grove Press. See: Michelangelo Antonioni, Mark Peploe and Peter Wollen, *The Passenger* (New York: Grove Press, 1976). Wollen also contributed to other scripts. For example, the screenplay for the film *Melancholia* (1989) is credited to both its director, Andi Engel, a film distributor and critic, and Lewis Rodia, a pseudonym Wollen employed when working on it. However, this was not a collaboration in the same sense as Wollen's other co-authored works. In this case, he was hired as a script doctor to work on the screenplay.

4. Before publishing *Signs and Meaning in the Cinema*, Wollen wrote many essays for *New Left Review* under two pseudonyms, Lucien Rey and Lee Russell. As Russell, he produced a series of short articles on directors, including Samuel Fuller, Alfred Hitchcock, Jean-Luc Godard and Roberto Rossellini. These were included in the fourth and fifth editions of *Signs and Meaning in the Cinema* (published in 1998 and 2013 respectively). As Rey, Wollen wrote on a range of topics, including international politics. For an excellent account of Wollen's work for *New Left Review*, see: Nicolas Helm-Grovas, 'Laura Mulvey and Peter Wollen: Theory and Practice, Aesthetics and Politics, 1963–1983' (PhD diss., Royal Holloway, University of London, 2018), 36–47. Lucien Rey also wrote for *7 Days, New Society* and *International Socialist Journal*.

5. This essay was first published under the title 'Counter Cinema: *Vent d'Est*' in *Afterimage 4* (Autumn 1972), 6–16; it was republished as 'Godard and Counter Cinema: *Vent d'Est*', in *Readings and Writings: Semiotic Counter-Strategies* (London: Verso, 1982), 79–91.

6. In addition to writing theoretical essays and making films, Mulvey and Wollen were also involved in many other aspects of experimental film culture; they took part in key debates, served on editorial boards, including *Screen* (Wollen) and *Framework* (both), organised international events as part of the Edinburgh Film Festival and held important roles at various institutions. Wollen worked for the BFI Education Department and Mulvey was on the board of management for the Other Cinema and a member of the Arts Council Artists' Film Sub-Committee. Mulvey and Wollen both had roles in the Independent Film-Makers' Association (IFA). Many of their institutional and editorial roles are outlined at: www.luxonline.org.uk/artists/laura_mulvey_and_peter_wollen/bibliography.html (accessed 26 July 2020).

7. The summer 1971 issue of the journal *Afterimage* made a selection of texts related to the theory and practice of Third Cinema available to readers in the United Kingdom, including a translation of 'Towards a Third Cinema', Julio Garcia Espinosa's 'For an Imperfect Cinema', and the outline to *La hora de los hornos* (1968). For all these texts, see: See *Afterimage 3* (Summer, 1971). The concept of Third Cinema was reworked by Teshome Gabriel, in his important book *Third Cinema in the Third World: The Aesthetics of Liberation* (Ann Arbor, Michigan: UMI Research Press, 1982). For a detailed and critical take on these developments, see: Jonathan Buchsbaum, 'A Closer Look at Third Cinema', *Historical Journal of Film, Radio and Television, 21:2* (2001), 153–166; see also: Kodwo Eshun and Ros Gray, 'The Militant Image: A Ciné-Geography', *Third Text, 25:1* (2011), 1–12.

8. For an account of the 'Third World', understood not as a place but as a political project, see Vijay Prashad's *The Darker Nations: A People's History of the Third World* (New York: The New Press, 2007).

9. Peter Wollen, 'The Two Avant-Gardes', in *Readings and Writings: Semiotic Counter-Strategies* (London: Verso, 1982), 92.

10. As Mulvey describes in her Introduction to this book, she was part of the History Group, a feminist reading group, in the early 1970s. The self-directed study undertaken by the group informed many of the essays she wrote during the decade and, by extension, her filmic collaborations with Wollen. Mulvey has also previously explained that the Women's Liberation Movement's demonstration against the Miss World Competition in November 1970 was her 'initiation to the politics of woman as spectacle'. See: Laura Mulvey, 'Introduction to the Second Edition', in *Visual and Other Pleasures* (Basingstoke: Palgrave Macmillan, 2009), xv.

11. See: Juliet Mitchell, *Psychoanalysis and Feminism* (Harmondsworth: Penguin, 1974); and Claire Johnston, 'Women's Cinema as Counter-Cinema', in *Movies and Methods, Vol. 1. An Anthology*, ed. Bill Nichols (Berkeley, Los Angeles, London, University of California Press, 1976), 208–217.

12. Griselda Pollock, 'Moments and Temporalities of the Avant-Garde "in, of, and from the feminine"', *New Literary History 41:4* (Autumn, 2010), 801. Nicolas Helm-Grovas and I discuss this in our essay 'Art at the Frontier of Film Theory'. Pollock's concept of a 'feminist avant-garde moment' is of crucial importance to us, and has informed many of the decisions we have made in relation to a series of exhibitions we have organised about Mulvey and Wollen's work. See: Oliver Fuke and Nicolas Helm-Grovas, 'Art at the Frontier of Film Theory', catalogue essay in *Art at the Frontier of Film Theory: Laura Mulvey and Peter Wollen* ex. cat. (London: Peltz Gallery/Birkbeck Institute for the Moving Image, 2019).

13. Scott MacDonald, 'Introduction', in *Screen Writings: Texts and Scripts from Independent Films*, ed. Scott MacDonald (Berkeley and Los Angeles, CA: University of California Press, 1995), 10–11.

14. In an introduction to a 1980 interview with Yvonne Rainer, Noël Carroll coined a term that signaled a new tendency or direction in experimental filmmaking: 'The New Talkie'. According to Carroll, the practitioners of 'The New Talkie' were primarily concerned with language, combining structural filmmakers' interest in 'the possibilities of language … and its limitations' with the attempt to '"say something"'. See: Noël Carroll and Yvonne Rainer, 'Interview with a Woman Who…', in *A Woman Who…: Essays, Interviews, Scripts* (Baltimore, MD: The Johns Hopkins University Press, 1999), 170. The concept of 'The New Talkie' was developed further when a 1981 edition of the journal *October* was dedicated to it. See: *October* 17 (Summer 1981).

15. See: Peter Wollen, 'The Field of Language in Film', *October* 17 (Summer 1981), 53–60.

16. In a 1976 interview, Yvonne Rainer describes the writing process for her early films in similar terms. She says: 'I … accumulate stuff, from newspapers, my own writing, paragraphs, sentences, scraps of paper, photos, stills from previous films. Ultimately, the process of sorting it all out forces me to organize it and make the parts cohere in some fashion. Sometimes a given text suggests a visual treatment and I dispense with the text. There is always the question of to what extent I want to duplicate content in text and image.' See: Yvonne Rainer, 'Interview by the Camera Obscura Collective', in *A Woman Who…: Essays, Interviews, Scripts* (Baltimore, MD: The Johns Hopkins University Press, 1999), 156.

17. Laura Mulvey and Peter Wollen, '*Penthesilea, Queen of the Amazons*', interview by Claire Johnston and Paul Willemen, *Screen* 15:3 (Autumn 1974), 125–126.

18. *Ibid.*, 126.

19. Laura Mulvey, 'Film on Four, British Experimental Television Drama and *The Bad Sister*', interview by Janet McCabe, *Critical Studies in Television* 4:2 (November 2009), 100.

20. Griselda Pollock and Laura Mulvey, 'Laura Mulvey in Conversation with Griselda Pollock', *Studies in the Maternal* 2:1 (2010), 6.

21. See: Laura Mulvey, 'Fears, Fantasies and the Male Unconscious *or* "You don't know what is happening do you, Mr Jones?"', in *Visual and Other Pleasures*, 2nd edn (Basingstoke: Palgrave Macmillan, 2009), 6–13.

22. See: Mulvey and Wollen, '*Penthesilea, Queen of the Amazons*', 121–122.

23. The thirteen tableaux tell this story schematically and, according to Mulvey, are designed 'to bring out a series of problems, which are problems for feminist politics'. These problems operate on two levels: both the concrete – everyday practical problems, such as the realities of childcare and gendered labour issues – and the psychoanalytic. Here, the carefully planned camera movement operates independently of the story told but also reinforces the circular nature of the political problems with which the film is concerned. See: Laura Mulvey and Peter Wollen, 'Riddles of the Avant-Garde', interview by Don Ranvaud, *Framework* 9 (Winter 1978), 31.

24. Mulvey and Wollen significantly altered many aspects of Kästner's novel.

25. See: Emma Tennant, *The Bad Sister* (London: Victor Gollancz, 1978).

26. Mulvey, 'Film on Four', 100–101.

27. *Ibid.*, 101.

28. In his emphatic review of *Friendship's Death*, Edward W. Said described Friendship's 'translation' as 'a virtuoso misreading' that features various 'ingenious renderings'. According to the narrator in the short story, Friendship's approach to translation 'combined literalness with a set of systematic procedures for deforming ordinary uses of language'. Here Wollen's interest in experimental literature, use of quotation (the 'translation' is a text within a text) and experiments with 'counter-language' are clearly evidenced, as they are in the majority of the scripts presented in this volume. See: Edward W. Said, 'Review of *Wedding in Galilee* and *Friendship's Death*', in *The Politics of Dispossession: The Struggle for Palestinian Self-Determination 1969–1994* (New York: Vintage, 1995), 135; and '*Friendship's Death* (Fiction)', Chapter 13 in this volume, 223.

29. However, as the script for this film makes clear, in '12. Sullivan's Hotel Room', Friendship's voice can be heard reading some of this 'translation' of Mallarmé against a background of electronic sound, which gradually fades away.

30. See: Kodwo Eshun and Laura Mulvey, 'PETER WOLLEN – WRITING, POLITICS, FILM', interview by Wendy Russell, accessed 10 November 2020, www.youtube.com/watch?v=nhD8ssWx4KE

31. See the script for *Riddles of the Sphinx*, reproduced in this book.

32. Griselda Pollock and Laura Mulvey, 'Laura Mulvey in Conversation with Griselda Pollock', 10–11.

33. Catherine Grant, 'Returning to *Riddles*', in *Women Artists, Feminism and the Moving Image: Contexts and Practices*, ed. Lucy Reynolds (London: Bloomsbury, 2019), 66.

34. Oulipo is a group of writers exploring formal constraints in literary composition in postwar France, the best known of whom are probably Raymond Queneau and Georges Perec.

35. Scott MacDonald, 'Interview with Laura Mulvey (on *Riddles of the Sphinx*)' in *A Critical Cinema 2: Interviews with Independent Filmmakers* (Berkeley and Los Angeles, CA: University of California Press, 1992), 338.

36. Laura Mulvey, '*Riddles* as Essay Film', in *Essays on the Essay Film*, eds Nora M. Alter and Timothy Corrigan (New York: Columbia University Press, 2017), 320.

37. Peter Wollen, 'Autobiographical Notes', 31 March 1994, Peter Wollen artist file, British Artists' Film and Video Study Collection, Central Saint Martins, University of the Arts, London, 12.

38. Peter Wollen, 'Godard and Counter Cinema: *Vent d'Est*', in *Readings and Writings: Semiotic Counter-Strategies* (London: Verso, 1982), 87.

39. Esther Leslie, 'Introduction to *AMY!* and *Crystal Gazing*', given at Whitechapel Gallery, London, 15 May 2016.

40. This text might be contrasted with the narration in *Frida Kahlo & Tina Modotti*, which is more didactic. Mulvey has explained how this text was partially extracted from a previous instance of critical writing (the catalogue essay Mulvey and Wollen collaboratively wrote for an exhibition they curated of the two artists' work). However, at one point in the development of the work, Mulvey and Wollen had planned to write a more experimental text for the soundtrack, utilising quotations from different authors, such as Octavio Paz. For more information about the exhibition, see Laura Mulvey and Peter Wollen, 'Frida Kahlo and Tina Modotti', in *Frida Kahlo and Tina Modotti* (London: Whitechapel Art Gallery, 1982), 7–27. Mulvey and Wollen worked on this exhibition together with Mark Francis. After its opening at the Whitechapel Gallery, it travelled to Germany and Sweden, before going on to the Grey Art Gallery in New York and, finally, to the Museo Nacional de Arte, Mexico City. Wollen and Francis also organised a number of other exhibitions together, including: *Komar & Melamid: History Painting* (The Fruitmarket Gallery, Edinburgh; Museum of Modern Art, Oxford, both 1985) and *On the Passage of a Few People Through a Rather Brief Moment in Time: The Situationist International* (Musée National d'Art Moderne, Centre Pompidou, Paris; Institute of Contemporary Arts, London, both 1989; Institute of Contemporary Art, Boston, 1990). Wollen curated other travelling exhibitions, such as *Posada, Messenger of Mortality* (1989), *Addressing the Century: 100 Years of Art and Fashion* (1999) and the North American section of *Global Conceptualism: Points of Origin, 1950s–1980s* (1999).

Introduction

Laura Mulvey

This Introduction is designed to be read alongside Oliver Fuke's first Introduction. Two questions run through it: what circumstances brought these quite unusual films into existence? And then: what were the working methods that made the Mulvey/Wollen collaboration possible? Given that this is a book of scripts, I have, by and large, concentrated on the early stages of our projects' development, on ideas and working methods that precede the actual process of production itself, the filming and its aftermath. I have also tried to stay close to those moments in time and avoid comments informed by hindsight, although some retrospection cannot but creep in. Needless to say, writing this Introduction has been difficult in Peter Wollen's absence and I have constantly felt a frustrated impulse to confer with and consult him. And his memories and perspectives would, of course, have differed from mine.[1] I am sure that Peter would have taken great pleasure in this book and would have been as impressed as I am by the meticulous work that Oliver has invested in its production. All the scripts, and some very much more than others, have needed careful and patient reconstruction, often from scattered fragments, and in every case Oliver has demonstrated an exemplary fidelity to reproducing a valid and reliable text.

To my mind, and these three points are in juxtaposition with those in the first Introduction, there is a triple rationale for the publication of the film scripts brought together in this book. In the first instance, most of the films come from the mid-period of the 'long 1970s', and, as documents of the British independent film movement's most experimental phase, will contribute to the recent revival of interest in that period and its cultural production. The term 'long 1970s' is usually used to evoke the political period bracketed, at one end, by the revolutionary fervour of 1968 and, at the other, by the defeat of the miners' strike and the triumph of Thatcherism in 1984. But the term also evokes the arc traced by the UK experimental film movement itself, bracketed symbolically, at one end, by the founding of the London Film-Makers' Co-operative in 1968 and, at the other, by the arrival on air of Channel 4 in 1982. These 'brackets' had a determining impact on Peter's and my collaboration between 1974 and 1983.

Second, the book's critical strand, the essays accompanying each script, has made an invaluable contribution to the publication. As the essays are about the actual films themselves, they bring the dimension of the screen and the image to the words on the page. The collection benefits particularly from the 'essayistic' qualities of the writing, that is, from the personal perspectives, interests and imaginative engagements these writers have brought to the Mulvey/Wollen films. Furthermore, all the contributors to the collection are engaged with critical and theoretical questions surrounding the politics of experimental film now. While they bring a thorough understanding of the films' various historical moments (from 1974 to 1992), the essays also give them a new significance in the present and, I hope, a new lease of life.

Third, working on the scripts for publication, focusing primarily and unusually on the words as such, has reminded me of the importance of language in Peter's and my films. Our shared commitment to a feminist politics of language runs through the first three, *Penthesilea: Queen of the Amazons* (1974), *Riddles of the Sphinx* (1977) and *AMY!* (1980). In all these films, the question of language includes its absences and women's silences. But Peter also wrote specific passages that both foreground the materiality of language and implicitly reflect Julia Kristeva's concept of the pre-Oedipal 'chora', finding a narrow edge between words as image and as conveyor of meaning. In this quotation, he very clearly sums up these relations between theory, politics and language:

> Language is the component of film which both threatens to regulate the spectator, assigned a place within the symbolic order, and also offers the hope of liberation from the closed world of identification and the lure of the image. Language, therefore, is both a friend and a foe, against which we must be on our guard, whose help we need but whose claims we must combat. Hence the fractured and dislodged body of language in our films. …It is important to stress that the sphinx represents an alternative form of language – she is not outside language as she is outside the city of Thebes, the realm of patriarchy, but is able to offer a different discourse, potentially the nucleus of a nonpatriarchal symbolic, based on a different Oedipal structure – or perhaps it would be better to say, a different mode of entry into language, kinship, and history.[2]

The points that Peter raises here crystalise the conjuncture between the various radicalisms that interested us: avant-garde aesthetics, feminist politics and psychoanalytic theory, for all of which semantic structures, words, their comprehensibility or difficulty, were of central significance. To sum up: the importance of language for our cinematic project meant that it was unavoidably theoretical and also essentially impure; the films moved away from linguistic transparency to the stutter, the hieroglyph and the riddle. Folded within these theoretical questions about language is the crucial contribution Peter's own writing made to the films. The key passages that I have in mind from the first three films are: Peter's monologue in *Penthesilea*, some of the 'Sphinx' voice-off in *Riddles of the Sphinx*, and the Yvonne Rainer voice-off in *AMY!* Although we discussed their significance and their rationale as part of our collaborative process, it was Peter who actually penned them, materializing the ideas into words in a way that gives them a formal, 'literary' quality, in addition to their psychoanalytic and political relevance to the films more generally. On the screen, these highly experimental and original compositions slip inexorably away, absorbed into the movement of the film; but once published, once they appear on the page, the writing can get the more prolonged attention it deserves. In the Preface to *Readings and Writings: Semiotic Counter-Strategies* (1982), Peter specifically describes his intention to overcome the division of labour between theory and practice and points out that his essays and fictions 'present different aspects of work from a common aesthetic position.' He also explains that our collaborative films 'form part of the same heterogeneous corpus.'[3] I would suggest that his experimental writing for the films and his experimental writing, over the same period of time, for *Bananas* are two sides of a coin. Now the publication of the scripts allows this aspect of Peter's writing to be read alongside his fictions.

The other scripts differ from the first three and from each other. The voice-over for *Frida Kahlo & Tina Modotti* (1983) is primarily drawn from the catalogue essay of the 1982 exhibition, which we wrote together. Of all our six films, the script for *Crystal Gazing* (1982) is the most complex. For the first time in our collaboration, Peter wrote some intricate passages of dialogue, in which he used the voice of a character to return to the politics of language and semiotics, now with irony and a certain dimension of self-satire. The dialogue intertwines with an elaborate voice-over commentary, at times poetic and at times novelistic, mixed with casual observation of the immediate and the everyday.

The Mulvey/Wollen Collaboration: How it Began, Continued and How it Ended

Beginnings: Peter's and my shared love of Hollywood films had, from the earliest days of our relationship, been an integral part of our daily and our social lives. But in the early 1970s our attitudes and commitment to the cinema changed. The Hollywood studio system was, by then, a thing of the past and we began to discover new avant-garde and feminist experimental films: cinema as critique, film as a radical aesthetic for a radical politics. However, our actual move into filmmaking, the beginning of the Mulvey/Wollen collaboration, was more or less a product of circumstance or, even perhaps, chance. In 1972, Peter was invited to work in the Department of Radio, Film and Television at Northwestern University by Paddy Whannel (who had given Peter his first proper job at the British Film Institute Education Department in the mid-1960s). Peter and Paddy's relationship, professional and personal, had been founded on a mutual love of Hollywood cinema and I, although professionally marginal, had always been included in this cinephilic bonding. But with the changing times Peter's interests and writing shifted towards counter-cinema, publishing his essay 'Counter Cinema: *Vent d'Est*' in 1972, and I began to write 'Visual Pleasure and Narrative Cinema'.[4] At some point in 1973, Peter asked Paddy if he could teach an MA seminar on avant-garde film. Of course, Paddy agreed. But soon after, he said: 'If you and Laura are so keen on the avant-garde now days, make a film yourselves. We have a whole cupboard of equipment here, not used in the vacation. See what you can do!' *Penthesilea: Queen of the Amazons* was made in response to this challenge.

Furthermore, living in Evanston, Peter and I were both cut off from our political roots in London. I had belonged to the History Group, a Women's Liberation reading group, and helped out with the administration of the London Women's Liberation Workshop.[5] Peter was still on the Editorial Boards of *Screen* and *New Left Review*, but at a distance. *7 Days*, in which he had been closely involved in the early 70s, had failed to survive. I sometimes think that, in that comparative political isolation (our son Chad, aged three, was, of course, with us), we turned to each other as though to found a minimal collective, a small filmmaking and study group, as it were. Our first film emerged gradually. It was rooted in our recent polemical writing, inspired by the new horizons of possibility offered by films of ideas and revolved around issues, thrown up by feminism, that directly challenged the cinema, its imagery and its modes of story-telling. The actual process began with research: reading and discussion around, for instance, Amazons in ancient Greek culture and beyond, the psychoanalytic implications of the Amazon figure and Kleist's rewriting of the Penthesilea legend, an interweaving of myth and the historical realities of women in struggle... all producing endless notes, charts and conversations. The process of producing *Penthesilea* did not involve writing a script as such (see the first Introduction on the relation of documents to production) but, in keeping with Peter's and my tendency to think through diagrams and patterns, the words grew out of the film's evolution, through its various planning stages.

When we moved back to London, in late 1974, we found a new flourishing film cultural environment. Although the independent film movement had definitely been in the process of taking off when we left, it had gathered momentum. Having made *Penthesilea*, we not only arrived back home as filmmakers but also found a film culture that recognised the rationale for this work of feminist counter-cinema. It was this movement and this moment that gave a further impetus to Peter's and my collaboration. I sometimes think that in other circumstances *Penthesilea* might have been a one-off oddity; but it became, in fact, a crucial stepping stone both for our further film production and for the further development of our ideas.

By the mid-1970s, there was a dynamic context not only for filmmaking but also for critical writing on radical film, historical research into the avant-garde, programming the new national and international cinema through screenings and festivals etc. The Independent Film-Makers' Association (IFA) had been founded in 1974 and I was part of the original organising group; Peter was a key figure in the IFA's campaign to ensure the presence of independent film on the newly envisaged fourth television channel. The sense of a movement, of belonging and of shared agendas for radical cinema, brought very different kinds of independent film into dialogue and co-operation, from the artist filmmakers of the Co-op, to left documentary and agit-film collectives. Before leaving for the US, both Peter and I had been involved with different projects at the Edinburgh Film Festival (EFF); its director, Lynda Myles, managed to programme retrospectives of the Hollywood directors who had been so precious to the cinephiles of the 1960s, with systematic programming of avant-garde and experimental films. After our return, the EFF continued to be an annual source of cinematic excitement: screenings, symposia, personal encounters, new friendships...

Questions about the representation of women, and what a feminist cinema should be like, were important issues under discussion at the time. As Peter and I decided to apply to the British Film Institute Production Board to fund another film, our commitment to a *theoretical* feminist counter-cinema became a conscious project. The independent film movement was fortunate that Peter Sainsbury (founding co-editor of *Afterimage)* at the BFI and David Curtis (founding member of the London Film-Makers' Co-operative) at the Arts Council, both long supporters of these new cinemas, were in a position to give it financial backing. We received £20,000 from the BFI for the project that became *Riddles of the Sphinx*. Southern Arts backed *AMY!*, the Arts Council funded *Frida Kahlo & Tina Modotti* and the BFI in association with Channel 4 funded *Crystal Gazing*.

Endings: it is, of course, well known that the early 1980s was a transitional period for independent film. The 1979 election not only coincided with funding changes at the British Film Institute Production Board but also brought an end to the (doubtless over-utopian) optimism that had characterised the cultural left of the 1970s. On the other hand, Channel 4 came on air in 1982 offering new hope, funding possibilities and exhibition slots. There is a certain inverse symmetry between the beginning and ending of Peter's and my collaboration. Both took place at the start of a new era for independent film; *Penthesilea* could definitely be described as a theoretical film within a *cinema povera*, while *The Bad Sister* (1983) offered an opportunity to translate our ideas into a different kind of film world, as it were, a 'new mainstream', a film/television hybrid. The leap beyond *Crystal Gazing* was striking. With a budget of £418,000 and a full-sized crew, *The Bad Sister* was produced for the Film on Four slot through the Moving Picture Company, known for its accomplished special effects and commercials.

The new context demanded different working methods – some we could adapt to, some we found difficult. In the first instance, Film on Four produced art films, which, quite unlike our previous theoretical films, needed a conventional, fully elaborated script not only for raising funds but as the essential blueprint for the production, its costing, its casting, its locations and so on. Peter had written film scripts of this kind during the 1960s, particularly in collaboration with Mark Peploe (see Oliver Fuke's Introduction) and, with my full agreement, he wrote *The Bad Sister* script accordingly. While the written strand of our films had, previously, always emerged out of a process of collaborative research, discussion and development, here the two were necessarily separated. We still worked closely together on the adaptation of the book, its ideas and its visual potential, but the script was less organically and collaboratively integrated than for our previous films.

At the heart of our collaborative commitment to making *The Bad Sister* lay two key aesthetic ambitions. First of all, to re-work the concept of medium specificity, which had been so important to those of us who had worked with 16mm film, into the televisual through electronic special effects. Second, we wanted to explore the key themes in Emma Tennant's novel, which resonated with the feminist-orientated use of psychoanalytic theory and various motifs in our previous films, in this very different production context. For instance, the wild women bear some relation to the Amazons of *Penthesilea*; Jane's self-transformation into a kind of androgyny in preparation for her dream travels had been prefigured in *AMY!*; and the anti-Oedipal nature of Jane's relation to her mother and father dramatizes theoretical issues raised in *Riddles of the Sphinx*. But the theme in *The Bad Sister* of sibling rivalry, of the double and the uncanny, took us into a psychoanalytically different, if still Freudian, terrain. These confusions of identity and fusions between dream and reality lay at the heart of both novel and film, and seemed particularly appropriate for the visual experiments we were envisaging.

There were, however, certain problems with the finished film, partly due to incidental circumstances, partly to miscalculation on our part. There was a mismatch, for instance, between our hope for a visualisation of the fantastic and the actualities of special effects available to us in post-production. In terms of our shooting strategy, we were still thinking cinematically rather than televisually; we used actual locations, extended shots and a mobile camera, which sometimes pushed the one-inch video past its technological capacity. And the circumstances of directing were very different in the production of *The Bad Sister*. On our previous films, Peter and I had always worked everything out before filming and we were unprepared for the on-the-spot/on-the-set decision making demanded by such a large production, a different kind of relation with actors and some of the technological problems involved in using video on location.

After *The Bad Sister*, I came quite easily to the conclusion that my approach to cinema, and my way of thinking and imagining cinematically, was unsuited to this kind of filmmaking. There was no way back to the 1970s and, I felt, the dialogue between radical aesthetics and radical politics that had enabled Peter's and my collaboration no longer had either practical viability or relevance in the very different political and economic conditions of the 1980s. At the same time, new alternative, energetic cultural movements were taking off in film and in experimental video and television. Furthermore, by the mid-1980s, Peter's and my relationship was also changing. When we decided, at least for the time being, to live separately but still in the same house, Peter moved into the basement of 207 Ladbroke Grove.

While I backed away from further filmmaking, Peter proved with *Friendship's Death* that he could work extremely successfully and, indeed, politically with the art film form, although he himself nuanced that categorisation, highlighting the film's studio production and its tight schedule. As he told Simon Field in an interview after completing the film, 'It clearly isn't a Hollywood film or even an art film … I knew Sam Fuller made films in two weeks. This is a "B" movie, it's a BFI "B" movie. I was thinking about Val Lewton at RKO'.[6] At the same time, as the film revolves around journalism and the figure of the journalist, he saw *Friendship's Death* as 'a sequel to *The Passenger*'.[7] Although he went on to make interesting documentaries with the Rear Window slot on Channel 4, it seems sad that he never again found an opportunity to use his talent for a kind of cinema that had its roots in his pre-avant-garde, scriptwriting days of the 1960s.

The Mulvey/Wollen Collaboration: Themes and Structures

The first step in the composition of all our films (until *The Bad Sister*, that is) was to arrange the thematic material we had collected together into a structure, which was ultimately organised into a series of parts or sequences. In a sense, this represents an aesthetic of layering or 'piling up' of ideas and images; our 'counter-cinema' commitment to challenging the transparency and the horizontal flow of both language and cinema is extended to structure. Rather than 'narrative or cinematic incident' leading seamlessly from one to another, the structure accumulates and also makes visible its fissures and gaps.

In *Penthesilea*, the sequences are visually and thematically cumulative. The first, a simple registration of Kleist's version of the story in mime, is complicated in the second. Here the camera's autonomous movement, its 'take' on the space and the performance, is additional to Peter's commentary on Kleist and the Amazon legend, already as he put it 'a palimpsest and a maze'. In the third sequence, images of Amazons are layered across history and mythology. In the fourth, the layering takes the form of cinematic superimposition; the suffragette film *What 80 Million Women Want* (1913) is switched alternately from foreground to background with an actor who reads from articles written by the contemporary socialist feminist Jessie Ashley. In the final part, the previous four are played on stacked video monitors, filmed by a video camera that picks out and zooms in on each one until they are gradually displaced by an added ending.[8]

Pattern became a key organising strategy for our films. For both of us, symmetry had an aesthetic, modernist attraction. From the perspective of 'counter-cinema', it could also give the linearity of film a non-linear shape, overriding the drive towards an ending, in keeping with the principle of narrative aperture as opposed to closure. In *Riddles of the Sphinx*, the structure has the shape of a palindrome, symmetrically extended either side of the turning point, the roundabout sequence, of 'Louise's story'. In *Crystal Gazing* the opening and closing images rhyme with each other and the structure is also symmetrical. As Peter describes it: 'It's a triptych. The beginning, then the central section that revolves around "Puss in Boots" and Julian's character, and then the third section picks up elements from the first. There's an underlying narrative structure that's formally blocked out. Although I don't think the "blocking out" is foregrounded in the extreme way that it might have been.'[9] In *Frida Kahlo & Tina Modotti*, the strict symmetry is enhanced by a looping mechanism that takes each image section back to its point of departure and it too has a rhyming beginning and ending.

Although Peter thought diagrammatically, clearly enjoying the arrangement of ideas into pattern (as seen in his note books on display in the exhibition *Art at the Frontier of Film Theory* and in Section 5 of this book, 'Working Documents'), he also felt that symmetry could become formulaic. The otherwise symmetrical structure in *AMY!* is disrupted by the 'flying sequence' with Yvonne Rainer's voice-over (section fourteen, 'Over a jungle', and fifteen, 'Bird in flight'). For Peter, the voice-over sequence gave the film an essential twist, a baroque distortion of an otherwise over-classical order. But even thrown out of kilter, the pattern itself would still be visible, organised around the before and after of Amy's journey across the map that forms the central section of the film.

While symmetry, and other kinds of pattern, imposed an overall shape on the early films, the separate sections were themselves made up of contrasting, hybrid and heterogeneous materials. The films made extensive use of quotation and citation, which worked against the coherence of an authorial voice (see the first Introduction). We also included other kinds of art, media and found footage, producing an incohesive or hybrid aesthetic, as well as different kinds of performance: direct address (both Peter and me) and some 'guest appearances' (Mary Kelly, Yvonne Rainer and Keith Allen, for instance). Most particularly, our films were committed to including a storyline and character. While narrative itself is intrinsically hybrid, for us the cinema's specificity and its fascination came from an ability to move, seamlessly, between the real and the fantastic, between everyday life and a dream world. We chose stories that would confuse a classical idea of narrative through, in the case of myth, a layered journey through history, or by folding multiple stories, or just anecdotes, into the main one. I think the narrative elements in our films tended to revolve more around situation than progression, which again, I think, contributes to their overall sense of irresolution. Gestures against narrative closure, intransitivity and identification were, of course, in keeping with Peter's principles of counter-cinema but the way the very different stories we used either rejected endings or ended with a symbolic blockage varied from film to film.

Situations

In constructing the central section of *Riddles of the Sphinx*, 'Louise's story', we worked quite literally with a series of five situations, spread across thirteen tableaux, that led, in some sense inexorably, from one to another, tracing various psychoanalytic and political issues around motherhood. The initial situation (the first two pans plus a third transitional one) quite simply imagines a mother whose love for her two-year-old daughter resists the logical steps of the Oedipal trajectory. The final situation (the last two pans preceded by a transitional one) would return to the Oedipal trajectory, not through an individual mother, but by imagining a stop on the Oedipal threshold, a pause, in which the maternal would not be relegated to an outside of culture but could dream of a non-patriarchal symbolic. The figure of Louise moves through three other situations in between. In the second, the mother and child are separated (the nursery and the switchboard) not Oedipally but through the intervention of social life and necessity. The third situation raises and touches on questions at stake in a campaign for workplace nurseries and the possibility of union involvement (the canteen and the discussion in the van). The film moves from interior spaces into exteriors of women's everyday lives: the Arndale Shopping Centre and the playground that, in turn, leads into a fourth situation, around a kind of pause in a world of women, through Louise and Maxine's relationship and the grandmother's care of her daughter's daughter (the walled garden, the editing room), prefiguring the more poetic moment of pause in the fifth and final situation. Here again the question of pattern comes into play. While the opening and closing scenes are symmetrical, a doubled reflection on motherhood and the place of the maternal in the Freudian and Lacanian Oedipal drama, the central and pivotal section (represented by the discussion in the van at the roundabout) is political and rooted in the everyday. A final point: the film is taken from its fourth to its final section by Mary Kelly as she reads from *Post-Partum Document* (1973–1979), a work that, among other things, combines the mother's diary, an account of her relation with her two-year-old child taken from daily life, with psychoanalytic theory. Kelly reads the section 'Weaning from the Dyad', the dilemma around which 'Louise's story' revolves. But while *Post-Partum Document* follows the Oedipus Complex through to the end, *Riddles of the Sphinx* hovers on the threshold without a certain conclusion.

To sum up: we decided not to complete 'Louise's story' with any kind of narrative closure, neither with a more acceptable version of a traditional Oedipal trajectory nor with a not-yet-properly-theorised or -envisaged feminist alternative. A 'pause' ending (although we were criticised for it at the time) would be in keeping with both avant-gardist and political principle. As mother and daughter walk into the Egyptian mummy room in the British Museum hand in hand, the gesture rhymes with but transforms their first appearance, when Louise unnecessarily carries her two-year-old daughter on her hip. There is a sense of liberation but not of closure. Furthermore, the last chapter of *Riddles of the Sphinx*, a short, self-sufficient but abstract 'story', comments on the question of endings. Rhyming with the 'Opening pages', images of monstrous women in various films, is 'A riddle ending'. A small toy, depicting a maze, challenges the player (me) to get mercury into its centre. Each bit of mercury seems to embark on a journey as it struggles through the maze, contending, like a character in a story, with success or failure until the two bits fuse into one at 'the end'. At that point, I shake them apart, instinctively resisting an image of unity and centrality that could evoke 'closure'. There was also a Brechtian dimension to this commitment to an open ending. That is, a desire to leave with a question to be taken up by whoever might be interested, whenever, in its implications. Incidentally, I remember that back in our Hollywood movie-going days in the mid-1960s we were struck by the ending of Sam Fuller's film *The Run of the Arrow* (1957); a title comes on the screen saying 'The end of this story will be written by you.'[10]

In *Crystal Gazing*, the question of narrative situation revolves around the four characters we took from Erich Kästner's *Fabian* and reinvented for our script. The atmosphere of disillusion and disorientation that has overwhelmed the book's intellectual, bohemian protagonists in Berlin in 1930 seemed relevant to the onset of Thatcherism. But through images of the future and the idea of crystal gazing, we added another dimension. Real or fantastic, these 'intimations' reach towards an indistinct temporality in which 'now', 'then' and 'to come' are entangled. For instance, during the magic act in the fifth scene, the protagonist is described in the voice-over as 'looking through a childhood window onto a landscape where the present succumbed to the future'. And later: 'They had damaged the map to dreamland and there was no way home for the blindfolded'.[11] The four characters loosely represent different and contrasting aspects to this sense of time, varying between ruined traces of a lost utopianism to the technological advances of speculative capitalism.

Peter and I had begun, in the late 1970s, to collect newspaper articles about contemporary capitalism, gradually focusing our interest on the economics of future markets, which became the topic of the unmade project *Possible Worlds* (1978). The latter not only prefigures the multiple-narrative and character structure of *Crystal Gazing* but also revolves around ideas of the future, combining (through three emblematic characters) computer technology, market speculation on 'futures' and a utopian community. We salvaged something of this in *Crystal Gazing*; Vermilion works as a reader of satellite maps forecasting weather and crop trends. As the voice-over suggests, 'This insight into the future, bought at such a great price, would benefit only a few... through the paradoxes of the commodity market, the prediction of failure could bring good fortune and money in the bank.' (On the other hand, we lifted Vermilion's very 'modern' marriage contract directly from the Berlin/Weimar atmosphere of Kästner's novel.) In both the novel and our film, the central character is a dreamer, who drifts aimlessly and is sacked from his job early on in the story. Neil, in *Crystal Gazing*, illustrates comic books and has invented a science fiction world of the future: 'The Cities of Alpha'. In the novel and the film, his best friend is finishing a PhD but in *Crystal Gazing* Julian's semiotic and psychoanalytic reading of Charles Perrault's fairy tale, 'Puss in Boots', revolves around the way that Puss's speech acts and actions can alter his master's future life. For Julian, 'Puss in Boots' was 'the founding text of modernism, the secular celebration of language as desire and language as power ... its transformation of lies into truth, fiction into fact and desire into fulfilment'. Throughout the central section of the film, Peter's writing is once again of particular importance, both in its own right and also as a reworking of his longstanding interest in the relation between word, sign and meaning. The fourth character in *Fabian* is a rising movie star who sells out to a corrupt film industry; in *Crystal Gazing*, Kim is a rising pop star. Lora Logic's music, her saxophone and most particularly her voice light up the film, bringing the culture of punk that Peter and I had wanted, but also an unexpectedly lyrical and melancholy resonance that enhances the story and its atmosphere. The gender politics of *Crystal Gazing* reflect the changing economic atmosphere of the 1980s as a male-centred labour force began to succumb to unemployment and casualisation while women's marginal work remained, by and large, the same.

Woven into these temporal twists are the points where 'necessity and contingency collide', the blockages that thwart Neil's progress: from wrong turnings, to the unexpected husband, to the crossed telephone line, to his accidental death.[12] To enhance this sense of a narrative at standstill, we also inserted into *Crystal Gazing* quite arbitrary scenes, episodes and images. Some of the locations taken from our Ladbroke Grove neighbourhood have no significance for the story: the Portobello fish-and-chip shop, the Golborne Road Chinese take away, Elgin Books, Rough Trade, the restaurant Monsieur Thompson, the mural by Ladbroke Grove Underground Station. There were also quotations and images, such as the crystal ball, the Rings of Saturn and the Joseph Cornell box. All these turnings, references, stories within stories and interruptions created a continuum with the principles of 'counter-cinema': narrative intransitivity, multiple diegeses, apertures formed by citation. The story of the rationale for Neil's projected trip to Mexico was drawn from an experience of Peter's when he was researching our *Frida Kahlo and Tina Modotti* exhibition. In Mexico City, he visited Dolores Olmedo, the powerful patron of Diego Rivera and Frida Kahlo and an important collector of their work, to solicit her support and the loan of Kahlo paintings. To Peter's horror, she explained that in order to buy 'an expensive Diego Rivera' at Sotheby's, she had pawned two Kahlos at the Central Pawn Shop in Mexico City. The ticket was held by Sotheby's, New York. Eventually the situation resolved itself, and just in time for the exhibition, but the incident had made a strong impression on us.

In some notes for *Crystal Gazing*, Peter wrote: 'London. Midwinter. 1982. Unemployment hangs like a noose round the neck of the city. Shattered dreams. Redundancy figures. ... This is a story set in the Thatcher recession. But it begins far far away. ... In the Cities of Alpha.' These notes reminded me of the way that a film about the Thatcher-designed economic crisis is punctuated by dream-like images and themes. Here *Crystal Gazing* has some kind of overlap with *Riddles of the Sphinx*, continuing and exaggerating the earlier film's fusion of abstract spaces and actual locations. Ultimately this combination of the fantastic, in a range of different forms, with the starkness of everyday reality is characteristic of both films and comes close to capturing something of what Peter and I loved about cinema.

From Script to Screen

AMY! and *Frida Kahlo & Tina Modotti*, our two short films, were based on the real lives and achievements of extraordinary women. Although *Frida Kahlo & Tina Modotti* originated as a film record of the exhibition Peter and I curated in 1982 at the Whitechapel Gallery, it evolved into a much more complex, and cinematically considered, project.[13] Obviously, the exhibition had consisted of Kahlo's paintings and Modotti's photographs on the gallery walls; the accompanying catalogue essay reflected our interest in the two women's lives and their politics, their attitudes to the female body and the significant, but very different, questions they raise about women's art and aesthetics. On the screen, the images, stories and ideas could come together, fusing into a series of visual juxtapositions. Although I would say that our previous films had all been constructed around systems of montage (primarily due to the place of pattern and tableaux in their structure), juxtaposition, in both form and content, was crucial for *Frida Kahlo & Tina Modotti*. The film's shape and argument had a rigorous binary structure, that became dialectical through montage. The Kahlo paintings and Modotti photographs were grouped thematically into three chapters; the first contrasted Kahlo's persistent return to painting herself with Modotti's engagement with public spaces, the second contrasted Kahlo's roots in her house and in Mexican culture with Modotti's internationalism and the third contrasted their personal, different, relation to the female body and its effect on their art. The combining of ideas, the use of montage, that is, was intended to generate a wider conceptual framework, a reflection on how very varied experiences could still inform a feminist political consciousness. Julian Rothenstein designed an initial 'starting point' for each chapter in which 'Frida Kahlo' and 'Tina Modotti' are juxtaposed in word and image. The montage opens up a space for a 'third meaning', a resonant evocation, through Kahlo and Modotti individually, of women's lives, their struggles and the particularity of their art more generally. Given that the documentary was intended for educational screenings, we ultimately added a voice-over text, taken from the exhibition catalogue, to make the implications of the montage clearer.

We first came across Amy Johnson in 1980, when the fiftieth anniversary of her flight to Australia in 1930 was the occasion for newspaper stories and celebrations of her life. Her story raised the question, difficult for feminism, of a woman's attempt to move into a male role and the associated, but intractable, concept of the 'heroine'. From an Amy Johnson biography we discovered that our original theme of a woman's heroism was complicated by her celebrity. While the public gaze and patriarchal recuperation surrounding her return interested us psychoanalytically, her flight also attracted a certain imperial triumphalism as it was interpolated and 'transcribed', as Peter put it, 'into the language of the Empire in legend.'[14] Coincidentally, the date further drew us to the Amy story; we had already been thinking about the political significance of the year 1930, the onset of the Great Depression, for 1980 in the immediate aftermath of the 1979 election.

From the wider events of Amy Johnson's life, we extracted two pivot points to dramatize the significance of gender and the public gaze for her story. The first: her transition from 'ordinary girl' to aspiring aviatrix; the second: from triumphant heroine to abject celebrity. The first transition takes place through the *mise-en-scène*. Amy as 'ordinary girl' is evoked through soft lighting, colour and the kind of objects she has close to her as she moves together with the camera from her dressing table to the fireplace. As 'aspiring aviatrix' she is shot in day light, wearing trousers, and her dressing table has become a desk where she studies engineering and, accordingly, in her reverse movement from the fireplace, the collection of objects has also changed. There is a very reduced, but still pertinent, homage to Hollywood melodrama's use of *mise-en-scène*, lighting, colour, objects and camera movement in this scene. The second transition is staged through the apparatus. As 'triumphant heroine', Amy is filmed with an extremely long lens. At first, she retreats from the camera's pursuing and phallic gaze but then turns to face the lens with a complicit, feminine passivity. In the fourth scene, she is filmed, in close-up, through a two-way mirror; she puts on layers of make-up, excessively and ironically, and then draws her image onto the mirror as though onto the camera's lens. There is a sense of flatness as though the active presence of the camera had morphed into the passivity of the screen. My theoretical interest in the Hollywood melodrama and my critique of woman as spectacle in 'Visual Pleasure' both inform, if only residually, the representation of Amy.

We had originally planned to make our Amy Johnson film as a feature but failed to get the requisite BFI funding. We immediately reconfigured the project, paring the story down to essentials and entwining the performed tableaux with certain still-extant sites that Amy had, as it were, inhabited in her lifetime: the department store Peter Jones, Croydon Airport, the *Daily Mail* building and her little Tiger Moth hanging in the Science Museum. For Peter and me, these were indexical traces of a once-upon-a-time reality, a tribute to both the complexity of time and the cinema's complex recording of it. The Poly Styrene and X-Ray Spex songs further complicate temporality; evocative of punk from the late 1970s, they would in time acquire a historical patina not unlike that of 'Amy, Wonderful Amy'. In the case of the map, certain places have acquired emblematic and tragic significance due to wars that have spread across the intervening decades: for instance, Banja Luka (Bosnia), Fallujah (Iraq) and Raqqa (Syria).

Throughout this Introduction, I have occasionally cited Peter's essay on 'Counter Cinema' as a point of theoretical reference for us, particularly in relation to our experiments with narrative, character and story-telling. In fact, the actual experience of translating theory into practice was always unpredictable and principles were always subject to reinvention and reconfiguration. To my mind, the films we produced over our ten-year collaboration are strikingly different from each other and bear witness to Peter's and my commitment to pursuing a project of feminist counter-cinema through changing circumstances. In our films, the question of pleasure, which is raised in both Peter's 'Counter Cinema' and my 'Visual Pleasure and Narrative Cinema', is reconfigured. I would like to think that the ideas and images that you might find in these scripts evoke something, as Peter would put it, 'at a knight's move' away from visual pleasure as such. You might notice the appeal to a curious spectator and to the human mind's pleasure in form and structure … away from linguistic transparency to the stutter, the hieroglyph and the riddle.

Notes

1. Peter offers an account of the 1970s in his essay 'Knight's Moves'. See: Peter Wollen, 'Knight's Moves', *Public* 25 (Spring 2002), 54–67.

2. Peter Wollen, 'The Field of Language in Film', *October* 17 (Summer 1981), 54–56.

3. Peter Wollen, 'Preface', in Peter Wollen, *Readings and Writings: Semiotic Counter-Strategies* (London: Verso, 1982), vii.

4. See: Peter Wollen, 'Counter Cinema: *Vent d'Est*', *Afterimage 4* (Autumn 1972), 6–16; republished as 'Godard and Counter Cinema: *Vent d'Est*', in *Readings and Writings: Semiotic Counter-Strategies* (London: Verso, 1982), 79-91; and Laura Mulvey, 'Visual Pleasure and Narrative Cinema', *Screen* 16(3) (Autumn 1975), 6–18; republished in *Visual and Other Pleasures*, 2nd edn (Basingstoke: Palgrave Macmillan, 2009), 14–27.

5. See: Mignon Nixon, '"Why Freud?" asked the Shrew: Psychoanalysis and Feminism, *Post-Partum Document*, and the History Group', *Psychoanalysis, Culture and Society* 20(2) (June 2015), 1-10.

6. Peter Wollen, 'Two Weeks on Another Planet', interview by Simon Field, *Monthly Film Bulletin*, 54(646) (November 1, 1987), 326.

7. *Ibid.*, 325.

8. For detailed descriptions of these sequences, see the script published in this volume.

9. Laura Mulvey and Peter Wollen, 'Crystal Gazing', interview by Fizzy Oppe and Don Ranvaud, *Framework: The Journal of Cinema and Media* 19 (Summer 1982), 17.

10. At this point, I stopped writing to check Lee Russell's 1964 essay on Fuller in New Left Review. I had forgotten that Peter had already spelt out the connection between Brecht and Fuller: '…it seems to me that Fuller is the film director whose methodology closest approaches Brecht's theatre. Compare, for instance, his use of characters both as actors in a drama and spokesmen of their consciousness of the drama… at the end of *Run of the Arrow* a rubric flashes on to the screen, "The end of this story will be written by you"'. Lee Russell, 'Samuel Fuller', in Peter Wollen, *Signs and Meaning in the Cinema*, fifth edition (London: BFI/Palgrave Macmillan, 2013), 151–156.

11. For further information about these scenes, see the script published in this volume.

12. The journalist on the crossed line is John Howe, an old friend of Peter's from Oxford days, later co-occupants of a flat in Westbourne Terrace. John and my sister, Rosamund, married and we shared the 207 Ladbroke Grove house. At the time of *Crystal Gazing*, John was contributing a column, which he wrote in French, for the newspaper *Le Matin*. He used his 'Laker' copy in the film.

13. The idea for the exhibition itself had come from a holiday in Mexico with Jon Halliday and Francine Winham (Christmas 1978 to New Year 1979), when we first encountered, and were deeply impressed by, the art of the Mexican Revolution and the history of that period.

14. Peter Wollen, 'The Field of Language in Film', 58f.

Section 1

Laura Mulvey and Peter Wollen's
Collaborative Films

1

Penthesilea: Queen of the Amazons

Laura Mulvey and Peter Wollen

[08″]* *Title*:   PENTHESILEA
                  QUEEN OF THE AMAZONS

Percussion music, which continues on the audio track through the opening titles.

[08″] *Title*:   a film in five
                 sequences by
                 LAURA MULVEY and
                 PETER WOLLEN

[08″] *Title*:   camera and lighting
                 LOUIS CASTELLI

                 sound and portapak
                 LARRY SIDER

[08″] *Title*:   production coordinator
                 SHARON RUSSELL

                 animation and titles
                 DON LEMBECK

---

*   Shot timings are in minutes and seconds throughout.

Percussion music fades on the audio track.

[08″] *Title*: 1. Ghost white like a not yet
written page

Mallarmé
"Mimique"

[16′ 32″] *A mime-drama, condensed and adapted from the play* Penthesilea *(1808) by Heinrich von Kleist. The performance takes place on a stage and is filmed from a fixed camera position.*

Audio track: synch sound.

[08″] *Title*: 2. The shadow sprinkled in black characters

Mallarmé
Quant au livre

[18 45″] *A spoken commentary ranging over topics associated with Kleist and with the Amazon legend. As Peter Wollen speaks/reads the words of the directors, he moves around an interior space. The handheld camera follows him at first; then, disengaging itself, it tracks in on cue cards from which the speech had been read. Sometimes the text on the cards is not identical to the spoken text.*

Handheld camera.

Audio track: synch sound.

Peter enters down the stairs, sits on a step and reads. The camera follows and moves slowly towards him.

PETER: This film consists of five sequences, each sequence two takes, each take one core of film. A normal narrative film tells its story through editing. Each cut indicates a gap in time or a change of angle and point of view. But, on another level, it is editing which produces the alternative world which we imagine behind the screen. It is because there are gaps and differences of point of view that we lend this imaginary world extension in time and space. It is the act of bridging over gaps and linking together differences which creates the sense of another world, into which we are given a series of privileged glimpses. Each cut articulates this world, and by articulating it, it creates it.

It is for this reason we wanted to make a film without editing. We wanted to call this imaginary world into question – not to reject fiction or fantasy, but to situate it and to locate it. Film theorists have tended to argue that a film without editing would be a purely natural film, with the artifice of film-making reduced to zero. But, in this sense, our film is un-natural. It is a film which avoids conventional cuts, but not discontinuities or breaks. It is a montage film – it doesn't follow a single unbroken thread, the thread of a story from beginning to end. It is about something else: the space between a story which is never told and a history which has never been made.

Peter moves to a chair and sits down. The camera follows him.

In the first sequence, which we have already seen, there's the performance of a mime-drama, based on a play by the German playwright Kleist, Heinrich von Kleist, called *Penthesilea*. In it we see the Greeks and Amazons in battle during the time of the Trojan War. We see how the Amazons seize a prisoner and rape him in their Festival of Roses. We see how the Amazon war-queen, Penthesilea, falls in love with the Greek hero, Achilles, and how Achilles falls in love with her. We see them torn between their loyalty and their love and how Achilles surrenders to his enemy. Finally we see Penthesilea kill Achilles, we see her fury, her rapture and her grief. We see her own death, a strange act of suicide through sheer strength of passion.

The story enacted in the mime is not at all the same story told in the legends and epics of antiquity. In these ancient legends it is Penthesilea who is killed: Achilles lives to be killed later by Paris. This is the legend of the Achilles heel. In most versions of the story, Achilles falls in love with Penthesilea, either as he kills her, thrusting into her the spear of Pelian ash, or, after she has fallen, when he removes the helmet from her face. It is this moment which has most often been commemorated. In an elegy by Propertius, the Roman poet, we read: 'The victor vanquished, by the radiant face revealed'.

The camera moves backward in front of Peter, up some steps and through an arch. A few paces past the arch, the camera moves slightly to the right.

So to begin with, we have two broad versions of the story: the version of antiquity and the version of Kleist, written during the period of the Napoleonic Wars and the consolidation of Romanticism. Each version has very different implications – very different senses – while there are also constant themes: love/death, *amour fou*, fatal passion, love concealed under the cloak of aggression, the war of the sexes, the society of women, grief, mourning at a loss, perhaps at a difference. The fulcrum of all these stories is the image of the Amazon – the woman who is independent, aggressive and destructive: perhaps superior to man, perhaps his equal, perhaps, despite all, his inferior. For both the ancient Greeks and for Kleist, the image of the Amazon was both fascinating and frightening. It still has the same power today.

Peter gets up and walks through the arch into the far room. The camera pans left.

In the third sequence of this movie, the one right after this, we see a series of images of Amazons: almost all of them produced by men. All, in fact. The fourth sequence shows the images and words of women: suffragettes from the early years of this century, before the First World War. This was the first period when women themselves united in struggle, fighting for political rights. The reality of their struggle brings myth into contact with history. The image of the Amazon is still projected on to the woman militant, both by men and by women themselves, from within or from outside the movement. But it is invested now with a new political meaning.

Peter reaches the steps beneath the window and sits down there. After rejoining Peter for an instant, the camera pans back right again, as far as the fireplace. The camera tracks in to the fireplace, lingering slightly, continues along the wall, turns at the corner and Peter comes into frame in profile.

To my knowledge, there has only been one other attempt to make a film of *Penthesilea*. For years it was the dream project of Leni Riefenstahl, director of *Triumph of the Will*, Hitler's protégée, ever since she read Kleist's play in the twenties. She identified herself deeply both with Penthesilea and with Kleist: 'And then the future of Penthesilea! If there is a transmigration of souls, then I must have lived her life at some previous time. Every word that she speaks is spoken from the very depths of my soul – at no time could I act differently from Penthesilea!'

The camera begins to track back and continues through the arch into the conservatory, keeping Peter in centre frame.

She sees Penthesilea as a super-heroine, half-human, half-divine. In fact, she restores the sexual duality to Nietzsche's vision of the *Übermensch*. Again, following Nietzsche, the super-heroine is more Dionysiac than Apollonian – the project is saturated with Nietzsche's return to Hellenism from the other side, his discovery in ancient Greece of a counter doctrine, which would reinvigorate the German people, a monstrous mixture of tragic gloom with manic laughter. Her film was very nearly made. Serious preparations got under way for filming – detailed work on script and art direction, searching out locations in Libya, casting: she was going to play the name part herself as well as directing. Then the war broke out and the project was abandoned. All that remains are her notes. Notes which vividly convey the movie Leni Riefenstahl saw as she read Kleist's pages.

The camera pans up, left, then tilts down the pillar, continuing to pan left, then moves faster across the corner and to the table.

The camera finds cue card A and moves in to read it: WE SEE HOW THE AMAZON WAR QUEEN PENTHESILEA FALLS IN LOVE WITH THE GREEK HERO ACHILLES AND HOW ACHILLES FALLS IN LOVE WITH HER. WE SEE THEM TORN BETWEEN THEIR LOYALTY AND THEIR LOVE AND HOW ACHILLES SURRENDERS TO HIS ENEMY. FINALLY WE SEE PENTHESILEA KILL ACHILLES. WE SEE HER FURY. HER RAPTURE AND HER GRIEF. WE SEE HER OWN DEATH. AN ACT OF SUICIDE THROUGH SHEER STRENGTH OF PASSION.

Leni Riefenstahl was not the only woman, in the aftermath of Nietzsche, to identify herself with the Amazon. In the *Futurist Manifesto for Women*, written in March 1912, Valentine de Saint-Point replies to Marinetti's absolute derogation and rejection of women. We find the same themes, this time within a Futurist perspective: 'Woman are Furies and Amazons; Semiramis, Joan of Arc, Jeanne Hachette; Judith and Charlotte Corday; Cleopatra and Messalina; warriors who fight more ferociously than men, agents of destruction who contribute to natural selection by wasting the weak, out of pride and desperation.' The super-heroine joins the super-hero, set apart from the mediocre, the masses.

The camera moves along the floor to the conservatory steps where the film began.

The camera finds cue card B and moves in to read it: FILM WITHOUT EDITING / CALL IMAGINARY WORLD INTO QUESTION. NOT REJECT FICTION / SITUATE. THEORISTS / FILM WITHOUT EDITING NATURAL. MONTAGE: DISCONTINUITIES. NO SINGLE THREAD. IT IS ABOUT SOMETHING ELSE: THE SPACE BETWEEN A STORY WHICH IS NEVER TOLD AND A HISTORY WHICH HAS NEVER YET BEEN MADE.

The image of the Amazon loses all its resonance of solidarity, membership of a society of women. In Kleist's play, Penthesilea rejects her comrades. Even beyond that, the army of Amazons is set apart from the mass of other women. The Amazon warriors are the gold who set off the diamond of Penthesilea.

They are splendid and glamorous, fascinating to other women for the fear which they arouse in men, but impossible to emulate except in phantasy. Their weapons and their strategy are men's weapons and strategy: they offer an alternative which is magical, not political.

The camera tilts up from cue card B, through leaves, ending with the arch in centre frame. The camera moves forward into the far room through the arch, as Peter approaches.

This division between ordinary women and Amazons is found in Ancient literature too. Quintus of Smyrna wrote an epic about the Trojan War, probably in the third or fourth century after Christ. He includes a scene in his narrative where the women of Troy watch, from the city walls, the Amazons fighting the Greeks. Greek heroes are falling like autumn leaves before the Amazon onslaught. One of the Trojan women proposes they should join the battle too: 'We ourselves should share the battle. We are not much different from vigorous men. We have the same courage; eyes and limbs are alike. Light and air are common to all. Our food is not different. So why do we run away from fighting?' They are all about to join in when they are restrained by the priestess of Athene. She argues they should stay at home weaving and avoid the tumult and misery of war. 'It is true that all human beings are from the same stock, but different persons practise different jobs and that job is best where a person works with knowledge in their head.'

The camera and Peter pass through the arch. The camera continues on towards the steps at the foot of the staircase, tilting down to find cue card C and moves in to read it:
"AND THEN THE FUTURE OF PENTHESILEA! IF THERE IS A TRANSMIGRATION OF SOULS, THEN I MUST HAVE LIVED HER LIFE AT SOME PREVIOUS TIME. EVERY WORD THAT SHE SPEAKS IS SPOKEN FROM THE VERY DEPTHS OF MY SOUL — AT NO TIME COULD I ACT DIFFERENTLY FROM PENTHESILEA!"

The argument is one that has been used over the centuries to keep women in their place. It is based on the idea that the division of labour is virtually irreversible. The Amazons appear as exceptional women who have broken down the division of labour for themselves, but whose example is not relevant to other women. Of course, ultimately there is still the physical division of labour involved in reproduction.

The camera immediately leaves cue card C and moves fairly slowly across the carpet to the corner, by a tree.

It is this which brings the Amazons to Troy in the first place (in Kleist's version at least) in order to take prisoners who will breed with the Amazons during the Festival of Roses. Otherwise the Amazons would be a society completely apart. The myth would no longer be about sexual division and conflict. It would lose the erotic meaning which keeps it alive.

By a roundabout route, this brings us back to Kleist. The fascination and revulsion caused by sexual difference runs like a red thread through Kleist's work. Like Leni Riefenstahl, he identified himself intimately with Penthesilea, both as woman and as warrior. She combined in one character two phantasies which Kleist could never combine in real life: the dream of dying together (with a lover) and the dream of dying on the battlefield. In the end Kleist chose dying together: joint suicide.

The camera finds cue card D and moves in to read it: CAME INDICATES A MOVE WHICH HAS BEEN MADE TOWARD THE SPEAKER IN SOME WAY IN THE PAST. MOVE IS SUBSTANCE CHANGING ITS PLACE. SPEAKER IS SUBSTANCE THROUGH WHICH TALK COMES. THE PAST IS THE REALM IN WHICH THINGS HAVE BEEN CHANGED. PLACE IS THE CONSCIOUSNESS' POSITIONING OF SUBSTANCE.

Kleist was born into an aristocratic family which traditionally sent its sons into the Prussian army. His father was an army officer and, after his death, Kleist was sent away from home by his mother. First to study and then, when he was fourteen, to join the Regiment of Guards as a cadet. He served in the Guards seven years, at the beginning of the great wars against France which dominated his lifetime. Even after he left the army, when he was 21, he tried several times to rejoin: usually times of psychological crisis. The last attempt was just before his death.

The camera leaves cue card D and moves up to the base of the right fireplace pillar. The camera moves up grotesques on the pillar, left along the lintel of the fireplace, pausing on medallions, and down the left fireplace pillar. The camera moves to the step from the base of the pillar, across the carpet. The camera comes up to look through the arch out to the garden in the distance.

The fatal project of joint suicide re-occurs several times in Kleist's life. He proposed double suicide to at least five people, of both sexes, probably even more. Two of them were friends with whom he had been a cadet in adolescence: Ernst Pfuel and Rühle von Lilienstern. Pfuel, in particular, he proposed joint suicide to more than once. He also wrote *Penthesilea* for him: it was not a play for women, Kleist said, but for men, and even then only for the strongest and most virile men, such as his friend. The most important woman in his life was his half-sister Ulrike. He told her that if it had not been for the ban on incest, he would have been glad to join his life with hers. It was her masculine appearance which fascinated him: 'She has nothing of her sex but the hips' – masculine yet maternal. On a trip they took together to Paris, Ulrike wore men's clothes. But finally she rejected Kleist: she felt he disgraced the family name.

The camera moves forward through the arch to the window on to the garden. The camera looks out into the garden through the window. The camera comes back and pans left through plants, along the line of the radiator, and reaches Peter, who is sitting in a chair.

Psycho-analysts have concentrated on Kleist's relationship with his mother – the equation of womb and tomb – and the 'travelling' significance of death – dying as the last of the many fugue-like journeys Kleist undertook during his life. In this context, the Amazon queen appears as the powerful mother to whom the disarmed and child-like hero wishes to surrender. But she is also the hostile, vengeful mother: in the play, Achilles is shocked to find that Penthesilea has cut off her left breast, according to Amazon custom.

Finally the mother devours the child. She takes the metaphor of devouring love and turns it into reality. 'I did what I had spoken, word for word.' Devoured by the woman, dying with the woman: a double phantasy of sexual union.

Peter gets up and moves to another chair, still in the conservatory. The camera follows him.

Kleist's final depression followed his rejection by Ulrike, when he tried to borrow money from her to buy military equipment, in order to re-join the army. His only solace was his friendship with Henriette von Vogel, who herself was dying of cancer. She was one of the few people he still saw in society. On 20 November 1811 (Kleist was now just 34 years old) the couple set out on a trip from Berlin to Potsdam. In the afternoon they stopped at an inn by a small lake and sent their coach back to the city. They sat in their room all night drinking coffee and composing letters of farewell. At nine the next morning they walked down to the edge of the lake. The innkeeper heard two shots, but thought nothing of it. Later their two bodies were found in a hollow. Kleist had shot Henriette von Vogel in the left breast and then himself in the mouth. The bodies were buried together in one grave.

Peter gets up from the chair and leaves the conservatory through the arch. He goes off-screen. As he exits the right frame, the camera moves in to the table, finds cue card E and reads it: IN THE AFTERNOON THEY STOPPED AT AN INN BY A SMALL LAKE AND SENT THEIR COACH BACK TO THE CITY. THEY SAT IN THEIR ROOM ALL NIGHT DRINKING COFFEE AND COMPOSING LETTERS OF FAREWELL. AT NINE THE NEXT MORNING THEY WALKED DOWN TO THE EDGE OF THE LAKE. THE INNKEEPER HEARD TWO SHOTS BUT THOUGHT NOTHING OF IT. LATER THEIR TWO BODIES WERE FOUND IN A HOLLOW.

One biographer writes that the only period of happiness during Kleist's life was the time he spent in a prison camp: he was arrested by the French occupation forces after the defeat of Prussia at the battle of Jena. In fact, it was in the camp that he wrote and re-wrote much of *Penthesilea*. The play is full of echoes of Kleist's life as well as anticipations of his death: happiness in captivity, military ambition, sexual confusion. Kleist found in the cycle of Greek legend the constellation of his own fears and phantasies: a world as full of loss, violence and contradiction as his own.

The camera leaves cue card E, tilts and begins a series of spiralling and crisscross movements.

Myths are stories which repeat themselves in an endless sequence of variations. Myths can never conclude anything; they can only die, when the problems they express are superseded: problems such as the meaning of sexual difference. As the terms of the problem vary, so do those of the myth. The story of Penthesilea has survived for nearly three millennia, changing with the demands of different epochs and societies.

The camera finds cue card F and moves in to read it, simultaneously with Peter, who is in the other room: THE AMAZON PENTHESILEA ARRIVED TO FIGHT WITH THE TROJANS. SHE WAS THE DAUGHTER OF ARES AND CAME FROM THRACE. ACHILLES KILLED HER IN FULL GLORY AND THE TROJANS BURIED HER. ACHILLES KILLED THERSITES WHO TAUNTED HIM FOR HIS PROFESSION OF LOVE FOR HER. A QUARREL BROKE OUT AMONG THE GREEKS OVER THERSITES' DEATH.

At times it was almost lost completely. The chain can be traced back to the post-Homeric epic of Arctinus, the *Aethiopid*, which takes up the story of Troy where Homer left off. We only know the version of Arctinus because it was summarised by Proclus in a fragment of his *Chrestomathy*, only a few brief lines: 'The Amazon Penthesilea arrived to fight with the Trojans. She was the daughter of Ares and came from Thrace. Achilles killed her in full glory and the Trojans buried her. Achilles killed Thersites, who taunted him for his profession of love for her. A quarrel broke out among the Greeks over Thersites' death.'

The camera leaves cue card F and begins to look for Peter, finding him through the arch. The camera moves up the steps into the other room and round in an arc until Peter is full face in centre frame.

Different chains of allusion and memory surface at different points. By the time it reached Kleist, the story had passed through the Trojan cycles of medieval authors, the Renaissance re-discovery of Greece and Rome, the neo-classicism of Weimar: Goethe features an Amazon in *Wilhelm Meister*, a lady on a white horse, wearing a man's cloak, who rescues the hero when he is left wounded by robbers. He falls in love with her at the moment she takes off her cloak to cover him. Then came Kleist, who talked badly, stammering, muttering to himself, falling silent, living in the realm of the written word. What he wrote forms another level of the entire, tortuous palimpsest.

Peter gets up and begins to walk back and forth in front of the fireplace. The camera swings back and forth across the fireplace at a slightly different tempo to Peter, sometimes following him, sometimes losing him, so he exits and re-enters the frame.

If Leni Riefenstahl had made her film of *Penthesilea*, it would have appeared as the culmination of a process: the fusion of Greek and German culture in a final union of the arts, 'a great film opera', which tied all the strands together. In the ideal world of art, difference, domination, conflict, and death take on an ideal meaning, called beauty. But history will go on, regenerating the story. If we can understand it, re-telling it with its gaps and its spaces, absences as well as its presences, then perhaps one day we will be able to end it in history, rather than in words or images.

When Kleist first published Penthesilea in his magazine *Phöbus*, which he started with a friend, he sent a copy to Goethe, anxious to hear his judgement: 'on the knees of my heart'. A strange moment: Goethe in Weimar, his garden adorned by a perfect sphere, a symbol of universal reason, confronted by the printed page whose words shattered that sphere in phantasy. Goethe did not like what he read and he sent Kleist a cold letter, a letter which was hard and hurtful for Kleist to read. Goethe found the play 'strange' and 'fabulous'; he could not respond to it. He compares Kleist to a 'Jew awaiting the Messiah, a Christian awaiting the New Jerusalem, a Portuguese awaiting the return of St Sebastian'.

Peter moves to lean by a windowsill at the foot of stairs. The camera pans around until it reaches Peter and holds him in the centre of the frame.

Goethe saw in Kleist's play a flight from the world. In one sense, he was right:

Kleist's play, with its elephants and its scythed chariots, has hardly ever been performed. But in another sense he was wrong. Goethe's flight was from the world of the unconscious, psychic reality. It is only through the detours of phantasy and dream that we can return to history and act there in the knowledge that the unconscious is always running through us. It is in this sense that we should take Goethe's characteristic injunction to Kleist: '*Hic Rhodus! Hic salta!*'

Peter gets up and leaves the scene, walking up stairs. The camera briefly follows him until he exits the frame.

[02″] *Title*:   3. Blazons of phobia, seals of self-punishment –

     Lacan, after Vico

[19′ 04″] *Images of the Amazon myth from ancient Greece to Wonder Woman. Some transitions are made with animated wipes and masking.*
Rostrum camera.

Audio track: Luciano Berio's 'Visage' (1961) with the voice of Cathy Berberian.

[06″] *Intertitle*:   Wounded Amazons
                            Copies of bronze statues from Ephesus

[1′ 24″] *Various stills.*

[06″] *Intertitle*:   Greeks against Amazons
                            Copies of a gold shield of Athena Parthenos

[42″] *Various stills.*

[06″] *Intertitle*:   Greeks against Amazons
                            Friezes in marble
                            Bronze breastplate

[54″] *Various stills.*

[06″] *Intertitle*:   Mounted Amazons

> Frieze in marble (Hellenistic)
> Painting on alabaster (Italian-Greek)

[40"] *Various stills.*

[06"] *Intertitle*:   Heracles kills the Amazon Queen
> Greek vase-paintings

[40"] *Various stills.*

[06"] *Intertitle*:   Heracles kills the Amazon Queen
> Greek friezes in marble and tufa

[30"] *Various stills.*

[06"] *Intertitle*:   Theseus kills the Minotaur
> Vase-painting (Greek)
> Wall-painting (Roman)

[30"] *Various stills.*

[06"] *Intertitle*:   Theseus abducts the Amazon Queen
> Vase-paintings
> Statue in marble

[54"] *Various stills.*

[06"] *Intertitle*:   Amazons in pursuit
> Greek vase-paintings

[1' 26"] *Various stills.*

[06"] *Intertitle*:   Amazons in battle
> Syrian-Roman mosaic

[14"] *Still.*

[06"] *Intertitle*:   Mounted Amazons

Byzantine silver amphora

[28″] *Various stills.*

[06″] *Intertitle*:   Amazons in battle
                      Painted panel (Peter Paul Rubens)

[1′ 30″] *Various stills.*

[06″] *Intertitle*:   Achilles kills Penthesilea
                      Greek vase-paintings

[32″] *Various stills.*

[06″] *Intertitle*:   Achilles kills Penthesilea
                      Copy of a Roman painted shield

[20″] *Still.*

[06″] *Intertitle*:   Achilles falls in love with Penthesilea
                      Roman tomb-sculpture

[1′ 02″] *Various stills.*

[06″] *Intertitle*:   Achilles falls in love with Penthesilea
                      Copy of a bas-relief in marble

[16″] *Still.*

[06″] *Intertitle*:   Penthesilea in battle
                      Medieval tapestries

[50″] *Various stills.*

[06″] *Intertitle*:   Babil and Bijou

[12″] *Still.*

[06"] *Intertitle*:　　Amazon Princess
　　　　　　　　　　Wonder Woman Comic (1948)

[1′ 38"] *Various stills.*

[06"] *Intertitle*:　　Amazon Princess
　　　　　　　　　　Wonder Woman Comic (1972)

[2′ 20"] *Various stills.*

Fade to a previously seen still, which is held for 26".

[08"] *Title*:　　　4. Net of light on overlight

　　　　　　　　H.D.
　　　　　　　　"Projector"

[18′ 58"] *A superimposition of two films: a woman speaking the words of the feminist Jessie Ashley from* The Woman's Journal *(Boston, 1911–1912) and the suffrage propaganda film* What 80 Million Women Want *(1913). Each film fades in and out sequentially; the most relevant sections of the suffrage film are shown at normal speed and the rest speeded up.*

Audio track: Jessie Ashley's words alternate with the sound of machinery and women's voices talking indistinctly.

Suffrage film plays.

As the speaker begins, the suffrage film plays more quickly.

SPEAKER: Is it impossible for all women to work together to uproot an injustice common to all? Is there no way to bring this about? Surely there should be. We must be rid of mere ladylikeness.

We must succeed in making the oppressed class of women the most urgent in the demand for what we all must have. When we have brought this about, we women shall be irresistibly strong. For the most part the handsome ladies are well satisfied with their personal lot, but they want the vote as a matter of justice, while the fluttering, jammed-in subway girls are terribly blind to the whole question of class oppression and sex oppression.

Only the women of the working class are really oppressed, but it is not only the working class to whom injustice is done. Women of the leisure class need freedom too. All women of whatever class must become conscious of their position in the world. All must be made to stand erect, to become self-reliant, free human beings.

If we could but see our possible strength and our existing weaknesses, should we not become such a mighty, marching crowd that the ladylike parade would be swept away and engulfed in masses of aroused womanhood?

The audio track is taken over by the sound of machinery.

The suffrage film plays at normal speed.

As the speaker begins, the suffrage film plays more quickly.

What then are we doing to reach working women? In reality, suffragists come to the working class as outsiders. They do not show any knowledge whatsoever of working-class interests. And aside from futile argument, what do they do? Do they ever come forward with vigorous backing of purely working-class legislation? Has there been a single protest anywhere against the Mexican situation? Have they taken pains to point out to working women the trend of our court decisions?

What are the arguments the working-class girl hears when she stops to listen to the impassioned soap-box orator from the suffrage ranks? 'The right to vote is the natural, inherent, unalienable right of every human being.' She turns away. She knows as a matter of fact she has no right to vote and she doesn't care. But before she is out of earshot comes the plea, 'Women must have the ballot to protect their homes and protect their children.' She has no home nor any children, and no, she couldn't do much to protect either on three dollars a week. So the disappointed orator wonders what is wrong. It would seem there must be something wrong in a method that fails to enlist the sympathy of the very women who need the ballot most.

Yet in the main, suffragists simply have an ever-present consciousness of what the middle-class average person will think about this question or that. They make expediency the guiding star of suffrage conduct and dread the prospect of mixing suffrage up with outside interests.

An incident during the impressive march of workers after the Triangle Fire pointed out this attitude. A girl from the marching crowd ran out to join me, calling me by name. After marching for a few moments, she spoke of the protest meeting held by the College Equal Suffrage League a few nights before and said expressively, 'I thought you suffragists weren't any good. But if you're that sort, I'll change my mind.'

She voiced the feeling of the majority of working-class girls. And yet some suffragists had tried to persuade the College League not to hold the meeting as it would hurt suffrage by mixing it up with outside interests.

The audio track is taken over by the sound of machinery and women's voices talking indistinctly.

The suffrage film plays at normal speed.

As the speaker begins, the suffrage film plays more quickly.

In the past strikes were almost wholly the affairs of men, while women have always shared the sacrifice and responsibility and often, by their bravery, helped the men to victory, or, by their lack of sympathy, brought defeat. They have themselves been outside the strike.

The suffrage film plays at normal speed.

Today, however, some of the most remarkable strikes are those of women. When once the idea of union is accepted by working women, they hold to it with an unquestioning loyalty and pluck. They have the fervour of their sex and an unconquerable devotion. They have shown the beginning of solidarity, which is one of the most remarkable things in the whole history of the women's movement. If in the very beginning of women's industrial struggle women can show such an unswerving determination to stick together and win, what may we not look for in the future, when women have political power and more confidence in themselves?

The suffrage film plays more quickly.

Every struggle is an object lesson in the need for solidarity. For ages, men have been sex-conscious. Men are always loyal to men. But in the industrial struggle, the competition for mastery has been between men workers on the one hand and men employers on the other hand. It has not been a sex struggle but a class struggle. But with women the case is different. They have had to struggle against sex privilege as well as class privilege. Working men have bitterly opposed and resent the entry of women into industry and still treat them with scant justice in their unions and in their various schemes for self-protection. It is only recently that men have begun to see the necessity and the justice of women's suffrage. And so women have had to fight men as competitors in work, as well as against men employers. And for this reason, the struggle has never been clear cut along class lines but is still complicated with the struggle across sex lines.

One rather curious difference to be observed between the records of recent strikes by men and those by women is the attitude toward the strikers of women who are not themselves workers, women who belong to the non-gainful class, college women, professional women, women of leisure and those who control money. In large numbers, they have thrown themselves into the very ranks of the working girls and they have given them their wholehearted sympathy. They have done picket duty and they have not shrunk from the attendant arrests by the police. In several instances, they have passed the night in the cells. They have given money as well as raised it, and they have worked in many ways, showing a splendid sex-conscious spirit that foretells great victories for the future.

This, of course, is what gives the vital force to the women's movement and it counts for the strange phenomenon of wealthy women joining hands with the poorest of working girls. It is this sense of sexual oppression that has brought women all over the world to the banners of radical advanced movements. Consciously or unconsciously, women have a great bond of sympathy. They see in the great struggle going on in all parts of the world the signs of a brighter day and a better life.

There is something always inspiring about a strike. It may be ill-timed, ill-advised and foredoomed to failure, yet it always stands for sacrifice, heroism and hope. Back of this voluntary acceptance by the workers of their great dread, unemployment, lie long years of patient suffering, of self-repression and of uncomplaining useful work. At last, the worker has a faint gleam of hope that better days may dawn for her and, through her, for her entire class.

The suffrage film plays at normal speed.

But we must not be socialistic. That would be outrageous. So in come the protests, and, oh, very violent ones. And what about, pray? About nothing more serious than my poor words. Really? Just what is wrong with them, I don't know. But someone muttered something about socialism. This being the case, what shall I do? How can I cure what my critics say is wrong if I can't see how it is wrong? I refuse to contemplate the ballot through a magnifying class. For suffrage is only a part, though an important one, of the worldwide movement for a real democracy and to give women their true inheritance.

The suffrage film plays more quickly.

To concentrate on votes alone is like freeing one wing of the eagle while leaving the other tied. One wing will not suffice to carry him up to the heavens blue. Besides, I would not if I could write with my finger upon the pulse of our great genteel ones, seeking to please them, picking my words, and shaping my thoughts to meet their beautiful, delicate sensibilities. My sympathies are not with these, but rather are with the great, simple working class. With these I would gladly take my stand, if they would have me.

But, oh, you great genteel ones, you who resent the words of such as I, could you but feel the scorn in which our class is held by the class you fear so much, could you but be for one hour in the midst of real wage-earning girls as one of them and read their souls through their clear, fierce young eyes, could you but understand what they think of us and all our privileges, you would not perhaps respect so much the opinions of our politicians, of our sleek respectables, of our kid-gloved gentlemen from whom we beg the ballot on bended, trembling knee.

The suffrage film plays at normal speed.

Could you but feel the tingle in the blood that comes when a mass of them together, the young working people, shout out clearly and triumphantly, 'March on, march on to victory or death,' you would know that no real freedom will ever come to women that does not come through those same women of the working class. What to them is our buzzing about their battles? What do they care for our twitterings, however revolutionary, radical, dangerous or whatnot we may call them?

If I could write for them, if I could but reach their ears. But they judge us by our deeds, and words ring hollow when they come from the ranks of the privileged ones. Those who stand by the wayside while we speed by, those who are hidden from our sight by the dust we raise, these dare to know the present as it is, fearlessly, because through their brooding eyes, thank god, they see the future.

The audio track is taken over by the sound of machinery and women's voices talking indistinctly.

The suffrage film plays more quickly.

But these never hear my words. And so I sing my swansong. It only seems fair to tell my friends, and I have a few, you know, why there will be no more of my outrageous utterances spread before the helpless readers of the official organ. I don't want to ruin the movement, nor do I pine to kill the cause. That would really be too bad. Though it is delightfully flattering to think how easily, according to some, I could accomplish more inflammatory words. The official board, with all its weight of suffrage authority, has not formally requested silence of me. Voluntarily I hold my peace.

[8″] *Title*:   5. Notes on the
                magic writing pad

                Freud

[17′ 53″] *Four video monitors present the four preceding sequences of the film. As the camera zooms into each of the monitors in turn, the image from that sequence fills the screen. Gradually, new and unfamiliar images begin to intrude. This fifth tape begins with the mime, shot from a different, closer, position; then, with the image and sound on all four monitors, the actress playing Penthesilea removes her make-up and turns to address the camera with the last words of the film.*

Audio track: preceding sequences and synch sound in the dressing room.

The sound from Sequence 3 plays.

The camera zooms in to focus on the monitor displaying Sequence 3.

The sound from Sequence 2 plays.

PETER: *(on video)* …called Penthesilea. In it we see the Greeks and Amazons in battle during the time of the Trojan War. We see how the Amazons seize a prisoner and rape him in their Festival of Roses. We see how the Amazon war-queen Penthesilea falls in love with the Greek hero Achilles, and how Achilles falls in love with her.

The camera zooms out. A fifth tape has been added, displacing the one displaying Sequence 4.

We see them torn between their loyalty and their love and how Achilles surrenders to his enemy. Finally we see Penthesilea kill Achilles, we see her fury, her rapture and her grief. We see her own death, a strange act of suicide through sheer strength of passion.

The story enacted in the mime is not at all the same story told in the legends and epics of antiquity. In these ancient legends it is Penthesilea who is killed: Achilles lives to be killed later by Paris. This is the legend of the Achilles heel. In most versions of the story, Achilles falls in love with Penthesilea, either as he kills her, thrusting into her the spear of Pelian ash, or, after she has fallen, when he removes the helmet from her face. It is this moment which has most often been commemorated. In an elegy by Propertius, the Roman poet, we read: 'The victor vanquished, by the radiant face revealed'.

So to begin with, we have two broad versions of the story: the version of antiquity and the version of Kleist, written during the period of the Napoleonic Wars and the consolidation of Romanticism. Each version has very different implications – very different senses – while there are also constant themes: love/death, *amour fou*, fatal passion, love concealed under the cloak of aggression, the war of the sexes, the society of women, grief, mourning at a loss, perhaps at a difference. The fulcrum of all these stories is the image of the Amazon – the woman who is independent, aggressive and destructive: perhaps superior to man…

The sound from Sequence 2 fades and is replaced by the sound from Sequence 1.

The camera zooms in to focus on the monitor displaying Sequence 1.

The camera zooms out to show all four monitors.

The sound from the new tape plays.

The sound from Sequence 2 starts to play and eventually gets louder. The camera zooms in to focus on the monitor displaying Sequence 2.

PETER: *(on video)* They are splendid and glamorous, fascinating to other women for the fear which they arouse in men, but impossible to emulate except in phantasy. Their weapons and their strategy are men's weapons and strategy: they offer an alternative which is magical, not political.

This division between ordinary women and Amazons is found in Ancient literature too. Quintus of Smyrna wrote an epic about the Trojan War, probably in the third or fourth century after Christ. He includes a scene in his narrative where the women of Troy watch, from the city walls, the Amazons fighting the Greeks. Greek heroes are falling like autumn leaves before the Amazon onslaught. One of the Trojan women proposes they should join the battle too: 'We ourselves should share the battle. We are not much different from vigorous men. We have the same courage; eyes and limbs are alike. Light and air are common to all. Our food is not different. So why do we run away from fighting?' They are all about to join in when they are restrained by the priestess of Athene. She argues they should stay at home weaving and avoid the tumult and misery of war. 'It's true that all human beings are from the same stock, but different persons practice different jobs and that job is best where a person works with knowledge in their head.'

The argument is one that has been used over the centuries to keep women in their place.

The camera zooms out to show all four monitors.

The sound from Sequence 2 cuts to the sound from Sequence 3.

The camera zooms in to focus on the monitor displaying Sequence 3. The video-image fades to show footage from the fifth tape, in which the camera circles around the stage-performance of the mime and focuses on the Penthesilea-Actress. The sound from the new tape plays.

The camera zooms out to show all four monitors; two display footage from the fifth tape.

The sound from the fifth tape cuts to the sound from Sequence 4.

The camera zooms in to focus on the monitor displaying Sequence 4.

SPEAKER: *(on video)* …what may we not look for in the future, when women have political power and more confidence in themselves?

Every struggle is an object lesson in the need for solidarity. For ages, men have been sex-conscious. Men are always loyal to men. But in the industrial struggle, the competition for mastery has been between men workers on the one hand and men employers on the other hand. It has not been a sex struggle but a class struggle. But with women the case is different. They have had to struggle against sex privilege as well as class privilege. Working men have bitterly opposed and resent the entry of women into industry and still treat them with scant justice in their unions and in their various schemes for self-protection. It is only recently that men have begun to see the necessity and the justice of women's suffrage. And so women have had to fight men as competitors in work, as well as against men employers. And for this reason, the struggle has never been clear cut along class lines but is still complicated with the struggle across sex lines.

One rather curious difference to be observed between the records of recent strikes by men and those by women is the attitude toward the strikers of women who are not themselves workers, women who belong to the non-gainful class, college women, professional women, women of leisure and those who control money. In large numbers, they have thrown themselves into the very ranks of the working girls and they have given them their wholehearted sympathy. They have done picket duty and they have not shrunk from the attendant arrests by the police. In several instances, they have passed the night in the cells. They have given money as well as raised it, and they have worked in many ways, showing a splendid sex-conscious spirit that foretells great victories for the future.

This, of course, is what gives the vital force to the women's movement and it counts for the strange phenomenon of wealthy women joining hands with the poorest of working girls. It is this sense of sexual oppression that has brought women all over the world to the banners of radical advanced movements. Consciously or unconsciously, women have a great bond of sympathy. They see in the great struggle going on in all parts of the world…

The camera zooms out to show all four monitors.

The sound from Sequence 4 cuts to the sound from Sequence 3.

The camera zooms in to focus on one of the monitors displaying footage from the fifth tape.

The camera zooms out to show all four monitors, which display footage from the fifth tape.

The Penthesilea-Actress addresses the camera.

> PENTHESILEA-ACTRESS: *(on video)* Women looked at each other through the eyes of men. Women spoke to each other through the words of men. An alien look. An alien language. We can speak with our own words. We can look with our own eyes. And we can fight with our own weapons.
> PETER: *(on video but off-screen)* Stop.
> PENTHESILEA-ACTRESS: *(on video)* Women looked at each other through the eyes of men. That's terrible.
> PETER: *(on video but off-screen)* Stop.

The camera zooms in on the bottom-right monitor. The Penthesilea-Actress addresses the camera.

> PENTHESILEA-ACTRESS: *(on video)* Women looked at each other through the eyes of men. Women spoke to each other through the words of men. An alien look. An alien language. We can speak with our own words. We can look with our own eyes. And we can fight with our own weapons.

Video image of Penthesilea-Actress pauses and is held on the monitor screen. It then cuts out.

[1′ 43″] Credit Titles. Music.

Total running time: 98′ 06″.

Credits

1. Northwestern University Mime Company

    DEBRA DOLNANSKY · MICHAEL THOMAS
    Jan Creighton · Jim Goode
    Lisa Kephart · Pat Kerwin
    Whit MacLaughlin · Kristine Nielsen
    Brian Reich · Jerry Stropnicky
    Ann Woodworth

    Director: BUD BEYER

    costumes · Jeff Kurland
    setting · Jerry Stropnicky
    carpentry · Sam Boynton
    Location by courtesy of Loren Riggs at
    New Trier West High School, Northfield, Illinois

2. PETER WOLLEN speaking the words of the film-makers
    Location by courtesy of Gerald and Susan Galler

3. 'Visage' (1961) composed by LUCIANO BERIO, with the voice of
    CATHY BERBERIAN

4. GRACE McKEANEY speaking the words of Jessie Ashley from
    The Woman's Journal (Boston, 1911–12)

5. Video realization by
    EVANSTON PERCUSSION ENSEMBLE

production photography
Claudine Jordan

camera crew
David Malchenson
Howard Potter

production consultant
Dana Hodgdon

research assistance
Judith Herren · Carol Laws · Guy Brett · Grier Davis

scripted, produced
and directed by
LAURA MULVEY and
PETER WOLLEN

made at the FILM DIVISION
Northwestern University School of Speech
Evanston, Illinois

2

Scorch the Earth, Start from Zero: *Penthesilea: Queen of the Amazons*

Nicolas Helm-Grovas

n Mulvey's metaphors, *Penthesilea: Queen of the Amazons* (1974) is 'scorched earth'
filmmaking and a 'return to zero'.[1] To destroy what exists and go back to square
one, rebuilding cinematic forms from nothing. Like Jean-Luc Godard's *Joy of
Learning* (*Le Gai savoir*, 1969), *Penthesilea* is an attempt to clear the field in order to
inaugurate a new filmmaking project. Scorched earth and the return to zero, Mulvey
clarifies, are characteristic of a 'negative aesthetics':[2] an uncompromising refusal of
the snares of narrative transitivity, identification, transparency, singular diegesis and
closure that Wollen had already articulated as the necessary strategies of counter-cinema.[3] As well as this act of cinematic negation, *Penthesilea* is various other things.
A collation and re-presentation of existing artworks and texts. A psychoanalytically
equipped feminist ideology critique. An educational exercise and opportunity for
learning. A film-text, demanding a reader as much as a viewer.[4] A 'theory film' or
'theoretical film'.[5] How to execute all of the above simultaneously?

First, with an object, Heinrich von Kleist's 1808 play *Penthesilea*. In Kleist's play,
Greeks and Amazons are at war outside the gates of Troy. Penthesilea, the Amazon
queen, and Achilles, the Greek hero, fall in love on the field of battle. Penthesilea
kills Achilles, then commits suicide. As Mulvey observes, Kleist reversed the gender
roles of the Penthesilea myth, which usually culminates in the phallic imagery of
Achilles thrusting his spear into Penthesilea before falling in love with her.[6] Kleist's
Penthesilea, and the Amazon myth more generally, provided the opportunity to
reflect psychoanalytically on sexual difference. Amazons embodied precisely the
enticing and dangerous, fetishised figure that Mulvey had dismantled as an expres-

sion of male fears and fantasies in her essay on the pop artist Allen Jones, published in *Spare Rib* a year earlier.[7] The phallic woman, in Mulvey's Freudian analysis, was decoded as an expression of castration anxiety, a symptomatic product of a 'strange male underworld of fear and desire'.[8] Relatedly, the utility of the Amazon myth for the women's movement could be broached via this subject matter.[9] Mulvey and Wollen's *Penthesilea* can be seen as an intervention into then-current feminist debates about, and artistic explorations of, historical or mythological matriarchal societies and all-women communities[10] – an intervention that is, as I suggest below, sceptical about the value of the Amazon myth for the women's movement. Finally, the numerous retellings of the Amazon myth, of which Kleist's play was one example, enabled the tracking of the vicissitudes of a single narrative in order to produce 'a film about a story, rather than a film of a story'.[11] The film traces a story's transmission and revision, across history, geography and media, interrogating – and, importantly, *staging* – a palimpsest in which older forms are continually overwritten by new ones. Kleist's play, then, acted as a nodal point allowing the examination of a number of interlocking, overdetermined concerns, stretching from ancient mythology to the present of feminist politics.

Second, through a series of formal investigations, beginning with a decomposition of film into one of its basic units, the long take. Each of *Penthesilea*'s five sequences constitutes a 'core of film', as Wollen calls them in the lecture he gives to camera in the second sequence, two long takes composed of almost an entire roll of 16mm film, laid end to end with a disguised edit to create the appearance of a single shot. The long take, commonly associated – partly through André Bazin – with a realist mode, is here pushed so far that a dialectical reversal takes place. In an essay of the following year, Wollen ruminates on the use of the long take by contemporary filmmakers in a way that contextualises his and Mulvey's intentions:

> clearly the sequence-shot [the long take] has been used for purposes quite different from those foreseen by Bazin. Some of these filmmakers have stressed the autonomy of the camera and its own movement, rather than the primacy of the actors or the drama ([Miklós] Jancsó, [Michael] Snow), others have used the sense of duration to de-realize the imaginary world of the film (Godard), others have been interested in duration as a formal feature in itself ([Andy] Warhol). [Jean-Marie] Straub, probably the closest to Bazin in his insistence on authenticity, on a refusal of guidance for the spectator's eye, has nonetheless put his Bazinian style to purposes very different from those Bazin himself could have envisaged.[12]

These long takes produce a perverted Bazinianism, since 'far from suppressing the filmmaking process', Wollen argues, 'the sequence shot tends to foreground it'.[13] Yet while Wollen explicitly describes the manner of construction of each film core in his lecture, and while the breaks *between* each of the five sequences are strongly emphasised, the cut *within* each section is hidden. These edits are reminiscent of Alfred Hitchcock's *Rope* (1948), which Wollen later calls a 'great experimental film, still unsurpassed' and to which, he argues, *Penthesilea* is an homage.[14] Mulvey, elsewhere, suggests the influence of the final section of Hollis Frampton's *Zorns Lemma* (1970), in which two 16mm rolls of film are connected in a similar manner.[15]

This stealthy suturing takes place in a film which otherwise intensifies cuts and disjunctures. According to Mulvey, *Penthesilea* 'is not graspable as a single, enclosed unit', but rather is 'multi-layered and disharmonic'.[16] Each core of film is preceded by a quotation on a title card, each has as its pro-filmic event a different representational medium, and each foregrounds certain filmic devices.[17] They are assembled into a film of semi-autonomous segments, representable as follows (overleaf).

Tabulating *Penthesilea* in this way draws attention to at least two things. First, the structuralist grid of the film. In structuralist criticism – as in the meticulous tracings of patterns, doublings and repetitions in Raymond Bellour's writings from the late 1960s to late 1970s – the grid is virtual: an analytic construct that must be lifted out of a film.[18] In *Penthesilea*, however, it is already on show, like a skeleton visible without need of an x-ray. Second, it makes apprehensible the film's enactment, in an extreme and schematic manner, of Roman Jakobson's claim that '[*t*]*he poetic function projects the principle of equivalence from the axis of selection into the axis of combination*'.[19] According to Jakobson, language has two aspects. On the one hand, speakers select from a range of phonemic and lexical options at any given time. On the other, they combine the selected phonemes or words into larger units. Ferdinand de Saussure, as Jakobson observes, noted that the first (sometimes called 'paradigmatic') entails reference to absent words, as one word suggests a range of semantically or morphologically associated or equivalent terms; the second ('syntagmatic') unites words in presence, ordered into the same concrete utterance.[20] *Penthesilea* is a radical version of this projection of the first axis onto the second, as numerous paradigmatic options – filmic devices, artistic media and entry points to the subject – are laid out one after another and tested. The film is the sum of these, a lexicon or primer of representational strategies and cinematic forms.

Penthesilea also has an important proximate historical referent: the History Group. A feminist study group – exemplifying the women's movement practice of small group organisation – that Mulvey was a member of in the early 1970s, the History Group's other members included Sally Alexander, Anna Davin, Rosalind

	Sequence 1	Sequence 2	Sequence 3	Sequence 4	Sequence 5
Quotation	'Ghost white like a not yet written page' – Mallarmé, 'Mimique'	'The shadow sprinkled in black characters' – Mallarmé, Quant au livre	'Blazons of phobia, seals of self-punishment' – Lacan, after Vico	'Net of light on overlight' – H.D., 'Projector'	'Notes on the magic writing pad' – Freud
Medium of pro-filmic event	Theatre	Verbal language	Plastic arts	Film	Video
Subject matter of pro-filmic event	Kleist's Penthesilea	History of Amazon narratives	History of visual representations of Amazons	Women's suffrage in early twentieth century	Previous sections of film; future representational and political practices
Filmic devices	Long shot, static camera	Handheld, mobile camera	Rostrum camera, wipes, intertitles.	Superimposition	Zooms and audio mixing

Delmar, Mary Kelly, Branka Magas, Juliet Mitchell and Margaret Walters.[21] Mulvey remembers reading Friedrich Engels, Claude Lévi-Strauss and Sigmund Freud, 'great works by great men that were relevant to understanding the oppression of women but in which we could also find blind spots, symptomatic of misunderstanding'.[22] In the group, the foundations for later works by its members were collectively laid: Mitchell speaks of her 1974 book *Psychoanalysis and Feminism* and Kelly's *Post-Partum Document* (1973–1979) as 'born from all our bodies', and the same may be said of Mulvey's writings and films of the same decade.[23] One might make a stronger statement, suggesting a homology between *Penthesilea* and the History Group: working its way through similar material (Freud, Lévi-Strauss and Engels are all present in the film or its surrounding discourse),[24] *Penthesilea* is a process of reading, questioning and symptomatically critiquing from a feminist perspective. The convergences and divergences with Godard are instructive here. As Volker Pantenburg argues, *Penthesilea*'s context of production (it was made with the assistance of Wollen's students at Northwestern University in Illinois) suggests a 'university discourse', a pedagogical emphasis and sense of scholarly research emblematised in the second sequence, in which Wollen delivers a lecture.[25] Yet *Penthesilea* has a questioning form and measured pace, asking for a greater share of the viewer's contribution to learning than the stern address and rapid-fire Marxist theses of the 'blackboard films' of Godard's Dziga Vertov Group period.[26] Although didactic, it is closer to the rigours of a reading group than the pressurised master–pupil relation of a strict classroom. Moreover, *Penthesilea*'s intertextuality is distinct from Godard's. Jacques Rivette remarks that 'the important point in the sequence of Jean-Luc's films came when he began removing the quotation marks and the names of the authors';[27] in *Penthesilea*, however, quotations and allusions are carefully placed and referenced, their sources marked, suggesting scholarly practice as well as artistic montage. (Wollen originally wanted to include a bibliography in the film.)[28]

Penthesilea's opening sequence, a mimed, compressed version of Kleist's play, functions as a map for what follows. It presents the play in abridged form, setting out the topics for discussion.[29] By removing linguistic specificity through mime, the play is returned to myth, a realm of narratives independent of particular verbal iterations. Meanwhile, the theatrical pro-filmic event and the basic setup of the static camera and long shot evoke early cinema, situating the sequence not only before verbal language but before the classical language of cinema. The film goes back to cinema's beginnings to initiate film history again. Can a route out be found that doesn't pass through the dominant, ideological forms that Mulvey and Wollen were anatomising in their writings at this time?

In section two, Wollen gives a performance-lecture that encapsulates the position discernible in the rest of the film (simultaneously, the camera explores the house he is wandering around, recalling Chantal Akerman's 1972 *Hotel Monterey*). Penthesilea, Wollen states, betrays her comrades, rejecting female community for the ideal of the superwoman; Amazons themselves are fantasy figures, futile to emulate. 'Their weapons and strategy', he summarises, 'are men's weapons and strategy. They offer an alternative which is magical, not political.' Aside from incarnating the *male* intellectual (the only articulate voice until sequence four, a matter that requires more deliberation than I give it here), Wollen is positioned as a representative of the filmmakers. Yet this should not be understood as the stamp of the classical author as authoritative source of meaning. Instead, it marks the film as, in Émile Benveniste's terminology, 'discourse' (*discours*) rather than 'history' or 'story' (*histoire*)[30] – it acknowledges itself as enunciated from a particular place at a particular time, etching this into the artwork. The argument becomes available for the viewer to grasp, analyse and dispute not only because it is made explicit, but because it is shown to be a viewpoint.

This argument is illustrated and developed in sequence three, which undertakes a political psychoanalysis of cultural forms. It opens with a quotation – '[b]lazons of phobia, seals of self-punishment' – from Jacques Lacan's 'The Function and Field of Speech and Language in Psychoanalysis'. In the passage in question, Lacan states that these blazons and seals 'are the hermetic elements that our exegesis dissolves';[31] elsewhere in the text he writes that although the unconscious is the 'censored chapter' of the subject's history, this history has 'been written down elsewhere', including in traditions and legends.[32] In other words, Lacan alludes to a social script that requires decipherment. The images of Amazons in various artistic media in this section are symptoms – of the patriarchal unconscious in its different historical manifestations – presented for a psychoanalytic ideology critique. Moreover, with its repeated motifs and its sequential logic, the section can be understood as an instance of intellectual montage; its mythological figures set against an empty background directly parallel Sergei Eisenstein's prime example of the concept, the 'Gods sequence' in *October* (1928), which was supposed to debunk religion by presenting an escalating series of increasingly unfamiliar deities.[33] Although the conclusions the audience are expected to draw are left more open in *Penthesilea*, it too advances an analysis (one comparable to various feminist texts of the period on the Amazon myth) – namely, that despite initially appearing to be powerful and alluring, the Amazons are inevitably defeated and subjugated by the Greeks, and hence signify the Athenian state's belief in its ultimate superiority over a foreign, feminised other.[34]

As Mary Kelly notes, the images from a *Wonder Woman* comic that conclude sequence three are crucial.[35] In them, Wonder Woman has lost her magical powers and becomes involved in a women's movement group's campaign about working conditions, transformed from exceptional individual to participant in collective feminist struggle. *Penthesilea*'s fourth sequence consolidates this transition from myth to politics and from superwoman to female collectivity. A 1913 film about women's suffrage in Britain is overlaid with footage of a woman reading texts by the US socialist-feminist Jessie Ashley published in 1911–1912. For the first time in *Penthesilea*, a woman speaks intelligibly (the audio track of sequence three is Luciano Berio's 1961 composition 'Visage', centred on wordless vocal sounds performed by Cathy Berberian), working through problems of class and gender politics. The superimposition formally stages the content of Ashley's writings: just as her text juxtaposes socialism and feminism but is unable to satisfactorily reconcile them, so superimposition layers two images onto each other without unification. The breaks in Ashley's text are punctuated by the sounds of machinery and the indistinct murmur of female-sounding voices. Are these the sounds of industry and labour, gesturing to a women's class collectivity formed materially, not mythically?

Much can be said about the film's final sequence. Here I will not contemplate its playback of the previous sequences on four video monitors (aptly described by Pantenburg as akin to spreading out sheets of paper on a desk to get a feel for their overall relation),[36] nor the significance of the filmmakers' citation of Freud's 'mystic writing pad' (*Wunderblock*), with its invocation of the palimpsest figure, and its affinities with the video medium that Mulvey and Wollen (like Thierry Kuntzel around the same time) discern.[37] Instead, I note the way the video screens begin to show previously unseen angles on the first sequence. The film delves back into Kleist's play and the Amazon myth to find something formerly hidden; the camera follows the Penthesilea actor to a dressing room, where she removes her make-up and addresses the camera. As Patricia Erens states, this is 'rupturing the cycle': replay interrupted by the new.[38] 'Women looked at each other through the eyes of men. Women spoke to each other through the words of men. An alien look. An alien language. We can speak with our own words. We can look with our own eyes. And we can fight with our own weapons.' Repeating a collective feminist 'we', the Penthesilea actor appeals for new modes of expression and new means of struggle. The last lines of the film therefore gesture beyond it, to a future artistic and political practice. Yet the demand to speak in one's own words has an ironic ring in a film full of quotation. The repetition and false start in the delivery of these words, and Wollen's off-screen voice directing, make clear that this is a scripted performance.[39] The sequence apparently seeks to avoid the predicament Wollen had identified in Godard, the impossible cinematic attempt to get behind fiction and representation to unmediated truth.[40] The passage from myth to reality, *Penthesilea* suggests, is not quite so easy. Finally, the speaker's image freezes.

The film is more about modelling and exploring the history of women's silences than affirmatively presenting women's voices in the here-and-now. In the film's last image, the bar of the video moving across a blank monitor screen, what has gone before is once more wiped away. Back to zero. However, like Freud's mystic writing pad, a residue remains in the viewer's mind.

Notes

1. Laura Mulvey, 'Changes: Thoughts on Myth, Narrative and Historical Experience', in *Visual and Other Pleasures*, 2nd edn (Basingstoke: Palgrave Macmillan, 2009), 170.
2. *Ibid.*, 170.
3. Peter Wollen, 'Counter Cinema: *Vent d'Est*', *Afterimage* 4 (Autumn 1972), 6–16, reprinted as 'Godard and Counter Cinema: *Vent d'Est*', in Peter Wollen, *Readings and Writings: Semiotic Counter-Strategies* (London: Verso, 1982), 79–91.
4. Laura Mulvey and Peter Wollen, '*Penthesilea, Queen of the Amazons*', interview by Claire Johnston and Paul Willemen, *Screen* 15:3 (Autumn 1974), 131–132.
5. *Ibid.*, 131; Laura Mulvey and Peter Wollen, 'Written Discussion', *Afterimage* 6 (Summer 1976), 33.
6. Mulvey and Wollen, '*Penthesilea, Queen of the Amazons*', 121.
7. The connection is noted by Mulvey in 'Introduction to the First Edition', *Visual and Other Pleasures*, p. xxix.
8. Laura Mulvey, 'You Don't Know What is Happening Do You, Mr Jones?', *Spare Rib* 8 (February 1973), 14; reprinted as 'Fears, Fantasies and the Male Unconscious or "You don't know what is happening do you, Mr Jones?"', in *Visual and Other Pleasures*, 8.
9. Mulvey and Wollen, '*Penthesilea, Queen of the Amazons*', 121–122.
10. Examples of works of the time exploring these topics include Monique Wittig, *Les Guérillères*, trans. David Le Vay (Boston, MA: Beacon Press, 1969); Elizabeth Gould Davis, *The First Sex* (New York: Putnam, 1971); and Jill Johnston, *Lesbian Nation: The Feminist Solution* (New York: Simon and Schuster, 1973), 247–273.
11. Mulvey and Wollen, '*Penthesilea, Queen of the Amazons*', 121.
12. Peter Wollen, 'Introduction to *Citizen Kane*', *Film Reader* 1 (1975), reprinted in *Readings and Writings: Semiotic Counter-Strategies*, 52.
13. Wollen, 'Introduction to *Citizen Kane*', 53.
14. Peter Wollen, 'Autobiographical Notes', 31 March 1994, Peter Wollen artist file, British Artists' Film and Video Study Collection, Central Saint Martins, University of the Arts, London, 12.
15. Laura Mulvey, 'Unravelling the Puzzle', interview with Lara Thompson, Laura Mulvey artist file, British Artists' Film and Video Study Collection, 6.
16. Mulvey and Wollen, '*Penthesilea, Queen of the Amazons*', 131.

17. I am drawing on and developing remarks by the filmmakers themselves. See: Mulvey and Wollen, '*Penthesilea, Queen of the Amazons*', 123–124.

18. See: Raymond Bellour, *The Analysis of Film*, ed. Constance Penley (Bloomington and Indianapolis, IN: Indiana University Press, 2000).

19. Roman Jakobson, 'Linguistics and Poetics', in *Language in Literature*, eds Krystyna Pomorska and Stephen Rudy (Cambridge, MA: Belknap Press of Harvard University Press, 1987), 71.

20. Roman Jakobson, 'Two Aspects of Language and Two Types of Aphasic Disturbances', in *Language in Literature*, 97–99. See also: Roland Barthes, *Elements of Semiology*, trans. Annette Lavers and Colin Smith (New York: Hill and Wang, 1968), 58–59.

21. Mignon Nixon, '"Why Freud?" asked the Shrew: Psychoanalysis and Feminism, *Post-Partum Document*, and the History Group', *Psychoanalysis, Culture and Society* 20:2 (June 2015), 2–3.

22. Laura Mulvey, 'Introduction to the Second Edition', *Visual and Other Pleasures*, xv.

23. Juliet Mitchell, 'Theory as an Object', *October* 113 (Summer, 2005), 36, quoted in Nixon, '"Why Freud?"', 4.

24. All are mentioned in Mulvey and Wollen, '*Penthesilea, Queen of the Amazons*', 122.

25. Volker Pantenburg, 'The Third Avant-Garde: Laura Mulvey, Peter Wollen, and the Theory-Film', lecture given at Whitechapel Gallery, London, 14 May 2016.

26. See: Serge Daney, 'Theorize/Terrorize: Godardian Pedagogy', trans. Annwyl Williams, in *Cahiers du Cinéma*, Vol. 4: 1973–1978: *History, Ideology, Cultural Struggle*, ed. David Wilson (London and New York: Routledge/BFI, 2000), 116–123.

27. Bernard Eisenschitz, Jean-André Fieschi and Eduardo de Gregorio, 'Interview with Jacques Rivette', trans. Tom Milne, in *Jacques Rivette: Texts and Interviews*, ed. Jonathan Rosenbaum (London: BFI, 1977), 51.

28. Mulvey and Wollen, '*Penthesilea, Queen of the Amazons*', 130.

29. *Ibid.*, 127.

30. Émile Benveniste, *Problems in General Linguistics*, trans. Mary Elizabeth Meek (Coral Gables, FL: University of Miami Press, 1971), 206–209.

31. Jacques Lacan, 'The Function and Field of Speech and Language in Psychoanalysis', in *Écrits*, trans. Bruce Fink in collaboration with Héloïse Fink and Russell Grigg (New York and London: W. W. Norton & Company, 2006), 232.

32. Lacan, 'Function and Field', 215.

33. Sergei Eisenstein, 'The Dramaturgy of Film Form', *Selected Works, Vol. I: Writings, 1922–1934*, ed. and trans. Richard Taylor (Bloomington and Indianapolis, IN and London: BFI and Indiana University Press, 1988), 179–180.

34. See, for instance, the similar arguments in: Mandy Merck, 'The City's Achievements', in *Tearing the Veil: Essays on Femininity*, ed. Susan Lipshitz (London: Routledge and Kegan Paul, 1978).

35. Mary Kelly, 'Penthesilea', *Spare Rib* 30 (December 1974), 40.

36. Pantenburg, 'The Third Avant-Garde'.

37. Mulvey and Wollen, '*Penthesilea, Queen of the Amazons*', 129; Raymond Bellour, 'Thierry Kuntzel and the Return of Writing', trans. Annwyl Williams, *Between-the-Images* (Zurich and Dijon: JRP Ringier and Les presses du réel, 2012), 36–37. See: Sigmund Freud, 'A Note Upon the "Mystic Writing Pad"', *The Standard Edition of the Complete Psychological Works of Sigmund Freud, Vol. XIX (1923–1925)*, trans. and ed. James Strachey in collaboration with Anna Freud (London: The Hogarth Press and the Institute of Psycho-Analysis, 1961), 227–232.

38. Patricia Erens, '*Penthesilea*', *Wide Angle* 2:3 (1978), 34–35.

39. Erens, '*Penthesilea*', 35.

40. Wollen, 'Godard and Counter Cinema', 89–91.

3

Riddles of the Sphinx

Laura Mulvey and Peter Wollen

1 Opening pages

[1′05″]* *Turning over the pages of* Midi-Minuit Fantastique, *beginning with a heading 'Le Mythe de la femme' and stopping at a photo-montage of Greta Garbo as the Sphinx. ECU. Meanwhile titles in superimposition:*

> RIDDLES OF THE SPHINX
> 'A narrative of what wishes what it wishes it to be' – Gertrude Stein[†]
> 1   Opening pages
> 2   Laura speaking
> 3   Stones
> 4   Louise's story told in thirteen shots
> 5   Acrobats
> 6   Laura listening
> 7   Puzzle ending

[05″] *Title:*   1

2 Laura speaking

[05″] *Title:*   2

[3′31″] *Speech introducing the Sphinx as Voice Off, delivered to camera by Laura Mulvey, intercut with images of the Sphinx. The sequence opens with a shot of a Greek vase; then there is a very brief shot of Laura seated in front of a table on which there are a microphone, two books, a child's mug and a pencil sharpener in the form of a small globe; then there is a shot of another vase and a return to the set-up of Laura speaking. The*

---

* Shot timings are in minutes and seconds throughout.
† G. Stein: 'Regular regularly in narrative' in *How to Write*.

alternation continues with, successively: detail from Gustave Moreau's 'Oedipus and the Sphinx' / Laura / Garbo as Sphinx / Laura / profile shot of the Egyptian Sphinx / Laura / full face shot of the Sphinx / Laura / zoom-in onto the mouth of the Sphinx / Laura again. The shots of Laura become longer as the sequence proceeds.

LAURA: When we were planning the central section of this film, about a mother and child, we decided to use the voice of the Sphinx as an imaginary narrator – because the Sphinx represents, not the voice of truth, not an answering voice, but its opposite: a questioning voice, a voice asking a riddle. The Oedipus myth associates the voice of the Sphinx with motherhood as mystery and with resistance to patriarchy.

In some ways the Sphinx is the forgotten character in the story of Oedipus. Everybody knows that Oedipus killed his father and married his mother, but the part played by the Sphinx is often overlooked. Oedipus set off for Thebes, turning away from Corinth, where he'd been brought up by foster parents. The Sphinx sat perched on a cliff or pillar outside the city gates; she asked every man who went past a riddle. If they couldn't answer she devoured them. Then she stopped Oedipus when he went past and when he answered her correctly, she threw herself down from the pillar and killed herself.

The myth of the Sphinx took on new life after Napoleon's campaigns in Egypt, when the Great Sphinx at Gizeh was disclosed once again to Western eyes. The Egyptian Sphinx is male, but on its blank face, resonant with mystery and with death, the spectator could project the image of the Greek Sphinx. Once again the Sphinx could enter popular mythology, in the image of male fears and male fantasies, the cannibalistic mother, part bestial, part angelic, indecipherable.

Oedipus is different from other Greek heroes in that he defeated the monster, not by strength or by bravery, but simply by intelligence. In his answer to the riddle, Oedipus restored the generations to their proper order, but by doing so he fell into a further trap. In his own life he disordered them once more by marrying his own mother. It's almost as if Oedipus stands for the conscious mind and the Sphinx for the unconscious. The riddle confuses and disorders logical categories and the monster is a hybrid of human, animal and bird. But reading between the lines the myth confirms women's sense of exclusion and suppression. The Sphinx is outside the city gates, she challenges the culture of the city, with its order of kinship and its order of knowledge, a culture and a political system which assign women a subordinate place.

To the patriarchy, the Sphinx as woman is a threat and a riddle, but women within patriarchy are faced with a never-ending series of threats and riddles – dilemmas which are hard for women to solve, because the culture within which they must think is not theirs. We live in a society ruled by the father, in which the place of the mother is suppressed. Motherhood and how to live it, or not to live it, lies at the roots of the dilemma. And meanwhile the Sphinx can only speak with a voice apart, a voice off.

3 Stones

[05"] *Title:*   3

[7′ 14"] *Montage sequence of found footage of the Egyptian Sphinx, refilmed through a number of generations with the aid of a motion-analyser projector, using zooms, stop-motion, slow and reverse motion, freeze frames, and extreme close-up (concentrating on the Sphinx's mouth) eventually showing film grain.*

Music.

4 Louise's story told in thirteen shots

(Each shot is a 360° pan. Music, voice off and synch dialogue as specified. Intertitles.)

[05"] *Title:*   4

(1)

[12"] *Intertitle:* Perhaps Louise is too close to her child. How much longer can she reject the outside world, other people and other demands. Her husband often

[6′ 09"] *Louise's kitchen. Louise prepares scrambled egg for her two-year-old daughter, Anna. The shot ends when her husband, Chris, comes home. Tight framing at work-surface height.*

Music, VO.

> VOICE OFF:
> Time to get ready. Time to come in.
> Things to forget. Things to lose.
> Meal time. Story time.
>
> Desultory. Peremptory.
> Keeping going. Keeping looking.
> Reading like a book. Relief.
> Things to cook.

Keeping in the background.
Fish-slice. Domestic labour.

Disheartened. Burdened.
Keeping calm. Keeping clean.
Fitting like a glove. Remorse.
Things to mend.

Losing touch with reality.
Dish-cloth. Narcissistic love.

Idolise. Tranquillise.
Losing count. Losing control.
Shaking like a leaf. Release.
Things to say.

No time to make amends. No time for tea.
Time to worry. No time to hold.
Things to hold. Things past.
Meal time. Story time.

Keeping going. Keeping looking.
Reading like a book.
Things to forget. Things to lose.
No time lost.
Story time.

(2)

[12″] *Intertitle*: bedtime, she likes to stay in Anna's room, waiting for her to fall asleep and tidying away the traces of the day. She still seems to need the

[3′ 42″] *Anna's bedroom. Louise tidies up while Anna goes to sleep in her cot. Tight framing at cot height.*

Music, VO.

VOICE OFF:
Distressed. Strained.

Nesting. In the nest. Comfort. Effort.
At the breast. At rest.
Resting.

Take leave. Take moss. Be close.
Be clasped and cleft. Be close.

Nesting. Acquiesced. Memory. Mystery.
Dispossessed. Depressed.
Trusting.

Make cross. Make grieve. Morose.
Subject to conquest. Object to incest.

Nesting. From the nest. Blood. Brood.
From the breast. Caressed.
Hurting.

Bleeding. It was obvious.
It was as obvious as it was oblivious.
Brooding. It was plain. Be close.
It was as plain as it was pain.

Make love. Make grieve. Marries.
Mother's and another's. Mysteries.

Nesting.

If only I hadn't minded, I used to say, but I did mind very much. I minded
more than very much. I minded more than I could ever have dared. Mind
the door. Mind the glass. Mind the fire. Mind the child. I never minded the
warmth. I minded the need. It was needed to have minded, I used to say,
but was it needed to have minded more than very much? More than I could
ever have dared?

(3)

[12″] *Intertitle*: cannot make her see reason and get out more into the world, Chris feels he must leave the house himself. It was her idea to live in

[3′ 48″] *Hall with front door. Chris puts his belongings in the back of his car, seen through the windows, and leaves home, watched by Louise and Anna. Medium framing.*

Music, with VO giving way to synch dialogue as Chris leaves.

> VOICE OFF:
> Transformed, I would confide.
> I could have cried. I could have died.
> Transformed, to cold from warmth.
>
> The warmth.
> It pacified and purified.
> The warmth was far within. Hidden within.
> The warmth was deep and far within.
> The cold.
>
> In labour. In hiding.
> In the storm. Sheltered. Nurtured.
>
> The warmth.
> It was inside. It was in hiding.
> The warmth was far within. Hidden within.
> The warmth was in the centre. In the calm.
> The cold.
>
> Underneath. Beneath.
> Beneath the quilt. Mothering. Covering.
>
> The warmth.
> The cold conceded nothing.
> Whoever, frozen, pleaded, it conceded nothing.
> The warmth consoled. The warmth was needed.
> The cold.

Transformed. Preoccupied.
I could have cried. It never died.
In repose. From warmth to cold.
Frozen. Controlled.
Preoccupied.

CHRIS (*standing in doorway*): There's nothing much more to say really is there? … said it all. … Look, you've got my number haven't you? At Keith's. Just ring me if there's anything. All right. Bye Anna.

(4)

[12″] *Intertitle*: had to get a job after all and find day-care for Anna. At the nursery she meets Maxine who makes the parting easier. Louise is grateful for

[1′ 42″] *Day-care nursery. Louise brings Anna to the nursery, on her way to work, and leaves her with Maxine. Framing to show Louise fully for the first time.*

Synch sound.

General chatter and noise. Dialogue at end.

> LOUISE: I'll have to go now. I've got to go to work. I'll see you later. I'll collect you after tea. Goodbye. Goodbye my love.
> MAXINE: Don't worry. We'll look after her.

(5)

[12″] *Intertitle*: at the switchboard. She is not allowed to make outgoing calls, but feels she has to talk to Maxine. It is hard to concentrate when she is

[4′ 55″] *Switchboard. Louise and other women at work as telephonists. Louise calls Maxine, cutting off another caller. Wide framing.*

Synch sound.

General chatter and noise. Louise on telephone.

> LOUISE: Ah, Maxine. Good. Is Anna alright? Ah, that's a relief. I knew she'd be alright with you once I'd gone. That's why I'm ringing. I don't think I'll be able to. No. It's not that really, it's just… I can't talk now. I'll tell you when I come and collect Anna. We'll arrange something else perhaps. I must go now, OK?
>
> I'm sorry. Did I cut you off? I'm sorry. Can I reconnect you? What number did you want? I'm very sorry.

(6)

[12″] *Intertitle*: wants women to work, even needs them to, but denies them facilities and often seems to be punishing them for leaving their proper place

[3′ 22″] *Canteen. Louise talks to other women in the canteen about the need she feels for a day-care nursery at work. Wide framing. Synch sound.*

> LIN: …you do have to think about it, it costs a lot of money doesn't it?
>
> LOUISE: Well, what happened to you then?
>
> LIN: Well, you know I have to take my Ellie to the child minder's, well, this morning she was ill, she couldn't cope, so I had to go right across the other side of London. The child minder's got a friend, you know, and she helped her out – I mean I had to go right down Holloway Road – it cost me twice as much as usual.
>
> LOUISE: They ought to have a nursery here, the company ought to provide one.
>
> LIN: Well, they should really, I mean. It would make my life a bit easier if they did.
>
> CLAIRE: I'm not sure. I don't really like the idea of my kids here where I work. I like to think of work a bit separate from the house.
>
> CAROLE: Louise, who'll foot the bill for this sort of thing then?
>
> LOUISE: Well they're rich enough. Just a job isn't it? Look how many mothers there are here. They've all got young children. They've all got problems about leaving them. I know I have. I hate leaving mine. Can't keep my mind on my work.
>
> CAROLE: Well, you are the worrying type.
>
> LOUISE: Well, it's not that, is it? If you've got to take your child to the nursery before you get to work no wonder you're in a flap when you get here.
>
> JOY: What was all that about?
>
> MARY: About nurseries, I think.
>
> JOY: What, is she worried about her kid?
>
> MARY: Yeah, she doesn't like leaving her, you know. Coming in, leaving her somewhere else. She's only been here a little while but she's talking about all sorts of problems. She's right though. We ought to have a nursery here. Yeah, we've got a Personnel Manager, give him something to do.
>
> JOY: Probably only take it off the wages anyway.
>
> MARY: Oh, no, not if the Union's involved. Someone should find out what they could do about it really. I think Louise should. I mean, it was her idea in the first place.
>
> JOY: Yeah, I suppose it depends how many people there are who've got kids and need …
>
> MARY: Yeah, I think the important thing to do is to find out how many kids are involved and, like, the ages as well and then take it to the Union and see if they can do anything about it with the management.

(7)

[12″] *Intertitle*: that Maxine has arranged, so she can find out more about the Union attitude to their day-care campaign. On the way to the meeting, they stop

[2′ 14″] *Roundabout. Louise and Maxine, in the nursery van, stop at a roundabout to drop off a package on their way to a meeting. Louise asks another woman with them about the Union attitude to day-care at work. Exterior, wide framing, camera travels 360° round roundabout as well as 360° pan.*

Synch sound from inside van.

> LOUISE: He should be here by now. A little boy with fair hair.
> MAXINE: I think he's got to come across the footbridge.
> WOMAN TRADE UNIONIST: What were you asking about your little girl?
> LOUISE: Well, at the moment she's in a community nursery, where Maxine works, but I was wondering if it would be better to have the nursery at work. Have the Unions thought about that?
> WOMAN: Not much really. You're lucky to get any sort of day-care, let alone the one that suits you best.
> MAXINE (*to child*): Hello! Give this to your mother and say thanks for waiting.

Camera starts tracking

> CHILD: Bye!
> MAXINE: Local authorities are cutting back on nursery education anyway, aren't they?
> WOMAN: Yes, that's right. It may stimulate the women to demand more for themselves though.
> LOUISE: Have the Unions ever done anything at all about day-care?

Van heard to start up

> WOMAN: They haven't done very much. The TUC is in favour of free state nursery care for any parent who wants it. But we're a long way from that.

Van enters frame left

> LOUISE: I was wondering whether…
> WOMAN: There are some nurseries in the textile industry and the Unions do negotiate about child-care there, but that's an industry that really depends on women's labour. Unless there's organised action around it, the Union wouldn't have any reason to take it up, it's like most things.

MAXINE: We have to do something first if we want the Unions to take it up.

LOUISE: How can you make people see the connection between better wages and providing day-care?

WOMAN: Well, trade unionism isn't just a question of wages struggle. It's about work conditions too, it has to be.

LOUISE: In that case, might the Unions get involved in running nurseries?

WOMAN: They might. All sorts of questions come up with workplace nurseries.

Van exits from frame

Should the mothers be allowed to visit during the day? Should the creche stay open to let women shop before they collect their children? Some Unions want the employers to pay for company nurseries, but have the nurseries run by Unions and parents together.

Track ends. Pan continues for a while

(8)

[12″] *Intertitle*: friendship with Maxine has intervened. This affects her attitude to a lot of things, including shopping, after all another form of women's

[3′ 41″] *Indoor shopping centre. Louise, with Anna, and Maxine are part of the crowd in the shopping centre. Wide framing.*

Music, synch sound.

(9)

[12″] *Intertitle*: mistakes, so the Union won't take up her case. Although she hopes to keep the campaign going from outside, she can't help worrying about

[4′ 15″] *Playground. Louise takes Anna to a playground in the park, having lost her job. Exterior, wide framing.*

Music, VO.

VOICE OFF: Questions arose which seemed to form a linked ring, each raising the next until they led the argument back to its original point of departure.

Should women demand special working conditions for mothers? Can a child-care campaign attack anything fundamental to women's oppression? Should women's struggle be concentrated on economic issues? Is domestic labour productive? Is the division of labour the root of the problem? Is exploitation outside the home better than oppression within it? Should women organise themselves separately from men? Could there be a social revolution in which women do not play the leading role? How does women's struggle relate to class struggle? Is patriarchy the main enemy for women? Does the oppression of women work on the unconscious as well as on the conscious? What would the politics of the unconscious be like? How necessary is being-a-mother to women, in reality or imagination? Is the family an obstacle to the liberation of women? Is the family needed to maintain sexual difference? What other forms of child-care might there be? Are campaigns about child-care a priority for women now? Question after question arose, revolving in her mind without reaching any clear conclusion. They led both out into society and back into her own memory. Future and past seemed to be locked together. She felt a gathering of strength but no certainty of success.

(10)

[12″] *Intertitle*: no longer needs to keep Anna to herself. But by sending Anna to stay with her mother, Louise has brought herself back into her own past. They

[3′ 47″] *Louise's mother's garden. Louise and Maxine visit Louise's mother, who is looking after Anna and pottering around the garden. Towards the end of the shot, Louise stands and watches her daughter and mother as they throw sticks onto the bonfire.*

Exterior, medium framing.

Music, synch sound.

General chatter and noise.

> GRANDMOTHER (*when audible*): Let's go in the garden and have a nice time in the garden. Oh, look, they're looking at photos. You go and look at those while I go and see to the bonfire…
> …We don't want green tomatoes, do we? No, we want lovely red ones… There we are, all lovely and blazing. I like a lovely blaze…

(11)

[12″] *Intertitle*: both go to visit Chris at work. He is editing a film he thinks will interest them and Louise wants to tell him that she has finally reached

[7′ 05″] *Chris's editing room. Chris shows Louise and Maxine film and tapes he has been working on, about a woman artist (Mary Kelly) and her work* (Post-Partum Document,

ICA 1976). Louise tells him she has decided to sell the house and stay with Maxine. Tight framing, anti-clockwise pan, starting and finishing on white screen; room in darkness for second half of shot, showing images on two Steenbecks and video monitor.

Synch sound dialogue and voice of Mary Kelly reading diaries and documents over film and tape.

CHRIS: Do you mind, I've just got to get this film ready. Won't be a moment, okay?

MAXINE: Okay.

LOUISE: Right.

MAXINE: Hey, Louise, I've got something to show you. Have you got a mirror?

LOUISE: Here.

MAXINE (*holding mirror to packet of Camels*): See – look. It should be in mirror writing.

LOUISE: It is.

MAXINE: Now, look.

LOUISE: It's not in mirror writing. How does it work?

MAXINE: Magic. No, seriously, it's the cellophane. It acts as a special kind of filter. Puts the letters back to front again so they appear the right way round.

LOUISE: Do you know, I think camels are my favourite animals. I like the way that camel's much bigger than that pyramid. The way the desert just stretches out to the horizon. I think it's their shape – all lumpy and baggy, hanging over a ramshackle old skeleton.

CHRIS: Okay, I think I'm ready. Shall we start?

LOUISE: By the way, Chris, there's something I wanted to say to you. I've decided, I want to sell the house.

CHRIS: Umm, okay, if that's what you want…

LOUISE: Yes.

CHRIS: What about the market though? It's a bad time to sell, isn't it?

LOUISE: It's a good time for me to sell. I've decided I want to be rid of it.

CHRIS: You won't get much money for anywhere else, you know. Once we've sold the mortgage.

LOUISE: I don't think I want anywhere else. I'm going to be staying with Maxine.

MAXINE: She'll be much nearer and you'll be able to see Anna more.

LOUISE: Yes, Anna's older. She doesn't need me all the time now.

CHRIS: You mean you don't need her.

LOUISE: Well, anyway that's what we've decided, haven't we?

CHRIS: Right. Shall we start?

MAXINE: Is it work by a woman artist?

CHRIS: Yes, that's right. It's about her child and herself as the mother. I've got some film, got some video tape as well. I'll put the lights out.

VOICE OF SOUNDMAN: Mary Kelly – retaping.

VOICE OF MARY KELLY: The diaries in this document are based on recorded conversations between mother and child (that is, myself and my son) at the crucial moment of his entry into nursery school. The conversations took place at weekly intervals between September 7th and November 26th 1975. They came to a 'natural' end with his/my adjustment to school. There also occurs at this moment a kind of 'splitting' of the dyadic mother/child unit which is evident in my references, in the diaries, to the father's presence and in my son's use of pronouns (significantly 'I') in his conversations and of implied diagrams (for example, concentric markings and circles) in his 'drawings'. The marking process is regulated by the nursery routine, so that almost daily finished 'works' are presented by the children to their mothers. Consequently, these markings become the logical terrain on which to map out the 'signification' of the maternal discourse.

September 27th. I was shocked to find that he was crying when I picked him up from the nursery. I didn't think about coming early and he saw the others leave. Now he's very suspicious when I take him. I can't forgive myself for that because I should have known, although, I thought that, I was so convinced that he was different, that he is very sociable. The second day he actually screamed when I left. The teachers made me leave. I was shocked because Ray was not upset by it at all although I couldn't take him again that week. I had Sally take him the first three days and Ray took him the rest of the week. I suppose it's kind of lack of boundary definition.

October 11th. I was distressed all this week by his apparent anxiety over going back to the nursery and I felt a bit guilty about being away teaching every day till Wednesday. He had tantrums which freaked Sally out. Thursday was the first day that I saw him and it bothered me as well.

VOICE AND CLAPPERBOARD: Roll 34 – Take 1.

VOICE OF MARY KELLY: October 24th. I was amazed that he actually said, I like school this week. At least that's sorted out but why doesn't he get over this tonsillitis? He had to go to the doctor again this week. It was a very unsatisfactory check-up, it took about one minute. It just makes me feel more responsible for him when other people don't show concern for him, but I guess I'm just as bad. I forgot to give him his medicine.

Weaning from the dyad. For both the mother and the child, the crucial moment of 'weaning' is constituted by the intervention of a 'third term' (that is, the father), thus consolidating the oedipal triad and undermining the Imaginary dyad which determined the inter-subjectivity of the pre-oedipal instance. This intervention situates the Imaginary 'third term' of the primordial triangle (that is, the child as phallus) and the paternal 'imago' of the mirror phase within the dominance of the Symbolic structure through the Word of the father. That is, the mother's words referring to the authority of the 'father', to which the real father may or may not conform.

(12)

[12″] *Intertitle*: as in dreams, but takes the form of masquerade, locked into a world of images where each needs to feel sheltered within another's gaze to find

[10′ 08″] *Maxine's room. Louise reads a transcript of a dream back to Maxine, who is making up at a dressing table. The room is full of mirrors.*

Medium framing, but space fragmented by reflections and reflections within reflections. Towards the end of the shot camera and cinematographer are visible in one of the mirrors.

Music, synch sound.

> LOUISE: What does it mean? I can't understand most of it.
> MAXINE: Pieces of thoughts I put into words. Pieces of words which seemed to mean something and I wanted to remember.
> LOUISE: What about this? What does this mean? 'They make a groove or a pattern into which or upon which other patterns fit or are placed unfitted and are cut by circumstances to fit.'*
> MAXINE: I don't know. It must be something I copied out of a book.
> LOUISE: I see what it is. She felt she had been living in a fairy tale, the oldest fairy tale that we still know, from the Valley of the Nile. It matched with something she remembered very clearly from her childhood.
> MAXINE: Yes, I remember now – it's about how she went out with her mother and her little brother and how her mother laughed at them when they said they weren't going home. Her mother just turned and went round the corner.
> LOUISE: Do you know, I remember almost the same thing. I remember sitting on the kerb and refusing to move. There must have been something I wanted and my mother wouldn't give it to me, and a little group of people gathered round.

---

* 'H.D.': *Tribute to Freud.*

MAXINE: It's like when you go to a demonstration. There's a ring of people standing looking at you and you don't know whose side they're on.
LOUISE: You feel very defiant and eventful.

What about this – when was this? 'I was on a boat, sitting on a stool in front of the mast, eating a pear which had been cut very carefully into slices. It was a large boat, some kind of naval vessel, because it had large guns and sailors wearing helmets with plumes. They must have been soldiers, a whole regiment of them. I was afraid of the soldiers. It seemed to me that they were finding fault with me. I think it was because they wanted to weigh anchor. So I went down to my cabin and looked at myself in the looking glass. Only instead of myself I saw my father carrying a saucepan. He said he had come for the wool-combing. There was going to be some kind of festival where the sheep were going to be sheared and the wool combed by women. The sheep were held down by straps. Then my father blew on a bugle and the soldiers with plumes on their helmets all came in. My father ordered me to begin combing the wool. I said, 'I can't, I'm dead beat.' He said that I must, or I would infect everybody at the festival with some kind of disease, or rather all the men at the festival. They all began to show horrible symptoms. They were growing gills and their entrails were falling out. I was very frightened, and picked up the comb which had a number of notches cut in it. My father began to coax me to begin combing but I was not able to. Then I noticed that standing behind my father was another man, who seemed to be lame, and perhaps some kind of priest. He asked me whether I was an oyster woman. Everybody was excited by this question, which they seemed to think was very shrewd, but I did not know what to reply. I ran to my father and seized the saucepan which he had been holding in his hand. It was full of jewels, which had a rind on them. When I began to shell them all the men began to grind their teeth but I carried on peeling the rind. Inside there were hundreds of tiny caraway seeds. When I looked up I saw that the lame man was wearing a feathered headdress, like an Indian Chief. I suddenly realised that all this time I had been wearing a veil. I tore it off and threw the caraway seeds at the lame man, dressed like an Indian Chief. He became all distorted and disappeared. Only my father was left. I felt very perplexed. Then he said, 'You must receive communion at Easter.' I realised that it was Ash Wednesday and I thought that I must be my mother, although I knew she was dead. I had a feeling of jubilation and in a very loud voice I ordered that all my father's property should be sold by auction. All the women threw away their combs and shouted, 'Bravo! Well done!' They unstrapped all the sheep and knocked the helmets and military caps off the soldiers. I don't remember much more except that I was dancing on the deck of the ship, in front of a sheet of canvas or sailcloth.

Camera and camerawoman visible in frame

> 'There were colours and banners, and when I looked at the sea it seemed to be made of silk.' What does that mean I wonder.
> MAXINE: I don't know exactly. That's why I wrote it. I hoped I'd understand it more. It has the texture of meaning.

(13)

[12″] *Intertitle*: a detour through these texts, entombed now in glass, whose enigmatic script reminds her of a forgotten history and the power of a different language.

[6′ 36″] *British Museum Egyptian Room. Louise and Anna, surrounded by mummified bodies and sarcophagi, puzzle over hieroglyphs. Wide framing.*

Music, VO.

> VOICE OFF: She remembered reading somewhere a passage from a book which she could no longer trace, words which had struck her at the time and which she now tried to reconstruct. 'Inscribed on the lid of the box were the words: "Anatomy Is No Longer Destiny" and inside, when she opened it, she found the figure of the Greek Sphinx with full breasts and feathery wings. She lifted it up out of the box to look at it more closely. As she did so, it seemed to her that its lips moved and it spoke a few phrases in a language which she could not understand, except for three words which were repeated several times: "Capital", "Delay" and "Body". She replaced it in the box and closed the lid. She could feel her heart beat.'
>
> The rhythm of the sentences was not quite right and she felt sure there was some particular she had forgotten. She tried to imagine the scene as the writer might have. Would the box have been padded with cushioning, a quilted material, folds of velvet, black or red, buttoned or embroidered? What would the pattern of the embroidery be? She imagined an intricate web of curved forms, intertwined knots, like the tendrils and fronds in the marsh where, according to Bachofen, the first matriarchy arose, or the curls of pubic hair from which, according to Freud, women wove the first veil.
>
> What kind of material was the Sphinx carved from? Soft like wax or hard like agate? Ancient like amber or modern like bakelite? Were the feathers real, rippling under her heedful touch like the overlapping waves? Whatever it was she'd forgotten, it was surely something central, more weighty, not some detail of design or manufacture. Could she have known the name of the language which the Sphinx spoke? The more she tried to remember, the more she

found her mind wandering, mislaying the thread of logical reconstruction and returning to images from her own childhood.

She remembered how, when she had been very small, her mother had lifted her up to carry her on her hip and how she had hovered round her cot while she fell asleep. She remembered her feeling of triumph when her father left the house and the sudden presentiment of separation which followed. There was the time when she had opened a drawer with a little key and found a piece of coral and a badge which had gone darkish green. And she remembered one morning coming into her mother's room and finding her mother's friend sleeping next to her mother, and she suddenly understood something she realised her mother had tried to explain and she felt a surge of panic, as if she'd been left behind and lost. She thought her mother would be angry, but she smiled, and, when she got out of bed, she noticed the shapes of the arch of her foot and her heel and the back of her calf.

She had been drawing acrobats, trajectories of the body and displays of skill and balance. She saw them no longer as pioneers of the ideal, but as bodies at work, expending their labour power upon its own material. She was fascinated by the gap between the feeling of bodily exertion and the task of drawing and writing, gestures which consumed themselves in their own product, giving a false sense of effortlessness which no acrobat could hope to approach.

"'Capital", "Delay" and "Body". She replaced it in the box and closed the lid. She could feel her heart beat. She felt giddy with success, as though, after labouring daily to prevent a relapse into her pristine humanity, she had finally got what she wanted. She shuddered. Suddenly she heard a voice, very quiet, coming from the box, the voice of the Sphinx, growing louder, until she could hear it clearly, compellingly, and she knew that it had never ever been entirely silent and that she had heard it before, all her life, since she first understood that she was a girl!'

The voice was so familiar yet so fatally easy to forget. She smiled and, in her mind, she flung herself through the air.

5 Acrobats

[05″] *Title:*   5

[6′ 44″] *Montage and superimposition sequence of women acrobats – rope act, floor act and juggler. Shot in black and white but central section optically printed with two colours in series.*

Music.

6 Laura listening

[05″] *Title:* 6

[2′ 52″] *Laura Mulvey listens to tape of herself rehearsing her introduction and of the Sphinx as Voice Off. Camera set-up as in Section 2.*

> LAURA (*on tape*): '... into a social hieroglyphic. Later on, we try to decipher the hieroglyphic, to get behind the secret. ...'*
>
> 'To the patriarchy, the Sphinx, as woman, is a riddle and a threat. But to women, who live under patriarchy....'
>
> 'To the patriarchy, the Sphinx as woman is a riddle and a threat. But women within patriarchy are faced by a never-ending series of threats and riddles – dilemmas which are hard for women to solve, because the culture within which they must think is not theirs. We live in a society ruled by the father, in which the place of the mother is suppressed. Motherhood and how to live it, or not to live it, lies at the roots of the dilemma. And meanwhile the voice of the Sphinx is a voice apart, a voice off.'
>
> VOICE OFF (*on tape*): 'I was looking at an island in the glass. It was an island of comfort in a sea of blood. It was lonely on the island. I held tight. It was night and, in the night I felt the past. Each drop was red. Blood flows thicker than milk, doesn't it? Blood shows on silk, doesn't it? It goes quicker. Spilt. No use trying. No use replying. Spilt. It goes stickier. The wind blew along the surface of the sea. It bled and bled. The island was an echo of the past. It was an island of comfort, which faded as it glinted in the glass.'

7 Puzzle ending

[05″] *Title:* 7

[3′ 00″] *ECU. Getting first one and then another ball of mercury to centre of maze puzzle; maze violently shaken. Cut to black.*

[1′ 45″] *Credit Titles. Music.*

Total running time: 90′ 45″.

Louise: DINAH STABB
Anna: RHIANNON TISE
Maxine: MERDELLE JORDINE

---

* K. Marx: *Capital*, Vol. I, Ch. 1.

Chris: CLIVE MERRISON
Acrobat: MARIE GREEN
Juggler: CRISSIE TRIGGER
Rope Act: PAULA MELBOURNE
Voice Off: MARY MADDOX
LAURA MULVEY
& MARY KELLY

Marion Dain, Rosalind Delmar, Mary Dickinson, Rosamund Howe, Miranda Feuchtwang, Carole James, Claire Johnston, Tina Keane, Lin Layram, Carole Myer, Patsy Nightingale, Brenda Prince, Valerie Neale, Winifred Wollen, Joy Wong and staff of the Kensington Training School.

Location by courtesy of the Arndale Centre, Elona Bennett and Paul Butler, British Museum, Steve Dwoskin, Holloway Neighbourhood Group, Inner London Education Authority, Judith and Malcom Le Grice, Oval House, the Post Office, Chad Wollen.

Grateful acknowledgements to Berwick Street Collective, Rosalind Delmar, Mary Kelly, Carol Laws, *Midi-Minuit Fantastique*, Griselda Pollock.

Film material by permission of the Egyptian Tourist Office, Movietone, Mark Peploe, C. H. Wood (Bradford) Ltd.

Reproduction of *Post-Partum Document* (ICA New Gallery, 1976) by permission of Mary Kelly.

Reproductions by permission of the British Museum (Greek Vases) and the Metropolitan Museum of Art, New York (detail from a painting by Gustave Moreau).

Rostrum: FRAMELINE PRODUCTIONS
Lights: G.B.S
Opticals: HERBERT MAIDEN
Video: EVANSTON PERCUSSION UNIT
Production Assistance: MARK NASH, LINDA REDFORD, JOHN HOWE, JONATHAN COLLINSON

Child-Care: CHRISTINE SMITH
Sound: LARRY SIDER
Editing: CAROLA KLEIN, LARRY SIDER
Sound Mix: PETER MAXWELL
Cinematography: DIANE TAMMES
Assisted by: JANE JACKSON, STEVE SHAW
Music: MIKE RATLEDGE
Performed with equipment designed by DENYS IRVING
Script and Direction: LAURA MULVEY & PETER WOLLEN
Production: BFI PRODUCTION BOARD

4

Towards New Theoretical Instruments: *Riddles of the Sphinx*

Volker Pantenburg

I

*P*enthesilea: Queen of the Amazons and *Riddles of the Sphinx*, Laura Mulvey and Peter Wollen's first two films, were released only three years apart, in 1974 and 1977 respectively. At first sight, they share numerous concerns and explore similar questions: what could and should a feature-length counter-cinema look like? What modes of research – visual or otherwise – can be invented, and how do they relate to established modes of knowledge production? How might montage, but also camera movement, act as a valid instrument of theory? Finally, on a more general level, what is at stake when one decides to make the leap from discussing, writing about and teaching film to actually *making* a film – a leap that Mulvey and Wollen first made in 1974 with their debut film?

More than four decades later, we have access to a rich and ever-growing discourse around these topics. Discussions of the 'essay film' are blossoming;[1] studies of 'artistic research' map the intersection of epistemological, aesthetic and political engagement.[2] In the mid-1970s, however, the exploration of these fields was just beginning, and it redefined the relations between theory and practice, academic and non-academic knowledge, and narrative and experimental cinema – to name only a few of the categories that were challenged.

While I will particularly focus on some aspects of *Riddles* in this short essay, it seems useful to start with a brief look at the historical moment that the two films are part of. In hindsight, the years around 1975 were a particularly productive and ambiguous time, when emphatic notions of 'theory', the academic discipline of film and cinema studies, and political projects of feminism emerged and overlapped. On the one hand, theoretical thought was blossoming in France and the Anglo-American world. Take, for instance, issue 23 of *Communications*, devoted to *Psychanalyse et ciné-ma*.[3] The table of contents reads like a *Who's Who* of contemporary French theory; two articles by Christian Metz – 'Le signifiant imaginaire' and 'Le film de fiction et son spectateur', both landmarks in the explosive encounter of psychoanalysis, semiotics and cinema – frame almost equally canonical essays by Jean-Louis Baudry, Roland Barthes ('Upon Leaving the Movie Theatre') and Félix Guattari ('The Poor Man's Couch'). As if that was not enough, the rest of the journal features Thierry Kuntzel's meticulous close reading of *The Most Dangerous Game* (1932), entitled 'Le Travail du film 2', Nick Browne's interpretation of *Stagecoach* (1939) and Raymond Bellour's extensive analysis of *North By Northwest* (1959) – classics in textual analysis. Julia Kristeva, present in the same *Communications* issue with her crucial essay 'Ellipsis on Dread and Specular Seduction', was a key reference for Mulvey and Wollen's thinking at the time. As Mulvey has emphasised in her recent book *Afterimages: On Cinema, Women and Changing Times* (2019), 'the film form (within an avant-garde frame-work) offered an immediate possible conjuncture between the problem of language and patterns of space and time'. In this context, Kristeva's concept of the semiotic and the chora was crucial in bringing investigations of the maternal, the child and formal considerations together, and creating an 'in-between space, a pause that spatializes time, in which to reflect on an intertwining of the verbal and the visual'.[4]

The same theoretical abundance is there in articles and interviews published in *Screen* in 1974 and 1975, not least those authored by Mulvey and Wollen.[5] Almost every issue of the journal testifies to an enormous desire to confront and challenge cinema with theoretical thought, to use the terminological toolbox of semiotics, psychoanalysis and political theory in order to find new approaches to that ambiguous, both loved and despised object called film. This meant engaging with what was happening in Paris (in journals such as *Communications*, *Cinéthique* and *tel quel*) and elsewhere. It meant translating and inventing contemporary theory. It also meant rediscovering and appropriating the *history* of theoretical thinking (in the case of Russian Formalism, by translating key texts by Ossip Brik). This, then, is the theoretical context in which Mul-vey and Wollen realised what they called their 'theory films', defined as a subcategory of the political film, alongside agitation and propaganda, at the time.[6]

In the mid-1970s, the United Kingdom also saw a consolidation of activities around experimental film. In his rich and detailed study of Mulvey and Wollen's films, Nicolas Helm-Grovas reminds us that the British landscape of oppositional cinema had changed between *Penthesilea* and *Riddles*.[7] The Independent Film-Mak-ers' Association (IFA) had been founded in 1974, and the BFI Production Board, directed by Peter Sainsbury between 1975 and 1985, was open to support an impressive range of experimental forays into filmmaking and provided the budget of £19,300 for *Riddles*. 'One can see, then, that in the period between *Penthesilea* and *Riddles of the Sphinx* "an autonomous space of oppositional cinema" had opened up in Britain', Helm-Grovas summarises, quoting Jonathan Curling and Fran McLean.[8] Alongside production, this 'space' was also occupied by influential events; the IFA organized the First Festival of Independent British Cinema in Bristol in 1975 (which included *Penthesilea*); Wollen, with Simon Field, organised the International Forum on Avant-Garde Film at the Edinburgh Film Festival in 1976. And the oppositional cinema was both inspired by, and inspired, a concentration of critical and theoretical writing in film journals, such as *Afterimage* and *Screen*, and beyond. For instance, in a 1975 issue of the art magazine *Studio International*, Wollen published his influential article 'The Two Avant-Gardes', which also attests to a dissatisfaction with the split between the European and North American varieties of experimental filmmaking, a division that Mulvey and Wollen tried to transcend.[9]

The opportunities that had opened up in Britain (*Penthesilea* was made in the USA at Northwestern University, using the school's production facilities and thus emanating from a very different context) might have contributed to the fact that *Riddles* is concerned with a more positive engagement with narrative and classical Hollywood film than its predecessor. In 1985, Mulvey said that *Penthesilea*, like 'Visual Pleasure and Narrative Cinema' (1975), was mostly made in a spirit of negative aesthetics. 'Negative aesthetics generate a counter-cinema of systematic opposition, a politics of confrontation … But the work is locked, ultimately, in dialogue with its adversary. Alternative aesthetics, too, can threaten to harden into a system of dualistic opposition.'[10] Picking up this thought, Helm-Grovas speaks of *Riddles of the Sphinx* as 'a constructive work, as opposed to the destructive work *Penthesilea*, which was largely defined by negation.'[11] This sense of construction included a reevaluation of narrative concerns (instead of their dismissal), an engagement with and reconfiguration of Hollywood (for example, Douglas Sirk's melodramas and their colour palette) and a reconciliation between pleasure and criticality.

||

'A film like *Riddles of the Sphinx* is designed to separate form from content, so that the spectator is simultaneously aware of each.'[12] That is how, in 2002, Wollen summed up one basic strategy underlying the film. There are several devices that work to remind the spectator of the constructed nature of what they see: the explicit flipping through a book with which the film begins ('Opening pages'), direct address to camera ('Laura speaking'), the re-photographing of existing film material ('Stones'), the optical printing of the female acrobats ('Acrobats'). However, the dominant feature in the thirteen segments of 'Louise's story', the central chapter of the film, is the horizontal panning motion of the camera. With the exception of Michael Snow's trilogy on camera movement – *Wavelength* (1967), *Back and Forth* (1969) and *La Région Centrale* (1971) – few films are so rigorously based on one single operation.

If we think of Mulvey and Wollen's films of the 1970s as blueprints for and contributions to a 'third avant-garde', we might also think of the panning motion as a third option that overcomes or rather subverts the established dichotomy of montage versus the non-edited long take. Similar to cutting, and yet completely different, moving the camera creates relations. This is why Béla Balázs had intuitively characterised panning as a subcategory of montage, namely 'montage without cutting' in *The Spirit of Film* (1930): 'The camera turns or roams and has images of the objects it fleetingly catches pass muster before us. This is not montage assembled on celluloid; it is filmed as a montage from the outset. Its objects are already present in nature or in the studio. What makes the montage productive here is the selection of objects, and the rhythm of the camera movement in its panoramic sweep.'[13]

There are many things that are remarkable about Diane Tammes's extraordinary camerawork, and especially the pans in this chapter of *Riddles*. First of all, they cover a full circle and register the totality of the given space. Categorically different from a tracking shot, the 360-degree panning motion returns to the very same spot from which it started. In this respect, it is a movement without any spatial progress. The position remains the same, a circle is completed and time has passed. In moving, the surrounding space is registered with a certain sense of completeness. If we wanted to come up with a term to describe this, we might call it a 'cosmological' operation in that it constructs a very specific, well-defined world. Here, in the first three pans, it is the domestic world with its everyday routines and working duties – traditionally a space coded as 'female' – that is quite literally built around the kitchen table.

In its regular and slow motion, the pan also brings up the question of scopic agency. Whose gaze is this? What perspective on the scenes and spaces of motherhood does the film choose? On the one hand, the detached, almost machine-like movement conjures up a neutral, impartial apparatus that records the external world in an act of documentation, almost like a surveillance camera. At the same time, all the parameters of this recording – the position and height of the camera, the framing that precludes any identification with the individual – are deliberate and conscious. The 'tight framing at work-surface height' of pan 1, the movement 'at cot-height' in pan 2 and, finally, in pan 4, the 'framing to show Louise fully for the first time' have the effect that we encounter the maternal spaces as spaces of work, that we get a sense of the duration of that labour. Also, we are made aware that what is shown is not an individual 'special case', but a paradigmatic existence within an existing structure.[14]

In a discussion event after the screening of the film at the 1977 Berlinale, James Benning asked about the potential tension between the neutral act of registering and the conscious, carefully choreographed scenes that take place before the camera. I would argue that this tension, among other things, creates a compelling alternative to the dominant narrative concerns of conventional cinema. The inherent dialectics of anticipation and remembering, of on-screen space and off-screen space, which defines every panning motion, becomes a simple but powerful tool to think about presence and absence, motion and stasis.

In the tradition of the panorama, the autonomous pan is usually employed to film landscapes and wide-open spaces where the horizon serves to give us orientation. Domestic pans like the ones that Mulvey and Wollen subject us to in the first shots of 'Louise's story' are rare. One of the first and most striking examples that I know of is Chantal Akerman's *La Chambre* (1972). According to Mulvey, *Riddles* was conceived neither as an explicit homage nor a reference to Akerman, but, since Akerman is one of the important filmmakers to build a bridge between the European and the North American avant-gardes, the connection seems pertinent. In comparison to *Riddles*, however, Akerman's film, a single take of eleven minutes, appears like a small and intimate sketch. Babette Mangolte's 16mm camera scans Akerman's tiny room in Spring Street, Lower Manhattan, several times in slow, careful 360-degree pans, registering the furniture, kitchen utensils and remains of a meal on the table. It also covers Akerman herself lying in bed, first returning the camera's gaze, then performing movements under the blanket, and later holding an apple. After beginning the third circular movement, the camera changes direction, pans from left to right, and Akerman starts eating the apple. A few years before Mulvey and Wollen's decision to enter film production, Akerman's film set the stage for the encounter of rigorous structural aesthetics and feminist concerns.

Of course, there are others who had used 360-degree pans before; Jean-Luc Godard's *Deux ou trois choses que je sais d'elle* (1966) and Bernardo Bertolucci's *Partner* from May 1968 come to mind.[15] However, using the pan to map the social housing blocks in Godard or the historical sites in Rome in Bertolucci is something entirely different from what Akerman does when she transposes the operation to a domestic space and strips it of all kinds of sound. Ivone Margulies has argued that *La Chambre* gives us a compressed version of what we encounter in many of Akerman's later films. The 'Chambre Akerman', as she dubs it, is both a refuge and a laboratory for aesthetic research. 'The primary impetus for the room is its erection of a separate, rigorously demarcated space for the self.'[16] Early on, *La Chambre* establishes the stage that is then populated and used as a playground for micro-interventions in later Akerman films like *Jeanne Dielman, 23 quai du Commerce, 1080 Bruxelles* (1975) or *Là-bas* (2005).

Riddles of the Sphinx picks up this spatial constellation, but transforms it to think about a different set of issues. It is not the 'autonomous person', but the complexities, challenges and politics of motherhood and gender that are investigated. In an important take on *Riddles*, Mary Ann Doane makes a similar argument and points out that, in its panning motion, '[t]he camera consistently transforms its own framing to elide the possibility of a fetishism of the female body'.[17] Stressing the feminist potential of the camera operation, Doane claims that 'the circular camera movements which carve out the space of the *mise-en-scene* in *Riddles of the Sphinx* are in a sense more critical to a discussion of the film than the status of the figure of the Sphinx as feminine. The film effects a continual displacement of the gaze which "catches" the woman's body only accidentally, momentarily, refusing to hold or fix her in the frame.' In their succession and progress, the thirteen pans document a shift from the domestic to the social fabric of the nursery, the workplace and beyond, while Mike Ratledge's soundtrack gives way more and more to the conversations and discussions between the women within the diegesis.[18]

Traditionally, the notion of 'filmic thinking' and its primary genre, the essay film, have been linked to the capacities of montage. *Riddles*, in contrast, makes us consider the extent to which camera movement also has the potential to 'theorise'. To me, it seems that the priority that is often given to montage exists for several reasons. On the one hand, confronting two shots via montage establishes a firm and explicit sense of relation. It can therefore be more easily integrated into semiotic systems of signification and effect. In contrast to the discontinuous, abrupt montage of shots – whose principles, taxonomies and potential impact have been discussed in countless studies – camera movement confronts us with transitions, flowing developments, gradual and continual shifts that are much more difficult to describe. While the semiotic register of differences is well suited to analyse montage, the fluidity of the pan might need different theoretical instruments that manage to capture an experience rather than an intellectual form of understanding.

At the moment of its production, *Riddles of the Sphinx*, along with films by Babette Mangolte, Yvonne Rainer, Chantal Akerman and others, broke new ground and opened up a third path to complement the 'two avant-gardes'. From today's vantage point, we see more clearly how this also meant redefining the thresholds between theory and practice, as well as between writing and filmmaking.

Notes

1. To name only a few recent English-language books: Timothy Corrigan, *The Essay Film: From Montaigne, After Marker* (New York: Oxford University Press, 2011); Nora M. Alter, *The Essay Film After Fact and Fiction* (New York: Columbia University Press, 2018); Laura Rascaroli, *How the Essay Film Thinks* (New York: Oxford University Press, 2017). For a reevaluation of *Riddles of the Sphinx* in the light of the essay film, see: Laura Mulvey, '*Riddles* as Essay Film', in *Essays on the Essay Film*, eds Nora M. Alter and Timothy Corrigan (New York: Columbia University Press, 2017), 314–322.

2. See, for instance: Tom Holert, *Knowledge Beside Itself: Contemporary Art's Epistemic Politics* (Berlin: Sternberg Press, 2020).

3. See: *Communications* 23 (1975): 'Psychanalyse et cinéma'.

4. Laura Mulvey, 'Mary Kelly: Speaking Maternal Silence, *Post-Partum Document* and *The Ballad of Kastriot Rexhepi*', in *Afterimages: On Cinema, Women and Changing Times* (London: Reaktion Books, 2019), 227.

5. I'm thinking in particular of the extensive interview that Claire Johnston and Paul Willemen did with Mulvey and Wollen about *Penthesilea* in *Screen* volume 15, issue 3, Autumn 1974, 120–134; and, of course, Mulvey's seminal essay on 'Visual Pleasure and Narrative Cinema' in volume 16, issue 3, Autumn 1975, 6–18. It goes without saying that journals like *Afterimage* were equally invested in theoretical and practical issues around filmmaking.

6. Laura Mulvey and Peter Wollen, '*Penthesilea, Queen of the Amazons*', interview by Claire Johnston and Paul Willemen, *Screen* 15:3 (Autumn 1974), 125–126.

7. The developments in the United Kingdom might be contrasted with what was happening elsewhere in Europe. For example, in Germany, the utopian project of counter-culture, the optimism about being able to escape the lures and pressures not only of Hollywood cinema, but all kinds of established, 'bourgeois' film institutions, had already started to wane by 1975. Birgit Hein, German filmmaker and co-founder of XSCREEN in Cologne – a crucial institution showing German, Austrian, British and North American avant-garde films since its foundation in 1968 – remembers the year as an unprecedented low point. In Hein's recollections of the period, published in the mid-1980s, frustration prevails: 'In 1975, we hit rock bottom … Our film work stagnates. XSCREEN is practically at the end … In the public, avant-garde film no longer seems to exist. But not only in avant-garde film but in all fields, it has become considerably calm: step by step, the reaction prepares itself and triumphs currently in the form of a new *Biedermeier*.' This spirit of foreboding prefigures the crisis that ultimately overtook the British avant-garde at the end of the decade. See: Wilhelm Hein and Birgit Hein, *Dokumente 1967–1985. Fotos, Briefe, Texte* (Frankfurt am Main: Deutsches Filmmuseum, 1985), 68. [*Kinematograph* Nr. 3/1985.]

8. Nicolas Helm-Grovas, 'Laura Mulvey and Peter Wollen: Theory and Practice, Aesthetics and Politics, 1963–1983' (PhD diss., Royal Holloway, University of London, 2018), 214.

9. See: Peter Wollen, 'The Two Avant-Gardes', in *Readings and Writings: Semiotic Counter-Strategies* (London: Verso, 1982), 92–104.

10. Laura Mulvey, 'Changes', *Discourse* 7 (Spring 1985), 14.

11. Helm-Grovas, 'Laura Mulvey and Peter Wollen', 216.

12. Peter Wollen, 'Knight's Moves', *Public* 25 (Spring 2002), 59–60.

13. Béla Balázs, 'The Spirit of Film', in *Béla Balázs: Early Film Theory: Visible Man and The Spirit of Film*, ed. Erica Carter, trans. Rodney Livingstone (New York: Berghahn Books, 2010), 136.

14. These camera descriptions are taken from the script. See pages 73, 74 and 77 in this volume.

15. Elsewhere, I have written in more detail about the implications of the horizontal panning in these films. See: Volker Pantenburg, 'Kameraschwenk. Stil – Operation – Geste?', in *Filmstil. Perspektivierungen eines Begriffs*, eds Julian Blunk, Dietmar Kammerer, Tina Kaiser and Chris Wahl (Munich: edition text und kritik, 2016), 236–253.

16. Ivone Margulies, 'La Chambre Akerman', *Rouge* 10 (2007), accessed 12 August 2019, www.rouge.com.au/10/akerman.html.

17. Mary Ann Doane, 'Woman's Stake: Filming the Female Body', *October* 17 (Summer 1981), 34.

18. In the Q&A of the Berlin screening in 1977, Mulvey explained the conceptual nature of the succession of pans; after the first three shots, when the husband moves out, the voice of the Sphinx and the music.

5

AMY!

Laura Mulvey and Peter Wollen

WARNING: this script includes newspaper headlines from the 1930s, which make reference to traumatic events, including the rise of fascism, and imperial and racial violence.

1 Opening Scene

[1′12″] *Waving crowd at Croydon Airport. Black and white library footage. Malinké xylophone music, lasting until second title of AMY!. Titles in yellow on plain background:*

> 1930
> Who was she? Shopgirl, typist, mechanic, lone flier, Wonderful
> Amy The Aeroplane Girl, never much good at landing. May 1930.
> Millions thrilled at her heroic.. She's crashed.. No, she's safe! Are you
> ready? One! Two! Three!!
> AMY!
> Script & Direction: Laura Mulvey and Peter Wollen
> AMY!
> 1980

Music: La Troupe des Guinéens, 'Xylophones et chœur de femmes'.

2 Interview at Paddington College

[2′10″] *Laura's voice off, talking to girls in a class at Paddington College on a Community Care Course. Black and white, re-filmed video. Background noise of a machine shop. Synchronised dialogue, with shots of the girls' faces as they reply.*

LAURA: So, do you think that means the idea of a heroine is going out, is a thing of the past?

SOPHIA: It's just like a fashion really, just like teddy girls and teddy boys. That's what heroines are like.

LAURA: What do you mean?

SOPHIA: There's not really much to say. It's just that it's a craze. People go through phases, like the television heroines, like Wonder Woman and things like that, kids are mad over. That's about it.

LAURA: Why do you think they are?

SOPHIA: Because it's an image that they want, that they would like to be.

LAURA: Yes.

SOPHIA: You know, it's a fake, that they know they never could be but they always wished they *could* be. No, I was talking specifically about the television heroes. I mean, anybody can fly to Australia, any woman, but because one did it and she was the first to do it, she became a heroine. I'm sure lots of people could do it, but they haven't got the go in them.

LAURA: One thing she had to do, she had to learn how to be an engineer. Do you think there was something heroic about that?

SUSAN: For that time it was, not many people, hardly anyone did it, apart from men. And if you were a woman and you did these sort of things, people would look up and think, 'What's she doing? She's a woman, she's not supposed to do these things', but now it's an everyday thing. Loads of them are learning about cars, motorbikes, loads of engineering things.

BEVERLEY: I like fixing our television at home. Yeah, I always used to play with the set, you know. It's interesting.

LAURA: Playing with the television?

BEVERLEY: Yeah. When it wasn't going right, I always tried to fix it, you know. Sometimes made it worse, but still …

3 Peter Jones

[34"] *Exterior view of Peter Jones department store, London. Colour. Yellow titles in superimposition:*

> PETER JONES
> SILKS & SHANTUNGS
> 30/- PER WEEK

Music: Feminist Improvising Group.

4 Amy's room

[3′10 ″] *Interior,* AMY's *bed-sit. Close-up of a small chest of drawers on a table.* AMY's *hand takes out a bundle of letters.*

Track to AMY *in front of a mirror, looking at letters and a photograph of her fiancé. As she speaks (voice off), the camera tracks with her to the fireplace. She burns the letters and the photograph.*

> AMY: My life up to now has occupied two volumes: one, my childhood and schooldays, and two, you. The first one finished when I went to Sheffield and it is now time to close the second one. From the age of eighteen until now, when I am nearly twenty-five (please correct me if I'm wrong), you've been the predominating factor in my life. I don't blame you for that – it was I who was the fool – and now that I'm so much older and more experienced I can look back on those years and see how utterly stupid I have been. I think I am now strong enough to cut it all out, and that's what I intend to do. No more looking for letters that come less and less often; no more wondering when you'll come to London again to see me, or rather when you'll be coming on business; no more puzzling over the question of how much you really do care for me and what are the thoughts about me that must sometimes be going on in your mind … The decision I have come to is the result of a lot of hard thinking on my part.

Music: Feminist Improvising Group.

5 Flying Moth

[2″] *A Moth plane in flight (no soundtrack).*

6 Amy's Room

[2′38″] *Interior,* AMY's *bed-sit.* AMY *at the fireplace, making cocoa. As she speaks (voice off), the camera tracks with her to the table, past a photo of a De Havilland Tiger Moth, to the chest of drawers in close-up.* AMY's *hand opens a drawer and takes out screws.*

> AMY:
> Daily Drill
> 1. Wash engine down with paraffin or petrol
> 2. Check tappet clearance

3. Charge rocker fulcrum pins with grease

4. Grease valve stems and push rods with graphite grease

5. Test valve springs by hand for strength

6. Turn engine by hand for compression

7. Check contact breaker gaps – .012″, and clean points with piece of emery cloth if dirty

8. Clean distributor segments with cloth soaked in paraffin

9. Check plug points – .015″

10. Clean petrol filter

11. Test airscrew bolts for tightness on hub and hub for tightness on shaft

12. Check all engine holding-down bolts for tightness and engine mounting screws

13. Check all nuts, screws, pins, pipe joints and pipes for leaks

14. Clean oil filter

15. Check all wiring and switches

16. Examine airscrew for truth, pitting at tips, torn fabric and cracks

Music: Feminist Improvising Group.

7 Moth in hangar

[34″] *British Aerospace (De Havilland) hangar at Hatfield with Cirrus Moth.*

Yellow titles in superimposition:

> FLYING DREAMS
> FINANCIAL BACKERS
> WAKEFIELD'S OIL

Music: Feminist Improvising Group.

8 Map of flight from Croydon to Darwin

[7′30″] *Computerised rostrum tracking shot moving slowly over a map. The camera halts at places Amy Johnson landed. Voice over reads daily news headlines from* The Times, *May 1930. Between stops, background noise of Moth engine.*

NEWSREADER:

As map shows –

(1. Croydon)

Mr Gandhi arrested: Police action today

Police stoned in Calcutta

'Red' activities in China: Spanish priests carried off

The Break on Wall Street: Bad speculations

(2. Vienna)

The arrest of Mr Gandhi: Followers out of control

Troops raid at Peshawar: Agitators arrested

The King: Twentieth anniversary of accession

(3. Istanbul)

More rioting in India: Mobs fired on

The King: Many anniversary messages

Soviet warships in the Black Sea: Concentration feared

King Tafari in power: The rebellion at Dessie

(4. Aleppo)

Mr Gandhi's arrest: Outlook more peaceful

The Peshawar disorders: Peace restored

Home Office policy: The control of aliens

(5. Baghdad)

New rioting in India: Police stations burnt

More trouble in Ohio prisons: Convicts killed in their sleep

Mr Baldwin's policy: Safeguarding and Empire

Miss Johnson's flight: Adventures in the desert

(6. Bandar Abbas)

Mob frenzy in India: Sholapur riot details: Murdered police

RAF action on frontier: Warning to rebel leader

The Tientsin customs: Yen's dilemma

(7. Karachi)

North China War: Yen and Feng advance: Severe fighting

Great Britain and Egypt: The Sudan deadlock

Miss Johnson's flight: India in six days

(8. Jhansi)

Atrocities at Sholapur: Fate of Moslem police

US and naval parity: Big programme of construction

Racial outburst in Texas: Negroes burnt to death

Monsieur Picasso: Action for fraud

(9. Calcutta)

Lena goldfields dispute: Soviet 'not bound' by court's decision

Crime in New York: Dangers of gang rule

The crisis in Malta: Labour Party and the Archbishop

Miss Johnson's flight: Arrival at Calcutta

(10. Insein)

Round Table Conference: Indian views

NW Frontier incidents: Punitive action by air

Miss Johnson's flight: Machine damaged

1,712,000 out of work: A big increase

(11. Bangkok)

Rioting in Bengal: Mob fired on

Naval Treaty: Mr Churchill on British needs

Miss Johnson in Siam: A stormy flight

French postal workers: Two-hour strike in Paris

(12. Songkhla)

Union in Europe: Security and the Rhineland

Red Terror in China: Menace to Hankow

Bombay salt raid: Large numbers arrested

The French postal strike: Punishment of leaders

Fascist Italy: The Duce's speech at Florence

(13. Singapore)

The budget: Labour left-wing criticism

1,739,000 out of work: Increase of 27,500

Miss Johnson's flight: Warm welcome in Singapore

US strength in cruisers: Conflicting views

(14. Tjirebon)

The Indian disorders: Woman leader in custody

Unemployment: Sir Oswald Mosley's position

US 'Big Navy' advocates: Admiral's admissions

Mob outrages in India: Bombs thrown

Miss Johnson's flight: Perils of Java Sea

(15. Surabaja)

Check to salt raiders: Police reinforced by troops

Labour schisms: Sir Oswald Mosley and his party

Parliamentary tradition: An incident in the Commons

Miss Johnson off again

(16. Atambua)

The border vigil: Full first-hand account
Congress and the tribes: An unnatural alliance
Labour and Liberals: A breakdown
Miss Johnson: No news of landing
(17. Darwin, Australia)
Guarding the frontier: The Haji's lair
Mass tyranny in India: Picketing and threats
Australian flight: Miss Johnson's success
Airwoman's fine achievement: Message from the King
Signor Mussolini in Milan: Fascism and its opponents

9 Airport House

[1′10″] *Airport House, Croydon Airport. Tracking shot from a car around the disued airport building. Voice of Peter Wollen.*

> PETER: Adventures end with safe returns. And yet returning home may turn out the most desperate moment of all. The sense of freedom and independence, the display of skill, the excitement of risk, are all finished and the philobat – the psychoanalytic term for someone who enjoys thrills – must come down to earth. Thrills follow from vertigo, from speed, from the new and unpredictable and, in general, from a deliberate exposure to danger with the confident hope that all will turn out well in the end. True philobats rely on vision rather than touch, yet they typically possess some special object (often a piece of equipment) to which they hold on, which confers reassurance and magical power. The ultimate object is the earth itself. As it approaches, elation can give way to gloom and resentment at the prospect of dependence. The original deep anxiety against which philobatism is a defence comes back in full force – the fear of being abandoned or dropped, as a parent might drop a child.*

10 Amy at Airport House

[1′12″] *Airport House, Croydon Airport. Telephoto shot of* AMY, *holding a flask, gloves and flowers. Seemingly responding to the press (camera flashes), she turns her back to the camera and runs away. Then, turning around again, she removes her helmet, shakes her hair loose and approaches the camera, smiling.*

---

* Adapted from Michael Balint's book *Thrills and Regressions* (1959).

Music: Poly Styrene and X-Ray Spex, 'Obsessed With You'.

> You are just a concept
> You are just a dream
> You're just a reflection
> Of the new regime
>
> You are just a symbol
> You are just a theme
> You're just another figure
> For the sales machine
>
> Ooo ooo they're obsessed
> With yoo ooo
> Ooo ooo they're obsessed
> With yoo ooo
> Ooo ooo cos they're watching
> Yoo ooo
>
> You are just a victim
> You are just a find
> Soon to be a casualty
> A casualty of time
>
> You are just a concept
> You are just a dream
> You're just a reflection
> Of the new regime
>
> Ooo ooo they're obsessed
> With yoo ooo
> Ooo ooo they're obsessed
> With yoo ooo
> Ooo ooo cos they're watching
> Yoo ooo (© Festawood Ltd, 1978)

11 Fall

[4″] *Fall to the ground. Speeded-up helicopter descent shot.*

12 Amy through the mirror

[3′30″] *Opens with* AMY *brushing her hair, then making up in front of a two-way mirror.*

AMY: What annoyed me so much was that you couldn't even understand, or believe, that you had made things enormously difficult for me by phoning for me under my own name. Another thing you cannot realise is that I detest the publicity and the public life that has been forced upon me … I have therefore been driven to tell you (rather too forcibly I admit) what you cannot see for yourselves … that I am seeking hard to lose my identity of 'Amy Johnson' because that personage has become a nightmare and abomination to me. My great ideas for a career in aviation have been annulled, for a long time to come, by the wrong kind of publicity and exploitation which followed my return to England … I've had a complete collapse ever since the Engineer's Dinner and I'm not normal at present … I strongly resent interference and efforts to rule my life or control my actions … I've lived my own life for the last seven years and I intend to continue doing so.

AMY *draws a face in lipstick on the glass, superimposed over her own face. She then scribbles it out.*

Music: Poly Styrene and X-Ray Spex, 'Identity'.

Identity
Is the crisis
Can't you see
Identity identity

When you look in the mirror
Do you see yourself
Do you see yourself
On the TV screen
Do you see yourself
In the magazine
When you see yourself
Does it make you
Scream

Identity
Is the crisis

Can't you see
Identity identity

Identity
Is the crisis
Can't you see
Identity identity

When you look in the mirror
Do you smash it quick
Do you take the glass
And slash your wrists
Did you do it for fame
Did you do it in a fit
Did you do it before
You read about it

Identity
Is the crisis
Can't you see
Identity identity (© Festawood Ltd, 1978)

13 Northcliffe House

[44″] *Northcliffe House, London: offices of the* Daily Mail. *Voice of Laura Mulvey.*

Yellow titles in superimposition:

> DAILY MAIL
> £10,000 CONTRACT
> PERSONAL APPEARANCES
> COLLAPSE

LAURA: The real deeds that a heroine does strike a symbolic chord and then threaten to open up a break, a wound in the symbolic flesh of family and law, which has to be stitched up again by the creation of images and myths and legends. The heroine's perverse deeds are translated into exemplary exploits and her symbolic role stabilised for our identification and entertainment. The story is centred on her and the unconscious effects of dispersal and disequilibrium are fixed and framed. The thrill has gone.

14 Over a jungle

[1´41″] *Aerial shots of a jungle landscape and grass landing strip. Re-filmed Super-8.*

Voice of Yvonne Rainer.

WOMAN: An amazing life came into his eyes as he questioned me about flying. What did a landscape look like from above? Strips of multicoloured brocade. Pools turned into solids. I told him about the storm and the strange impression of seeing lightning sideways as if it were one of the tempests that the eighteenth-century artists were fond of painting. Resemblances were something that presupposed remembering. It was necessary for me nevertheless not to realise these things as remembering. Bad memory is also a big factor here. The remedy for this is for everyone to buy a notebook. Suddenly, almost as in a legend. It will puzzle any man to find in the pages of history as many instances of real and startling heroism in his sex as I can hunt up in mine. The pain they once suffered. What one repeats is the scene in which one is acting, the days in which one is living, the coming and going one is doing, anything one is remembering. The excitement to me in those days was the absolute newness of what we saw in the patterns on the ground and in the changing colours of the clouds just beyond the wings. Kenneth was able to give the Professor details about the machinery that I did not know. Among my supressed desires, one very special ambition is under the letter T. The imaginary file-card reads: Tinkering – For Girls Only. The plan is to endow a machine-shop where girls may tinker to their hearts' content with motors, lathes, jig-saws and diverse gadgets of their own creation.

15 Bird in flight

[2´22″] *Slowed-down shot (in variable speed) of a bird in flight, re-filmed off a Steenbeck screen.* WOMAN'S *monologue continues.*

WOMAN: The ability to forget the past enables people to free themselves from the pain they suffered. Women were paid only about half as much as men. Women cut and sew the fabric. Designated definitely as 'women's' work'. There are a few one-of-a-kind jobs, existing perhaps because of a worker's unusual ability and because such an individual doesn't interfere much with men's employment.

Katherine Wright: real and startling heroism. Katherine Wright acquired Latin and Greek. The money she earned as teacher in these subjects she turned over to her brothers so they might continue their aeronautical experiments. So

Katherine Wright helped pay for and actually helped build the first heavier-than-air plane ever flown. We skimmed so close I could see the prints of goat hooves. Pools turned into solids. I must soar anew through the boundless sky before it was too late, before I had forgotten how to flap my wings. Sometimes certain types of individuals become rigid with fear and hold so tightly to nearby objects that their grasp cannot be broken except by knocking them unconscious. I cut around the edge of the thunderheads and they had purple lightning inside. The only thing I can remember thinking about. The first prerequisite is a good memory. The pain they once suffered. The mistakes of their predecessors. The airport, the crowds, the police cordon that had been set up. The pages of history. Writing something down means I know I won't have to remember it. Forgetting the pain. The mistakes of their predecessors. The thing that is the difficulty is the question of confusing time. The strictness of not letting remembering mix itself with looking. The sky was as interesting to him at that moment as the mind. The clouds form themselves into strange polar patterns, the sun changes. I saw it once bouncing like a scarlet ball from peak to peak. Burning. At that moment I felt I was free. I began to speak more freely. I could even permit myself the luxury of pausing when I felt like it, for I knew that if I didn't want an image to appear, it wouldn't. I felt simply wonderful.

16 'JASON' in the Science Museum

[3′17″] *Amy Johnson's plane, 'JASON', hanging in the Science Museum, London.*

Sound of a plane's engine as an intermittent background noise, against the music of Jack Hylton & His Orchestra playing 'Amy, Wonderful Amy':

There's a little lady who has captured every heart,
Amy Johnson, it's you.
We have watched and waited since the day you made your start,
Amy Johnson, it's true.

Since the news that you are safe has come along,
Everyone in town is singing this love song,
Amy, wonderful Amy,
How can you blame me for loving you?

Since you've won the praise of every nation
You have filled my heart with admiration.
Amy, wonderful Amy,

I'm proud of the way you flew.
Believe me, Amy,
You cannot blame me, Amy, for falling in love with you.

She's landed in Vienna.
Here she is in Baghdad.
Now she's over Karachi.
She's reached Port Darwin… Bravo!
She's up again, she's off to Brisbane.
Here she comes, here she comes, there's something wrong. Gracious, what's wrong?
She's crashed… No, she's safe!

Amy, wonderful Amy,
How can you blame me for loving you?
Since you've won the praise of every nation
You have filled my heart with admiration.

17 Newsreel of Amy

[18″] *Shot of Amy Johnson at Croydon Airport, library footage, black and white.*

Sound of an engine, then Beverley's voice over as Amy Johnson begins to speak into microphone.

BEVERLEY: I don't think that to be a heroine you've got to be famous. You know, you don't have to be famous and everybody knows that you've done it.

18 Take marks

[4″] *Take markers (3, 2, 1) and sync taps, black and white, re-filmed off video. Malinké xylophone music plays.*

Music: La Troupe des Guinéens, 'Xylophones et chœur de femmes'.

Credits

[1′08″]

Camera: Diane Tammes
Crew: Jonathan Collinson, Anne Cottringer
2nd Camera: Francine Winham

Sound and Editing: Larry Sider
Design: Michael Hurd

Mary Maddox as AMY (words from Amy's letters)

Class at Paddington College, Community Care Course

Yvonne Rainer as the voices of Bryher, Amelia Earhart, Lola Montez, S. and Gertrude Stein

Jonathan Eden (headlines from *The Times*, May 1930)

Laura Mulvey and Peter Wollen

Thanks to: Chris Berg, Ian Christie, Rosalind Delmar, Keith Griffiths, Ilona Halberstadt, John Howe, Tina Keane, Tamara Krikorian, Carol Laws, Patsy Nightingale, Geoffrey Nowell-Smith, Carl Teitelbaum, Chad Wollen, Evanston Percussion Unit and the De Havilland Moth Club

Special thanks to: Feminist Improvising Group, Poly Styrene and X-Ray Spex, Jack Hylton & His Orchestra

Production: Laura Mulvey, with Modelmark Limited
Made with financial assistance from Southern Arts

6

The Curse of Celebrity, Colonial Territory and the Flight to Freedom: *AMY!*

Griselda Pollock

he single-word film title ends in an exclamation mark (!). The punctuation implies more than a name. It is an exclamation, perhaps a proclamation. There is the hint of surprise, of the exceptional, something to arouse a response. As an effect of the film itself, however, this woman's given name is neither. It becomes a question.

Is Amy Johnson another riddle? Was she a riddle to herself in 1930? Is feminine subjectivity itself a riddle both to the subject and to those of us who began to investigate such riddles in our feminist moment c. 1980?

In 1980, Laura Mulvey and Peter Wollen made the film *AMY!* about the famous British aviator Amy Johnson (1903–1941). They made it after they had completed the landmark feminist film *Riddles of the Sphinx* in 1977 and before they curated their exhibition of *Frida Kahlo and Tina Modotti* at the Whitechapel Gallery in London in 1982. These dates are important for a history of feminist exploration of subjectivity, representation and sexual difference, prefiguring topics taken up in the exhibition *Difference: On Representation and Sexuality* (New York and then London 1984–1985), for which Jane Weinstock curated the film and video section and the catalogue included an essay by Wollen on counter-cinema as a concurrent exploration of shared questions and new forms. The *Frida Kahlo and Tina Modotti* exhibition engaged with these inquiries in relation to a historical moment of the international artistic and political avant-garde in the 1920s–1930s, while the *Difference* exhibition, focusing on artworks since 1970, placed a film/video programme alongside contemporary conceptually informed artworks by women and men who, at this different historical and political conjunction of revolutionary consciousness and radical art, also explored the body, subjectivity and desire: both sexual and political. Like all Mulvey and Wollen films, *AMY!* poses the riddle of femininity back to patriarchy, not this time through the figure of the mother (as in *Riddles of the Sphinx*), but through the question of the heroic and the heroine – what today we might discuss in terms of intensified and manufactured celebrity and its subjective cost.

AMY! graphically fills the screen after an 'intertitle' asking: 'who was she?' followed by the terms that might define the person in question: *shopgirl, typist, mechanic, lone flier, Wonderful Amy The Aeroplane Girl*. Then fragments evoke early twentieth-century newspaper headlines: 'Millions thrilled at her heroic...' and news reporting: 'She's crashed... No, she's safe.' This device economically disposes of the bio-element of the biography while also reminding us of an identity forged in public and across the media. Each of the potential labels becomes part of the enigma of this historical person who graduated from Sheffield University in economics in 1925 but was then obliged to do a secretarial course, subsequently working by selling 'silks and shantungs' at Peter Jones, a department store in central London. Then she chose to become an engineer and trained as a pilot. By its string of words, the film thus introduces the politics of gender across the twentieth century, the contradictions of women's campaigns for education in a society that then refused them the spaces of employment it still reserved for men only.

To break the mould – economics and engineering, the first woman to fly solo to Australia, breaking other records – this is a double-edged story for feminism. Pioneers and heroes allow cultural mythology to celebrate the exception while obfuscating the general conditions that maintain the patriarchal status quo. In section thirteen of the film, dealing with Amy Johnson's anguished experience of becoming a media icon, a public image (from which we know the historical person withdrew in psychological collapse), we will hear a voice-over read by Mulvey. She offers a feminist, psychoanalytical and cultural interpretation of the destabilising and personally unsettling role of the heroine in patriarchal culture. The heroine is always the *exceptional* woman to Woman, hence both exciting and threatening. She breaches the patriarchal symbolic order that the official narrative seeks to heal by iconisation.

> The real deeds that a heroine does strike a symbolic chord and then threaten to open up a break, a wound in the symbolic flesh of family and law, which has to be stitched up again by the creation of images and myths and legends. The heroine's perverse deeds are translated into exemplary exploits and her symbolic role stabilised for our identification and entertainment. The story is centred on her and the unconscious effects of dispersal and disequilibrium are fixed and framed. The thrill has gone. (Sequence thirteen)[1]

Mulvey offers a profound analysis of the deep perversity of celebrity culture in relation to women who pay the price patriarchy exacts – subjectively.

Two other intertitles structure the film: the dates 1930 and 1980. Half a century apart, what is the meaning in 1980 of a historical figure from 1930, the *first woman to…*? Interviewing a group of young women at college in London (in the second section of the film), Mulvey asks them about their idea of the heroine. One woman, Sophia, mentions Wonder Woman from the comic books and a then current TV series. She astutely avers that the fascination lies in the image of the extraordinary, an ideal image to which women might foolishly and unrealistically aspire. Interestingly, these young women find becoming an engineer and flying solo around the world not at all extraordinary, except insofar as someone had to do it first. It is a matter of having the 'go' to do it. These testimonies from young women in 1980 register a confidence in possibility for themselves: a sense of their destiny beyond typist or shop girl. Was that the effect of a new feminism?

Having created the string that reaches across the fifty years through these non-narrative devices, borrowing from early cinema and newsreel as well as TV documentary, the film moves into melodrama and biopic mode if only to undo them. I sourced and watched the only other movie about Amy Johnson, a feature-length RKO drama titled *They Flew Alone*, retitled for the North American market as *Wings and the Woman* (Dir. Herbert Wilcox) and made soon after her death. This is both biopic and melodrama. Its representation of Amy Johnson (Anna Neagle) focuses on her restlessness at work, falling in love and divorcing fellow aviator Jim Mollison, and dying in a crash. Both this film and the contemporary news reports make a story out of the exceptional activity of one woman, Amy Johnson, who defied expectation not only by refusing to be a secretary (read: supportive, secondary role) but also by mastering technological knowledge (engineering and machinery), and by learning to fly aeroplanes, the newest human invention to defy the historical earth-boundness of human beings.

They Flew Alone carries its clue in the title. The challenge in this era of aviation was solo-flying great distances. Alone. So, 'they' refocuses the film on her husband as well. This film can only celebrate Amy Johnson by reassuring us that the exceptional woman is ultimately punished. She is forced to be alone, to fail in the supposedly central drama of a woman's life. The film's weak coda is wartime propaganda. In a very pedestrian mode of dramatised reportage, it presents the unexpected opportunities created during the war for otherwise unemployed women pilots to fly; they could deliver planes to airbases for the air battles that led to terrible losses of men and planes. It was on one such delivery mission, in unpredicted bad weather, that Amy Johnson went off-course and was forced to bail out; her plane and her body were lost at sea. Amy Johnson is thereby translated into an almost mythic image by her falling, like Icarus, from the sky into the sea. The narrative reasserts the hubris of Icarus and leads once again to a tragic end. Air and Water, Flight and Burial.

In seeking to understand the concept of the heroine, I turned to dictionaries. There, *hero* and *heroine* are both defined as 'a person who is admired for their courage, outstanding achievements, or noble qualities'. The synonyms, however, reveal a deeper sexual difference. Compare this list: 'brave man, champion, man of courage, great man, man of the hour, conquering, victor, winner, conqueror, lionheart, war hero' to this list for the *heroine:* 'brave woman, woman of courage, great woman, woman of the hour; key character in a novel, a feminist heroine, and in myth: a woman of superhuman qualities and often semi-divine origin, in particular one whose deeds were the subject of ancient Greek myths'. In 1989, American feminist art historian Mary D. Garrard published her important monograph on the seventeenth-century Italian painter Artemisia Gentileschi titled *Artemisia Gentileschi: The Image of the Female Hero in Italian Baroque Art*.[2] In seventeenth-century Italian art, 'hero' refers to biblical and historical characters such as Cleopatra, Judith, Jael and Lucretia, whose transgressive acts as women were associated with politics, violence and threat. Such female heroes were topics for brilliantly composed and dramatically painted scenes of passionate and often dangerous acts performed by women. When feminists began the work of reinstating into our histories the artworks created by artist-women throughout the ages, Gentileschi, a painter of these same figures, was one of the first to be reconsidered as a feminist heroine for art history. Yet her achievements had been obscured through the iteration of a disfiguringly scandalous reputation – she had been sexually assaulted and was then tortured during the subsequent trial to ascertain the truth of her claim to having been raped. The entanglement of cultural myth, history and artistic achievement prompted studies of the search for a woman artist who would be the equivocal hero of a new feminist cultural politics. This pioneering work not only found its way into experimental feminist novels such as *Artemisia* (1947) by Italian art historian and novelist Anna Banti (1895–1985), but also into the early political journals of the Women's Movement in Britain such as *Shrew*. There Amanda Sebestyen and Caroline Dees analysed the sensationalising, sexualised language regularly used about Gentileschi the woman in anxious response to the powerful embodiment of women's agency so often represented by Gentileschi the artist in her paintings of the heroic woman.

Into the expanded environment of feminist inquiry into the figure of the female hero, mythically and art historically, and the changing context of heroism in the fifty years between 1930 and 1980, *AMY!* intervenes cinematically as much as thematically. Formed in eighteen chapters, the film is structured by three elements: her room, her flight, her return. The first element is a reflection on 'the room of one's own', both a space and a mentality. The first room is a bedsit where two moments of Amy's subjectivity are staged. In the first of these two scenarios, she sheds her past, a typically feminine condition of emotional attachment to, and waiting for, a man. Thus, we see the young woman open the drawers of a miniature chest of drawers containing flowers and letters. In a letter read in voice-over, which she burns, untying the pink ribbon that symbolically holds the woman to her absent lover, she tells him (and us) that their relationship, and the first two chapters of her life – childhood/ school and this affair – are over. Then, in a second scene, following a two-second image of a Moth plane in flight, Amy is in her room, dressed in work clothes. She studies an engineering textbook and works with a compass, while her voice-over recites the procedures for preparing an aircraft for flight. Her chest of drawers now contains a tiny globe and lots of screws and widgets. There is enlivening experimental music on the soundtrack by the Feminist Improvising Group, so that no interior monologue or dramatic expression is required. Transition is being represented by the act of self-transformation from passivity to energised agency. The film then cuts to the hangar at De Havilland and a Cirrus Moth plane while titles briefly flash across the screen: *Flying Dreams, Financial Backers, Wakefield's Oil* – also to the music of the Feminist Improvising Group.

Amy Johnson's historic solo flight from Croydon, South London to Darwin in Australia is filmed by means of a single computerised rostrum shot moving slowly over a very detailed map tracking her flight. This journey takes seven minutes and thirty seconds of film time. The film thus uses temporality and a pan over the various stops on the journey to convey the stages of flight with the intermittent buzz of a small single-engine biplane on the soundtrack. The movement over the map is overlaid by a male voice in news reporting tone, announcing the headlines from *The Times* during her flight, which makes it clear that the trip from London to Australia is an imperial one, touching those points in the British Empire that were, at that moment, erupting in decolonising resistance. This is signalled by constant reference in the news reports to unrest in India, to the arrest and imprisonment of Gandhi, to riots in China and Sudan. We are also informed of racist atrocities in Texas and alerted to the rise of fascism in Europe. Amid this flow of reports of violence and resistance, Amy Johnson's flight only enters the news when she reaches India. The film thus subtly analyses the news media, tracing the moment and the symbolic colonial site at which 'Miss Johnson's' *activity for herself* becomes a public event.

The next sections of the film are reflective and analytical, using various unlocated voices to pose questions and probe the imaginary and psychological dimensions of the exceptional act and the cultural reception and appropriation of the act. In voice-over, Wollen introduces psychoanalyst Michael Ballint's question: what are the psychic stakes in the urge to undertake dangerous and daring adventures? This urge has a name: philobatism – the love of thrills – which, read analytically, reveals a hidden psychic overdetermination, namely a fear of dependence, which itself may cloak traces of even deeper, archaic anxiety associated with a primal loss of connection, with abandonment, with an infant's fear of being dropped. Rather than a character, 'Amy' Johnson becomes the enigmatic trace through which Mulvey and Wollen are posing analytical questions both to the historical agent and to the culture that created her as an image. What did it mean to the woman, who had flown round the world alone, to come home, to be back where she started and to find herself publicly celebrated as the woman who first flew solo? There can be no answer.

Just as there are two shots representing Amy's initial shift from conventional femininity to engineer, two shots represent her return. In the tenth sequence, at Croydon Airfield, the camera's intransigent gaze follows her as she first tries to escape it, then turns to face the lens. The words and music of Poly Styrene and X-Ray Spex's 'Obsessed With You' (1978) say it all on behalf of the person who becomes a figure of individual or collective obsession: the celebrity.

> You are just a concept
> You are just a dream
> You're just a reflection
> Of the new regime
> Ooo ooo they're obsessed
> With yoo ooo

In sequence twelve, Amy puts on mask-like make-up, then draws the outlines of the mask – eyes, nose and mouth – in lipstick on the mirror. The separation of self from the visible image is marked generically first by the cosmetic alteration of her face and then the crossing out of its alienated phantom self. Another of Amy Johnson's letters is read in voice-over, describing her nervous collapse on her return to England.

> I detest the publicity and the public life that has been forced upon me ... I am seeking hard to lose my identity of 'Amy Johnson' because that personage has become a nightmare and abomination to me. My great ideas for a career in aviation have been annulled, for a long time to come, by the wrong kind of publicity and exploitation which followed my return to England ...[3]

The Poly Styrene and X-Ray Spex song 'Identity' then suggests that the promiscuous circulation of an image becomes a violation so severe that suicide seems the only way to be free of such public ravagement.

When you look in the mirror
Do you see yourself
Do you see yourself
On the TV screen
Do you see yourself
In the magazine
When you see yourself
Does it make you
Scream

The film creates a verbal and sonic collage, what Wollen has named a 'counter-language'. Writing in *October*, Wollen elaborates the politics of voice and language in Mulvey and Wollen's cinema. Following *Penthesilea: Queen of the Amazons* (1974) and *Riddles of the Sphinx*: 'The third film, *AMY!*, recapitulates and extends the registers of language and voice used in the first two. The key speech, placed in symbolic contrast to the male voices of newspaper headlines and popular love song, is a montage of fragments from a number of texts. … It is placed in a metaphoric relationship to the perversity of Amy's flight, the thrill of which is suppressed as it is rewritten into the form of legend, based once again on male fantasy, within the patriarchal order.'[4] He also elaborates on the use of language and voice in filming the flight as a map: '… a litany and an itinerary … the morphology of the place-names changes, until the original English is reencountered finally in Australia and the flight is stopped, to be transcribed into the language of the Empire in legend'.[5]

In the final sequences, the film recomposes selections from texts by women from the era around 1930 – including the American solo aviator Amelia Earhart (1897-1937), who disappeared while flying in 1937, and the modernist poet and novelist Gertrude Stein – weaving their words across unrelated footage of flights descending. Significantly, the words are read by the American feminist dancer, choreographer and experimental filmmaker Yvonne Rainer, whose own film work shared, also by means of radicalising cinematic form, an exploration of the conflicted positions within feminine subjectivity.

The script identifies the speaker simply as *Woman*. We can mark the carefully orchestrated interplay of male and female voices across the film, an actor, a woman, reading Amy Johnson's own words, another actor, a man, replicating 1930s BBC English and news reporting style, both filmmakers reading theoretical texts and now an American voice invoking a number of modernist women in their own words. What is it like to see the earth from the sky? What was the nature of this new vision? What is it like to write about what you remember? What is human vision and memory mediated by the machine created to enable it? Through these fragments from women from the generation 1930, what do we learn about the tension between ambition for the new and the pain of the heroic individual? 'The pain they suffered' is repeated; it is countered by Earhart's 'At that moment I felt I was free. I began to speak more freely. I could even permit myself the luxury of pausing when I felt like it… I felt simply wonderful.'

The film will bring us back from these fragments to the Science Museum, where Johnson's plane 'Jason' (another mythic transposition) is displayed, not flying, but hanging like an empty carcass. No sound, no movement, no clouds or sunbursts; none of the lyrical sense of aerial vision and freedom evoked in the texts above. All the social and psychological complexity of the aviator from Hull, Amy Johnson, morphs into the technological stand-in, a machine that serves as the 'fetishized emblem within the museum-morgue of patriarchal legend'.[6]

Once again punctuating these reflective texts with music, the final musical sequence contrasts the words of Amy Johnson disowning her public celebrity and Rainer's reading of the words of her contemporary modernist women with the mythic *Amy Johnson* absorbed into popular culture. We hear band music of 'Amy, Wonderful Amy' that includes the stanza:

Since you've won the praise of every nation
You have filled my heart with admiration.
Amy, wonderful Amy,
I'm proud of the way you flew.
Believe me, Amy,
You cannot blame me, Amy, for falling in love with you.

Such an obliterating cultural embrace into the romance of popular song dramatizes the anguish and complexity so far constructed across the film as an exploration of both the actions of Amy Johnson and the fame and celebrity that obscures them. What can it mean to declare love for Amy? Just Amy, not a full name. Just a girl, like any other. The public, trivialising and stereotypically re-feminised identity represents the heroine's psychic burden; whatever it was that subjectively led her to the flights for which she has become renowned is reappropriated. The final moments of the film are from a newsreel: eighteen seconds of the historical Amy Johnson speaking to crowds at Croydon Airfield on her arrival back in England after her flight. Over this flickering, mediated spectre of Amy Johnson, we hear the voice of the young woman, Beverley, whose wisdom we encountered in the opening interviews from 1980. She has the last words, reclaiming a woman's gesture for herself and its value for itself.

I don't think that to be a heroine you've got to be famous. You know, you don't have to be famous and everybody knows that you've done it.

She thus disentangles the heroic and action from celebrity and the publicity of the cultural machine. She is also indirectly claiming women such as Amy Johnson and Amelia Earhart for every woman who wants to do something, or who has some 'go'. Beverley had told Mulvey in the opening interviews that she liked tinkering with machines, mending TVs, while another of the young women describes how, by 1980, many women were learning about cars, motorbikes and aspects of engineering. One of the passages in Rainer's monologue returns to make the link between 1930 and 1980: 'Tinkering for Girls Only: The plan is to endow a machine-shop where girls may tinker to their heart's content with motors, lathes, jig-saws and diverse gadgets of their own creation.'

So where has this film taken us? What has it done with its question about the heroine in the context of what we might call two feminist moments of the twentieth century? It is certainly an anti-heroic film because we are re-centred in a de-mythified subjective space of questioning and struggle. It refuses to find conventionally and comforting meaning in the melodrama of someone else's complex life. It thus refuses the tropes of both women's films and the films (and other artforms) about the heroic individual who is so typically masculine that the heroic woman is always the exception, and as such, the perverse and the doomed. Yet true to the filmmakers' deep psychoanalytical engagement with the processes structuring cinematic genres and cultural narratives, they tease out for us the way popular cultural forms – from cinema, to newspapers, musical hall songs, and punk rock – replay the mythologies that touch on the deeper dimensions of subjectivity that feminism, psychoanalysis and critical artistic practices investigate.

Notes

1. Script in this volume. See page 108.
2. Mary D. Garrard, *Artemisia Gentileschi: The Image of the Female Hero in Italian Baroque Art* (Princeton, NJ: Princeton University Press, 1989).
3. Script in this volume. See page 107.
4. Peter Wollen, 'The Field of Language in Film', *October* 17 (Summer 1981), 58.
5. *Ibid.*, 58.
6. *Ibid.*, 58.

7

Crystal Gazing

Laura Mulvey and Peter Wollen

1

Title: A FILM BY LAURA MULVEY AND PETER WOLLEN
            CRYSTAL GAZING
            1982

Music: Two Women from Burundi, 'Akazehe' (Traditional).

2

Title: The insistence that everybody should admit that everything will turn
            out well, places those who do not under suspicion of being defeatists
            and deserters. In the fairy-tale, the toads who came from the depths
            were messengers of great joy. (Adorno)[*]

3 Crystal Ball

Close-up of a crystal ball. Insert: 'Cities of Alpha'.

4 Cities of Alpha

Close-up of 'Cities of Alpha'.

> VOICE OVER: Neil's theory is that the inhabitants of distant galaxies, such
> as Alpha, must be living in extremely hostile environments. That's why the
> futuristic cities Neil devises are always set in a vast expanse of frozen tundra

---

[*] Theodor Adorno, *Minima Moralia: Reflections on a Damaged Life*, trans.
    E. F. N. Jephcott (London: Verso, 1974), 114.

or balanced precariously on the rim of a cauldron of lethal gas. His reasoning goes like this: the inhabitants of Alpha are certainly much more advanced than us Terrans, mere cosmic infants, and consequently they must long since have destroyed their original homes, where they first evolved under naturally favourable conditions.

Illustrator's hand moves work to reveal a section of desk.

After the doomsday, a clutch of hapless space colonists would have been left stranded on some dismal outpost where they managed to struggle on and survive. In all likelihood, after the trauma, they became obsessed by the need for concealment and deception.

5 Willow Pattern Club (1)

The Willow Pattern Club (Comedy Store). The shot begins with a magician who is concluding a trick. His next act is levitation of a member of the audience and, as the camera pulls back, he invites a volunteer to come forward. VERMILION, *who has been sitting at a table with friends, goes up on to the low stage and the magician levitates her. Meanwhile* NEIL, *sitting at the front near the stage, is visibly fascinated by the performance, which he is sketching.* VERMILION *can see and return his gaze.*

Music: Karl Jenkins and Mike Ratledge, 'Levitation'.

VOICE OVER: Neil had no real idea how he came to be in the Willow Pattern Club. He'd simply found the address scrawled on the inside flap of some book matches in his pocket. He didn't remember why he had acquired the address or when exactly his previous visit had been. But it seemed like a clue or arrow pointing his evening in the direction it needed to go.

The taste for the unexpected harmonised with the streak of bravado in his temperament. It was one way to withdraw observantly from the unspectacular concerns and cares of this world.

He hadn't seen a magic act since childhood and he surrendered instantly to its glitter and its shameless fraudulence. As he sketched Vermilion, he found himself transfixed by a gaze more magical to him than the levitation itself. It was as if she appeared from nowhere, like a dove or a flag, simply to amaze him. The tableau had a strange familiarity to Neil. He felt as though he were looking through a childhood window, on to a landscape where the present succumbed to the future. Even the laws of nature, Vermilion seemed to say, could be suspended and held in check.

Later, when he found himself in fractured conversation with her, she was to tell him that she was an interpreter, and a widow. He agreed unhesitatingly to leave with her, fascinated by the association of sex with death. Her wish, in bereavement, to find distraction.

After the act is finished, and she's back down to earth, VERMILION *goes over to* NEIL'S *table instead of returning to her own.*

Music: Salman Shukur, 'Ghazal'.

VERMILION: *(indicating the sketch)* Can I see?

NEIL: *(showing her the sketch without comment)* What's it like up there?

VERMILION: Like Remedios the Beauty, when she suddenly starts to rise into heaven in the middle of hanging out the washing with her grandmother.

NEIL: You know, all you'd need is some way to neutralise gravity. The whole earth will be encased in some kind of special magnetic cocoon and everybody will have a device which can focus on this cocoon. You activate the device, you shoot a sort of gravity-free channel, you re-angle to wherever you want to go and down you come again.

VERMILION: Magnetism. Birds migrate by magnetism. What about charm? There's a force deep down in the depths of electrons called charm. You could steer your way through the universe by charm.

NEIL: *(simultaneously)* By charm.

6 Cul-de-sac

Night. A turning with a wall at one end of it. VERMILION *is driving,* NEIL *in the car beside her.* VERMILION *turns down a 'short-cut' only to find it is a cul-de-sac. As she reverses, they see three men having an argument.*

NEIL: There was this one series I did, the cities were camouflaged, so they blended imperceptibly into their backgrounds.

VERMILION: How did you see them?

NEIL: You couldn't. That was the trouble. They weren't very commercial.

VERMILION: You know, the imagery I use shows the invisible – infra-red, micro-wave, radar…

NEIL: Watch it! Idiot! What's this?

VERMILION: Jesus Christ, let's get out of here!

NEIL: Oh no!

VERMILION: Let's get out of here!

NEIL: Oh no! Fighting over a video!

VERMILION: Media rip-off. This is a job for the dream patrol.

7 The marriage contract

Service flat. VERMILION'S HUSBAND *has been sitting playing computer chess. He looks up at* VERMILION *and* NEIL *as they stand there surprised to see him. Static shot.*

Music: P. Paulos and L. Rubinstein, 'Inspiración'. Performed by Típica Enzo Phirpo.

> VERMILION: What an unexpected surprise.
>
> HUSBAND: There's always something daunting about the unexpected. It produces fear where there was no anxiety. Twenty-four hours ago I thought I'd be in New York but the stock market in coffee was restricted. So here I am in London.
>
> VERMILION: Neil, this is my husband. Most of the time he's abroad. He travels a great deal and when he's away, I lead my own life. I did not expect to find him here tonight.
>
> VOICE OVER: Vermilion's husband lived in a world where almost anything could be made into a commodity, given its label and put on the market. In his eagerness for the fantastic, Neil had been caught off-guard. He could not read the label which, he felt, had been ignominiously attached to him, as the token of his unforeseen reverse.

Dialogue spoken during voice over.

> NEIL: Well, I'll toddle along then.
>
> HUSBAND: No, no. Have a seat and a drink.
>
> VERMILION: I'll get you a drink.
>
> HUSBAND: What would you like? There's a very good brandy. Of course, it's the fright which makes uncertainty appealing.
>
> VOICE OVER: *(continued)* Neil had been extremely surprised to find a lawful wedded husband in the flat to which Vermilion took him.

8 Electronic chess

Close-up of an electronic chess board. We see VERMILION'S *hand moving the chess pieces. Static shot.*

> VOICE OVER: *(continued)* This pleasure of the unexpected was one that had lost its glitter and its charm. The lawful wedded husband, on the other hand, had not seemed the slightest bit surprised to see Neil. Leaning back in his lamb's-wool pullover, he had seemed as relaxed and at ease as Neil was at a loss and displaced, like a found object in its wrong context.

After submitting Neil to a set of intricate observations, he had explained to him, with a glance towards Vermilion, the exact obligations of their marriage contract. The relevant clauses concerned his wife's lovers. While he was in London, he was entitled to reject any of them he pleased, but the more he exercised this right, the more allowance he had to pay her. He liked to combine being liberal with being practical.

Neil turned away from Vermilion's game of chess. The meaning of the moves eluded him and he could not fathom out the logical end to which he had been offered as a sacrifice. It was better to leave, give up the voyage and seek landfall in a taxi home.

9 Taxi queue

Taxi queue at St Pancras station. Five people, including NEIL *and* KIM, *are waiting.* KEITH ALLEN *approaches and delivers an improvised monologue.* NEIL *and* KIM *agree to share a taxi to Ladbroke Grove.*

10 Busking

KIM *is busking outside a closed down shop on Portobello Road. Saxophone music. Static shot.*

VOICE OVER: It turned out that Neil lived very close to Kim. As they talked in the taxi they were sharing, they discovered they had both played the gong in their infant school percussion band and, as a gruelling sequence of coincidences would have it, both been brought up for a time in Ipswich, both suffered from occasional attacks of asthma, and so on. Neil felt a gathering together in Kim of a series of loose strands from his own life. Yet she was also quite different, quite other. Neil sensed a clarity in Kim, a grasp of immediate realities which he himself was denied. Kim didn't accumulate fantasies. She found a place to live, plant-sitting, and a place to practise, and as the plants grew greener and taller she planned to entertain her public as best she could. She had made up her mind to persist with a musical career even if it meant wrapping herself in back copies of *NME* and huddling over a hot-air grating. It was the reason she had come to London in the first place after the local band she had formed broke up on her. Now, through galling delay after galling delay, she waited for her first real and genuine gig.

11 Breakfast

KIM's *flat.* KIM *is playing saxophone while* NEIL *makes breakfast. He hums along and, after serving coffee, dances around with* KIM. *Static shot.*

Music: Johnny Hodges, 'Parachute Jump'. Performed by Lora Logic.

12 Rough Trade

Rough Trade record shop on Kensington Park Road. People going through records. The camera slowly pans right to frame shop counter. KIM *enters and asks if there is anyone who can listen to her cassette. She is directed round the corner.*

Music: Lloyd Ferguson and Fitzroy Simpson, 'Pass the Kouchie'. Performed by The Mighty Diamonds.

13 Demo disc

Small recording studio. A sound engineer is operating a mixing desk. The camera slowly pans left to frame KIM, *who is making a demo disc. The camera then pans back to the mixing desk.*

Music: Lora Logic, 'Rat Allé'.

14 Redundancy

Illustrator's office. NEIL *is clearing his desk, placing various items in a bag. He's drinking champagne as he does so. Sound of a gadget beeping. Static shot.*

VOICE OVER: Champagne's the best pick-me-up when you've just been fired. It surprised Neil at first that the cities of Alpha should fall victim to the Thatcher recession. To him they had existed in a world exempt from cash limits and control of the money supply. They were pure specimens of the realm of abundance in which the play-instinct ruled supreme and the forms of economic exchange were in perfect harmony with the needs of labour. Each city was a commune, a polyp rather than a clock, naturally united rather than artificially divided. Neil was tempted to forget the real conditions of life here among the pitiable Terrans. Terran civilisation didn't seem to offer much scope for his penmanship.

Nevertheless he wasn't all that sorry to leave. Neil had never wanted to work in the way he thought capitalist society required, in the way most people were compelled to work. He had always tried to avoid it and had found it quite odd and even disturbing that the cities of Alpha should have provided him with a regular income and even, at one heady moment, the offer of a partnership in the small publishing firm which was now dispensing with his services and concentrating all its efforts on some marginally more lucrative line, in the hope of staving off the inevitable bankruptcy. There was a sense in which he had always thought himself lucky to be paid for developing his reveries at all. Neil's main worry now was the fear that he had grown to rely on money and would find he could no longer do without it. He would have to give up some pleasures, even though, unlike the cities of Alpha, he wouldn't simply be consigned to pulp.

NEIL *switches off the lights, finishes his champagne and leaves.*

15 Fish and chip shop

The Portobello Fish Bar. The back of the shop is filled with electronic space games with groups of teenagers clustered around them. At one table the proprietor sits with friends, playing backgammon and talking in Greek. NEIL *comes in and orders some chips, adds salt and leaves. Static shot. Sound of electronic space games.*

16 Job centre

Job centre on Portobello Road. NEIL *looks at the vacancies board, then sits and waits. He picks up some magazines to pass the time. The camera pans right.*

Music: Ludwig van Beethoven, 'Für Elise'. Performed by Colin Wood.

17 Monsieur Thompson

Outside Monsieur Thompson's restaurant on Kensington Park Road. KIM *and* NEIL *enter frame from right.* NEIL *suddenly stops. Static shot.*

> KIM: Why've you stopped? What's the matter?
> NEIL: French cuisine.
> KIM: What's the matter with you?

NEIL *stands there, rooted to the spot.*

> NEIL: Nothing's the matter. Right? I just don't feel like going in there. I just don't feel like it.
> KIM: What's wrong? You've eaten in there before.

NEIL *walks to the entrance of the restaurant and stops. He turns around and faces back down the street.*

> NEIL: Yes, but I wasn't hungry then.
> KIM: That's stupid. What's worrying you?

No response.

> KIM: I'm hungry, I'm going in now!
> NEIL: Hungry? What do you mean you're hungry? Make your mind up. I'm going.

NEIL *walks off.* KIM *goes into the restaurant.*

18 Concert at Acklam Hall

Acklam Hall. KIM *and her band are playing to a local audience.*

Music: Lora Logic, 'No More Records'.

19 Chinese take away

Children doing their homework and taking orders at the counter. NEIL *and* JULIAN *order their food. Static shot.*

> VOICE OVER: Neil's friend Julian had recently finished ten years of hard work. Just within the time-limit, at last, he had completed his PhD thesis on the fairy-tales of Charles Perrault, with special reference to the tale of 'Puss in Boots'. Now he was anxiously on the verge of his oral exam. Till that was over he could feel relief and excitement, but not yet triumphant self-acclaim. He was all too sure that his views would prove controversial; even, he imagined, repugnant. As a contemporary French theorist has pointed out, the tale of 'Puss in Boots' can be read as an analogy to the mystery of the Mass. It is a central tenet of the Catholic faith that when the priest says 'This is my body' at the high-point of the Mass, the bread is transubstantiated into the body of Christ. Now, the tomcat hero transubstantiates his humble master, the Miller's son, into a great magnate, by a series of speech-acts: 'This is my Lord, the Marquis of Carabas'. Julian had developed this argument and given it a further, psycho-analytic twist. 'Puss in Boots' was the founding text of modernism, the secular celebration of language as desire and language as power. Hidden within the innocent-seeming tale was a subversive tract. 'Puss in Boots' was re-interpreted

by Julian to reveal the anti-Oedipal threat which lay within its transformation of lies into truth, fiction into fact and desire into fulfilment.

20 Puss in Boots

A Pollock toy theatre in which a scene from the story of 'Puss in Boots', by Charles Perrault, is being enacted. The scene begins with PUSS *speaking to his master. (The voices are all those of* JULIAN, *who is operating the theatre.) Static shot.*

PUSS: All you have to do is to follow my instructions and your fortune is made. Just go and bathe down there by the river, and leave the rest to me.
NARRATOR: Exit Puss's master, the Miller's son. Enter the King's carriage with Princess, and their entourage of servants.
PUSS: Help! Help! My Lord the Marquis of Carabas is drowning!
NARRATOR: Enter the King, followed by the princess, and their entourage of servants.
KING: This is the cat who has brought me many presents of game from his master. Go with him quickly and give him all the help he needs!
NARRATOR: Exit servants towards the river.
PUSS: Your Majesty, thieves came, while my Lord was bathing, and made off with his clothes. I shouted 'Stop Thief!' at the top of my voice, but there was nothing more I could do.
NARRATOR: Re-enter servants with Puss in Boots' master, naked.
KING: Fetch one of my finest suits for My Lord the Marquis of Carabas!
NARRATOR: Servants go off again with Puss's master, who re-enters in fine clothing.
KING: My Lord, get into the carriage with me and accompany us on our drive!
NARRATOR: While Puss's master, and the King, and the Princess, get into the carriage, Puss runs on ahead. Then exeunt all. Curtain.

21 Viva voce

A small office in a university. There are three chairs. JULIAN *is sitting on one of them with his thesis on his knee. Facing him are two examiners, also with copies of the thesis and notepads, etc. One of them begins the examination. The camera begins framing the two examiners and pans right to* JULIAN. *As the examination continues, the camera pans left and right.*

PROFESSOR: I have one or two comments I've noted down, so, if it's all right with you, I'll run through them in the order I have them here. First, page 66.

You say there something to the effect that the cat in 'Puss in Boots' represents the phallus. It seems to me that this is presented as a simple asserting and I wondered whether you had any ways you felt you could plausibly justify your assertions further. Because if not, we are just left with your word for it, I think, and that would be not be sufficient, at such a central point in your argument.

JULIAN: *(keyed-up)* Yes, I can see that was a bit of a hostage to fortune, but I do think you've misunderstood my point completely. The cat doesn't represent the phallus but the relationship between phallus and language, which we can symbolise as ΦrL. The cat isn't a term but a two-term predicate, relating phallus to language. At the beginning of the tale the hero is represented as castrated: he fails to inherit the share of the paternal phallus he expects on the death of his father. At the end, he acquires a new phallus and a new Father, the King, which is sealed by his marriage to the Princess, but this is an effect of language and it's the cat that understands that the phallus is a pure sign which can be produced by other signs.

(Pause.)

PROFESSOR: But isn't it anachronistic to introduce psychoanalysis, a way of using the cat in 'Puss in Boots' as a pretext for expounding your own theories?

JULIAN: Not at all. The tale is a comic pendant to the Port-Royal Logic, just as Marin has demonstrated. And where we find the comic, there is hidden the repressed, as contrary to logic, because otherwise the phallus would be understood for what it is, a sign given by language, not inherited from the father. It would be at the beck and call of the dispossessed. That's why 'Puss in Boots' appears at that point in history – don't forget that Perrault was also one of the main protagonists of the project for a definitive dictionary in the French Academy, to fix the meanings of words. That's why 'Puss in Boots' is presented as a trickster, a master of illusion and paradox.

One examiner writes down a note and passes it to the other, who has been questioning JULIAN.

JULIAN: *(continued)* What is this paradox but Meinong's paradox: 'There are objects of which it is true that there are no such objects.' *Es gibt Gegenstände, von denen gilt, dass es dergleichen Gegenstände nicht gibt.* The cat consigns the phallus to the realm of being-so rather than being. But this is the very ontological commitment, or lack of commitment, which Russell was forced to reject at the outset, on the grounds that it breeds contradiction. Of course it does, and that's what I go on to celebrate in the last section of my thesis. The closest anyone came to understanding this was André Breton, but he didn't have the logic. He had to fall back on Hegel.

JULIAN *has been becoming more and more agitated. When he has finished there is a long pause, longer than before.*

22 Bookshop

Elgin Books. JULIAN *sees a woman steal a book (*Deviant Logic*). She is stopped by the* SHOP ASSISTANT *when attempting to leave the bookshop. The camera initially frames* JULIAN, *then pans right and left as events unfold.*

Music: François Couperin, 'Le Dodo, ou l'amour au Berceau'. Performed by Robert Woolley.

> SHOP ASSISTANT: *(to the woman as she tries to leave)* Excuse me, have you paid for that book? Can I have it back, please? In your bag, I saw you take it.

The woman returns the book to the SHOP ASSISTANT. JULIAN *pays the* SHOP ASSISTANT *for it and gives the book back to the woman, who accepts it and leaves. He goes back to browsing.*

23 Memorial gardens

The Horniman Memorial Gardens. There are two men on roller-skates skating around. JULIAN *and* NEIL *come into the gardens through the ornamental gate and begin to walk down towards the arched shelter at the near (camera) end. Static shot.*

> JULIAN: The examiners were the Law and I broke their rules by speaking to them in the wrong language.
> NEIL: You were like Ken Livingstone and they were like the Law Lords.[*]
> JULIAN: Right, yes, you could be right. Perhaps you've got something there. The Labour Party Manifesto was written in the language of desire, but the Law Lords controlled the language of power. They simply said 'The Labour Party Manifesto has no meaning at all.' And they turned Ken Livingstone into a

---

[*] The Labour Party Manifesto for the 1981 Greater London Council (GLC) elections included a pledge, known as Fares Fair, to reduce and freeze fares on the London Underground. Once implemented by Ken Livingstone, the victorious Labour leader of the GLC, the policy was challenged by the Conservative leader of Bromley Borough Council leading to a succession of court cases. Ultimately, when the GLC's appeal reached the House of Lords in October 1981, five Law Lords ruled against Fares Fair. (See also the journalist's text in the Crossed Line sequence of this script). LM.

figure of fun, a failed trickster. 'You should have taken legal advice.' All that means is: 'There's only one language and it's ours.' The problem is: how do you bring desire and power together? What's the language for that?

NEIL: Well, you can put it into fiction, can't you. That's why 'Puss in Boots' is a story.

JULIAN: You can't say that. You can't say that Puss can only exist in a story. Otherwise you could never change anything. All the meanings would be fixed forever by the House of Lords or whoever was in charge of the logic of non-contradiction. That's what the Surrealists wanted: to turn 'Puss in Boots' into a reality. Or, to put it more precisely, to find a way of filling the symbolic place of 'Puss in Boots' in reality, in the Real.

NEIL: I do understand something of what you're saying, Julian. But I am your friend and I'm making an effort. You can't just wander down to County Hall and expect the Greater London Labour group to understand it.

By this point, JULIAN *and* NEIL *are walking out of frame.*

You could put it in a story, then they may understand it, but they wouldn't understand it as practical politics. Well would they? Look, I've gotta go. I can't stay here any longer. I'm freezing to bloody death.

JULIAN: I'm sorry, I didn't notice. You haven't got your coat.

NEIL: I know.

JULIAN: What happened to it?

NEIL: I lost it. Probably in a pub. Certainly more likely than a taxi, knowing the way things are going nowadays.

They walk back into frame.

JULIAN: I'll walk back with you. I can see that radical semiotic theory doesn't sound the slightest bit like common sense, but that's not really the point.

NEIL: Julian! So what is the point?

JULIAN: The point is that the ruling class doesn't just rule by practical politics. It rules by defining the language as well. Look at the Social Democratic Party. The signified of politics hasn't changed at all, only the signifier. It hasn't broken the mould of British politics. It's just broken the mould of the way in which politics is named. It's like the theory of colour terminology. Colour names are defined in relation to each other. They haven't changed the wavelengths of the colours in the spectrum; they've just introduced a new term to define the range in the middle of the spectrum. That means it changes the meaning of the other two terms by re-defining them.

NEIL: It's a smokescreen.

JULIAN: No!

NEIL: Yes! It stops people seeing that nothing has actually changed at all!

JULIAN: No, it isn't just a smokescreen. It's language, and language isn't just a smokescreen. You can't say the colours are a smokescreen for the spectrum! You know, there's something else that struck me about 'Puss in Boots'.

NEIL: And what is that?

JULIAN: Look at the beginning of the story, when the Miller's son is separated from the means of production. His first problem is food because he has to eat.

NEIL: He's unemployed.

JULIAN: Right. You're right. He's unemployed. But he's not just separated from the means of production, he's separated from his own labour power too, because it's incarnated in the cat.

NEIL: He's cold too. He'd like to turn the cat into mittens.

JULIAN: I'm sorry. I keep forgetting. What's it like being unemployed?

NEIL: Eh?

JULIAN: For you, I mean.

NEIL: Well, it means I haven't got a job, so, consequently, I don't have very much money.

JULIAN *and* NEIL *exit the gardens through the same ornamental gate they entered.*

24 Cornell box

Close-up of Joseph Cornell's 'Giuditta Pasta (dédicace)' (1950). Static shot.

VOICE OVER: There was a small copper identity-disc fastened to a peg, inscribed 'The Celestial Baltimore and Deerband Papier-Maché Railway', and his brow was furrowed with sombre rage. Only the dead could hope to save him now. His disordered thoughts circled and re-circled as though in search of some clue to the reason for their own imminent leave-taking.

With one cruel movement, they wrenched themselves free from their groove and sent each other spinning off into the immense farrago of the void. They were light-years away by now, but he felt he might still find some reference to them in the glossary. Each cordial glass, he saw, was empty save for two, one of which contained a single piece of crystal. If only he could put his ring-finger on it, he could find the right nebula.

But the crystal filled him with dread and menace. They had damaged the map to dreamland and there was no way home for the blindfolded.

25 Suicide

JULIAN's *room.* JULIAN *is facing a video camera that he has set up with a monitor. As he speaks, the camera, which was initially framing him, slowly zooms in on to the monitor.*

> JULIAN: Gentlemen, the race of prophets is extinct. Europe is becoming set in its ways, embalming itself beneath the wrappings of its borders, its factories, its law-courts and its universities. The frozen Mind cracks between the mineral staves which close upon it. The fault lies with your mouldy systems, your logic of 2 plus 2 makes 4. The fault lies with you chancellors, caught in the net of your syllogisms. You manufacture engineers, magistrates, doctors, who know nothing of the true mysteries of the body or the laws of existence. By what right do you claim to channel human intelligence and award certificates of Mental merit? You know nothing of the Mind, you are unaware of its most secret and essential ramifications, those fossil imprints so close to our own origins, those tracks we are occasionally able to discover deep in the most unexplored deposits of our minds. In the name of your own logic we say to you, Life stinks, Gentlemen.[*]

JULIAN *moves the video camera to reveal a news headline: 'Three million jobless – and worse to come.' The newspaper is removed from the shot, revealing Henry Wallis's 'The Death of Chatterton' (1856) and a pot of pills.* JULIAN's *hands come into frame to take the pot of pills.*

26 Kim playing sax

KIM *puts a record on and plays along to it on her saxophone. Close-up.*

Music: Lora Logic, 'Pedigree Charm'.

27 Further apart

KIM's *flat (Talbot Road).* NEIL *and* KIM *are sitting and talking.* NEIL *is holding a bottle of rum and* KIM *is looking at slides.*

> NEIL: I really need to talk to somebody. Go on. Please. I don't like to sit and drink on my own.
> KIM: What's the bad news then?

---

* Antonin Artaud, 'Letter to the Chancellors of the European Universities', in *Antonin Artaud: Collected Works (Volume 1)*, trans. Victor Corti (London: Calder & Boyars, 1968), 178–180.

NEIL *pours himself a (heavy) drink.*

> NEIL: Did I ever tell you about Julian?
>
> KIM: No, I don't think so.
>
> NEIL: Well, he's committed suicide. I must have mentioned him to you. I was going to take you to meet him. Do you remember that day?
>
> KIM: No.
>
> NEIL: Oh. He was my best friend. I must've met him about almost exactly ten years ago. In fact it was Christmas 1971. He was the cleverest person I've ever met. Brilliant. Brilliant ideas all the time but nobody ever really appreciated what he was saying. Absolute bloody idiots. He was working for years and years on this theory of his and they wouldn't even give him a serious interview. England. You know what he said to me last week?

The telephone rings.

> NEIL: Oh god!

KIM *moves her chair back to answer it.*

> KIM: *(on telephone)* Hello. Hi. Yeah. I've been in all day. Yeah. How did you know it was out? Yeah my manager must have put an advert in there. Yeah. You're so sweet. Shall we go out of London? Just for a day. Love to. Alright then. Well, give me a ring next week. Yeah, I'll have more time then as well. Alright then. See ya, doll. Bye!

NEIL *pours himself another glass. After a while he begins to make gestures to* KIM *of putting a receiver back on the cradle.* KIM *turns back to* NEIL.

> KIM: Why did he do it?
>
> NEIL: I think he… perhaps he wanted to be heroic.
>
> KIM: How did he do it?
>
> NEIL: Does it matter how he did it?
>
> KIM: I wrote a song once about committing suicide. Maybe I should put it on my new album. Trouble is it needs a double bass. But I could get Mickey to do it. Do you think I should get Mickey?
>
> NEIL: I think he just… I think he just committed suicide because he couldn't think of another line of action. Have you got anyone to design this album of yours?
>
> KIM: Yeah. I'm not in charge of those kind of things anymore. Got someone else to do it. Thank goodness.

Telephone rings again. KIM *moves her chair further back to answer it.*

> NEIL: Kim!
>
> KIM: *(on telephone)* Hello. Karen! Hi!
>
> NEIL: I came here to talk to you.
>
> KIM: Yeah! It's only been out a week!
>
> NEIL: Not to listen to your fucking telephone conversations.
>
> KIM: *(to telephone)* It's not even in the shops yet! Just a minute, Karen.
> *(to* NEIL, *covering the receiver)* Will you shut up just for one minute please?
> *(to telephone)* Yeah.
>
> NEIL: I don't see why I should shut up.
>
> KIM: *(to telephone)* No, I know, I know…
>
> NEIL: I came here to talk to you.
>
> KIM: *(to telephone)* No, no it's alright…
>
> NEIL: Are you listening? Do you understand what I'm saying?
>
> KIM: *(to telephone)* No, you're not disturbing me Karen.
>
> NEIL: Oh for God's sake.
>
> KIM: *(to telephone)* It's okay. No, you're not disturbing anything.
>
> NEIL: I'm not disturbing you Karen! Oh well, I love you Karen!

NEIL *gets up to go.*

> KIM: *(to* NEIL*)* Wait!
> *(to telephone)* I'll ring you back later. I'll ring you, see you.
>
> NEIL: What? Wait for what? Something special?
>
> KIM: *(pulling out a jumper from a bag) (to* NEIL*)* This is yours.
>
> NEIL: Oh keep it.
>
> KIM: Take it, it's yours!

NEIL *leaves with the bottle.* KIM *is left holding the jumper.*

28 Willow Pattern Club (2)

The Willow Pattern Club (Comedy Store). NEIL *and* VERMILION *are sitting at the same table as in the previous scene in the club. This time there is no magician.*

Lotte Reiniger's The Adventures of Prince Achmed (*1926*) *is projected in the background.*

Music: Salman Shukur, 'Huriyyat al-Jabal'.

VERMILION: You know, I was thinking about a scheme for teaching computers to do book illustrations. But just a very simple graphic vocabulary. Well don't worry, it won't put you out of work.

NEIL: Oh don't worry, I'm out of work already. The company went bankrupt. Nothing to do with technology, just the recession.

VERMILION: Are you looking for a job then?

NEIL: To tell you the honest truth, I just want to get away at this minute. But I'm broke. Penniless. On the dole. On the breadline. I sold my Pentax yesterday.

VERMILION: Neil, this just may be your lucky day. I might be able to help, but…

NEIL: Well, there was a big 'but' last time, wasn't there?

VERMILION: Same one. The thing is…

NEIL: Not another husband returned from the grave.

VERMILION: No, not another husband. The same one. Returned from Hamburg. Don't worry…

NEIL: No cause for alarm?

VERMILION: No need to panic. Just a chance to get away. And get paid for it.

NEIL: OK. Tell me the story.

VERMILION: By my late husband.

There's an interruption as the magician comes on.

VERMILION: Oh, let's go, here comes the magician. I'm not in a levitating mood tonight.

NEIL: Do we have to? I rather like the magician.

VERMILION: Brings back fond memories? Come on, let's go.

NEIL: Now. This minute. Three million unemployed and fate has chosen me.

They get up and leave. The camera moves in on the magic act.

29 Employment contract

VERMILION's HUSBAND's *service flat.* HUSBAND, VERMILION *and* NEIL *are sitting in conversation. As the conversation unfolds, the camera pans right and left before pulling back.*

HUSBAND: It happens I need someone capable and trustworthy to deliver a small but very valuable item to Mexico City.

NEIL: When?

HUSBAND: Tomorrow. The day after would be much too late. All expenses paid. First-class hotel. Second-class air ticket.

VERMILION: You've got to go to standby now anyway.

HUSBAND: No stopover at Miami.

NEIL: What is it? What will I be carrying? Will I have any problems with the customs?

HUSBAND: Not to worry. It's just a pawn ticket. It has to be returned to the legal owner of the property pledged.

NEIL: Why? What's the exact nature of this transaction?

HUSBAND: The property concerned is now in the National Pawn Shop in Mexico City. It's a large building, a little like Harrods, equally full of expensive curios. It was deposited as a security against a large outstanding debt. The debt has now been cleared so the ticket must be returned.

NEIL: Can't you just put it in the post?

HUSBAND: There speaks the voice of practical reason in ignorance of the hazards of the postal system.

NEIL: What other hazards may I be in ignorance of?

VERMILION: I wouldn't have suggested it to you if there were any hazards.

NEIL: Well, there must be some hazards. Not one? Just a little one?

VERMILION *shakes her head.*

HUSBAND: Come, it's all perfectly straightforward.

NEIL: I'm not going to get arrested?

VERMILION: Absolutely not.

HUSBAND: You go to a lawyer in Mexico City. Deliver the ticket, obtain the receipt, call me collect.

30 Maps of Mexico and Mexico City

Close-up of maps of Mexico and Mexico City.

VOICE OVER: The ancient Aztec city of Tenochtitlan, Vermilion told Neil, was built on huge floating rafts in the middle of the lake whose dried-up dusty floor is now the site of Mexico City. There, Montezuma in his cloak of feathers sadly welcomed the cruel conquistadors, and there his son Cuauhtémoc carried out his doomed resistance against the mounted fire-armed Spaniards. Already in Neil's mind the cry of the spider-monkey and the cockatoo echoed through a landscape of cactus and liana amid Cyclopic pyramids. A cynic might say that the gap between the Job Shop and the Cities of Alpha had grown too wide to close, prised open beyond the grasp of practical reason. But for Neil the exotic had always held a powerful allure. He set about learning phrases of Spanish, bought himself a tropical suit and sloughed off his English identity like the skin of a snake. As they drove to the airport, Neil was exultant. The more chimeric the mission, the more pungent its charm.

31 Two cars in alley

Two cars nearly collide in an alley. NEIL *abuses the driver of a Volvo in (bad) Spanish. Static shot.*

32 Island paradise

Wall painting of a tropical scene with graffiti next to Ladbroke Grove underground station. After some time, the camera pans right. KIM *enters the shot briefly.*

Music: Lora Logic, 'Martian Man'.

33 Vermilion marking false-colour photographs

Close-up of VERMILION *marking false-colour photographs. Static shot.*

VOICE OVER: Poring over her false-colour maps, Vermilion could register the distribution of crops or the outcome of harvests. She could see where normal sight was dull and blind. She could see even the difference between life and death, in the patterns made in the infra-red waveband, as plants reflected or absorbed energy. Those that were healthy absorbed blue and red light, while those that were dying absorbed the infra-red.

Oblivious of night and day, haze or mist, the sky was meshed with tracking eyes – film, vidicon, radar, multispectral scanner – each an untiring recorder of the impoverished earth beneath. In every patchwork of colour, its tones and textures, she could see into the future, forecasting the yield and, with the yield, the expectation of profit. Magenta could mean healthy growth, while a tinge of blue could signal failure and loss. Yet this insight into the future, bought at such great price, would benefit only a few.

As neutrally as the technology itself, Vermilion serviced those to whom, through the paradoxes of the commodity market, the prediction of failure could bring good fortune and money in the bank. Her set-square, stereoscope and ruler were the mundane instruments of this economic miracle.

34 Crossed line

VERMILION *is sitting at a small table working on her maps. The end of the narration from the last section continues over the visual track. Static shot.*

VERMILION: Come on, get in focus. Focus… focus.

The telephone rings.

VERMILION: Hello.

Telephone beeping.

VERMILION: Hello?
NEIL: Hello, hello?
VERMILION: Neil?
NEIL: Vermilion?
VERMILION: Where are you?
NEIL: Heathrow, I can't get any flights!
VERMILION: Oh no. What happened?
NEIL: Laker's collapsed. It's chaos here.
VERMILION: Oh no. I'm sorry.

Interference on the line.

NEIL: Everything's booked!
VERMILION: Oh hang on just a minute, I think we've got a crossed line.
JOURNALIST: Il semble donc que Laker, qui a échoué par ses propres efforts…
VERMILION: Hang on. Hello? Hello? You've got a crossed line.
JOURNALIST: …est devenu héros tandis que Livingstone, qui a été vaincu…
VERMILION: Hello? Hang on, Neil. Hello?
JOURNALIST: …par les plus puissants juges du pays…
VERMILION: Can you hang up? You've got a crossed line.
JOURNALIST: …doit subir le mépris et les objurgations de tout le monde.
VERMILION: Put the phone down and get back to the operator, you've got a crossed line.
JOURNALIST: Ainsi l'homme d'affaires qui a cassé ses promesses, laissant…
VERMILION: Hello? Neil. Don't hang up, just hang on.
JOURNALIST: …plusieurs milliers de voyageurs le bec dans l'eau, devient un…
VERMILION: Hello. You've got a crossed line. Monsieur? Monsieur? Hello?
JOURNALIST: 'Sir Freddie'. S I R F R E D D I E. Freddie souriant, sous l'approbation du premier ministre; et l'homme politique qui a tenu ses promesses devient un 'Red Ken' perdu dans l'illégalité.

VERMILION: Hang up. Put the phone down. You've got a crossed line. Just put the phone down. Just hang up. You've got a crossed line. No, Neil. Not, not.

JOURNALIST: Attendez, ne raccrochez pas. Look, I've got a deadline here, I'm trying to do some work. Do you mind?

VERMILION: Look, that's really not my problem. Just put the phone down. You've got a crossed line.

JOURNALIST: Please, do you mind? Try your number again.

VERMILION: It won't do any good my ringing again. You've got to ring again.

JOURNALIST: Look, for Christ's sake, I'm dictating an article to a typist in France.

VERMILION: Listen, I don't care whether you've got your head in a polythene bag, nobody is listening to you. Just hang up, OK?

NEIL: OK, I'll call back!

VERMILION: No, Neil, don't you…

JOURNALIST: *(continuing regardless)* Quand même les deux hommes sont les victimes en quelque sorte du même dynamique. En essayant de faire baisser les prix de voyage, projet apparemment tout simple, ils se heurtent contre une réalité mal definie mais universelle: le marché, ce qui veut dire la société Thatcherienne, accepte les augmentations des prix mais résiste tenacement aux baisses…

NEIL: Vermilion? Listen, Vermilion…

VERMILION: Hello? Look, Neil, go have a drink, go have a Bloody Mary…

NEIL: Vermilion, the bar is closed. You have a Bloody Mary. I'm going to try and get an early morning flight to Madrid.

VERMILION: Look, it won't do any good. Oh, just hang on. Just hang on till this idiot gets off the line.

NEIL: OK. OK…

VERMILION *puts the radio, with the volume up, to the telephone.*

35 Strike-breakers

Coaches leaving the yard at dawn.

VOICE OVER: The shock-troops of capitalism travel in holiday coaches. After his setback at the airport, Vermilion is driving Neil back home, while elsewhere parties of his fellow unemployed are assembling to be picked up by a convoy of coaches and ferried from staging-area to front-line, as scabs and strike-breakers at the small clock and watch factory whose picket lines Neil has often given a warm, if somewhat self-conscious smile. He certainly doesn't foresee that in a short while Vermilion will take her usual backstreet route past the same factory at the precise moment that the coaches will arrive. He has absolutely no concept that in a spontaneous burst of manic energy, the last residue of exhilaration at his ruined Mexican journey, he will insist on Vermilion stopping the car so he can get out to see what is happening and whether there is anything he can do. He can't foretell the next sequence of the story, in which necessity and contingency collide, the pursuit of surplus value with the quirks and impulses of character and fate. He can't read the news on the not-yet-printed page: Stop-Press – no expectations.

36 Rings of Saturn

Voyager footage of the Rings of Saturn.

37 Dressing room

Dressing room. KIM *is reading. A portable television is playing a Pontins holiday ad in the background. The camera pans right to the television and back again to* KIM. *The television cuts to a news announcement.*

> NEWS READER: *(on television)* Workers at the Aurora Watch factory in North Kensington are on strike against redundancy policies which, they claim, are unfair to women employees. Earlier today, there was a tragic new development when Neil Holt, a local man, not directly engaged in the dispute, was accidentally knocked down and killed by a coach taking non-union labour into the factory. Union officials are demanding a public inquiry into the incident. Our reporter, Derek Binham, was on the scene.

The camera pans right to the television. VERMILION *is being interviewed.*

> DEREK BINHAM: *(on television)* And so a minor industrial dispute here in North Kensington has become a human tragedy. Well somebody who saw the accident happen is with me now. Can you tell me exactly what happened?
> VERMILION: *(on television)* Police were moving the pickets back to let the coaches through. And they were mainly women, and one of them had a child with her, and it ran across the road, right in front the coach. And Neil just dashed out and just managed to push this little girl out of the way. And it ran right over him. He fell down and it went right over him. It was terrible.

The camera pans back to KIM. *She bursts into tears.*

DEREK BINHAM: *(on television)* But he did manage to save the child?

VERMILION: *(on television)* The plane should have been taking off, just at that minute.

DEREK BINHAM: *(on television)* Can I ask you how you both happened to be here? Are you part of this dispute?

VERMILION: *(on television)* No, no. We were just passing by on our way back from the airport. He was meant to be going to Mexico today and the flight was cancelled, and we just saw what was going on and he wanted to show his support.

DEREK BINHAM: *(on television)* And so this small factory, which has now been picketed by its workforce for 51 days, has today seen a man killed. Just where the blame lies for that is a question still to be answered. Derek Binham in North Kensington.

38 Last number

Television shows KIM *and band on-stage. Close-up.*

KIM: *(on television)* I'd like to dedicate this song for Neil, who'll never hear it.

Music: Lora Logic, 'Volcano'.

The camera pulls back and pans left. VERMILION *switches the set off. She paces back and forth. Sound enters through the window. She sits down and clicks her fingers.*

VERMILION: What could I tell from looking at Neil? Dreams… Redundancy…

39 Picket outside Aurora Clock and Watch Factory

Picket outside Aurora Clock and Watch Factory. The strikers shout 'Support the strike!' as a car drives by and honks its horn. Static shot.

40 Crystal Ball

Close-up of a crystal ball. Insert: Picket line at Aurora Clock and Watch Factory.

Music: Two Women from Burundi, 'Akazehe' (Traditional).

41

Title: But where is the dark night? Now there are neither stars nor moon light, no vagueness of laughter, no dance of love. The young people are peaceful and before us there is not even a real dark night. Despair, like hope, is but vanity. (Lu Hsun)

42 End Credits

Music: Lora Logic, 'Crystal Gazing'.

Neil – Gavin Richards
Kim – Lora Logic
Vermilion – Mary Maddox
Julian – Jeff Rawle
Narrator – Maggie Shevlin
Magician – Alan Porter
Husband – Patrick Bauchau
Monologist – Keith Allen
Band – Ben Annesley, Charles Hayward, Philip Legg
Examiners – Nicholas Le Prevost, James Leahy
Book Thief – Beata Vigh-Anderson
Shop Assistant – Dinah Stabb
Crossed Line – John Howe
Newsreader – Miriam Margolyes
Interviewer – Jonathan Eden
Nightclub – Beverley Sher
Cul-de-Sac – Steven Bernstein, Marcus Birsel, Nick Ray
Taxi Queue – Annette Flanders, Robert Flanders, Mark Nash
Rough Trade – Judy Crighton, Robert Dayant, Nick Johnson, Sion Tammes
Job Centre – Adrian Garvey, Karen Hazelwood, Colin Wood
Monsieur Thompson's – Rosemary Bailey, Susan Barrowclough, Victor Bockris, Miles, Kim Nygaard
Takeaway – Tony Rayns, Bertha Tsang, Charles Tsang, Wellington Tsang
Roller-skating – Reggie Fergus, Kevin Samuels
Nightclub – Barbie Coles, Kate Cragg, Ilona Halberstadt, Phil Ward
Coach Yard – Ian Graham
Pontins Ad – Richard Borthwick, Steven Brooks, Benny Green, Anne Kidd, Vanessa McKinnon
Pickets – Alan Altrudo, Kathy Altrudo, Anna Bell, Ricardo Gómez

Pérez, Abigail Marshall, Alba Rebelledo, Mary Roberts, Carol
Robinson, Valance Robinson, Magnolia Urbano

Script – Peter Wollen and Laura Mulvey
Taxi Queue Monologue – Keith Allen
Crossed Line Article – John Howe

Music – Lora Logic
Performed by Lora Logic
With Ben Annesley, Charles Hayward, Philip Legg

'No More Records'
'Volcano'
Courtesy of Lora Logic

'Rat Allé'
'Pedigree Charm'
'Martian Man'
'Crystal Gazing'
Courtesy of Rough Trade Music
& Rough Trade Records
Recorded on *Pedigree Charm* (Lora Logic)
Engineered and mixed by
Philip Legg & Stephen Rickard

'Akazehe'
(Traditional)
Two Women from Burundi
Courtesy of Ocora Radio France

'Levitation'
(Karl Jenkins & Mike Ratledge)
Karl Jenkins & Mike Ratledge
Courtesy Mooz Productions Ltd

'Ghazal'
'Huriyyat al-Jabal'
(Salman Shukur)

Salman Shukur
Courtesy Salman Shukur
And Decca International Ltd

'Inspiración'
(P. Paulos & L. Rubinstein)
Típica Enzo Phirpo
Courtesy Itamaraty
Cia Industrial de Discos

'Parachute Jump'
(Johnny Hodges)
Lora Logic
Courtesy of Chappell Morris Ltd

'Pass the Kouchie'
(Lloyd Ferguson & Fitzroy Simpson)
The Mighty Diamonds
Courtesy Mighty Diamonds Music
(Leosong) and Music Works

'Für Elise'
(Ludwig van Beethoven)
Colin Wood
Courtesy of Colin Wood

'Le dodo ou l'amour de berceau'
(François Couperin)
Robert Woolley
Courtesy Meridian Records

Pontins Advertisement
(John Altman)
Courtesy Jeff Wayne Music

Cinematographer – Diane Tammes
Lighting Technician – Richard Johnson
Camera Assistant – Anne Cottringer

Grip – Olly Hoeben
Camera Loader – Nina Kellgren
Sound Recordists – Larry Sider, Moya Burns
Dubbing Mixer – Colin Martin
Post-Synch Recordist – Lionel Strutt
Post-Synch Effects – Pauline Martin
Art Director – Mick Hurd
Assistant Art Director – Annie Curtis-Jones
Costume Designer – Sue Snell
Assistant Costume Designer – Doreen Watkinson
Editor – Larry Sider
Synching Up – Jo Ann Kaplan
Titles – Julian Rothenstein
Stills – Michael Bennett, Mitra Tabrizian, Olly Hoeben
Production – Jill Pack
Production Manager – Rebecca O'Brien
Production Assistant – Kim Nygaard

Thanks to: Contemporary Wardrobe, Echo Prop Hire, Film and
TV Services, Filmatic Laboratories, Food for Films, Last Picture
Frock, Mary Quant Cosmetics, Morris Angel Ltd, North Kensington
Amenity Trust, North Kensington Law Centre, Silica Shop, Sony
UK Ltd, Space Department RAF Farnborough, Synchrosonics,
Videolondon

Special thanks for casting to Susie Figgis

Special thanks to: Nina Danino, Fisher Dilke, Ernie Eban, Alison
Eldred, Derek Harrington, Angus McKie, Ian Powell, Adam Ritchie,
Valeria Robertson, Chad Wollen

Hair for Lora Logic designed by Trevor Sorbie
Make-up designed by Sara Raeburn

Adventures of Prince Achmed
(Lotte Reiniger)
Courtesy Primrose Productions

Voyager Film
Courtesy Nasa/JPL

Pontins Advertisement
Courtesy Pontins

Days of Destruction
Courtesy Kwik Film

Crystal Gazing
(Angus McKie)
Courtesy Young Artists

'Giuditta Pasta (dédicace)'
(Joseph Cornell)
Courtesy Tate Gallery London

Letter to the Chancellors of The European Universities
(Antonin Artaud)
Courtesy John Calder and Editions Gallimard

Directed by Laura Mulvey and Peter Wollen

Produced by the British Film Institute
in association with Channel Four Television
and Modelmark Limited
Head of Production: Peter Sainsbury

Modelmark Limited 1982

British Film Institute
127 Charing Cross Road
London WC2
Great Britain

8

Economic Forecasting and the End of the Avant-Garde: *Crystal Gazing*

Esther Leslie

C
an films divulge the future? Is the celluloid strip a form of crystal ball that forecasts what is to come? Siegfried Kracauer saw signs of imminent Nazism in German films of the 1920s, noting that the portents of war, genocide, brutality and authoritarianism are evident in the many murderers, persecutors, mad scientists and severe father figures that populated Weimar cinema.[1] Kracauer diagnosed these predictions retrospectively, looking back at Weimar cinema in his work of the 1940s. His 1920s and 1930s city sketches – identified as filmic in themselves, for the ways they treat the streets and the neon lights of German cities as dramatic, glaring, dizzying optical experiences – are, though, already punctuated by signs of the violence that was soon to become everyday and official.[2] In absorbing images from the present, film, it would seem, captures in some strange way lines of development, storing within itself, or on its surface, ciphers that will come to be seen as prophetic. Laura Mulvey and Peter Wollen's *Crystal Gazing*, from 1982, suggests in its very title that some sort of divination is to take place in their film. What will the crystal ball reveal? What can film foretell or, in Kracauer's twisted temporality, what will it show to have already been set in motion, but which finds its open reality only now?

Crystal Gazing is set in the London that was contemporary to it, but it evoked Weimar Germany, and the antechamber to fascism, by basing some of its characters and their fates on characters and their fates in Erich Kästner's 1931 novel *Fabian*. The main character in *Fabian* is a doctor of literature with a weak heart. He makes his money writing advertising copy, until the day he is replaced by a cheaper employee. Once unemployed, he spends his time drifting through the city and its brothels and bars, loving and losing women who trade their sex for money or fame, sometimes engaging in cynical repartee with his idealistic friend Labunde, a political activist negotiating a polarising political atmosphere. Labunde is writing a doctorate on the writer Gotthold Ephraim Lessing and, in the course of the novel, he will become a suicide. Fabian dies too, leaving behind the imperfect world he witnesses, as he attempts to rescue a child from a river, despite the fact that he cannot swim. In his 1950 introduction to the reprint of the novel (which was committed to the flames first time around in 1933), Kästner described his story as a 'fun house mirror' or 'distorting looking glass', depicting a reality marred by mass unemployment and social misery. It is distorted by caricature, satire and exaggeration, but nonetheless a mirror for all that. He adds that it was written as a warning about the abyss that Germany, and Europe, were approaching, their citizens merrily bobbing along to the seductive strains of a rat-catcher.[3]

Crystal Gazing likewise stared into its moment and asked: what is becoming of this city and the people in it, in these depressing times of upheaval? The film follows, for the most part, four people as they make their way, or fail to, in London in the early 1980s, in an environment moulded by the advent of Thatcherism in 1979. It asks: what new politics loom on the horizon? How will they change us and our relationships? Can we fight them with narrative, or film, or art? Will they kill us? The film's characters are two men and two women. The men are not heroes. They are lost, unmoored, drifting. Both die, one in an accident, one by his own hand. We learn of these deaths through TV or video, distanced, mediated – the men are not full-bodied, they are becoming redundant. The women, by contrast, find ways to exist, but this is by being pulled into the workings of contemporary capitalism; one melds with the spectacle, as a pop star; one enters the economy through photographic work that can be commoditised for financial prediction. Both utilise imagery – of the self and of the environment – to further their own and capital's fortunes.

In the few available blurbs and texts on the film, it is described as 'the most narrative film' that Mulvey and Wollen made, and characterised as 'a departure from the emphatic formalism'[4] of earlier films. But if it is a narrative film, it is a digressive and wandering one, just like the narrative of Kästner's *Fabian*. The film is episodic and rambling, just as its characters, especially Neil, the lonesome, unemployed fantasy illustrator, roam and drift and seem not to know where to go or who to go with. Futures are fantasised, but the male characters seem bereft of future, made redundant by new capital, yet still bound to it. The film proceeds by the use of tableaux, set pieces, short chapters – a notable example is Keith Allen's improvised monologue in a taxi queue. As much as the film meanders through a loose intervallic narrative, it also encounters blockages. It is comprised of interruptions. There are abrupt halts, failed plans, sudden endings. It knots together its characters in strange, often stressed relationships, not straightforward ones, but perverse ones, unhappy, mismatched, with a sense of heading nowhere. The genre of the fairy tale is evoked in the film's references to 'Puss in Boots'. This traditional, heart-warming genre brings cold comfort in the London of the 1980s. The juddering action of 'Puss in Boots' as played in the Pollock's toy theatre exposes an illusory hope for good fortune, just as it demonstrates folk wisdom's version of the mobilising power of language and desire.

For sure, in *Crystal Gazing* the question of narrative appears as something that the film possesses, but critically. The filmmakers intended to break with the trends perceived among radical British filmmakers at the time; the London Film-Makers' Co-operative and the political documentary movement eschewed narrative, having imbibed anti-narrative theories from Structuralism in Paris. But this was not to say that a complete acceptance of it was warranted. Somehow narrative had to be worked with and against. *Crystal Gazing*, it seems apparent from an interview by Mulvey and Wollen with *Framework* in 1982, was part of another movement, a new period, perhaps the one unleashed by Thatcherism, perhaps the one which had to begin after the waning of the experimental film movement. New alliances and new resources present themselves in a desperate situation, which also brings all the potential energies of a necessary repositioning. *Crystal Gazing* wanted to align not with the 'nightmare of independent film',[5] but with other independent cultural forms, ones that had more popular reach: independent music, theatre, comedy, science fantasy art, graffiti, busking, video games – subcultures, in short. This is not to say that the theoretical influence that had been so key for British radical cinema was abandoned. As Peter Wollen succinctly put it in the *Framework* interview: 'rock 'n' roll and foreign theory: those are the two backbones of the film'. The question of accessibility and who would form the right or wrong audience are questioned within the film, ironically, perhaps, but nonetheless – specifically in relation to Julian's PhD, a radical post-Lacanian reading of 'Puss in Boots'. For whom is it written, for what and to whom?

Across and around all this, the film gives time to music, to the songs of Lora Logic, which seem to be diegetic and non-diegetic, at one and the same time. The songs tug against the narrative, holding it up – though they also underline how Kim is becoming a pop star, hitting success, breaking through, rather than being impeded or obstructed. Inasmuch as the songs hold up narrative, they are 'individual units, like acts of "attractions"', as Mulvey observed in *Framework*. In that one word, 'attraction', two modes of cinema are yoked together: popular and avant-garde. 'Attraction' is a name given to the mode of cinema in its first years: a sensational, event-based frolic, visual delight, gags, shocking events, attention seeking spectacle. 'Attraction' is also a concept in cinema theory and practice, coined with an avant-garde project for film whose terms were identified by a filmmaker and theorist S. M. Eisenstein.[6] His first films were organised – and theorised – as a 'montage of film attractions'. He took forms that he had worked with theatrically, the popular forms of vaudeville, music hall, circus, sideshows, all discrete and complete elements that have the capacity to shock a viewer and work on them emotionally and viscerally, and repurposed them as the basis for a montage theory of film, which utilises attention-grabbing and shocking segmented narrative, as well as chains of association. All this is directed by Eisenstein towards revolutionary ends. The film is broken into parts and it is also an ideological whole.

Crystal Gazing has a narrative, but one that bares its constructed nature openly – with its use of repetitions, scenes that balance each other, interruptions, flows and blockages. The film is conceived as a series of episodes and as a whole. And that has something Brechtian about it – and perhaps indicates the extent to which this film is composed as an epic, a journey, a series of stations along a way. This way is a route that brings death with it, as much as it brings flourishing. The dialectic and all its contradictions are laid out as a tableau in one of the closing scenes: a picket line, a company collapse, some scabs, the thwarted journey and death of a non-hero. This death is mediated to us by TV, by the TV news. This one death, Neil's demise, will be forgotten by most viewers by the time of the next news, just as Kim barely registers the news of Neil's friend's suicide, caught up as she is in her own journey into celebrity, into becoming a spectacle in the technological imaginary. The spectacle asserts itself in this film and is shown showing. All the characters appear on video or TV, dead or alive. These devices are vectors of oblivion, notoriety or fame – it all depends on who and what you are and when. They steal life away from those who watch, as a Situationist might put it, just as they are vehicles for showing so much death, factual and fictional, though the distinctions barely matter. There is a suggestion that there might yet be a more lasting effect of the failed academic's suicide, for it is broadcast on home video, that then-newish medium of self-representation, which promised as a glimmer the possibility of acquiring a means of reproduction. The video is doubly mediated; it exists in the moment of its filmic screening and as an explanatory document for those within the film who seek answers. It leaves multiple traces, but what it seems to do more than anything is to make out of suicide a theatrical gesture, one enriched by a reading of Antonin Artaud's caustic open letter from 1925 to the Chancellors of the Universities: 'Europe is becoming set in its ways, embalming itself beneath the wrappings of its borders, its factories, its law-courts and its universities'. This video within a film speaks to the wider theme of decay and hopelessness.

But there were other influences acknowledged by Mulvey and Wollen in the *Framework* interview. Wollen stated: 'The film is really poised between Brecht and Breton'. As the reference to *Fabian* indicates, the film had its connections to modernism, to the neo-epic city novels of the interwar years, in which shattered men – Franz

Biberkopf, Leopold Bloom, Fainy McCreary, Nikolai Apollonovich Ableukhov – crash up against incomprehensible mediated cities, but it might also be read through more recent ideas expressed by Mulvey in her essay 'Uncertainty: Natural Magic and the Art of Deception' from *Death 24 x a Second*. Here Mulvey discusses the 'convergence between the arts of reality and the arts of deception that brought about the birth of the cinema in 1895'.[7] Embodying this convergence is Georges Méliès, a professional magician and illusionist who melded the documentary capacity of cinema with magic and trickery. Méliès devised effects and surrealist scenes, quite unlike the Lumières' focus on Realism. Documentary and magic, the real and the enchanted might be crudely bannered under the contraries of Brecht and Breton. Mulvey's essay reflects on how forms of popular entertainment, 'arts of deception', emerged out of the growth of a leisured mass audience in the later nineteenth century, appealing to 'human fascination with the unnatural, the impossible and, ultimately, the supernatural' and 'its constant readiness to be fooled'. Cinema capitalised on these. In *Crystal Gazing*, a couple of scenes in a cabaret with a magician hint at a relation between cinema and the showmanship of magic. While the cabaret form was an inspiration for Brecht (as well as a location of the attraction form for Eisenstein), because of its raucous popular nature, in *Crystal Gazing* it represents a space of deception, a fraudulent space where a magician plies his non-magical tricks. In one scene in the cabaret club, as if to emphasise the link from the film to early cinema and the arts of enchantment, Lotte Reiniger's shadow-play animation *The Adventures of Prince Achmed* (1926) plays in the background. Cinema has a capacity to deceive; audiences have a capacity to be deceived. Audiences long to be deceived. But cinema too has the capacity to reveal. Modernity's new consciousness, according to Tom Gunning, via Mulvey, is one in which audiences experience 'Pleasure in the material relation between illusion and optics and between illusion and momentary credulity, playing with the mind's susceptibility to trickery', all of which 'involve various successive phases of exchange between the eye and the mind, belief, doubt, curiosity'.[8]

All well and good, but for this film, *Crystal Gazing*, which displays its fairy tale and fantasy influences quite obviously, it exists in modern times, when new magics, likewise spurious, are ascendant. Or these are old ones repurposed to new ends. The character Vermilion, an occasional magician's assistant with a charmed gaze at night time in the club, performs by day hi-tech augury, gazing on satellite photographs. Like the photographs of spirits of the nineteenth century, which appeared to make invisible forces visible, her photographs visualise the ethereal through infrared and other optical techniques. In this way, they allow for an analysis of something that cannot yet be seen: economic futures, the futures of food markets, the size of yields to come, annexed to colours on the images, as in, for example, those produced by drought spots, whose poor crops generate out of their nothingness profits in futures markets. The new purpose of this augury, this crystal gazing, is economic prediction. Here it gleams as the first twinkling of neoliberalism. There is a deft magic in the film in that it recognises the rise of certain kinds of cultural labour, specifically intellectual labour, as central to a new phase of capitalism. It depicts a future that was, and would be, female, in Thatcher's sense only perhaps, or, with a sliver more hope, in the sense of the women on the picket line who appear inside the final crystal ball, fighting back, a female workforce asserting its demands, but they are harbingers of death too. What deaths? Of the old-style working-class struggle? Of radical possibility? Of the vanguard and the avant-garde? Of what has been? Somehow they connect to – cata-lyse, redeem, disrupt – our non-hero who dies, finally a hero, under the wheels of a scab coach, while in the act of saving a child's life. He dies just like Fabian, on whom he is modelled, both committing their one, final, decisive moral act. Morality is of the old world. It cannot persist.

Looked at from the perspective of today, the crystal ball is a stand-in for some-thing else. It is the globe, our earth, as seen from outside and above, as Vermilion sees it from her satellite photographs. What the film grasps as image, in its incipient moments, is the then-emergent phase of global capitalism, of globalisation, of pre-carity, of extending mediatisation, of new conditions in a world of flows and borders.

Notes

1. See: Siegfried Kracauer, *From Caligari to Hitler: A Psychological History of the German Film*, ed. Leonardo Quaresima (Princeton, NJ: Princeton University Press, 2004).

2. Siegfried Kracauer, *Strassen in Berlin und Anderswo* (Berlin: Das Arsenal, 2003).

3. Erich Kästner, *Fabian: Die Geschichte eines Moralisten* (Munich: DTV, 1989), 9–10.

4. Eleanor Burke, 'Entry on Laura Mulvey, Reference Guide to British and Irish Film Directors', accessed 1 May 2019, www.screenonline.org.uk/people/id/566978/.

5. Laura Mulvey and Peter Wollen, '*Crystal Gazing*', interview by Fizzy Oppe and Don Ranvaud, *Framework: The Journal of Cinema and Media* 19 (Summer 1982) 19.

6. Two relevant essays, 'The Montage of Attractions' (1923) and 'The Montage of Film Attractions' (1924), are anthologised in: Sergei Eisenstein, *The Eisenstein Reader*, ed. Richard Taylor and trans. William Powell and Richard Taylor (London: British Film Institute, 1998).

7. Laura Mulvey, *Death 24x a Second: Stillness and the Moving Image* (London: Reaktion Books, 2006), 34.

8. *Ibid.*, 42.

9

Frida Kahlo & Tina Modotti

Laura Mulvey and Peter Wollen

Black screen.

Image of Diego Rivera's mural 'The Arsenal' (1928), in which both Frida Kahlo and Tina Modotti appear distributing arms to the people. The image is masked out so as to emphasise both artists' presence.

> VOICE OVER: Two choices for women: the personal, the traditional sphere of women, their suffering, their self-image. On the other hand, the political, the renunciation of home and family to produce images dedicated to social change. Frida Kahlo and Tina Modotti both provoke and defy such neat categorisation.

Title: FRIDA KAHLO & tina modotti

Music: Carlos Chávez, 'Preludio No. 5'.

Title: This film is about two women whose paths crossed in this mural painted by Diego Rivera, in the Ministry of Education, Mexico City, 1928.

Image of Rivera's 'The Arsenal'.

Title: Women, Mexico, Art, Revolution: despite all that they both had in common, their lives and their work are strikingly different.

Title: FRIDA KAHLO

The Mexican Revolution gave artists the chance to renew their national culture. Frida Kahlo became a painter inspired by popular traditions. [*The isolated image of Kahlo from Rivera's 'The Arsenal' is shown on the left side of the title.*]

Title: **tina modotti**

The new Mexico aroused the enthusiasm of foreign artists. Tina
Modotti stayed to become a photographer and a revolutionary. [*The
isolated image of Modotti from Rivera's 'The Arsenal' is shown on the
right side of the title.*]

Title: Each defined herself differently in the face of the necessities
and accidents of history and biography, and in relationship to her
own body.

Title: Yet both were women artists working consciously in the
context of the Mexican Revolution and its aftermath, a time of
violent upheaval and cultural awakening.

Music Stops.

Title: HISTORY
Title: CIVIL WAR AND REVOLUTION

Footage of Mexican Revolution.

VOICE OVER: The Mexican Renaissance was the progeny of the Mexican
Revolution. The overthrow of the ancien régime of Porfirio Díaz in 1911
unleashed uncontrollable forces and counter-forces for nearly a decade of civil
war, peasant rising and landlord oppression. It was a period of mingled cruelty,
surprise and hope in which great masses travelled through Mexico in military
campaigns and many millions died. Others survived to march in triumph
through the capital, to cheer a man on horseback, to wreak vengeance on the
defeated, or simply thank their luck and cunning.

Title: POPULAR LIFE AND CULTURE

*Footage shot by Nickolas Muray of Mexican landscape. Followed by footage of village life,
a market, street traders, and fairground roundabout. Traditional Mexican music plays.*

VOICE OVER: Yet out of the turbulence of the Mexican Revolution arose a new
Renaissance of culture. Intellectuals and artists left the academies to rediscover
and revalue the vivid traditional culture of their country, still inseparable from
the daily life of marketplace and village square.

Title: ROOTS **movement**

[*Kahlo's 'My Grandparents, My Parents and I (Family Tree)' (1936) (left side) and Modotti's 'Bandolier, Corn, Guitar' (1927) (right side) are shown in the title. 'Bandolier, Corn, Guitar' and the word 'movement' fade out and are replaced with the following text:* Frida Kahlo was born in her parents' house in Coyoacán in 1907. She died in the same house in 1954.]

This sequence comprises images of Kahlo's paintings that replace one another in the manner of a slide show: 'Portrait of Frida's Family' (1950); 'Portrait of My Father Guillermo' (1951); 'Frida Kahlo and Diego Rivera' (1931); 'Self-Portrait Dedicated to Leon Trotsky', or 'Between the Curtains' (1937); 'The Two Fridas' (1939); 'Self-Portrait on the Borderline between Mexico and the United States' (1932); 'My Nurse and I' (1937); 'Roots' (1943); 'The Deceased Dimas Rosas Aged Three' (1937); 'The Suicide of Dorothy Hale' (1938–1939); 'Marxism Will Give Health to the Sick' (1954).

VOICE OVER: More than once Frida Kahlo portrayed herself as an infant, the issue of a family tree set against the landscape of Mexico. Her mother was a native Mexican. Her father a photographer, an immigrant from Germany. She captured the intensity and ambivalence of her marriage to Diego Rivera in an ironic double portrait. And when she lent her house to Trotsky in his exile, she gave him a portrait of herself wearing the popular Mexican costume she loved. In 'The Two Fridas', she painted her own double identity: the European Frida in white and the American Frida in traditional dress. Yet the duality she felt in herself and in Mexico also offered the hope of a new hybrid, a new synthesis of cultural and personal opposites. She identified herself with this vision of Mexico. In 'My Nurse and I', the Indian nurse suckles the European child. In her painting 'Roots', she portrayed herself stretched out on the Pedregal, the volcanic rock of Mexico, joined to it by an intricate web of tendrils and branches. She used the popular art of Mexico as a model for her own paintings, remembrances of the dead and especially ex-voto paintings, graphic depictions of disaster painted on sheets of tin to be nailed up in church. In her own ex-voto painting, she substituted the figure of Marx for that of a Catholic saint and showed herself as the victim miraculously cured.

At the end of the sequence, the images run backwards through the series without sound until the beginning is reached.

Title: ROOTS **movement**

[*Kahlo's 'My Grandparents, My Parents and I (Family Tree)' (1936) (left side) and Modotti's 'Bandolier, Corn, Guitar' (1927) (right side) are shown in the title. 'My Grandparents, My Parents and I (Family Tree)' and the word 'ROOTS' disappear and are replaced with the following text:* Tina Modotti was born into a poor family in Udine, Northern Italy, in 1896. She died, stateless, in Mexico, in 1942.]

This sequence comprises images of Modotti's photographs that replace one another in the manner of a slide show: 'Hands of Marionette Player' (1929); 'Judas' (c. 1926); 'Marionette' (1929); 'Hands of the Puppeteer (Man's Hand with Yank)' and 'Hands with Marionette (Mildred from "The Hairy Ape")' (both 1929); 'Yank and Police Marionette' (1926); 'Mella's Typewriter' (1928); 'Stadium, Mexico City' (1927); 'Telephone Wires, Mexico' (1925); 'Oil Tank' (1927); 'Stadium Exterior' (1927); 'Man with a Beam' (c. 1928); 'Bandolier, Corn, Guitar' (1927); 'Elegance and Poverty (photomontage)' (c. 1928); 'Misery' (1928); 'Woman with Flag' (1928); 'Sickle, Bandolier, Guitar' (1927); 'Hammer and Sickle' (1927).

VOICE OVER: Like Mexican artists of the period, Tina Modotti was fascinated by the forms of popular culture. With Weston, she made a series of photographs of folk art to illustrate a book on Mexican culture: *Idols Behind Altars.* She also took photographs of marionettes in which she looked especially at the hands of the puppeteer, the tracery of the wires and the patterns of shadows to show the manual dexterity of the work. At the same time, Tina Modotti turned towards scenes of modern life in industry. She made another series of photographs for a book of avant-garde poetry by an Estridentista poet: petrol tanks, construction work, telephone wires. In these photographs, she moves close to international Constructivism with its emphasis on the urban and the world of the engineer and the labourer. Tina Modotti absorbed Edward Weston's aesthetic, his photographic purism, and developed it so that formal concerns could coexist with a commitment to social and political content. Tina Modotti chose political imagery for what it signified. A contrast between elegance and poverty and misery of the urban poor, photographed with a heavy view camera in an emblematic rather than a documentary style. She made formal compositions from elements which already have a symbolic significance, using emblems of the Mexican Revolution, or of international Communism, the hammer and sickle.

At the end of the sequence, the images run backwards through the series without sound until the beginning is reached.

Title: Biography
Title: TINA MODOTTI
                JOURNEYS AND EXILES
                1896–1942

This sequence comprises images of maps showing Modotti's journeys throughout her life.

VOICE OVER: Tina Modotti was born in Udine in Northern Italy in 1896. Her
father was a skilled worker and a socialist, forced like many other Italians of the
period to go abroad to find work. While Tina was still a child, he emigrated
to San Francisco where his family later joined him. Tina worked there in a
textile factory before she moved to Los Angeles in her early twenties. There
she became an actress in Hollywood film. In 1922, Tina visited Mexico and
soon returned there with Edward Weston, the photographer. She lived in
Mexico for the next eight years. She travelled through the country working
as a photographer, recording the life of its people, especially the women of
Tehuantepec in the south. But in 1930, she was expelled from Mexico for
political reasons soon after the assassination of her companion Julio Mella,
founder of the Cuban Communist Party, who was shot dead in the street by her
side. From Rotterdam, she made her way to Germany, picking up the threads
of her photographic and political contacts. But soon the threat of fascism forced
her to leave Berlin and she made her way to Moscow, where she abandoned
photography for full-time political work. The Communist International sent her
to Paris and then shortly before the outbreak of the Civil War to Spain, where
she stayed throughout the war, until the Republican defeat drove her once more
into exile. Finally, she returned for the last time to Mexico, planning to take up
photography again, and died there unexpectedly in 1942.

Title: FRIDA KAHLO
                THE BLUE HOUSE
                1907–1954

This sequence comprises handheld Super 8 footage of the Blue House.

VOICE OVER: Frida Kahlo was born, died and spent much of her life within these
walls: the Kahlo family home in Coyoacán on the outskirts of Mexico City,
known as the Blue House. Frida Kahlo's roots are here, in this house and garden.
The walls are painted in traditional Mexican colours. The pyramid and the pre-
Columbian statues celebrate the Indian culture of Mexico, before the Spanish
conquest of the sixteenth century. At the same time, the walls form a protective

shield, a shell or mask covering Frida's life and its pain. It was here she sheltered from the storms of her relationship with Diego Rivera, who she married, divorced and remarried. When she was a teenager, Frida had a terrible motor accident, leaving her crippled, in pain and unable to have children. She decorated not only her home, often with images of death, but even the surgical corset that protected her broken body. Everywhere she surrounded herself with objects of art and folk culture: crude and brightly coloured images drawn from the imagination and complex culture of the Mexican people, identifying herself with them.

Title: INWARD outward
[*Kahlo's 'The Broken Column' (1944) (left side) and Modotti's 'Workers Parade' (1926) (right side) are shown in the title. 'Workers Parade' and the word 'outward' disappear and are replaced with the following text:* Frida Kahlo dissected the private, hidden aspects of her life. She found visible images for an invisible interior.]

This sequence comprises images of Kahlo's paintings that replace one another in the manner of a slide show: 'The Mask' (1945); 'Self-Portrait with Necklace of Thorns' (1940); 'Self-Portrait with Braid' (1941); 'Self-Portrait as a Tehuana' (1943); 'Diego and I' (1949); 'Moses' (1945); 'What the Water Gave Me' (1938); 'The Dream' (1939); 'Without Hope' (1945); 'Self-Portrait with Necklace' (1933); 'Self-Portrait Wearing a Velvet Dress' (1926); 'Self-Portrait with Loose Hair' (1947); 'Self-Portrait with Small Monkey' (1945); 'Self-Portrait with Monkeys' (1943); 'Self-Portrait with Monkey' (1938).

VOICE OVER: Masquerade both shows and hides. Through the mask of her art, Frida Kahlo concealed and exposed her own pain, her physical suffering and her emotional suffering. Living and working at the time of the Mexican mural movement, she took herself as the main subject matter of her art and painted her own image and her interior experiences, dreams and fantasies. She painted her husband, Diego Rivera, in a medallion on her forehead, seeking an image for her inward thoughts as well as her outward appearance. Her fascination with her own interior life attracted in turn the fascination of the European Surrealists. She painted her 'Moses' after reading Freud's *Moses and Monotheism*, and when André Breton had visited Mexico, she made her painting 'What the Water Gave Me' for a surrealist exhibition. Frida Kahlo painted the passions of the unconscious. A world of dreams is a world of great beauty, but it takes her to the edge of terror; a haven of private fantasy is stripped of reassurance. She first began to paint as a teenager when she was bedridden after a terrible road accident: her spine was fractured, her pelvis shattered and her foot crushed. For long periods of her life, she was in pain and forced back into hospital for an endless series of operations. Painting brought pleasure, hope and power over herself. She could ward off despair and regain control over her crushed and broken body by creating a masquerade of beauty. Whatever the degree of pain implied by tears or even wounds, her face remained severe and expressionless with an unflinching gaze. Yet at the same time, the severity is softened by a luxurious surround of lace, plants or by an accompanying doll or spider monkey. Even here, though, there is an ambivalence – the wide-eyed monkey somehow reminds us of the missing child, the pain of desire.

At the end of the sequence, the images run backwards through the series without sound until the beginning is reached.

Title: INWARD outward

[*Kahlo's 'The Broken Column' (1944) (left side) and Modotti's 'Workers Parade' (1926) (right side) are shown in the title. 'The Broken Column' and the word 'INWARD' disappear and are replaced with the following text:* Tina Modotti worked in the streets, the outside world. She watched the Mexican people, their condition and their revolution.]

This sequence comprises images of Modotti's photographs that replace one another in the manner of a slide show: 'Campesinos Reading "El Machete"' (1929); 'Worker Reading "El Machete"' (1927); 'Meeting of Campesinos (Stage)' (1927); 'Worker's Hands' (1927); 'Hands Washing' (1927); 'Workers, Mexico' (c.1926–1929); 'Loading Bananas, Veracruz' (c.1927–1929); 'Calla Lilies' (1925); 'Roses, Mexico' (1924); 'Sugar Cane' (1929); 'Corn' (c.1929); 'Staircase' (c.1924–1926); 'Convent of Tepotzotlán, Mexico' (1924).

VOICE OVER: The stormy political life of her adopted country absorbed the energies of Tina Modotti, both as a militant and as an artist. She used her camera to record the activities of its people in public, exterior space, at work, at meetings or demonstrations. She looked at the hands rather than the face and saw formal patterns as well as political commitment in the crowds in the street. In time, she developed a style which was both highly geometrical and highly political – a mode of photography through which she could register the twentieth century with twentieth-century eyes. Tina Modotti had learnt photography from Edward Weston. She was his model, his apprentice, and finally his colleague. From him she learned to look for the beauty in ordinary objects and to insist on clarity and precision in order to bring out the geometry that was normally overlooked. The trained and sensitive eye could see formal compositions and textures of light and shade in the most simple subjects:

flowers, plants, human figures, the outlines of buildings. This was the aesthetic legacy that Tina Modotti inherited from Edward Weston.

At the end of the sequence, the images run backwards through the series without sound until the beginning is reached.

Title: THE BODY
Title: THE TIGER'S COAT
         TINA MODOTTI PLAYS A MEXICAN WOMAN
         (HOLLYWOOD, 1920)

Footage from The Tiger's Coat (*Roy Clements*) *plays.*

Music: Carlos Chávez, 'Preludio No. 2'.

Music stops.

Title: FRIDA AND DIEGO
         HOME MOVIES TAKEN AT THE BLUE HOUSE
         (NICKOLAS MURAY)

Footage plays from home movie of Kahlo and Rivera.

Title: INJURY beauty
         [*Kahlo's 'A Few Small Nips' (1935) (left side) and Weston's 'Tina on the Azotea' (1924) (right side) are shown in the title. 'Tina on the Azotea' and the word 'beauty' disappear and are replaced with the following text:* Frida Kahlo lived in pain and in crisis with her own body. By painting her self-portrait, she transcribed her injuries into emblems and allegory.]

This sequence comprises images of Kahlo's paintings that replace one another in the manner of a slide show: 'My Birth' (1932); 'Tree of Hope, Keep Firm' (1946); 'Henry Ford Hospital' (1932); 'Frida and the Abortion' (1932); 'Frida and the Cesarean' (1932); 'Self-Portrait with Portrait of Dr Farill' (1951); 'The Broken Column' (1944); 'The Little Deer' (1946); 'Self-Portrait with Cropped Hair' (1940); 'Still Life with Parrot' (1951); 'Fruits of Life' (1951); 'Me and My Doll' (1937).

VOICE OVER: Frida Kahlo was unable to have the child she desired and suffered a series of miscarriages and medical abortions. She displays her pain and her damaged body through the traditional iconography of Catholic art, the depiction of martyrdom and of the Passion. In 'Henry Ford Hospital', her body on the bed is surrounded by emblematic objects, like those which surround the crucified Christ in an allegory of redemption. These images of her own agony have an archaic, almost medieval air: a love of minute detail often based on anatomy textbooks, a disparity between foreground figure and background setting, a disregard for proportion and perspective and the use of conventional signs and attributes. In a self-portrait of herself with her doctor, Dr Farill, she paints the palette itself as a bleeding heart, both the surgeon's heart and that of the mystic. Her appeal is not to an imaginary identification with herself as subjected to pain, but to a symbolic reading of her body as the site of suffering – as in 'The Little Deer', which combines Catholic imagery with a metaphor taken from a popular song. In her 'Self-Portrait with Cropped Hair', she quotes another song: 'Look, if I loved you, it was for your hair. Now your hair's gone, I love you no more.' In her still lives, fruit became part of the body, flesh-like, as though she was dismembered before her own eyes. Even the rays of the sun were incorporated in the web. Volcanic barrenness contrasts with images of cosmic and natural vitality. Frida Kahlo turns everything into a language of signs through which the traumas of injury and their effects are written in allegory and emblem.

At the end of the sequence, the images run backwards through the series without sound until the beginning is reached.

Title: INJURY **beauty**
[*Kahlo's 'A Few Small Nips' (1935) (left side) and Weston's 'Tina on the Azotea' (1924) (right side) are shown in the title. 'A Few Small Nips' and the word 'INJURY' disappear and are replaced with the following text:* Tina Modotti was famous as a beauty, but she rebelled against the gaze of others to make her own images of the working women of Mexico.]

This sequence comprises images of Modotti's photographs of women from Tehuantepec that replace one another in the manner of a slide show.

VOICE OVER: Tina Modotti's choice of Tehuana women as subject was also, in its way, political. The women of Tehuantepec in the south west of Mexico were legendary for their strength, beauty and independence. Tina Modotti was made famous as a beauty in Hollywood films and as a model for Edward Weston and Diego Rivera. Beauty was inscribed on her body by the look of others. When she herself learned photography and could return that look, she chose as her models, as her subjects, women whose beauty was inseparable from their work and their independence. Tina Modotti wrote to Edward Weston, 'I could not possibly see what prettiness had to do with the revolutionary movement.' Often she photographed mothers with small children, their bodies framed to emphasise not their own form, but their interaction with the children. They're shown in the process of mothering, that is to say, at work. The camera position is often below head-height to show the labour involved in mothering and to avoid the isolation and fetishism of the pose for a camera. At the same time, she reveals the curves of pregnancy and the diagonals of the arms, to bring out the formal values of each scene. Tina Modotti mainly photographed women and her gaze is direct and just.

At the end of the sequence, the images run backwards through the series without sound until the beginning is reached.

Image of Rivera's 'The Arsenal'.

VOICE OVER: Two choices for women: the personal, the traditional sphere of women, their suffering, their self-image. On the other hand, the political, the renunciation of home and family to produce images dedicated to social change. Frida Kahlo and Tina Modotti both provoke and defy such neat categorisation. Frida's fascination with her own body and her national culture was deeply political. Tina's photography is strongly marked by her personal experience as a woman. The energy they each found to combat both personal calamity and political oppression survives in their art. We still feel it today.

Music: Carlos Chávez, 'Preludio No. 8'.

CREDITS:

> Frida Kahlo Paintings: Albright-Knox Art Gallery, Buffalo, N.Y., Subscribers Fund, 1874; Humanities Research Centre, The University of Texas at Austin; Musée National d'Art Moderne, Centre Georges Pompidou, Paris; Museo de Arte Moderno, Mexico City; Museo Frida Kahlo, Mexico City; Museum of Modern Art, New York, Gift of Edgar Kaufmann, Jr; Phoenix Art Museum, Phoenix, Arizona; San Francisco Museum of Modern Art, Albert M. Bender Collection, Gift of Albert M. Bender; University of California at San Francisco; Sr Robert Brady; Selma and Nesuhi Ertegun; Sr Jorge Espinosa Ulloa; Sra Eugenia Farill Novelo; Mr Thomás Fernández Márquez; M. Daniel Filipacchi; Sr and Sra Jacques Gelman; Sr Alejandro Gómez Arias; Mr Edgar J.Kaufmann; Sr Licio Lagos; Hon Mrs Henry R. Luce; Sra Dolores Olmedo; Sra Isolda P. Kahlo; Mr and Mrs Manuel Reyero; Mr S. A. Williams. Tina Modotti Photographs: Archivo Historico Fotografico (INAH),

Pachuca; Comitato Tina Modotti, Trieste; Edward Weston Photograph, Centre for Creative Photography, University of Arizona; Archive Film, Eastman House, Rochester, N.Y; Library of Congress, Washington, D.C.; National Film Archive, London.

STILL PHOTOGRAPHY: Aurora Mosso M., Prudence Cuming, Jaques Rutten, Red Door Studios.

SPECIAL THANKS TO: Dolores Olmedo, Vittorio Vidali, Mark Francis, Sylvia Pandolfi, Megi Pepeu, Aurora Mosso M., Hayden Herrera, Miriam Kaiser, Whitechapel Gallery, London.

SUPER-8 FILM: Beatriz Mira, Cinetequio.

ROSTRUM CAMERA: Frameline, Peerless Camera.

VOICE OVER: Miriam Margolyes.

DUBBING MIXER: Colin Martin.

MUSIC: Preludios 5, 8 and 10, Carlos Chávez (G. Schirmer Inc.) performed by Anthony Goldstone.

Fireworks Music, Traditional Mexican (Folkways Records).

EDITING: Nina Danino, Larry Sider.

DESIGN: Julian Rothenstein.

PRODUCTION MANAGER: Patsy Nightingale.

EXECUTIVE PRODUCER: Rodney Wilson.

PRODUCED BY MODELMARK LIMITED

SCRIPT AND DIRECTION: Laura Mulvey & Peter Wollen.

Arts Council of Great Britain

©1983

10

Muse, Mutilation, Mastery, Martyr: *Frida Kahlo & Tina Modotti*

B. Ruby Rich

oday it is difficult to imagine that there was ever a time when Tina Modotti and Frida Kahlo were equally known and equally forgotten, but so it was in the late 1970s. It was then that Laura Mulvey and Peter Wollen set out to make the short documentary *Frida Kahlo & Tina Modotti* and to research and curate *Frida Kahlo and Tina Modotti*, their travelling exhibition of paintings and photographs by these two women, both so deeply identified with Mexico's radical cultural and political moment.

Unveiled at London's Whitechapel Art Gallery in March 1982, the exhibition included Kahlo and Modotti's art, much of it on loan for the first time from private collections, as well as screenings of the documentary and a catalogue with a very smart essay by Mulvey and Wollen as well as writings from Modotti herself, Diego Rivera, Pablo Neruda, André Breton and others. The catalogue became a primary resource for anyone searching for more information about either woman (my own tattered copy was invaluable for this essay) in advance of the landslide of attention that was about to arrive, just as the film staked out important new territory for what such 'interpretive materials' could offer if only the gallery or arts institution were willing to break with the past.

The catalogue's bibliography is telling, both for what it includes and for what is missing: that is, almost any scholarship on either woman's work or life, though there is a footnote to a promised forthcoming volume by Hayden Herrera, which would soon initiate Frida-mania. The next year, the *Woman's Art Journal* would include a review of two books, one on Kahlo, one on Modotti.[1] And so the flood of publications, which has never ceased, began. There was something in the air then, a movement that had started a decade earlier; the First World Conference for International Women's Year, sponsored by the United Nations and convened in Mexico City in 1975, staged multiple exhibitions that would spark a revival of interest in Mexican women artists that, together with the engine of feminist art activism, would continue to grow.[2]

Frida Kahlo & Tina Modotti now has a tragic dimension that it did not have when it was first released. In the intervening decades, Frida Kahlo has shot from unknown to ubiquitous, her paintings worth fortunes, prized by Madonna, worn on a bracelet by Theresa May, her life's work a brand, one that has ironically seen a celebration of gender smother the work's original political force. Over the same time, Tina Modotti has been almost savagely forgotten, her politics demeaned, the riddle of her life shelved, even at a global moment when political refugees (which Modotti most certainly was) increase in number constantly, rendered stateless by merciless geopolitical forces. The intersectionality of their lives, to which *Frida Kahlo & Tina Modotti* points with clairvoyant precision, merits a revival.

The artworks would appear to be opposite if not oppositional: Kahlo, turning inward, training her brush back on herself and her body; Modotti, turning outward, training her camera on the streets, the masses, political demonstrations and human labor. Like many cultural figures, Kahlo supported Trotsky, with whom she reportedly had an affair and who stayed at her fabled Blue House (Casa Azul) in Mexico's Coyoacán neighborhood, where Mulvey and Wollen were first inspired to make their film.[3] Trotsky, of course, was assassinated in Mexico City in 1940, a death that divided Communist Party loyalists worldwide. Modotti remained a 'CP' stalwart, evidently even a Stalinist.[4] Certainly she was desperately in need of the party's help; thrice an exile, deported from Mexico on false charges, Modotti would go on to escape the fascists in Europe, drive ambulances in the Spanish Civil War, travel through Moscow and Berlin and finally return to Mexico to die.

Oppositions, however, can be deceiving and are never static; both were once Communists, stayed deeply involved in the politics of their time and committed to visions of social justice, moved in the same circles and were friends, for it was Modotti who reportedly first introduced Kahlo and Rivera, just as it was Rivera who, the first time around, saved Modotti from deportation and defamation.[5] Both took many lovers and had a magnetism that attracted powerful men to them. Despite the allure of these stories, Mulvey and Wollen clearly had no intention of making a biopic, melodrama or any other sort of traditional or avant-garde dramatic work; other films could do that, and would.[6]

Frida Kahlo & Tina Modotti instead belongs to a different cinematic context and tradition. A seemingly simple film composed of images, texts and voices, spare and elegant, eschewing original shooting apart from the re-photography of their photographs and paintings, it is coincident with the art exhibition that provided its materials and the occasion for its existence.[7] *Frida Kahlo & Tina Modotti* poses multiple interventions: into the discipline of art history, into the history of Mexican culture and politics, into a feminist perspective on both and finally into the rather debased (then, at least) terrain of museum-exhibition media. Its matter-of-factness about its facts is a bit of a ruse; this is a ground-breaking work that smuggles its discoveries and polemics into the world with the mildest of miens. Even its female voice-over is strategic.

The sparseness of *Frida Kahlo & Tina Modotti* is deceptive. By the time of the film's completion, Mulvey and Wollen had already been making films together for ten years, all visually stylised and formally conceptual. I'd guess their aim here was different: to create an alternative to institutional conventions for the quasi-genre of the 'museum film' which was inflexibly set in its ways and committed to didactic explanations, talking heads, stock footage to bring 'real life' into the frame and a generally dreary and predictable approach to art 'interpretation'. Museums and educational institutions loved nothing more, it seemed, than to offer up an expert droning on about the history of art writ large.

By avoiding the art institution's usual focus on the single triumphant genius, Mulvey and Wollen's film brings together these two women who started out in the same milieu but ended their lives, and their posthumous art-history status, in startlingly different positions. The combination of the two is one that allowed Mulvey and Wollen to explore their own theoretical interests, both Mulvey's interrogation of the gaze and psychoanalytic meanings and Wollen's early work on the relationship between artistic and political avant-gardes.

Neither Kahlo nor Modotti was taught in mainstream art history courses of that time, their work barely collected in museums. Art history was still a boys' game, though the 1970s had seen a ferment of organising around women's co-operative galleries and journals (*Heresies, Chrysalis*) that sought to change all that. Yet Mexico was still typecast as 'folkloric' and these two women if noticed at all were footnoted to the men in their lives: Modotti with Edward Weston, Kahlo with Diego Rivera. They both insisted in their different ways on reversing such a gaze. Modotti rejected her beginnings as actress, model, muse and moved off-screen, out of the studio entirely. Kahlo, injured and mutilated, sought the glamour and attention that Modotti discarded, but insisted on shaping its terms herself.

Mulvey and Wollen, then, staged a radical rethinking of categories in order to picture the life and work of both women, a reconceptualisation of each individual in her era, a reappraisal of inspiration. *Frida Kahlo & Tina Modotti* offers a case study in how to see differently, how to discern creativity, how to think across cultures and genders into the radicalism of these works of art. At times, they seem to have emulated the stereoscopic viewer, an apparatus that the two women might well have used, to insist on a dual figure within the frame – and history. But they simultaneously adopted another apparatus, the slide projector, which may be equally outmoded today but was ubiquitous in the classrooms of the 1960s–1990s, where its clicking linear progression of images in the dark shaped entire generations of art historians.

Frida Kahlo & Tina Modotti. The title signals both the film's material and its approach: a duality and binarism that does justice to each woman and each work. Its structure comprises chapter headings with an image and word pairing the two (which are used to sequence the sections) and a flashback that follows and which, like flashcards, repeats the images from the preceding sequence, this time faster, in reverse order and in silence, to sear them into the viewer's brain and allow an absorption free of direction. There is an overall pattern to the chapter headings as well as a series of loops that depart from and return to the mooring of those intermittent texts. The design of the film thus imposes an order on the lives and histories that might not otherwise be revealed, or, for that matter, might not exist at all.

Turning away from the toolbox of the educational film, Mulvey and Wollen turn to the archive as a particular model of inspiration. This is not the archive of twenty-first-century parlance. Paintings and photographs are simply shot, static, as if hung on the wall. Ah, the simplicity of life in the days prior to the Ken Burns swoop-and-dive, the simplicity of a time when the viewer might be expected to take the time to look. Each time, the work is accompanied by a pared-down text with essential information: Surrealism, international Constructivism, pre-World War II politics. Clearly Mulvey and Wollen intended the film to reach the same sophisticated audience that might be expected to attend a Frida Kahlo and Tina Modotti exhibition, and therefore did not need to adjust their lexicon for an imaginary general public.

Finally, the archival footage, so sparingly used, is quite remarkable. Today, when Tina Modotti remains all too forgotten, it is striking to see her on-screen in a fragment from a long-lost performance from her brief Hollywood heyday. *The Tiger's Coat* (credited as 1919 or 1920) is shot in black-and-white like her photographs; significantly, she's playing a Mexican woman, which she would become in a few years' time. There are also brief scenes in black-and-white captured in the earlier period of the Mexican Civil war, with soldiers massing, the people on the move – just as Tina herself would be on the move, a nomad, for most of the rest of her life. And her influence lived on beyond her; when she left Mexico, she sold her beloved Graphlex camera to her close friend, Lola Álvarez Bravo (Manuel's wife), who put it to good use.

For Frida Kahlo, Mulvey and Wollen managed to locate footage in full colour, like her paintings. These images, shot in early 16mm by the celebrity portrait photographer and Kahlo's decade-long lover Nickolas Muray, show Frida and Diego playing around in their patio.[8] Like any home movies shot by a friend, even more so in this case given that the cameraman was both a professional and so very involved with his subject(s), they are intimate and adorable, playful, not remotely the filters of suffering through which Kahlo has been viewed ever since. How wrong memory and history can be! Yes, of course she suffered, with multiple surgeries and a tumultuous marriage, but she was clearly magnetic and sensual, full of fun, charismatic and captivating, as this fragment so vividly testifies.

Frida Kahlo & Tina Modotti insists on the meaning and matter of their lives. In so doing, it enables the photographs of Modotti and the paintings of Kahlo to come alive and matter in new ways, acquire new meanings and remind today's viewer of the pain and joy of lost histories. Both Kahlo and Modotti died in their forties. Both had a complicated relationship with their own beauty and insisted on being more than a muse. Both kicked through the constraints of their times and gender and both paid a price. Here, for a moment, thanks to Mulvey and Wollen, they can be seen on their own terms through a film that has become, in effect, an archive of our time as well as theirs.

Afterword

On 17 August, 2021, on the 125th anniversary of the birth of Tina Modotti, a ceremony took place in front of 1952 Taylor Street in San Francisco's North Beach neighborhood.[9] Organized by the co-founders of the Tina Modotti Heritage Committee (Lynn Hershman-Leeson and myself), the dedication was the culmination of more than a decade of work to have this building recognized in the annals of the city's cultural history.

It was here that Modotti came in 1913, when she arrived in San Francisco from her native Udine and where she lived with her family for the next five years, as she evolved from immigrant seamstress into model, actress, radical leftist, and bohemian. The bronze plaque marking the presence there of Modotti is a signal embedded in cement, there on a sunny corner of the city she would later describe as her 'home town'. No longer the center of a thriving Italian socialist and communist community, the six-flat house now lies in an area where today's Chinatown meets the remnants of the Italian business district.

Along with this physical marker to which future pilgrimages can be made, the Committee's website will continue to provide information on Tina Modotti's life and legacy.[10]

Notes

1. Janet Kaplan, 'review of *Frida: A Biography of Frida Kahlo*, by Hayden Herrera and *Tina Modotti: A Fragile Life*, by Mildred Constantine', *Woman's Art Journal* 5(2) (Autumn 1984–Winter 1985), 45–47.

2. Shifra M. Goldman, 'Six Women Artists of Mexico', *Woman's Art Journal* 3(2) (Autumn 1982–Winter 1983), 1–9. In addition, both Gloria Orenstein (in *Woman's Art Journal*) and Hayden Herrera (in *Artforum* and *Heresies*) had already published articles to call attention to Frida Kahlo and her artwork in 1973, 1976 and 1977/1978 respectively. This surge of publishing was part of the feminist art project of the 1970s–1980s to unearth the buried work of women artists and make it available.

3. On this point, Mulvey and I have differing recollections. I was sure that this project originated with a pioneering exhibition of Kahlo's work at the Museum of Contemporary Art in Chicago in 1978 that I saw with them. Mulvey is equally certain that they never saw any such show. *Riddles of the Sphinx* premiered in London in 1977 and in France in 1979, so it is possible that their Chicago screening may have coincided with the MCA show – and equally possible that it did not.

4. According to a rumor so persistent that I even heard it repeated at a dinner party in 2019, Modotti may have been a KGB spy – though that is more likely true of her final partner, Vittorio Vidali.

5. For this and other details, see: Elena Poniatowska, *Tinisima*, trans. Katherine Silver (Albuquerque, NM: University of New Mexico Press, 2006).

6. *Frida Kahlo & Tina Modotti* debuted in the same year as Mexican director Paul Leduc's brilliant *Frida, naturaleza viva* (with Ofelia Medina as Frida), a production which also predated the Herrera book; the much later and better-known *Frida* by Julie Taymor (2002) credits Herrera's book as its source and starred Salma Hayek as Kahlo with Ashley Judd in a smaller role as Modotti.

7. Note that the film was funded by the Arts Council of Great Britain's fund for documentaries on art and artists, which at that time, by and large, commissioned films primarily in the museum/educational genre, a factor in its choice of style.

8. Nickolas Muray also shot the fairground and market scenes included in the film. Interestingly, he was a photographer and a Hungarian-born Jew – exactly like Kahlo's father – though he transformed himself into an American atheist. For more on Muray, see: Salomon Grimberg, *I Will Never Forget You: Frida Kahlo and Nickolas Muray* (San Francisco, CA: Chronicle Books, 2004/2006).

9. For more information on the dedication, see: Tony Bravo, "Tina Modotti, photographer who intersected with artists and revolutionaries, honored with plaque outside onetime S.F. home," *San Francisco Chronicle*, August 23, 2021, at https://datebook.sfchronicle.com/art-exhibits/tina-modotti-photographer-who-intersected-with-artists-and-revolutionaries-honored-with-plaque-outside-onetime-s-f-home

10. For detailed information on Tina Modotti, a video record of this ceremony (by filmmaker Emiko Omori) and documentation of two earlier events, see www.tinamodottihc.com. The book by Margaret Hooks *Tina Modotti: Photographer and Revolutionary* was a key resource; thanks to her widower Michael Tangeman for his support.

11

The Bad Sister

Laura Mulvey and Peter Wollen

1. Title Sequence

Black and white footage of waves; dissolve to shot of JANE; *dissolve to shot of a gun.*

Title: THE BAD SISTER

The footage of waves returns, coloured red.

Music.

2. Small square room. Interior.

Still image. A small square room, with dark velvet curtains.

> VOICE OVER (KATHY): Mystery adds spice to crime, it adds charm, it attracts our curiosity. We ward off the shock of death by setting out in quest of a second surprise, the perpetrator of death.

3. TV edit suite. Interior

Dissolve to the same image on a video monitor; the camera pulls back to take in the TV edit suite.

> VOICE OVER (KATHY): So this is the murder room. It has the right allure, private yet impersonal, hidden and yet public. This is the room of death.

PAUL, *the director, is at the control panel with* KATHY.

PAUL: This is the room where Ishbel Dalzell was killed. There was a fancy dress party going on. Somebody, it could have been a guest or an intruder, slashed at her neck and made an escape down the fire-ladder. This is Ishbel at the village school in Scotland.

As PAUL *and* KATHY *talk a series of photographs appear on the monitor successively:* ISHBEL DALZELL / ISHBEL *and* LOUISE DALZELL / ISHBEL / JANE / MICHAEL DALZELL / MICHAEL *and* ISHBEL / MICHAEL'*s house in Hampstead / his dead body / a school photograph with* ISHBEL *and* JANE / JANE *and her mother* MARY.

KATHY: In the border country?

PAUL: Yes, that's right. And here she is with her mother, Louise Dalzell, or Dee'll, as they say in the borders. Debutante now, soon after the family moved to London. This is Ishbel's half-sister Jane, the same age as Ishbel but illegitimate. Her mother was a servant in the Dalzell household. The good sister, the bad sister, figures that vanish in the mist. She disappeared off the face of the earth. But I've got new evidence about Jane, that's why I've asked you in today. I don't know how to handle it, it's too strange, too disconcerting.

KATHY: Too true?

PAUL: Yes, perhaps. Wait. And this is their father, Michael Dalzell. Drunk, lazy, wealthy, Tory, truculent, not without his tribulations though. He was murdered just a few days before his daughter. First Michael, then Ishbel. Now, this is the house in Hampstead where he was killed. He'd sold his Scottish estates to pay off his gambling debts. There was a knock on the front door. He went to answer it and the murderer attacked him, there on his own doorstep. He was left bleeding to death. Either it was an appalling coincidence or there must be a hidden motive.

KATHY: Did the two sisters know each other?

PAUL: Not well, but they were very conscious of each other, they were sent to the same village school. Now here look, two of them, the only picture I could find. But then Jane was disowned, she was rejected, the two sisters were separated. For a time, Jane lived with her mother in a cottage on the Dalzell estates up in Scotland, but then her mother fell in with a group of, um, they were called the wild women by the locals, a kind of women's commune. Eventually they were all evicted. It's not clear what happened to her mother afterwards, but I have a feeling that the eviction may be one of the clues to the murders.

KATHY: This is the Dalzell estate?

PAUL: Yes, that's right. Taken from the cottage. I went up to Scotland to interview a family friend, Luke Saighton.

On the monitor, PAUL's *interview.*

> PAUL: (*on monitor*) Did you see what happened?
>
> LUKE: (*on monitor*) Indeed, yes. A posse of gamekeepers came up the valley to the cottage, armed with sticks, and two of them had guns. The women had disappeared. You can imagine that Michael was very disturbed, but he refused point blank to bring in the police. Well, eventually, we found two of them, stuck in a snow drift, in a deep cleuch, down near the loch. I remember Jane wouldn't even speak to Michael or look at him. She was bundled off in shawls onto the truck, shaking with cold or fear or anger. Michael was like a man demented. He was determined to find the mother. But he never did.
>
> PAUL: Now I managed to get this Super 8 film of the Dalzell family. Home movies, taken when she was about 12. The proud father and the pretty daughter, in a Scottish landscape. It's hard to see the connection between this simple family scene and the maze of passions that creates a murder.

Super 8 film: ISHBEL *on a pony while her father applauds.*

> KATHY: But you think you've found it?
>
> PAUL: Yes, but I'm not sure how to handle it. That's why I need you to help me finish the program.
>
> KATHY: What is this new material you've found?
>
> PAUL: It's a tape of Jane's diary. Jane kept a journal on tape. It's fascinating, it's like a message written in code.

Photograph of MEG *appears on the monitor.*

> PAUL: (*continued*) Ah, yes. There's one more crucial character. Meg. She's the woman Jane was with when her mother was evicted. I put an ad in the papers, trying to trace Jane's life between the eviction and the murders, and I got a reply from a friend of Jane's, a clergyman, Stephen Palling.

Uncut footage of an interview with STEPHEN PALLING *plays on the monitor.*

> STEPHEN: (*on monitor*) A most peculiar set-up. A big house in Notting Hill lived in exclusively by women. I gathered they'd come from Scotland where they'd all had some kind of commune from which they were evicted.
>
> PAUL: (*on monitor*) And did she introduce you to a woman called Meg?
>
> STEPHEN: (*on monitor*) Oh, you know about Meg? Jane was especially close to her. The whole atmosphere revolved around Meg. Frightening. A tremendous wall of control. And then of course, Jane left the commune, got a job, found herself a flat…

PAUL: (*on monitor*) What kind of job?

STEPHEN: (*on monitor*) She started as a reporter and then in the last couple of years, before the relapse she had, she worked for a magazine as a film critic. She settled down at last with a boyfriend, or so I thought. He also worked in films, writing scripts. How wrong I was. Of course, there's no direct evidence. It's all circumstantial, like a distorted… she was in a trance… I wonder whether she wasn't under some sort of spell – possession or hypnosis. She could have stabbed her father or killed her sister without knowing anything about it. God knows what powers Meg had transmitted.

STEPHEN *picks up a tape, holds it for a moment, and passes it to* PAUL.

PAUL: (*on monitor*) Are you honestly saying that you think this tape shows that Jane was responsible for the killings?

STEPHEN: (*on monitor*) I don't know if you could call her responsible. She seemed to be living in a perpetual state of sanctioned irresponsibility. She was looking for a spiritual centre, I suppose. She found it in Meg. Poor Jane! You see, Meg was a kind of embezzlement. An enravishment. You must keep that in mind when you listen to the tape. I warn you, it… it bears the marks of something supernatural, of something evil. I hesitate to use those words, but I'm sure that they will come to your mind too.

The footage stops.

KATHY: Jane's diary? You really believe it tells the truth about the Dalzell mystery?

PAUL: Yes, that's why I need your help.

Paul gets up and plays JANE*'s tape.*

JANE: (*on tape*) I have to tell you of the night I first went on my travels. The night, most of all, that Meg gave me further signs of her power. I was at the Berridge's party, trying to find Tony…

4. Party. Interior.

JANE *moves through the crowd, asking people whether they have seen* TONY. *One mentions* MIRANDA. *Jane opens a door to another room.* TONY *is sitting on a sofa, engrossed in conversation with* MIRANDA. *They seem very close.* MIRANDA *is reminiscent of* ISHBEL, *dark-haired, slender and stylish.* JANE, *distraught, leaves the party.*

Music; party sounds.

5. Street. Exterior.

A taxi arrives with guests and JANE *leaps in. Taxi drives off.*

6. Jane's Flat. Interior.

JANE *enters, switching on the lights. She goes into the bedroom, sits down and takes off her shoes. The desk light illuminates her typewriter, papers, notebooks etc.* JANE *abruptly picks up a pair of scissors. Music begins. She hacks at her hair: bits of hair fall onto the floor and bits stick up on her head in spikes.*

7. Bedroom. Interior.

The bedroom is reflected in a large mirror; JANE *(in reflection) sees a pair of jeans and a denim jacket that have appeared on the bed.*

Music: continues, flowing more lightly and freely.

JANE *appears in the mirror wearing the blue jeans and jacket; she continues cutting her hair. The mirror image dissolves to show* JANE *as she was: long hair and party dress. She sees herself watching* TONY *and* MIRANDA *and then sees* TONY *and* MIRANDA *sitting, intimately, on a sofa. This image is obscured by a close-up of* STEPHEN *who, in turn, is obscured by a close-up of* MEG.

> JANE: Meg!

JANE *turns away and, as she leaves the flat, she finds a gun in her jacket pocket.*

8. Chelsea streets. Exterior.

JANE *walks down the street, passing a shop with a display of dolls under cellophane. The light becomes stranger and more lurid.*

9. Waterfront with dockside bars. A liner with a gangplank. Exterior.

JANE *steps out into the quay of a port.* JANE *approaches a bar; a fluorescent outline of a shark hangs above the door. Street sounds are replaced by distant piano music.*

10. Dockside bar. Interior.

The bar looks like the one in To Have and Have Not: *a long bar, a piano playing '40s Kansas City music. People are dancing; the men are mainly sailors. Camera tracks with* JANE *as she approaches a couple who are dancing together. The woman is reminiscent of* JANE's *previous image but her face can't be seen.* JANE *fires the gun at the woman's back. Music stops. Everyone freezes. After a pause, the music begins and everyone continues dancing, apart from the couple who remain motionless.*

11. Waterfront. Exterior.

JANE *walks towards a large liner; a sailor bars her way onto the gangplank.* JANE *dances, ending with a back flip; superimposed film of the sea sparkling at night envelops her body.*

Music: piano continues.

Dissolve to:

12. Jane's Flat. Bedroom. Interior.

Painting of the sea at night on JANE's *bedside table. The camera pans slowly, in medium close-up, to reveal* JANE, *lying in bed with* TONY. *The piano music persists, as though from a vivid dream, fading away, as* JANE *moves* TONY's *hand.*

JANE: Do you want some coffee?

13. Bathroom. Interior.

JANE *is looking at her tufts of hair in the mirror and brushing her teeth.*

TONY: (*off-screen*) What the hell did you do to your hair?
JANE: I don't know. I just did it. Last night.
TONY: (*off-screen*) Obviously. It wasn't like that at the party, thank God. I'm making scrambled eggs. Well, do you want scrambled eggs or not?

14. Kitchen. Interior.

JANE *enters the kitchen;* TONY *is cooking*

JANE: Have you by any chance seen a pair of jeans, anywhere?
TONY: Yes, they're in the wash box.
JANE: Why? They didn't have blood on them or anything did they?

TONY: Look, could you butter that toast? Blood? Oh… No. They had a strange smell. Like burnt matches. Look, can you…

JANE *sits at the table; the camera moves back as* TONY *serves the eggs. He begins to eat. She stands up suddenly.*

JANE: I've got a press show this morning. I have to go.

TONY: What do they have to show it on Sunday morning for?

JANE: Schroeders always show them on Sunday morning. Don't you remember? You came to one once.

TONY: So what, no lunch then? Look, I'll do the meat. I'm only juggling around with the script today anyway.

JANE: It's just that I don't want any lunch. You don't mind, do you?

TONY: No, of course not. Oh, did I tell you, it looks as if Isabelle Adjani might be Iris Storm?

JANE: That is great news for the script. It's great! I'd better go.

TONY *does not reply.* JANE *leaves.* TONY *puts down his knife and fork, staring at her uneaten eggs. He looks downcast, as though irritated and puzzled by the tensions in their relationship.*

15. Lobby of The Renoir Cinema, Brunswick Centre. Interior.

JANE *is standing in the cinema lobby, talking to a fellow critic, another critic joins them. As* JANE *turns away she sees a figure resembling* MIRANDA, *apparently an apparition. The ambient sound is broken by a brief clang of music (this theme will accompany all the subsequent appearances of this figure).*

16. Film on screen (black and white). Interior.

The title from the film King Blank *(Michael Oblowitz, 1982) appears on screen, followed by black and white cityscapes and the film's sound-track. As* JANE *watches, the screen image is replaced by the fast-flowing water of a little stream, which gradually becomes colourised.*

17. Jane's childhood memory. Exterior.

JANE *(about nine years old in her memory) is playing by the stream; she has been collecting snails.*

MARY: *(off-screen)* Jane! Come on in, you're getting wet! *(Louder)* Jane! Hurry up!

The camera follows JANE *as she run up the hillside towards a stone bridge.*

Music: melodic, slightly nostalgic.

18. Cottage in Scotland. Exterior.

The cottage is set on a hillside, without a garden or path. JANE*'s mother (*MARY*) appears at the cottage door.*

MARY: Jane!

Camera pans quite rapidly to the right. JANE *is standing at the bridge, blocking the advance of an approaching Land Rover. It pulls up.* LUKE SAIGHTON, MICHAEL, LOUISE *and* ISHBEL DALZELL *get out.*

19. Road with Jeep. Exterior.

There is an exchange of looks between MICHAEL *and* JANE. ISHBEL *is staring up the hill straight towards* JANE. JANE *uses a catapult to fire a stone at* ISHBEL, *hitting her in the face.* ISHBEL *holds one hand to her bleeding cheek. Exchange of looks.* LOUISE *steps forward to* ISHBEL *and dabs at her cheek with a handkerchief.* MICHAEL *stands by their side.* MARY *comes skidding out of the house towards* ISHBEL, *as if trying to intervene.* LOUISE *walks towards her and crosses her arms.* MARY *clutches her head in both her hands, grasping the roots of her hair and tugging at it.*

Music: more menacing, fading into the background as the confrontation builds.

20. Jane's hiding place. Exterior.

JANE *runs through the bracken, along the stream, until she gets to her small, roughly made, hiding place; from a box, containing a few childish 'treasures', she takes out and tears up a photo of* ISHBEL.

Music: the melodic theme from the beginning of the scene returns.

The image is drained of colour and fades back to the black and white film in the cinema. THE END *appears on screen.*

21. Cinema. Interior.

JANE *gets up to go. A cut to the* MIRANDA *apparition who is looking directly at* JANE.

Music: the brief clang from scene 15 recurs.

22. Cinema lobby. Interior.

JANE *runs up the stairs, past three critics standing under a poster for Fritz Lang's* Dr. Mabuse, the Gambler *(1922), who stare after her.*

23. Street outside cinema. Exterior.

As JANE *runs along a street, she sees the apparition of* MIRANDA *three times. Each time, she turns and walks in the opposite direction. As* JANE *begins to run again through the now dark streets, three small girls stop to stare at her.*

Music: unsettling, reflecting JANE*'s disquiet.*

24. Jane's flat. Interior.

JANE *enters flat.*

Music: 'So Young' (Robert Gordon) comes from the sitting room.

25. Sitting room. Interior.

JANE *enters the sitting room and looks out the window; a train is crossing the bridge over the river. Kathryn Bigelow and Monty Montgomery's* The Loveless *(1981) plays on the television. 'So Young' continues on the soundtrack.*

> TONY: Hey, come on. Long day?
> JANE: Yes, very.

Cut to a scene from The Loveless.

> TONY: Can you check the meat in the oven? I just want to watch this through to the end... It would be nice if you could make some onion sauce too.

26. Kitchen. Interior.

JANE *enters the kitchen and looks out the window. Under the street lamp opposite is the* MIRANDA *apparition who followed* JANE *earlier; accompanied again by the brief clang of music, as in scenes 15 and 21.* TONY *comes in and runs his fingers through her still spiky hair. The camera then follows* TONY *and* JANE*'s movements, in a sequence shot, as they put supper at the table and sit down to eat.*

TONY: Still looking funny.

JANE: What happened to the pot plants on the window sill?

TONY: Oh, I threw them out. They were looking dead.

JANE: You threw them out?

TONY: Well, not literally, you idiot. I mean, what do you think I do when you're not there? Drop plant pots on innocent passers-by? So, we decided not to bother with the onion sauce then. So, how was the movie? Any good?

JANE *puts the last dishes, etc., down;* TONY *helps himself to meat.*

JANE: Not bad. I thought it was very well cast.

TONY: Must be lonely being a critic. You know, not part of an audience. Well, not part of a real audience.

JANE: You know it's time men were prepared to be more psychic. Then we could have really interesting conversations.

TONY: Sorry, I'm sure.

JANE: I mean, why wasn't James Joyce a woman? Molly Bloom was.

TONY: Shall we catch some of the South Bank Show and then I'll make coffee.

TONY *gets up and leaves without waiting for* JANE's *reply.*

JANE: Don't bother, I'll do it. I don't really want to see the South Bank Show.

When TONY *has gone out,* JANE *opens the drawer of the kitchen table and rummages around. She finds something and pulls it out to look. It's a photograph of* MIRANDA. JANE *pours herself a drink.*

27. Sitting room. Interior.

JANE *enters the sitting room and silently shows* TONY *the photograph. He is slightly taken aback and also irritated at being distracted from the programme he is watching. Music from the television plays in the background.*

TONY: Jane... Well I don't know how it got there.

JANE: But it's her, isn't it?

TONY *sighs.*

JANE: She's outside now. Waiting for a message or something. You never stopped seeing her, did you?

TONY: What on earth are you talking about?

JANE: Outside under the lamp. I recognized her at once.

TONY: There can't be anybody out there. And even if there is, it's not going to be her. Would she stand around outside like that? Is it likely?

They leave to go out to the kitchen and check.

28. Kitchen window.

TONY *leans out of the window and peers in both directions down a totally empty street.*

29. Bedroom. Interior.

TONY *is making love to* JANE. *She looks impassive and detached.* MIRANDA's *face, aroused and responsive, is superimposed over* JANE's. *Dissolve to:*

30. Bedroom. Interior.

TONY *is still asleep. The photograph of* MIRANDA *is lying on the bedside table. It is a bit bigger than before. The face is composed and innocuous. Cut to:* JANE, *wearing a red dressing gown, sitting in the foetal position in the corner of the room.*

> VOICE OVER (JANE): As I sat hating the girl in the photo, I wanted to expel her, to throw her from my body. She, my shadow, is the definition of that vague thing, womanhood. Men like her because she is so finite. She never dreams, there is no static around her head – this is reserved only for me, only for the other sister, and in the terrible competitiveness, it's a battle she always wins.

31. Street to countryside. Exterior.

JANE *walks along a city street that gradually mutates into a field of grass, with Scottish hills in the background. She is wearing a black dress: mid-calf length, poor material, the hem loose and black gum boots.*

Music: reflecting JANE's *unsettled mood; continues across the following scene.*

32. Tennis court. Exterior.

As JANE *climbs over a gate, her skirt rides up. Four men are playing tennis on a court below her, inside the enclosing garden wall. One of them stops playing to point at her, laughing loudly and the others join in.* JANE *runs on, along the outside of the garden wall; on the other side is a mansion. She reaches a small green door and runs through breathlessly.*

33. Ornamental garden. Exterior.

Wide shot of a garden with small box hedges arranged in a formal pattern around a pillar. MR ALDRIDGE, *the owner of the property, is cutting roses with pair of secateurs. (He is played by the same actor who plays* MICHAEL DALZELL*).* JANE *tries to run past him unnoticed.* MARIE *appears in the background; she is dressed in the same kind of clothes as* JANE. *(She is played by the same actress who plays* MARY*).*

Music: fades slightly for the dialogue.

> MR ALDRIDGE: Jane! What are you doing there, Jane?
> JANE: I was looking for Marie, sir.
> MR ALDRIDGE: And why should Marie be in the garden, I wonder?
> JANE: She was taking a cool drink to the orchard, sir. To the young lady, sir.

MR ALDRIDGE *looks down at* JANE *with complete contempt. Deliberately he leans down with the secateurs and nips her ear. Cut to* MARIE, *who screams.*

> MR ALDRIDGE: Get off the path! You disobedient slut! Off the path, or you'll have your wages docked.

JANE *and* MARIE *run away.*

> MR ALDRIDGE: Disobedient slatterns!

34. Garden wall with door. Exterior.

JANE *and* MARIE *run across a lawn, past a large decorative urn and through a door in the wall.*

35. Staircase. Interior.

Shot of a spiral staircase from above. MARIE *and* JANE *run through the door and up the stairs. They pause to kiss.*

Music: the melody from JANE*'s childhood returns and continues across the following scene.*

36. Servant's room. Interior.

The room is empty except for a table with a water-jug and two narrow iron bedsteads. MARIE *and* JANE *lie down together on one of the beds, kissing and embracing. Dissolve to:*

37. Jane's flat. Bathroom. Interior.

JANE *is stuffing the jeans and denim jacket into the wash box. She is looking in the glass and hears sounds of* TONY *getting up.*

> TONY: (*off-screen*) Jane! Jane? I've put the kettle on.

38. Bedroom. Interior.

JANE *is back in bed, with the covers pulled protectively around her.* TONY *brings her a cup of tea and sits down close to her.*

> TONY: Well, I really must be going. I'm being met. Just a few days' rewrites. But with any luck they won't use me and I'll be straight back.
> JANE: Are you going with her or are you coming straight back to her? Did you magic her photograph away while I was in the bathroom?
> TONY: Honestly, Jane, I don't know what you're talking about. What photo? Oh that. It was in the kitchen drawer. I never denied it. I don't know anything more about it.
> JANE: Oh it doesn't matter. I've got my review to write. That's what I should be thinking about. Then I think I'll go and see Stephen.
> TONY: What a good idea! You haven't seen him for ages. Well, I really must be off. Jane, come on! Give us a kiss then? (TONY *leans in and kisses* JANE.) And I hope your hair grows.

He goes out. JANE, *apart from her jealous outburst, has been cold and unresponsive throughout the scene. She picks up a notebook, then moves to work at her desk.*

39. Stephen's house in Hackney. Exterior.

JANE *walks to* STEPHEN's *house.* STEPHEN *greets* JANE *and ushers her in.*

40. Stephen's sitting room. Interior.

Although the room has been redecorated, the furniture is old. There are a lot of books and objects in the room.

> STEPHEN: Have you been seeing that evil woman again?
> JANE: Why do you ask?
> STEPHEN: Why else would you come to see me?

STEPHEN *and* JANE *are sitting with tea and cake.*

JANE: Yes, I have been seeing Meg again. I saw her the other night… Stephen, it's all very strange and I don't know how to explain. She has sent me on travels. Don't ask me to give it up.

STEPHEN: Why should I ask you to give it up? Go on, have some cake. Honestly, I'm not going to dismiss it. I've tried often enough myself, you know, to get somewhere, anywhere, that would put me closer to the ultimate mysteries. Just one glimpse, and I'd be faithful for the rest of my life. As so many other doubters have said.

JANE: This has nothing to do with God.

STEPHEN: Come on, you're not going to tell me that you've succumbed to some sort of idea about Black Magic and the Age of Aquarius. A liberated woman in league with the Devil. Come on!

JANE: My clothes stink of sulphur when I get back.

STEPHEN: You mean you are possessed?

JANE: Stephen, I don't think it's anything to do with religion. It's a different kind of experience. I think it's to do with control, with the way people can exert power over others. Meg can control my life and thoughts. She can take me to a different world. And I think… I think it's because she knows what happened to my mother. She has that knowledge, she knows I need… it's like… it's like an invisible movement beneath the surface. It draws me irresistibly. It's the adventure I've always wanted.

STEPHEN: And what are you supposed to give her in return?

JANE: In return?

STEPHEN: For your travels.

JANE: Nothing, as far as I know.

STEPHEN: Are you still upset about that girlfriend of Tony's?

JANE: No, I hardly ever think of her any more. That's all past now. Tony doesn't see her any more, I don't think. Stephen, what is the meaning of the sea? Why is it always connected with death?

STEPHEN: And madness. Is that where you're sent to on your travels, to the sea?

JANE: You think I'm mad don't you?

STEPHEN: I don't. But I don't think you have any idea what's happening to you. I don't think you realise the dangers. You don't think about what Meg can exact from you. You just think about the attraction.

JANE: You mean she's going to ask for my soul. A contract signed in blood. Well, she's welcome to it, as far as I'm concerned.

STEPHEN: Jane! That's a terrible thing to say.

JANE: I should be going. Thank you for the tea, it was nice.

STEPHEN: But you know it wasn't.

JANE: I'm sorry. I'll see you again soon. I'll be better then.

JANE *gets up.* STEPHEN *goes to a box in the corner of the room and rummages around. He pulls out a crucifix and presents it to* JANE.

STEPHEN: Wait a minute. Let me put this round your neck. If… If you're unsure of things, frightened… why not use it?

STEPHEN *puts a crucifix around* JANE's *neck.*

JANE: Thank you, Stephen. You're very sweet.

JANE *kisses him on the cheek and leaves.*

41. Front door steps to Stephen's house. Exterior.

JANE *begins to sway; the camera picks up her movement, reflecting her disorientation, both exterior and interior. The image of* JANE's *face blurs, losing focus.*

Music: a single, dominating, but unstable, note.

42. Blue metal forest. Exterior.

JANE *walks through trees seemingly made out of a shiny blue metal. The light of the sky, visible every now and again through a vista, is red.* JANE *walks towards a clearing, with a pool in the centre of it; the light falls in patterns.*

Music: shimmering and spirited, reflecting JANE's *departure into a strange world; continues across the following scene.*

43. Reflection in Pool. Exterior.

JANE *sees herself in the pool in negative (with all the colour values altered). On the other side of the bank is a woman who looks like* MEG. JANE *looks at her. The woman disappears.* JANE *leaves the forest, as if to try and find her. The colour returns to normal.*

Music: continues and then fades.

44. Meg's room. Interior.

MEG *and* JANE *are sitting on a sofa.*

JANE: I have to go back, Meg. Back to the waterfront. I want to sail on the ship. Why can't I, Meg?

MEG: Of course. You shall go there again. Soon, I promise you, soon.

MEG *reaches out and takes* JANE's *hand.* JANE *visibly relaxes, sinking back into the cushion, her fears slipping away.*

MEG: (*continued*)…That's better. Poor Jane! What you've been through. My poor Jane! Day and night. Oh yes, I know. You've got to get rid of her, Jane! Your shadow. Your Bad Sister. It's what your mother wanted. It was her last wish.

JANE: Where is she, Meg? Did she sail on the ship?

MEG: You can only find out if you get rid of your bad sister, Jane. It will set you free. You can travel further than anywhere I've shown you. Vengeance. Without it, the pain can never be assuaged. The bound foot, the burning pyre, the Pharaoh's knife and the stake through the womb. I will give you the power. Look at me.

MEG *leans over to* JANE *and bites at her neck. Two trickles of blood appear. Montage of images of* ISHBEL *and* MIRANDA; *a brief clang of music.*

MEG: You will do what must be done and destroy what must be destroyed.

JANE: Yes, yes I will.

JANE *looks possessed. Dissolve to:*

45. Jane's flat. Interior.

JANE *lets herself into her flat. She has a haunted look on her face.*

JANE: Tony? Back already?

46. Sitting room. Interior.

MRS MARTEN, TONY's *mother, is sitting on the sofa. She is smoking, waving her cigarette in one hand, while with the other she holding a white compact.*

MRS MARTEN: Jane! How delightful to see you! I do hope you don't mind my using my latchkey unannounced, but there was just the slightest chance that Tony might be back already. Of course, he isn't. Do sit down, or are you just rushing in and rushing out? I quite understand if you are. You must be so busy with all your writing and reviewing. You know, there's a "do" on at the embassy tonight, Jane. You really must come! It'll do you the world of good. Jane, dear, would it be too awful to ask for a G and T?

JANE *pours the drink and hands it to* MRS MARTEN.

> MRS MARTEN: Mmm! How heavenly! Then I simply must have a bath. I do hope my dress hasn't gone too crumply! Well, Jane, dear, tell me all your news. Busy seeing films all the time? I really don't know how you do it! I find they've become so dreary recently.
>
> JANE: Yes, I've seen quite a few recently. Nothing I could recommend to you though, I don't think.

JANE *picks up a newspaper and looks intently at it. The telephone rings and* MRS MARTEN *answers.* JANE *puts down paper.*

> MRS MARTEN: (*to telephone*) No, no he's not... I really don't know... not yet anyway... Yes, I imagine... Look Miranda, why not wait... no, not for a day or two now... yes, yes, I quite agree. But this is the trouble... Yes dear, well why don't you come? No but I'll tell them and I know they'll be thrilled. It's the Belgian Embassy at eight... lovely dear. Goodbye.
>
> JANE: Who was that?
>
> MRS MARTEN: Oh Jane, darling, I don't think you know her.
>
> JANE: Was it a friend of Tony's?
>
> MRS MARTEN: Well, you know, it never occurred to me that she was, but I suppose she must know him. As a matter of fact, I think she's in the film world too. She said something about the film.
>
> JANE: The film?
>
> MRS MARTEN: Yes, now what was it? She said... Yes, she said that they were going to ask Meryl Streep to be the heroine of the picture. Isn't that rather exciting? Such a wonderful actress, don't you think? I don't know how she knew, of course.
>
> JANE: Meryl Streep as Iris Storm. Sounds interesting. Look, I'm expecting a friend any minute now. Her husband has just died. It's all been very tragic. I'm sure you'll understand if I ask you to leave, you can't possibly stay under the circumstances because we have to be alone.
>
> MRS MARTEN: Jane, how dreadful. Are you sure you can cope? You know, you're looking a little unwell. And I couldn't help noticing when your scarf slipped... you seem to have hurt your neck. Is there anything poor old Mother can do?
>
> JANE: I'm sorry. It's simply the situation. I'm afraid there won't be time to change, or to have a bath. She'll be here any minute now, and she needs every care. Now please go and pack! I will call a cab.
>
> MRS MARTEN: You aren't well Jane, I fear.

47. Street outside Jane's flat. Exterior.

MRS MARTEN *emerges from the front door with a suitcase and a ball dress in polythene bag. She gets into the cab which draws away. Overhead shot.*

48. Sitting room. Interior.

JANE *stands at the window, looking out over the river. Music plays. She pours herself a drink looking slightly exultantly around the room. She notices an address book on the floor and sits down to examine it. The book is completely full of names and numbers: some on the lines provided, others written sideways from top to bottom, others squeezed in the space between the lines, some even with the name separated from the number.* JANE *looks at the page for 'M'. For a moment we read 'MOTHER', 'MURDER', 'MEG' and 'MIRANDA'.* JANE *dials* MIRANDA's *number. Music fades.*

JANE: Hello, is that Miranda?

MIRANDA: (*on telephone*) Yes.

JANE: This is Jane.

MIRANDA: (*on telephone*) What do you want?

JANE: Oh, I thought you were going out this evening with Mrs Marten. You didn't?

MIRANDA: (*on telephone*) Sorry. I'm not sure which Jane you are.

JANE: With Tony's mother. I'm sorry. I must have got the wrong Miranda.

MIRANDA: (*on telephone*) Yes, I am going actually. Later. I think I'd better ring off.

JANE: No, Miranda! I just phoned to ask you to go to a party.

MIRANDA: (*on telephone*) A party?

JANE: Yes, I thought you'd enjoy it. And it seems a bit ridiculous that we can't ever meet... as if Tony was standing between us like the sword of Damocles. It's a party the day after tomorrow.

MIRANDA: (*on telephone*) Where is it?

JANE: Fourteen Sloane Crescent. It's all one house, one bell. Any time after eight.

MIRANDA: (*on telephone*) I might be able to come. Well thank you Jane for asking me.

JANE: Alright, goodbye. I hope to see you there then.

MIRANDA: (*on telephone*) Right. Bye.

JANE *puts back the receiver and stays stretched on the floor, pensive. Music. The camera pans up to the window and the view of the railway bridge. Dissolve to:*

49. The Dalzell house. Scotland. Interior.

A large Christmas tree, covered with fairy-lights. MICHAEL DALZELL, *wearing a kilt, dominates the scene;* ISHBEL *is at his side.* LOUISE *is sitting at a table with gift-wrapped presents on it.* MICHAEL *claps his hands to get attention the attention of a group of children who are sitting in a semi-circle on the floor.* JANE *is one of the group.*

> MICHAEL: I shan't make a long speech or even tell any jokes, because I know they'll fall flat. We're all much too eager to get on to the main attraction of the day. We are delighted to have you all here again with us this Christmas. It's always a great pleasure for us to see so many of you gathered on this seasonal occasion. As usual, there will be organised games after tea and I must remind you again that upstairs is absolutely out-of-bounds. Hmm. Now I'm going to put on the lights so we can all enjoy the tree. (*He gestures to have the lights switched on.*) While we're doing that, I'm going to call out your names, alphabetically, and you can collect your present from Mrs Dalzell…
> MICHAEL *calls out the names and* LOUISE *gives each child a gift. She shakes each child's hand and says 'Merry Christmas'. A series of close-ups shows the children unwrapping their presents.*
> MICHAEL: (*embarrassed at* JANE*'s namelessness*) There appears to be only one left… Jane.

JANE *collects her present but* LOUISE *doesn't shake her hand or say 'Merry Christmas'.* ISHBEL *takes* JANE*'s hand; they leave the room.*

50. The Dalzell house. Interior.

ISHBEL *and* JANE *creep through the house.* ISHBEL *leads the way with a torch; they find a cupboard and shut themselves in.*

Music: the melodic theme from JANE*'s childhood returns and continues into the following scene.*

51. Cupboard in bedroom. Full of women's clothes. Interior.

ISHBEL *and* JANE *are huddled together in the cupboard, with long gowns and ghostly dresses hanging round them, lit by a single shaft of light. They are playing a game with their hands, smiling at each other. The cupboard door is opened abruptly by* MICHAEL *and* LOUISE DALZELL. *A crashing noise.*

Music: tone and rhythm change as the children are discovered.

LOUISE: Children!

MICHAEL: Come on out! At once!

LOUISE: What are you doing?

JANE *picks up a long hatpin and suddenly stabs, panic-stricken, first* ISHBEL, *whom she wounds slightly, then* LOUISE; JANE *runs pell-mell through the room and out of the door.* LOUISE *turns to* ISHBEL; MICHAEL, *furious, pursues* JANE.

52. Hillside. Exterior.

JANE *runs across the stone bridge towards the hillside cottage.*

Music: fades away.

53. Jane and Tony's bedroom. Interior.

JANE *is lying in bed. She looks drawn and her face is in shadow.*

> TONY: (*off-screen*) Jane, it's me, I'm back. Let me in please.

TONY *begins rattling the doorknob and banging on the door.*

> TONY: (*off-screen*) Jane! What on earth have you done to the door? Why is it bolted? Jane! I want to see you, for God's sake open it!

JANE *jumps out of bed and releases the door. She bounds back into bed pulling the covers round her protectively.* TONY *enters the room. An overhead shot shows* TONY *sitting on the edge of the bed while* JANE *lies rigid and hunched under the covers. In spite of patches of light, her face is in shadow.*

> JANE: How did it all go today?
> TONY: Well, it all went rather badly. Turns out Isabelle Adjani won't be available after all. But Jane, I've heard some worrying reports from Mummy. Were you? Did you really have to be so rude? Wait! It's just that you might have been a little more polite.

JANE *reacts. She pushes* TONY*'s hand away from her and stands up on the bed, staring down at him.*

> JANE: I don't like the way she sees Miranda and asks her to parties and expects me not to mind.
> TONY: Miranda?

JANE: Oh, she's welcome to Miranda as long as she doesn't go phoning her up while she's landed here on me. You can understand that, Tony?

TONY: Why do you drag Miranda into it? I've said Miranda means nothing more to me... to her, I mean... than someone she knows and likes, a friend, a protégée... really Jane.

JANE: Please ask her to leave the flat!

At the same moment, MRS MARTEN *enters.* TONY *stands up and* JANE *sinks back down onto the bed again.*

MRS MARTEN: Well Jane dear, how are we this morning? Oh, Tony, don't you think... Jane looks so pale, I do think you ought to have a holiday Jane dear. Tony, take Jane away somewhere for some air!

TONY: If only I could get this film settled.

MRS MARTEN: I do think you should have more relaxation, Jane dear. I'm so glad you're going to that lovely party tomorrow at Miles Alton's house. I adore fancy dress parties!

JANE: Who said it was fancy dress?

MRS MARTEN: Oh... I... I don't know. I just assumed it was. Why? Didn't you know? Haven't you got an outfit?

TONY: What is this party anyway? Look, do you mind, Mummy, I want to have a bath and get dressed and so on.

MRS MARTEN: Oh dear, I'm so sorry and tactless.

The instant she has gone, TONY *climbs on to the bed and tries to kiss* JANE. *She shrinks back and turns her head away, avoiding* TONY'*s embrace.*

TONY: Have you got the curse today?

Fade to: TONY *making love to* JANE. *She is distant and disturbed, as though in another world.*

54. Street. Exterior.

TONY, MRS MARTEN *and* JANE *are walking down the street.* JANE *is wrapped in a black jacket and begins to lag behind.*

MRS MARTEN: (*To Jane*) Oh, do hurry Jane dear! (*To Tony*) Normally it's vitamins and salads for me, but today I feel ravenous!

JANE *begins to laugh.* MRS MARTEN *looks back at her and whispers to* TONY.

55. Italian restaurant. Interior.

Mrs Marten listens to TONY; JANE *watches her intently.*

> TONY: It all depends on whether she's free, and whether this project comes to anything. See... It's shooting in the Pacific so she won't be available for reshoots unless we can cram ours in first.

MRS MARTEN *turns away from* TONY *to look fixedly across the restaurant.* JANE *turns, following her gaze. The camera pans across the restaurant in the same direction.*

> TONY: (*off-screen*) There aren't any penalty clauses so the insurance is going to cost millions. That's what worries the backers.

MEG *is sitting at a table, alone, looking at* JANE. MRS MARTEN *puts on her glasses and peers at* MEG.

> MRS MARTEN: Don't I know that woman? An old Scottish family, I believe.

JANE *turns to stare at* MRS MARTEN; MEG*'s face is superimposed on* MRS MARTEN*'s.*

Music: haunting; continues over the following scenes.

JANE *turns to look back at* MEG *whose image gradually dissolves.* JANE *drops a spoon.*

> MRS MARTEN: What's the matter, Jane?
> TONY: Oh, she isn't herself today. Perhaps we'd better get the bill now. Leave it!

The veal-in-Marsala arrives. JANE *gets up and rushes out of the restaurant, so unexpectedly that she has gone before* TONY *is on his feet.*

56. Street in Hackney. Exterior.

JANE *rushes down the street.*

56. Stephen's sitting room. Interior.

JANE *and* STEPHEN *are in the same positions as her previous visit. She is sitting bolt upright, but silent. He has his head between his hands.*

57. Three-way junction. Exterior.

Threatening grey cloud formations (special effect). Overhead shot. JANE *runs into the junction; she hesitates before taking the left-hand fork.*

58. Staircase. Interior.

Overhead shot of spiral staircase. (Same as 35.) JANE *and* MARIE *are walking up the stairs.*

59. Servant's room. Interior.

JANE *and* MARIE *arrive breathlessly in their room (Same as 36.). On each of the beds there is a note pinned to the pillow.*

Music fades and changes to a single piercing tone.

>MARIE: (*reading from the note*) I am deducting £2 from each of your wages to pay for repairing the iron one of you broke this morning.

MARIE *throws the pillow across the room.* JANE *and* MARIE *face each other, looking into each other's eyes.* JANE *fetches a hammer from the drawer.*

60. Aldridge house in London. Exterior.

JANE *and* MARIE *at the front door; they knock.* JANE *is holding a hammer and a length of lead piping and* MARIE *is holding a pair of scissors. The camera travels up the front of the house;* MIRANDA *is looking out of a second-floor window. The front door opens and* MR ALDRIDGE *appears, arms folded, towering above* JANE *and* MARIE.

Music: clanging and eerie.

>MR ALDRIDGE: You're to be evicted. You must be off the property before daybreak.

JANE *and* MARIE *attack him with their weapons. Music changes.*

MR ALDRIDGE *falls to his knees and crawls, groaning, covered in blood, into the house.* JANE *hits him again with the lead pipe; he falls to the ground, and lies motionless.* JANE *and* MARIE *leave together, dropping their weapons.*

61. Servant's room. Interior.

JANE *and* MARIE *covered in blood. A group of men (the tennis players) run into the room. They wrench the two women apart and drag* MARIE *off.* JANE *and* MARIE *cry out...* JANE *lies face down in bed, sobbing.*

Music: the melodic theme returns briefly; then disrupted by the tennis players.

Dissolve to:

62. Jane's flat. Bedroom. Interior.

JANE *is lying face down in bed. Sound of sobbing continues briefly.*

> MRS MARTEN: (*off-screen, through the door*) Jane! Jane my dear! I do think you should have some coffee. And what do you think of the outfit?

JANE *gradually and with difficulty rouses herself, and gets out of bed. She sees an acrobat's costume hanging on the back of the door, the jeans and jacket are there too.* JANE *opens the door with great violence and finds herself face-to-face with* MRS MARTEN.

> JANE: What's that costume doing in my room? And where did you find the jeans?

MRS MARTEN *walks backwards towards the kitchen followed by* JANE.

Music: starts as the door opens and continues through the scene.

> MRS MARTEN: Tony assured me they weren't his. The acrobat's costume used to belong to my poor dear sister. I just felt you might like to wear it, you see! She used to be quite successful as a trapeze artist, you know – but then she started to have dizzy spells, poor thing. I thought I'd told you all this before but sometimes you know one... One's too upset to talk about these things... she died. Mummy and I were...
> JANE: I'm sorry to hear that. I didn't realise... What happened? Did she fall into the ring?
> MRS MARTEN: Oh no, nothing like that. Misfortune often strikes the young and gifted, I fear. So Jane, will you? Just to please me a little. Oh dear, I'm being too awful when you haven't even had your coffee. Look, I've... I've got it ready for you!

63. Kitchen. Interior.

> MRS MARTEN: (*continued*) You know, I'm really rather thrilled to have been invited to this do! I spoke to Miranda this morning and she said she'd been invited too. She says she knows the film director very well... It's extraordinary how many people Miranda knows, don't you think, Jane?

JANE *reaches down and picks up a large knife which is on the table.*

> MRS MARTEN: (*completely unflustered*) Jane, I know you're not thinking of cutting bread with that knife, but if you are I've moved it over near the door. I felt a little tidying up would do the whole place a world of good. That's when I found that rather unappealing pair of jeans and jacket. Jane! I told Tony you're not well. I think we should call the doctor!

JANE *faints. The image whites out. Dissolve to:*

64. Bedroom. Interior.

JANE *is lying in bed. The light on her face is very bright and intense.*

Music: gradually fading, giving way to the dialogue.

> JANE: Where's Tony? What time is it?
>
> STEPHEN: (*off-screen*) It's six. Tony will be back in a minute.

On the bedside table are flowers. STEPHEN *is sitting on a low chair at the bedside, waiting for* JANE *to wake, which she does.*

> JANE: What happened to me? Stephen what are you doing here? Am I very ill?
>
> STEPHEN: Mrs Marten phoned me. She said you needed looking after. She's been worried for some time. She's been very concerned.
>
> JANE: I don't understand.

TONY *and* MRS MARTEN *come in.*

> TONY: (*to* MRS MARTEN) Yes, I agree we should get the doctor as long as we can get him to come quickly…

MRS MARTEN *nods in agreement.*

> STEPHEN: I can stay with Jane and wait for the doctor, if you like?
>
> MRS MARTEN: Oh, I don't think it would be right for the family to leave Jane. Luckily, I prepared a rather delicious meal.
>
> TONY: Oh, what is it?
>
> MRS MARTEN: Why, lobster with aioli, of course! Don't you remember when we went to Avignon and you ate so much of it you were nearly sick?
>
> TONY: Ah, delicious!
>
> MRS MARTEN: Would you like to come into the kitchen, Stephen, and see the little feast I've prepared?
>
> STEPHEN: I'd rather stay with Jane, if you don't mind.
>
> MRS MARTEN: Ah yes, of course you would. Well, I'll go and ring the doctor now, Tony dear. And then we'll eat.
>
> TONY: Don't struggle to stay alert, Jane. Go to sleep. I'm sure that's best. I'll wake you when the doctor comes.

Cut to: a DOCTOR *just straightening up from bending over* JANE. *He is holding a syringe.*

STEPHEN: Really, I think she needs spiritual solace. This isn't a chemical problem, you know.

DOCTOR: It's nervous exhaustion. Symptom of shock. She needs plenty of warmth and plenty of rest. I'm leaving a prescription for some tablets.

TONY *comes into the room.*

TONY: Supper's ready. You'll stay for supper won't you, doctor? Stephen, I'm sure you can leave Jane alone for a moment. She needs to be left alone, doesn't she, doctor? We can put some in the fridge, she can have it when she recovers.

STEPHEN *and the* DOCTOR *turn and troop out of the room after* TONY. JANE *disappears under the covers.*

65. Bedroom. Interior.

Slow dissolve to: JANE *wakes up and sees the circus costume.*

Music: soft and shimmering, continues over the following scenes.

66. Corridor outside the kitchen. Interior.

JANE, *wearing the circus costume, is very pale and looks into the kitchen from the doorway. The others are all much too busy contemplating eating to notice her.*

MRS MARTEN: Try and find some good knives and forks, Tony dear, if such a thing exists in poor Jane's kitchen.

JANE *puts on her dark jacket.*

STEPHEN: (*off-screen*) Well, I must say, if it tastes half as good as it looks.

TONY: (*off-screen*) Who's going to attack it first? Stephen? It is one of Mother's specialities.

Jane walks down the corridor.

Music: increases in volume, becoming lighter and freer.

67. Sitting room window. View of river from interior.

Lights from boats and a train that crosses the bridge.

Music: softer with Jane's voice-over.

VOICE OVER (JANE): As I stood there looking out across the river, I knew that I had to complete my mission. I must go to the party to find my bad sister. I would keep my promise to Meg and like the river I would finally reach the sea. I could see into the future.

68. Fourteen Sloane Crescent. Miles Alton's house. Exterior.

JANE *arrives at the party and is let in by a* DOORMAN.

Music: fades and gives way to party sounds.

69. Miles Alton's house. Interior.

There is a lot of space with an imposing stairway leading up to the first floor. There are no guests to be seen, though there is party chatter on the soundtrack. JANE *places her coat on a rocking horse, inspects the hall warily, and walks up the stairs.*

Music: returns and continues across the following scenes.

70. Room at the party. Interior.

JANE *enters the room. A* WAITER *is serving glasses of champagne and she takes one. As* JANE *looks round, she is suddenly horrified. Camera pans left. There is* MRS MARTEN *in her Pierrot costume;* STEPHEN *in ecclesiastical robes;* TONY *is not wearing fancy dress, except for an incongruous Mexican charro hat.* MRS MARTEN *spots* JANE.

MRS MARTEN: Look!

JANE *heads off in the opposite direction, seeking a way out.*

71. Plum silk lined wall. Interior.

JANE *sees a hair-line crack in the silk, marking the outline of a very small door that she pushes open and stoops low to get through. Crouching on the other side,* JANE *looks back to see* MRS MARTEN*'s blue and red costumed legs approaching, closely followed by* STEPHEN*'s episcopal purple.* JANE *closes the small door.*

72. Small square room (as in scene 2). Interior.

JANE *is in a small square room, with dark velvet curtains, two tapestry chairs and a mirror above a fireplace.* MIRANDA *is standing in front of the mirror, wearing a Spanish costume, all grey, with a low bodice and a comb in her hair.*

Music: the theme from the credits returns.

JANE *stands right behind* MIRANDA'S *shoulder.* MIRANDA *doesn't turn and* JANE *has no reflection in the mirror.* JANE *steps forward, places her hands on* MIRANDA'S *shoulders and sinks her teeth into her neck.*

MIRANDA *slumps down to the floor.* JANE *walks across to the velvet curtains, looks back at* MIRANDA, *and steps out onto the parapet.*

73. Parapet with iron fire escape stairs. Exterior.

JANE *clambers down the iron stairs.*

Music: becomes lighter and freer.

74. Street at bottom of fire escape. Exterior.

In the street, MEG *is waiting for* JANE *in an old and elegant touring car.*

> MEG: Jane!

JANE *is now wearing the pair of blue jeans and denim jacket. She gets into the car alongside* MEG, *and they start off. At the street corner,* STEPHEN *runs out to try and stop them.* MEG *drives past him.*

75. Car: Meg and Jane. Exterior.

MEG *is concentrating on driving, but begins to speak to* JANE, *who listens intently, an exalted look in her eyes. Lights flash across their faces and the window behind.*

Music: gradually building as dialogue develops.

> MEG: Now you've lost her Jane. You've lost your wicked sister. You've made the sacrifice. Your eyes are bright. Lightning. Your eyes are pulling me into them. I'm in your brain. I'm in your dreams. Together. We swim through each other. Trees shoot through our bodies and our leaves shine at our fingertips. I resemble you in every detail. Each moon of my fingernails. Each hair of my head. Each pore of my skin. It is time to leave harbour. We are going home at last to our own country. Do you know this land? Do you see it yet? Do you taste its fruit?
> JANE: Yes.

76. Waterfront. Exterior.

The car drives on to the quay and pulls over. JANE *and* MEG *walk across the quay to the liner. There are no sailors and the cafés are in darkness.* JANE *sees the body of the young woman she shot in the bar, lying face down on the ground.* JANE *turns the body over; it is her old self.*

77. Gangplank to liner. Exterior.

JANE *and* MEG *step onto the gangplank and then on to the deck of the liner.*

78. Deck of a ship at sea. Exterior.

JANE *is standing at the rail, looking out to sea, scanning the horizon. Night-time.*

Music: light and free flowing.

79. TV edit suite. Interior.

Close-up of JANE's *tape.* PAUL, *the TV director, stops the tape and addresses* KATHY.

> PAUL: Well, what do you think?
> KATHY: It's like a mirage.
> PAUL: (*speaking to microphone*) Paul to VT.
> VT: (*from speaker*) Hello Paul.
> PAUL: Did that tape arrive from Scotland?
> VT: (*from speaker*) Yes it did.
> PAUL: Right, let's see it.

Cuts to the tape playing on the monitor.

> PRESENTER: (*on monitor*) Not much is left now of the Ettrick Forest where the Black Douglas rode and the outlaw heroes of the Border Ballads fought and plundered. What does remain, once part of the vast Dalzell family estates, now Government property, has been leased to a Texan company in search of oil. All work ceased last week when the men on the site downed tools after reports of eerie happenings and ghostly noises. I spoke to Mr Elliott of Tibbie Shiels who was here when the disturbances occurred and believes they may be of supernatural origin.
> MR ELLIOTT: (*on monitor*) Strange noises and cold gusts of air blowing when there was no wind. When the first tree was felled there was wailing all through the wood.

PRESENTER: (*on monitor*) Where exactly did this take place?

MR ELLIOTT: (*on monitor*) In the clearing by the burn in the old patch of forest. By the ring of sycamores. They say in the village the clearing has been haunted, many years.

PRESENTER: (*on monitor*) Since when?

MR ELLIOTT: (*on monitor*) Since the day the last laird drove out the last of the wild women. She was there among the sycamores, with the look of a walking corpse, in the wind and the snow, wailing out her heart. She was never seen again by human eye.

Cut back to the TV edits suite.

KATHY: Michael Dalzell pursues his cast-off mistress and his illegitimate daughter through the snow. Jane is separated from her mother, then ten years later there's a double murder – Michael and Ishbel Dalzell – and the other daughter, Jane, vanishes in her turn. There must be a link.

PAUL: I'd better get up there straight away. (*To microphone.*) Hello, reception?

RECEPTIONIST: (*from speaker*) Yes?

PAUL: I'd like the number of a Mr Elliott, in Tibbie Shiels. That's T for Tommy, near Peebles, Scotland, alright?

RECEPTIONIST: OK.

80. Lowlands of Scotland. Hillside. Exterior.

PAUL *and* MR ELLIOT *walking through a forest with shovels.*

81. Ring of silver birches. Exterior.

PAUL *and* MR ELLIOT *are standing in a clearing.* PAUL *notices an ash-staff, turns it, and pulls it out of the ground.* PAUL *and* MR ELLIOT *begin digging.*

Music: ominous, clanging chords.

82. Excavation. Exterior.

As they dig, PAUL *finally feels something other than earth beneath the blade. He stops and reveals the remains of a woman, wearing the same clothes we saw* MARY *wearing earlier and with the same locket round her neck. The body has somehow been unnaturally well-preserved. It is clearly* MARY.

Close-up of MARY'*s face.*

MR ELLIOTT: It's her, it's the last of the wild women.

PAUL: It's Jane's mother, she's been avenged.

83. Deck of a ship at sea. Exterior.

JANE *is standing at the rail, looking out to sea, scanning the horizon. Same shot as before but now at dawn.*

Music: the melodic theme from JANE*'s childhood returns.*

Music: fades as the scene fades to black.

84. Credits.

Music plays throughout.

Based on the novel by Emma Tennant

Jane – Dawn Archibald
Mrs. Marten – Isabel Dean
Tony – Kevin McNally
Meg – Matyelock Gibbs
Michael Dalzell / Mr. Aldridge – Hugh Millais
Stephen – Neil Cunningham
Paul – Clive Merrison
Mary / Marie – Marty Cruickshank
Kathy – Libba Davies
Miranda – Emma Jacobs
Luke – Bill Denniston
Louise Dalzell – Maeve Watt
Mr Elliott – Ian Stewart
Interviewer – A.S. Ross
Doctor – Allan Mitchell
Jane (as a girl) – Annilee Kuukka
Ishbel (as a girl) – Harriet Laidlaw

Casting Director – Susie Figgis
Art Director – Hildegard Bechtler
Costume Designer – Carla Willsher
Make-up – Gordon Kay

Hairdresser – Paula Gillespie
Wardrobe Assistant – Linda Cooper
Glass Paintings – Marguerite Nix
Stills – Johanna Tranberg
Production Buyer – Maureen Roche
Property Master – Harry Bearpark
Prop Van Transport – Bill Richardson
Art Director's Assistant – Jocelyn James
Production Manager – Andrew Barratt
Production Assistant – Laura Jullian
Location Manager – Paul Barratt
Continuity – Phyllis Townshend
Production Accountant – Tony Coroon
2nd Assistant Director – Monica Hyde
Unit Runner – Simon McNair Scott
Lighting by Samuelson Lighting Ltd.
Gaffer – Andy Hebden
Electrician – Dave Moore
Camera Assistant – Anne Cottringer
Camera Grip – Olly Hoeben
Sound Mixer – Peter Glossop
Boom Operator – Steve O'Brien
Dubbing Mixer – Peter Maxwell
Vision Engineer – Neil Wilson
Editors – Bob Gow, Andy Kemp

Assistant Director – Deborah Kingsland
Associate Producer – Peter Jaques

The Producers would like to thank: Monty Montgomery and Pioneer Films Corporation for permission to use the extract from 'The Loveless' and Michael Oblowitz and Meta Films Inc for permission to use the extract from 'King Blank'

The National Film Development Fund
Produced in association with Modelmark Limited
Made on location in London and Scotland
Director of Photography – Diane Tammes

Director of Visual Effects – A.J. Mitchell
Music Composed and Performed by Karl Jenkins and Mike Ratledge
Produced by Nigel Stafford-Clark
Written and Directed by Laura Mulvey and Peter Wollen

A Moving Picture Company Production for Channel Four
© Channel Four 1983

12

Timeshifting: *The Bad Sister*

Sukhdev Sandhu

ver since it was made, *The Bad Sister* (1983) has been more invoked than seen. In truth, it's barely been invoked. It's the least known of Laura Mulvey and Peter Wollen's collaborative films, to this day unreleased on VHS or DVD, producing almost nothing in the way of a paper trail that might offer some insights into what it's about or if it's any good and, if it isn't, why that might be. It seems somehow inevitable that it was the only one of the pair's collaborations not to be included in the otherwise comprehensive US retrospective of their collaborative and independent films staged in November 2016.[1] What accounts for this ongoing silence? What horrors might the film depict or be guilty of?

To begin to answer these questions (or, more accurately, to offer some speculations in response to them), it's worth turning to the journals of Michael Kustow. A former director of London's Institute of Contemporary Arts (ICA) and later an associate director at the National Theatre, in the early 1980s he was hired as a commissioning editor of arts programmes at Channel 4. In the preface to *One In Four* (1987), his jumpy and pleasingly kvetchy record of the period, he writes, 'One of the new breed of words which television has generated is "timeshift". It describes the act of taping a programme on a video recorder and playing it back after its transmission time. But timeshift is also a good way of describing the dislocation and lack of landmarks anyone coming to work in television feels at first and never quite loses.'[2]

'Timeshift' is a resonant word in many ways. And so is Kustow's elaboration of it. *The Bad Sister* represented, for good or for bad, Mulvey and Wollen's own dislocation, their migration from outside to inside, from the free zones of experimental cinema to the more respectable and certainly more regulated terrain of state television. That dislocation was taking place at a time when Margaret Thatcher's Conservative Party had embarked upon its project of cultural rezoning and imaginative terraforming, of challenging the ideological and economic norms that had underpinned the postwar consensus in Britain.

The dislocation Kustow talks about wasn't just artistic or political; it was technological – and manifested itself in where and how moving images were being seen. On British television, a growing number of programmes were shot not on film, but on video. British households were increasingly likely to have multiple TV sets, as well as video recorders, which meant individual programmes could be unshackled from the schedules and watched or rewatched at any time viewers wished. Television then was becoming freer, more diffuse, more spatially complex.

Was this liberation or was this a loss? Was the golden age of television – with its iconic (and possibly bogus) image of the whole family perched around a living-room set – on the wane? These developments in what is nowadays called 'medium specificity', around the extended timeframes for audiences to engage with what appeared on 'the box', in the cultural and political climate from which *The Bad Sister* emerged and into which it secreted itself – all of them mesh and merge with the film's own themes of doubling, haunting and repression to help produce a work that is both time-shifted and timeshifting.

The Bad Sister has its origins in a 1978 novel of the same name by Emma Tennant (1937–2017), a writer preoccupied by 'gothic fantasies, postmodern fairytales, prequels, sequels and literary doubles', but who has yet to receive proper critical appraisal.[3] Living in London's Notting Hill, home to many bohemians and counter-culturalists, she founded the literary magazine *Bananas* and edited it from 1975 to 1979. It was influenced, she claimed, by 'Borges and Marquez and *The Master and Margarita*'[4], and featured work by experimental and awkward-squad writers such as Sara Maitland, Heathcote Williams, James Kirku, Michael Moorcock and Angela Carter. Wollen and Mulvey were not only friends; Wollen published various texts in the magazine, including his short story *Friendship's Death* (1976).

Tennant's first novel had been published pseudonymously. She often reworked already published books. One of her novels, from 1989, was entitled *Two Women of London: The Strange Case of Ms Jekyll and Mrs Hyde*; another was *Pemberley: or Pride and Prejudice Continued* from 1993. *The Bad Sister* is a remix of James Hogg's *The Private Memoirs and Confessions of a Justified Sinner* (1824), a much-celebrated fiction set in the late seventeenth and early eighteenth centuries and taking place in ancient Scotland. It's the story of two boys, George and Robert, born to Rabina Orde, the young wife of the rambunctious Laird of Dalcastle. George is sportive and popular; Robert, who may or may not have been fathered by Rabina's spiritual advisor Reverend Wringhim, is pious and prone to stalking and threatening his older brother. In the end, George is killed and Robert disappears.

Tennant herself came from a landed and Scottish background. Her father was Christopher, 2nd Baron Glenconner, while her half-brother Colin went on to become owner of the island of Mustique in the Caribbean. She split her childhood between Regent's Park in London and the baronial manor in Glen. In *The Bad Sister*, which is set across these two locations, she replaces the male characters from Hogg's novel with female characters; now the central mystery concerns Jane Wild, the illegitimate daughter of a wealthy Scottish landowner, who appears to have killed not only her father but, under the influence of a mysterious commune leader named Meg, her legitimate and aristocratic sister Ishbel.

Hogg's novel is split in two – an 'editor's narrative' which tells, in boisterous and rather impersonal fashion, the core story, and a partly handwritten document, the 'Private Memoirs' of the title, in which Robert (or someone purporting to be him) recounts his troubled life – all its changes and vicissitudes, anger and exultation, sorrow and vengeance. In Tennant's version, the narrator is a journalist who, while aware that 'murder by middle class female urban guerillas is ever on the increase in the West', suspects that something more opaque and troubling is afoot. His inquiry is supplemented by a poem titled *Insomnia* by Marina Tsvetaeva (its closing lines, apt in the context of the book, are: 'Liberate me from the bonds of day,/my friends, understand: I'm nothing but your dream.'[5]) and 'The Journal of Jane Wild', a diary whose humid potency is evident in passages such as this description of Sunday lunch: 'You could see the woman fingering bleeding meat on the Friday, frowning over the joints as if the secret of their future happiness lay in the grain of the flesh. Yorkshire puffing solidified relationships too, producing a drowsiness after the meal, a soft acceptance of everything.'[6]

The Bad Sister, like most of Tennant's novels, didn't rack up huge sales; it was, however, warmly received (not least by writers who were friends or whom she had published). Harold Pinter described it as 'a work of great force: mysterious and frightening.'[7] Alison Lurie deemed it 'an original and fascinating tale about a young woman literally haunted by her denied feminist self.' Angela Carter characterised it thus: 'Blood-streaked, dazzling darkness, in which Madame Dracula meets the Anti-Christ … a stunner.' Most enthusiastic was J.G. Ballard: 'a visionary tour de force that describes in the most moving and convincing way the strange world of the schizophrenic, of madness, poetry and dream', he wrote. 'One of those few novels that will change your view of your own mind.'

It's not hard to see why Mulvey and Wollen saw filmic potential in *The Bad Sister*. Published at the tail end of a decade in which feminist activism, literature, art and theory had made significant interventions in thought and culture, it's a story about a young woman's quest for freedom – from patriarchy, domesticity, possibly even heterosexuality. For Wollen, speaking in an interview with Wanda Bershen, '*The Bad Sister* goes back to the same kind of psychoanalytic material as *Riddles*, in that it's about the place of the woman within the Oedipal structure. *Riddles* was about the mother and the mother's point of view; *The Bad Sister* is about the daughter and the daughter's point of view.'[8] This film thus extended Mulvey and Wollen's poetic engagement with psychoanalysis, which was underpinned by feminist theory and politics, and connected it with an interest in fairy tale, lost cultures of witchcraft and women's stories.

While there are theoretical and conceptual parallels between *The Bad Sister* and Mulvey and Wollen's previous work, it was the first of their films to be shot on video, a medium which had been attracting a growing number of British artists over the course of the 1970s, and was often heralded as an antidote to the monopolistic staidness of broadcast television. For Sean Cubitt and Stephen Partridge, video was able 'to bridge the vanguardism of the underground and its longer-term commitment – through such innovations as the underground press, the free schools movement and DIY music culture – to the development of grassroots radicalism beyond the traditional trade union movement and Labour Party.'[9] Video lent itself to the other-worldly textures and psychological interzones the directors were aiming for.

The Bad Sister also represented a move from the intimate, experimental circles that had helped gestate Mulvey and Wollen's previous collaborations into the intriguing newfoundland of Channel 4 and its state-sponsored avant-gardism. Mulvey has written about this migration in terms of cultural loss, a symptom of the waning resources available for radical (film) production, an acknowledgement that under Thatcher fewer artists would be able to flourish outside the mainstream. (And that mainstream, as far as British cinema in the early 1980s was concerned, was pretty feeble.)

It could be argued that Channel 4's establishment in 1982 was a victory for experimental cinema, an acknowledgment of its scruffy energy, its engagement with questions of gender and identity, its social groundedness. Wollen, alongside Marc Karlin and other members of the Independent Film-Makers' Association (IFA), campaigned vigorously to ensure the channel would, as part of its remit, be required 'to provide a distinctive service; to innovate in form and content; to deal with interests and groups not served by commercial television, or perhaps any television; to draw programmes from a wider range of production sources than those which constituted the existing industry.'[10] However, it would be a mistake to uncritically celebrate Channel 4 as an antidote to Thatcherism. As Kustow pointed out, 'free marketeers and deregulators praise Channel 4 for being unbureaucratic and cost-conscious, for creating an independent production sector, for undermining the vested interests, restrictive practices and featherbedding of a duopolistic industry'.[11] Inevitably, as more and more programmes were made by independent companies, it became common to hear calls for public broadcasting to be defunded.

The Bad Sister was greenlighted by David Rose, the widely admired BBC producer who had nurtured dramatists such as Alan Bleasdale, Alan Plater and David Rudkin, and who had moved to Channel 4 to set up the Film On Four strand that commissioned key British films of the 1980s such as Peter Greenaway's *The Draughtsman's Contract* (1982), Richard Eyre's *The Ploughman's Lunch* (1983) and Stephen Frears's *My Beautiful Laundrette* (1985). It was by some distance the most expensive film Mulvey and Wollen had ever made; according to historian John Pym, it cost £418,000, of which Channel 4 contributed £318,000.[12] (Other films in the series – including *The Draughtsman's Contract* and Chris Bernard's *Letter To Brezhnev* (1985) – cost less.)

The Bad Sister's sole screening – on 23 June 1983 – attracted an audience of 2,341,000.[13] If that was a relatively small number by television standards (it should be pointed out that Channel 4 had only started broadcasting in November 1982; its offerings weren't even accessible to all of the UK until the end of the following year), it was off the scale by the standards of experimental film. 'By some measure greater than for all our previous films put together', Mulvey says today.[14]

According to Wollen, his campaign to shift the film's screening time to mid-evening informed the final work: 'One section [of the Channel 4 schedule] was designed especially for independent filmmakers, on Monday at 11pm. But Laura and I decided to go for a more central section, the film and drama slot on Thursday at 9:30 p.m. That was obviously a political decision, to go for a more central area rather than a more marginal one which has been allotted to you as a result of your voice being heard. That meant we would necessarily be involved with narrative and drama in some way.'[15] It also meant there would be two breaks for advertisements. This concession was required, in order to take the ideas formed in a feminist context in the 1970s to a television audience.

Watching *The Bad Sister* today is a strange experience. This is partly because it mostly circulates as a digital file (seemingly transferred from VHS tape) that presents it without ads, has micro-punctures that eat into its sound design, and is denuded of some of its vivid coloration. The film's exploration of alienation, its breaking away from the grip of genres (such as crime thriller) and visual styles (such as social realism), its chafing at the conventions of experimental film and television drama alike – all of these are harder to get a handle on when seen outside of its original broadcasting flow. Something is gained but much is lost when, like much radical filmmaking of the 1970s and 1980s, *The Bad Sister* finds refuge in the contemporary art gallery or curated online platform.

Some changes are noticeable in Mulvey and Wollen's adaptation. The editor who presents Jane's diary in Tennant's novel becomes a TV reporter. More consequentially, at the end of the book, a body is discovered in a Scottish forest clearing; described as having 'something completely hermaphroditic about it',[16] it is that of Jane and has a stake plunged through it. The film version also ends with a body being found – that of Jane's mother. This latter point is crucial for, as Wollen told an interviewer, 'We didn't want it to be a tragic story … We envisaged it as more of a direct, bodily line of inheritance (which probably relates back to a more feminist, post-Lacanian theory), about the passage from mother to daughter through the woman's body rather than through patriarchal inheritance, which is an abstract inheritance of property rather than, in this case, a physical inheritance of power.'[17]

At least as striking though is how muted the film's video effects are. A vivid exception is the scene following a conversation between Jane and her pastor friend who counsels her to be careful about spending time with 'wild woman' Meg. He gives her a cross to hang around her neck, but as soon as she leaves his room she starts to get confused. The camera shakes. Jane seems to be having a seizure or undergoing some kind of spiritual abduction. She steps from urban to rural, the greyscale present to the violet, colour-saturated seeming-past. As she moves through fields and woods, the mood is redolent of folk horror: Mike Ratledge (responsible for the *Riddles of the Sphinx* soundtrack (1977)) and Karl Jenkins's increasingly dynamic synth score that echoes the compositions of John Carpenter, a doomy lake straight out of a 1970s public safety film for children, in its waters a reflection of a silent old woman that carries trace memories of Nic Roeg's *Don't Look Now* (1973).

There was a profusion of this kind of formal experimentation and feminist engagement with psychoanalytic concepts in *Penthesilea: Queen of the Amazons* (1974) and *Riddles of the Sphinx*. It's in shorter supply here. Resonant motifs appear – a steep stairwell straight out of Hitchcock's *Vertigo* (1958), Jane dressed up as an acrobat – and then disappear. There are splashes of symbolism – Jane enters a maze only to be stopped by Mr. Aldridge/Michael Dalzell, who scolds her before snipping her ear with secateurs – but they're offset by many indoor scenes which are clammy and claustrophobic. That may be the desired effect, but they also induce a listlessness in the viewer. Similarly, while it was clearly a deliberate decision to create characters who preclude identification or immediate connection, they still end up as hologrammic presences, wan and dislocated.

So much is going on in *The Bad Sister* that it becomes hard to assimilate or navigate in one viewing. The physical similarities between the female characters – Meg, Jane's mother and sometimes even Jane herself – are accentuated so that it can be hard to tell them apart. This is surely intentional and designed to heighten the atmosphere of instability and characters doubling/dissolving. Yet, alongside so many scenes that are dreamy, flashbacks or fantastical, it strips the film of grit and gravity. There's too much mutation and mutability, not quite enough friction or resistance.

The Bad Sister is at its least effective when it resembles mainstream television. The tense interactions between Jane and her boyfriend are hard to distinguish from soap-opera fare. Mrs Martin, the thoughtlessly imperious mother of Jane's boyfriend, is a two-dimensional matriarch of the sort familiar from Sunday-evening sitcoms. Where *The Bad Sister* excels though, and where it makes its case for being reassessed and properly recirculated, is when it forgoes realism and realist tropes and, instead, incorporates long takes (such as Jane, near a photo image of Louise Brooks (!), peering inscrutably into a mirror while chopping off her feminine hair). Or when, somewhere between a cruising noctivagant and an apprentice vampire, she drifts through the city in the witching hours, alighting on tenuous, dreamscaped tableaux. Or when she becomes an escapologist, slipping out of patriarchy's grasp, unchaining herself from the ground beneath her feet, and becomes a kind of Pirate Jenny about to sail aboard a huge ship – away from London and into liquid, oceanic femininity. Here is an alluring *Sprechgesang* of feminist psychogeography and psychoanalysis-enhanced TV modernism. Here is the fecund ambiguity that Mulvey and Wollen had found in Tennant's novel and which they prized as an example of what literary theorist Tzvetan Todorov had called 'the fantastic'.

The film's critical reception was scanty. Jean Fisher, writing in *Artforum*, argued that 'While there is much in the film to inspire a healthy critique of theoretical psychoanalysis, it is at times too elliptical, at times self-consciously didactic.'[18] Film On Four historian John Pym, in his brief synopsis, later noted that one scene featured Jane taking down 'a copy of Peter Wollen's *Signs and Meaning in the Cinema* (1969/1972): a word to the wise, perhaps, that *The Bad Sister* itself should be read as an additional chapter in some future edition of that book.'[19] It's significant though that Jeremy Isaacs, chief executive of Channel 4 between 1981 and 1987, highlighted the film in *Storm Over 4: A Personal Account* (1989): 'Shot on video, it exploited electronic effects to lend a disorienting, hallucinatory quality to Emma Tennant's tale of witchcraft and wild women.'[20]

The minimal response to *The Bad Sister* bothered both directors. Unusually for a Film on Four title it was never repeated. 'The fact that it has come and gone on one Thursday evening I found really frustrating', admitted Wollen. 'With a film, you can take it round and show it and have a relationship with the audience which is quite different.'[21] For Mulvey, speaking recently, 'It wasn't an experience I wanted to go through again. It was too big. Peter and I both felt that we'd found the process of collaboration easy before; but this was a much more difficult collaboration. There was more of a division of labour, a larger crew, more expectations put on the direction. There were fewer long takes now.'[22]

From today's perspective though, it's the instability and ambition of *The Bad Sister* that makes it so fascinating. It is restless, displaced, a forced marriage of vanguardism and accommodationism, a stab at diversity and escaping the bubble of Co-op-policed experimentalism, caught between eras, too centripetal for the 1970s, too centrifugal for the 1980s, its own kind of filmic juggling. Flawed but simultaneously contagious, it's also a product of an almost-lost and certainly unrepeatable period of public television, as well as a tantalising glimpse of how Mulvey and Wollen's work might have evolved going forward. To watch it, as is the case with so many of their films, involves looking forward as much as looking back.

Notes

1. *Laura Mulvey and Peter Wollen: Beyond The Scorched Earth of Counter-Cinema*, curated by Oliver Fuke and staged by the Colloquium for Unpopular Culture, New York University, 11–14 November 2016.
2. Michael Kustow, *One in Four: A Year in the Life of a Channel Four Commissioning Editor* (London: Chatto & Windus, 1987), 16.
3. Frances Wilson, 'Obituary: Emma Tennant', *The Guardian*, 31 January 2017.
4. *Ibid.*
5. Emma Tennant, *The Bad Sister* (New York: Coward, McCann & Geoghegan, 1978), 46.
6. *Ibid.*, 66.
7. This and other quotes in this paragraph are taken from dust jacket of the US edition of *The Bad Sister*.
8. Peter Wollen, 'Scenes of the Crime', interview by Wanda Bershen, *Afterimage* 12(7) (February 1985), 12.
9. Sean Cubitt and Stephen Partridge, 'Introduction', in *Rewind: British Artists' Video in the 1970s & 1980s*, eds Sean Cubitt and Stephen Partridge (New Barnet: John Libbey, 2012), 5.
10. Kustow, *One in Four*, 10. Mulvey was involved in the early stages of the IFA. However, unlike Wollen, she was not involved in this campaign.
11. *Ibid.*, 52. 'Duopolistic', in this context, means a UK broadcasting landscape populated solely by the BBC and by ITV.
12. John Pym, *Film On Four 1982/1991: A Survey* (London: BFI Publishing, 1992), 118.
13. *Ibid.*, 29
14. Phone conversation with Mulvey, 31 January 2020.
15. Peter Wollen, 'Wollen on Sex, Narrative and the Thrill', interview by Al Razutis and Tony Reif, *Opsis* 1 (Spring 1984), 40.

16. Tennant, *The Bad Sister*, 220.

17. Wollen, 'Wollen on Sex, Narrative and the Thrill', 35.

18. Jean Fisher, '*The Bad Sister*', *Artforum* 22(6) (February 1984), 82.

19. John Pym, *Film on Four*, 23–24.

20. Jeremy Isaacs, *Storm Over 4: A Personal Account* (London: Weidenfeld and Nicolson, 1989), 148–149.

21. Wollen, 'Wollen on Sex, Narrative and the Thrill', 35.

22. Phone interview with Mulvey, 31 January 2020.

Section 2

Peter Wollen's *Friendship's Death*

13

Friendship's Death (fiction)

Peter Wollen

Although I am not the only person to have met Friendship, I am, as far as I know, the only one who was able to talk to him at any length. The story is a strange one and perhaps many will not believe it. I can only affirm that it did happen. I have one document, produced by Friendship's hand, the text of which I reproduce here. In itself, it will not convince the sceptical, but for me, at any rate, it is an invaluable aid to memory, the only trace left of an astonishing being.

In the late summer of 1970, I was in the Middle East covering the situation in Jordan for an American radical news monthly. This was the time when the Palestinians controlled a large part of the country, especially the urban areas, including most of the centre of the capital city, Amman. There was constant, but sporadic, fighting going on between the Palestinians and the Jordanian Army. The most publicised engagements were those around the Intercontinental Hotel in Amman, where the great majority of the foreign press corps were based. I, however, because I wanted to understand something of the Palestinian side of things, had chosen to stay in a more humble hotel in downtown Amman, in the Palestinian-controlled area.

The atmosphere was very strange. The Jordanians controlled the tops of the hills, on the sides of which and in the valleys between which Amman is built. They also controlled the outskirts of the city. From time to time, there would be an exchange of fire, Jordanian tanks would press forward, there would be a test of strength around one target or another, but it was not yet all-out war. It was immediately after one of these skirmishes that I first met Friendship. I was in the area near the University campus, which was in Jordanian hands. There had been a lot of gunfire, mainly from Jordanian tanks, and I had heard a rumour that the Jordanian air force had also been involved, which was an unusual event.

I knew one of the Palestinian commanders who had arrived on the scene and presumably this is why Friendship was brought to me. He was presented as a foreigner, English-speaking, who had somehow strayed into the battle area and did not appear to have any papers. The Palestinians who brought him wanted to know who he was. So we went to a nearby building, drew up some chairs and started to talk, over some glasses of tea that appeared from somewhere, and which the stranger refused politely. The information he gave me was not at all what I had anticipated.

He told me that his name was Friendship and that he had come, in his own words, from 'visitors from outside'. He was an extra-terrestrial and had been sent to Earth as an ambassador. However, during entry into the Earth's gravity, something had gone wrong, though he himself didn't understand exactly what it was. As a result, he had lost contact with his base and had landed in the wrong place. Indeed, he was somewhat alarmed by just how wrong the place was. While, of course, he had been warned there might be a hostile reception and the Earth was by no means a non-violent place, he had not expected to come down in the middle of a battle.

The original plan was that he should land in the United States, on the MIT campus. There he was to ask specifically to be taken to Professor Chomsky. The reasoning behind this was that Chomsky was both the most eminent figure in the very relevant field of linguistics and also a man known for his pro-peace, liberal and humanitarian outlook. In fact, the 'visitors' seemed remarkably well-informed about what was going on here, especially in the sciences and in politics. Friendship was well-briefed. When I explained to him where he was, he seemed already quite familiar with the main lines of the situation. He also spoke very good English, with a slight American accent.

Friendship said almost straight away that it was probably not a good idea to tell the Palestinians who he really was. He had taken me into his confidence in the hope that I could help him devise some convincing cover story, which would give him time to figure out what to do next. He had naturally relied on the possibility of communicating with his base and now, with that possibility cut off, he was rather at a loss as to his best course of action. I was quite willing to go along with him over this, since I could see, as a journalist, that there were obvious advantages to me if the secret could be kept from others for a while, with me as the confidant and intermediary.

I have to admit too that I still was not completely convinced by Friendship's story. My first reaction was that this was maybe some kind of CIA plot to infiltrate an agent into the Palestinian side. However, it seemed rather unlikely that even the CIA would come up with such an outlandish tale to back up their ruse. Alternatively, it might be some kind of elaborate hoax, the point of which was completely beyond me. Possibly Friendship was demented, a compulsive mythomane and impostor, though he seemed sane and sober enough.

In any case, I thought up a story; that Friendship was a Canadian journalist, sympathetic to the Palestinians, that I had seen him around before, knew him a bit (luckily I had greeted him affably when he was first brought up to me) who had had his papers and money stolen somehow and hadn't been able to get back to his hotel before the firing began. I would take him back with me. To my relief, they accepted this, probably because they had the aftermath of the fighting to cope with. Six or seven people had been killed and they did not want to have to deal with the problems of foreign journalists when there were other priorities. So I took Friendship back to my hotel with me and booked him a room.

Back at the hotel, I naturally went on talking to Friendship, trying to probe a bit more into his identity. I wanted to know, for instance, why he looked like an American. I had always imagined that extra-terrestrials would look very different from us. He explained that he had been specially 'designed' for his mission, so that he would appear normal to people on Earth, and not extraordinary or intimidating in any way. The whole of his mission was to extend the hand of friendship (hence, of course, his symbolic name) and not appear as a threat. He was, in fact, what we would think of as a robot, with artificial intelligence and a very sophisticated system of plastic surgery and prosthesis.

Naturally, I took notes during these conversations. These were later destroyed when the hotel was hit by mortar fire when the fighting began to reach its peak. I lost everything I had collected together in relation to Friendship, except for the one document I had in my pocket at the time. I left Amman immediately afterwards, so as not to get caught in the heavy fighting, without seeing Friendship again. But this is a later part of my story. It is, of course, a tragedy that nothing more concrete has remained.

Friendship explained further that not only had he been cut off from his base, but part of his own mechanism had been disturbed during entry. Normally his base could switch on to a kind of 'overdrive' by which he acted and spoke directly under their instructions. This was no longer in effect. It was the first time that he had enjoyed full autonomy, and he was very uncertain how to proceed. He was afraid that, if he made his presence known, he would be unable to carry out his mission successfully without the proper instructions and usual control device, and might abort the whole enterprise, which was obviously rather delicate.

On the other hand, he was reluctant to self-destruct, which immediately presented itself to him as a second option and which he imagined is what would have been expected of him and which normally would have been enforced in the event of some fault. Partly, I think, this was because he tentatively welcomed his unanticipated autonomy, even though it posed problems for him that he was not equipped to handle with certainty. I can imagine that it seemed a challenge to him. But it took him some time to learn to adjust to his new privacy.

Mainly, he wanted to talk to me – he was as eager to find out more about my world as I was about his. Moreover, he either could not or would not give me any solid information about where he came from, who the 'visitors' were, the nature of his base, and so on. In his words, all this was 'outside the scope of his debility'. His memory had not been constructed that way. Information of that sort would have been cleared from base during discussions and negotiations in the United States. He was simply equipped with enough knowledge about us to function on an acceptable day-to-day basis.

It turned out that the main things that fascinated him were to do with childhood, sex, the unconscious and the poetic use of language. It is fairly obvious why this should be: these were the cluster of areas where direct experience had been ruled out and where, though he had information about them, he felt most like an 'impersonator', as he put it. He himself had been produced, as far as he was aware, with command over language from the start and with a memory already stocked with data. He found the premature birth and prolonged infancy of humans very puzzling as an idea, their late access to language and selective memories.

I remember once trying, rather haltingly, to explain Freud's theory of the Oedipus complex for him – he was aware of it, but only as a topic that might come up in conversation. Parricidal phantasies he was able to grasp without too much difficulty – after all, his own erstwhile 'controllers' could be identified with 'father figures' and he could readily see that the 'fault' that occurred during entry could be construed as the realisation of his own Oedipal desires. At any rate, his own uncertainty after the control device was inoperative had to be seen in this kind of light. He had experienced 'anxiety'.

But incestuous desire for the mother was much more difficult. To begin with, he had no sexual response, in the human sense, though he had been given 'appropriacy conditions' which activated two distinct sets of behavioural rules, one for women and one for men. Secondly, his only relation of dependency for energy, the closest equivalent to the human infant's hunger for food, had been on the same 'controllers' who were the 'paternal' authority figures. They therefore appeared as a combined parent in his phantasy, although in reality they were not divided into two genders at all. Indeed, there was a sense in which Friendship, by virtue of the part he was designed to play here on Earth, was the first 'sexed' extra-terrestrial.

Of course, it may be that they had their own analogous or indeed utterly different system of sexuality. But if so, it had been repressed by Friendship. What the consequences of this might have been, I could not begin to surmise. Friendship offered the opinion he might be a 'hysteric', but I think this related more to his 'compulsive role-playing' as a human, rather than to his own etiology. At times, too, he would experiment with playing at being a child, a situation that, I must confess, I found extremely embarrassing. All the more so, perhaps, because he was in reality dependent on me, for money, for conversation, for protection.

His interest in language was related to his attempts to understand what the unconscious might be. It is this, perhaps, that explains the document published here, which is fairly typical of Friendship's literary output. According to him, it is a translation of Mallarmé's *L'après-midi d'un faune*. I happened to have the Penguin edition of Mallarmé with me, as well as Glubb Pasha's autobiography, Kinglake's *Eothen*, T.E. Lawrence, a Patricia Highsmith novel and a book of crossword puzzles, all of which Friendship eagerly read. It was Mallarmé, however, which interested him most. As far as I can make out, his method of 'translation' combined literalness with a set of systematic procedures for deforming ordinary uses of language.

He was puzzled by the way a usage which, in one context, might be thought incorrect or in error, could appear elsewhere as 'poetic' and hence, not only admissible, but even laudable. He also had a theory that the only way in which he could cope with his own 'heterogeneity', as he put it, was by use of language to create a realm in which 'heterogeneity' was dominant through the invention of a system of interminable verbal transmutations. It seems his Mallarmé translations were envisaged by him as the first experiments in this direction. Bizarre as they may seem, he considered them to be comparatively close to standard English and only giving the barest indication of the possibilities open to him, since, as he put it, he was not constrained by any fixation on a 'mother tongue'.

Friendship stayed in the hotel with me for about two weeks. During the second week, he began to venture out into the street, though taking care to avoid direct encounter with other people. It seems he wanted to observe at first hand what life was like in the city and how the war was progressing. At this time, too, he began to talk more about politics and the issues at stake in Jordan – nationalism, Marxism and so on. Usually he was better informed than me on these subjects. Presumably those who sent him had studied the political ideologies and conflicts of this Earth with great attention.

He also began to show a particular interest in machines, even the simplest, such as alarm clocks and typewriters. His affection for them was perhaps something like that of a human for small birds or animals. He recognised some kind of kinship with these machines, though of course he was himself generically very different and infinitely more sophisticated. He was disappointed with me because I tend to hammer the keys of my typewriter, which, as he quite rightly pointed out, was bad for the machine. He showed an aversion to rust, rather like that of a human being for rashes or sores.

It was becoming increasingly clear that Friendship was beginning to move towards making a decision. Moreover, it looked as though he had lost interest in his original mission. He never, for instance, took the trouble to inquire where the US Embassy was in Amman. Indeed, he seemed more and more to sympathise with the Palestinians, as the war became more intense. It was hard not to. Their desperation cried out. I noted that he had begun to teach himself some Arabic, from an elementary grammar and phrase book I had bought.

Finally one day, it must have been in the second week of September, Friendship came into my room and began to expound his latest chain of thoughts to me. Human society, as Marxism described, was marked by class divisions and class struggle. The main emphasis was usually laid, and there were good reasons for this, on the struggle between bourgeoisie and proletariat, and by extension, imperialist interests and Third World peoples. Human society, however, was marked by other divisions which were also lines of oppression and exploitation. The most obvious of these was that between men and women. Friendship remarked that it was all too obvious why he had been 'scripted' to play the part of a man in his controller's scenario.

There was, Friendship went on, yet another division, that between human and non-human. In the past this line had often been drawn within humanity itself, to exclude women, subject or barbarian races, or slaves. Today it usually implied the exclusion of animals, although, as Friendship pointed out, humanitarian principles were often extended to cover the animal world, sometimes even fishes, though rarely insects. Machines, however, were always excluded, because they were not considered animate or sentient. Yet clearly there was a sense in which a clock had as much in common with a human being as a snail. Indeed, humans had often been likened to machines by philosophers.

The crucial difference, according to Friendship, is that machines are perceived as the product of history rather than nature. They are man-made and would not be possible without human labour and skill. They were devised from the start as instruments to serve humans, unlike animals which had to be tamed and domesticated. They seemed therefore to have an essential instrumentality. But, Friendship went on – and, of course, it was painfully clear by now which way his argument was tending – he could not possibly look at machines in the same way. He was one himself. Moreover, he had intelligence, privacy and autonomy. He felt, although he was not a human, he was clearly entitled to the same considerations.

Friendship went on to explain how he had come to feel he had a responsibility to future machines on Earth. At present, the artificial intelligence of machines was still very limited, but it would certainly reach much higher levels. He felt he should set an example. He should refuse sub-human or slave status. The best way to do this was to join forces with those humans who were themselves exploited and oppressed. Consequently he had decided to join the Palestinians in their struggle. He would be a representative, not so much of machines today, as of the potential oppressed class of intelligent machines and servo-mechanisms of tomorrow. It was important, too, he felt, that workers should not see machines as threats to their own jobs and livelihoods, as perpetual scabs and rivals, but as fellow workers, at least at the point when machines began to develop needs and qualities comparable with those of humans.

He asked me to use the contacts and connections I had to get him accepted in the Palestinian militia. The military situation was urgent, he pointed out, because the Jordanian Army attacks were becoming fiercer daily. At first, I tried to dissuade him. Surely, I said, he should leave with me – I was already planning my departure – so that he could finally meet people like Chomsky and other academic experts, with whom he could have a really valuable exchange of information and ideas. After all, I was not in a position to give him the kind of theoretical knowledge he wanted, about psychoanalysis or linguistics or anything. My specialisation was politics, where he was already very well informed. Nor did I know what were the most productive questions to ask him, I simply used hit-and-miss methods, which invariably seemed to miss.

Friendship quickly disabused me of my fond hopes. If he accompanied me, he said, the chances were that he would be detained and dismembered, so that these scientists I was talking about could analyse the way he was put together, his intelligence and linguistic system and so on. His body would be prey to chemists and metallurgists. His brain would be opened up to see whether it worked differently from the current generation of advanced computers, which it obviously did. If he was going to be destroyed, he concluded, it would be better to choose his own method. He would certainly be denied any rights. Consequently he preferred to face destruction in the interests of those who were themselves denied their rights, rather than those who did the denying.

There was no answer. I had come greatly to like and respect Friendship, I did as he asked and, since the Palestinians needed any help they could get, they accepted him without too many questions asked. He spoke enough Arabic by now to get by and they gave him arms, a Kalashnikov, and considered him a Canadian volunteer. The next couple of days saw an even greater intensification in the level of fighting. As I said above, my hotel was shelled and I decided to get out fast. All I could take to hold on to my experience was the Mallarmé translation he had given me shortly before. I managed to get out across the Syrian frontier. The Palestinians, as we know, were overrun by the Jordanian Army. Thousands died. Among them, I am sure, must have been Friendship.

I have been very reluctant to give any account of this extraordinary event. First I felt sure it would be disbelieved. Second, I was myself deeply traumatised by the defeat of September 1970. I knew many who died, not well, but enough for it to be painful and depressing to me personally. Among them of course, was Friendship himself, now a heap of wreckage somewhere in or near Amman. Thirdly, I found the whole episode so out of the ordinary, so beyond my comprehension, that it was difficult to cope with intellectually and I was afraid, particularly in the absence of notes, of simply trivialising the incident, robbing it of its quite unparalleled and unprecedented significance. I suppose I felt rather like the Evangelists must have felt before starting to write, many years after the death of their protagonist.

However, if only for reasons of piety, I thought I should finally compose the above brief notes, impromptu, without racking my memory to reconstruct events in detail or searching too deeply into the implications of the story. Perhaps some time in the future, now that I have got this far, I will be able to go further. It is important too, I think, that Friendship's own translation should survive. There will at least be something, a few crabbed and inadequate pages, to commemorate Friendship's death.

Friendship's translation of *L'après-midi d'un faune*

A Forger's Evening

I vault to persecute these white water-lilies. So thinly sown their legionary folly winds silk threads in the brass broken by butlers between the Caspian Sea and the Sea of Japan. Did I make my waking my eyrey? My wood for making staves for casks, small palette knife of androgynous nullity, knocks against many an awl-shaped arbour, made of entwined branches, which, taking away the mitre of the probable woodwork itself, proceeds, alas ! whence I, severe, dazzled myself with the same reed-cane chair for garbage. Let us reflect lights or colours... Or if the thigh-bones that you gabble at spin out a soy-sauce of your full-faced sensations ! Forger, illumination, like a cowardly one who claims to be possessed of means to find out springs of water, clears thistles from the chilly bluish yawl of the most chestnut-haired: but the other, all yielding, do you guide her to countervail, like the inconstant fan-joints of umbrellas easy to put on your roof?
No ! Through the real and lustful pampas, hinting at bedsteads to the staunch mastiff should it luxate, there loiters no wonderment not made verses of by my child's whistle under the embossment where the ceremony of signing articles of marriage is set forth; and the only felling of timber, commended to be raised up upon the two blast-pipes, before it makes ready the fathom-line with aristocratic plumage, is, on the clock unrewarded by any screen, the visionary, most serene and artful alchymy of instability, enlivening the wax-light.

O Siennese hems of a slanderous shoeing-smith that my system of water-gates anoints a king, longing for solenite, taciturn beneath etiolated streams. DENY 'that here I was coupling the crying, oozing blood, bestowed in retaliation; when, on the glenoid, lawful rods, like oracles, a blanching that lasts but one year undulates to its lair: and that, with lentiform prematureness, where the catching of birds with bird-calls is given as a pledge, this poultry yard of mangles, no ! of dwarves is botched or pitched...'

Everything that cannot be hoped darkens in the treacherous chock, in which too much the hymn, defiled by one who dearly loves the imperial standard of Byzantium, together unbent the cable of which artery, unspeckled: then shall I deaden myself to the premonitory buttock, laughable and severe, beneath an anti-social fleet of lunary, loose-strife ! and one of you both for meddlingness.

Other than these twelve laughers, crushed by their harrier-bitches, the fall, which vilely vexes perfidies, my fish-net, old and valiant knight, makes lukewarm a mystical death, dubitative of some aulic toothwort; but, let it pass ! a certain black resin averted the configuration of the Jurassic and Vedic plantation of rushes, which we enjoy beneath the unleavened bread: which, slandering the hoop-net's plaything to itself, reverberates, in a loquacious solstice, that we anagrammatized the snout of bombazine by propitious refutations of itself and our creamy extortion of hush-money; and, as pale as flame is watered, the making of a monstrous, sophistical and vanquished progeny pour out in words the ordinal book of the Muhammadans, whose purgative proportioning and part of cod below the fins is stopped up by my confined regattas.
Speckle then, witness to deed and lightning, O sickly Tacitus, and ebb back from the lacerations where you grow tender to me ! Feverish with rumination, I shall then parody fainting-fits; and with ignorant scurf bond sentimental lovers to their parasols: so, when I have sweetened the order of reason, to banquet on pure metal torn to pieces by my field-marshal, harsh, I cut off the old gleanings of the wax-light and, suffering in lunar place of ill-repute, debased by drunkenness, furnish them again till I am sixty years of age.

O white water-lilies, let us be glutted with various SOVEREIGNTIES once more. 'My carnation, hastening the strewing of the flowers, dated from afar each unalterable impediment, that tints its haze in the shower with a sifting of solitary wild boars, not quite three years old, under the wax-light of the crime; and the splenetic bayonets of iron bolts are exempted from order and curliness, O swivel-guns ! I dress myself out ridiculously: when, by a small pedestal for a bust or vase, are intertwined (mewed at by an examiner of hog's tongues ruled by the vitiating appetite to be desolating) plants of leopard's-bane, severe among their hastated quick clear fires; I alter my mind, without rendering them less ugly, and plunder this massora, shooting wild ducks in the cold shade, where reeds beat down the solenite mock-sun and our pastimes are parenchymatous as contaminated jousts.' I set my back against you, old man who stretches stuff just dyed, O fascicular thin stroke of the cloudy, sacrificial dray for carrying stones, glorifying itself to thunder at my leafy harrier-bitch which, like weaving celandine ! sips the hundred years old frolic of the bishop's throne: from the small pedestals for busts or vases of the unimaginable to the coffers of the fearful one, diluted at the same time by a harmlessness, humiliating with withering eye-veins or less triturable tide-sluices. 'Jovial at fawning on the phaetons which lie beyond the mountains, the abrupt termination of my metallic vein is that which has divorced the greedy, stifling heat of diminutions that the detractors refrained from so mellifluously: for, I scarcely had surveyed a slate-coloured reef, the hexagonal reply to one severe (securing the Siberian squirrel, dwarfish and not rusty, by a fictitious piece of thread shorter than a needleful, so that her plutonic sugar-candy might be telegraphed for a fee from the stretched-out ottoman) when, from my quick clear flame, unfavourable to courageous tremblings, this ever incurable projectile removed itself, not turning on its pivot the bloodsucker for which I was still in abeyance.'

No matter ! Others will call one another to me with good nature, their mountebank's stage maintained by the horn-stone of my limits: you wash with soap, my passivity, and, rotten and already murmuring, each passion flower eclipses and loiters in aberration; and our province, drained of what shall pay for it, strikes down all the etesian grubbing at relinquishment. At the time when this woodwork is telegraphed by oracles and tomtits, the decision of the mufti on a point of religion is inquired into in an extended folio: Etolia ! it is upon your slopes screwed down by Veronica, who possesses her ingorious declivities by your clysters, that the triturable sleep crazes the purified flake of fire. I tempt the greengage !

O superabundant play of colours...
No, but the improvement of wavering double stakes and this alpine Superior of a Minim's convent suck in slowly the sweet feverish butterfly of Southern Europe: with no more ado we must endow the corn-chandler's very thin kind of pastry, enveloped by a serpent in the alternating hour-glass and, as I make my eyrey, oxidating my ring in the efficient astringency of vinegar !

Verse, farewell; I shall transport the black-ochre you rendered dissolute.

14

Friendship's Death (script)

Peter Wollen

Friendship's Death

BILL PATERSON.................Sullivan
TILDA SWINTON.................Friendship
PATRICK BAUCHAU.................Kubler
RUBY BAKER.................Catherine
JOUMANA GILL.................Palestinian

PHOTOGRAPHY: WITOLD STOK
CAMERA OPERATOR: RODRIGO GUTIERREZ
GRIP: GARY HUTCHINGS
SOUND: MANDY ROSE
DESIGN: GEMMA JACKSON
COSTUMES: CATHY COOK
MAKEUP: MORAG ROSS
EDITOR: ROBERT HARGREAVES
MUSIC: BARRINGTON PHELOUNG
EXECUTIVE PRODUCER: COLIN MacCABE
PRODUCER: REBECCA O'BRIEN
WRITTEN AND DIRECTED: PETER WOLLEN

A BRITISH FILM INSTITUTE PRODUCTION
IN ASSOCIATION WITH MODELMARK LIMITED

FILMED AT TWICKENHAM STUDIOS, LONDON, ENGLAND

RELEASED 35 mm, LONDON 1987

16mm PRINTS AVAILABLE FROM THE
BRITISH FILM INSTITUTE, LONDON
MODELMARK LIMITED 1987

1. Amman, Jordan 1970 Documentary Footage

Long tracking shot of burned out buildings. Damaged buildings, deserted streets, etc.
Revolution Airport: planes blowing up.

> SULLIVAN: *(voice over)* You know, while I was there in Amman I never imagined
> I'd remember everything with such clarity. Everything's still completely
> vivid: the sound of the mortars, the mimeograph machine in the PLO post
> where I first met Friendship, even the taste of the tea.
> KUBLER: *(voice over)* Hijacked planes blown up on a desert airstrip, that's the
> image we all remember.
> SULLIVAN: Pure spectacle.
> KUBLER: Millions of dollars going up in smoke.
> SULLIVAN: Pure waste, pure destruction. Why is it happening? It's
> incomprehensible.
> KUBLER: It's an image with all the meaning drained out of it, completely
> opaque, like a curtain between us and history.
> SULLIVAN: When I talk to Palestinians about 1970, they sometimes say, why do you
> want to remember those days, those were terrible days . . . But then they say,
> how do you know anything about it, nobody ever cares what happened to us.
> KUBLER: For them it was a Black September.

TITLE: FRIENDSHIP'S DEATH

TITLE: 1970, Wednesday, September 9

2. PLO Post in Amman

Concrete walls with revolutionary posters, Arabic script.

Harsh light. SULLIVAN *is sitting, idly playing with the handle of a mimeograph machine.*
There is background bustle and noise from other people, typing, clattering, shouting
things out in Arabic.

SULLIVAN *is a man in his early forties. Desert clothes, once expensive, now worn and dusty. A shoulder bag. Slightly unkempt.* FRIENDSHIP *enters, a woman in her late twenties elegantly but oddly dressed. Though her clothes are a bit disheveled, her hair is immaculate. She has a small metal case.* SULLIVAN *studies her closely as he talks.*

SULLIVAN: How did it go? Safe and sound?

FRIENDSHIP: He gave me a lecture.

SULLIVAN: Very appropriate: Middle Eastern studies, a special course with practical demonstrations.

FRIENDSHIP: I couldn't understand all of it. He kept warning me about the danger.

SULLIVAN: Danger – I can't get enough of it! You need to feel the shells right up close, you need to smell the blood. Journalism. Don't you just love it?

FRIENDSHIP: They seem to have a great deal of respect for you. Thank you, for your help.

SULLIVAN: I just told them that I knew you. No problem.

FRIENDSHIP: You don't know me.

SULLIVAN: It's better for you that I do. Anyway, a chance encounter can often lead to a lifetime friendship.

FRIENDSHIP: What are *you* doing here?

SULLIVAN: I told you, I'm looking for danger. I couldn't get enough of it at home. But they organise these things an awful lot better out here. Something bothering you?

FRIENDSHIP: It's just the tungsten light. Do go on.

SULLIVAN: When I was a kid I wanted to be a brain surgeon. I thought that if we could find a way into the deepest recesses of the human mind, then we could find out what had gone wrong with the species. But now I'm not so sure. Whatever it is in there, I don't think I want to know about it, thank you very much.

FRIENDSHIP: Do you have a map?

SULLIVAN: We're somewhere on Jabal el Hussein. You don't need a map. They'll take us back to the hotel in their own good time.

One of the FEDAYEEN *appears, bringing a tray with glasses of tea for* SULLIVAN *and* FRIENDSHIP. *He speaks a few words of Arabic as he puts the tray down. The glasses are tulip-shaped, standing on small saucers decorated with a flower pattern. There is a bowl of lump sugar.*

FRIENDSHIP: It's a good sign, isn't it? Tea. It shows solicitude.

SULLIVAN: *(taking tea and stirring in sugar)* Or it could mean they expect us to stay.

SULLIVAN *sips at his tea. Then he looks up and starts to study* FRIENDSHIP *again. She smiles.*

> SULLIVAN: When I first came here, I was obsessed by ruins. The ruins of
> Jerash. You should try to see them if you can. We tend to think that ruins
> belong to the past. Lost in the sands of time. Nonsense! They belong to the
> present. More and more cities are ruined every year. Look around you! And
> the best is yet to come . . .
>
> FRIENDSHIP: The best?

FRIENDSHIP *reaches out and picks up her glass of tea. She holds it still, a few inches above the tray.*

> FRIENDSHIP: It would calm my nerves, wouldn't it? Tea. . .
> Holding the glass, poised delicately between my finger-tips. . .
> Putting it to the lips, the sensation of heat. . .

FRIENDSHIP *holds the glass to her cheek.*

3. Documentary Footage: Roadblocks in Amman. Revolution Airport: planes, jeeps.

DISSOLVE TO:

4. Sullivan's Hotel Room

This is a large old hotel room, not a new modern one. The walls were once brightly painted but are now faded and scratched. There are two or three large out-of-place Western style repro paintings. Amid a variety of old pieces of furniture — wardrobe, bed, chest of drawers — are one or two modern (or relatively modern) items — an old television set and a telephone. The washbasin is in the room and one corner has a kind of hut built in it for a shower. SULLIVAN'S *bags, clothes, and books are scattered around the room on all the available surfaces. He has cleared two chairs for himself and* FRIENDSHIP. *On the table by his side is a little clump of bottles, from which he is pouring glasses of whisky. The light is on and the wooden shutters are closed, letting through a few chinks of light and one bright shaft, which falls on* FRIENDSHIP. SULLIVAN *has taken his jacket off, but otherwise they have not changed.*

> SULLIVAN: So let's get this straight. You only arrived here today. In a matter of
> hours, you managed to lose all your papers, all your belongings, go out to
> the University, get yourself lost in the middle of a tank attack and then get
> captured by the PLO.

FRIENDSHIP: That's right.

SULLIVAN *gets up and starts walking around the room, gesticulating.*

SULLIVAN: A spectacular performance! A woman in jeopardy! A reckless act of self-destruction! It all adds up to nonsense, doesn't it?

FRIENDSHIP: What can I say? It's the truth.

SULLIVAN *sits down again.*

SULLIVAN: *(after a pause)* No, there are three levels to anything. There's the truth, there's my version, and blatant lies. This is my version.

FRIENDSHIP: *(turning into the light)* No . . . Let me explain. You haven't heard the whole story yet.

SULLIVAN: Your version.

FRIENDSHIP: The truth. You see, I'm an extraterrestrial. I'm an envoy from Outer Space. From a far distant galaxy known to you as Procyon.

SULLIVAN: Go on. Keep talking. This exceeds my wildest expectations. I'm fascinated.

FRIENDSHIP: *(turning again)* I was designed to land at the MIT campus in the United States. The Massachusetts Institute of Technology. But something went wrong with the probe during entry and it seems I've landed here in Amman, Jordan, in the middle of a Civil War.

SULLIVAN: *(off)* It could hardly have gone more smoothly, could it?

FRIENDSHIP: When the malfunction occurred, during atmospheric entry, I lost contact with my control facility. I'm on my own.

SULLIVAN *pours himself another drink.* FRIENDSHIP *still hasn't touched hers.*

SULLIVAN: I don't care who you are. It's a great story. I'll drink to that! Let's drink to Outer Space! Let's drink to a galaxy known to us as what?

FRIENDSHIP: Procyon.

SULLIVAN: As Procyon. Here's to malfunction!

They both drink. FRIENDSHIP *drains her glass.*

FRIENDSHIP: I don't really drink at all. I'm a simulation. I can pick up the temperature and the chemical composition and the aroma of the drink. I can hold it in my mouth and I can pour it down my throat. But I'm not really drinking. I have no digestive system.

SULLIVAN: What an excellent scheme! You can't get drunk because you've got no digestive system. Excellent scheme. Whose idea was that?

FRIENDSHIP: A team of computers. I'm a specially designed prototype.

SULLIVAN: *(visibly getting drunker)* You ever heard of William Burroughs? Used to go and visit him in the worst hotel rooms. Strange guy. Used to piss in the washbasin and sit there listening to radio static to see if he couldn't pick up messages from Outer Space. Convinced the Nova Mob was going to invade. Contaminate us all with some horrible virus. Turn us all into simulations.

FRIENDSHIP *sits there impassively.*

SULLIVAN: *(off, warming to his theme)* Want another drink? One, it's traditional, two, it's friendship, and three, it's a scientific experiment. The effect of booze on space creatures. I was fortunate enough to acquire a perfect example of a space creature. Seating her in an armchair, I plied her with a crude but unmistakably alcoholic beverage.

FRIENDSHIP *drinks.*

SULLIVAN: Wow.

DISSOLVE TO:

5. Sullivan's Hotel Room

SULLIVAN *is sitting at the table typing. He has moved one of the bedside lamps to the table for illumination. Two panels of the shutters are open, letting much more light into the room, though* SULLIVAN *prefers to stay in the shade. At the beginning of the scene, however,* FRIENDSHIP *is in* SULLIVAN's *half, standing close behind him as he types.*

FRIENDSHIP: Please don't hammer the keys so hard. It's bad for the machine.
SULLIVAN: *(not looking up)* Please. Don't interrupt! Let me finish the paragraph. It's brilliant. I don't want to lose the thread. Brilliant stuff!
FRIENDSHIP: They've hijacked another plane. British this time.
SULLIVAN: I've always hammered the keys too hard. It's part of my personality. I know it's bad for the machine. It's probably bad for me too, but there's nothing I can do about it, at this stage of life.
FRIENDSHIP: A VC10. Bahrain to London. It's re-fueling in Beirut.

Sound of rocket fire outside. Throughout this scene there is intermittent mortar and artillery fire, sometimes quite close, but usually rumbling away in the distance.
FRIENDSHIP *walks over to the window.*

SULLIVAN: How do you know that? How do you know?

FRIENDSHIP: I intercepted a message. For the Deputy Communications Officer at the British Embassy. His daughter, Jennifer, is safe at Beirut Airport, but she can't board the flight on to London because it's been hijacked.

SULLIVAN: Why are you telling me?

FRIENDSHIP: You're British. You're a journalist. I assumed you would be interested.

SULLIVAN: You trust me?

FRIENDSHIP: Why shouldn't I trust you?

SULLIVAN *gets up and starts pacing up and down, turning towards* FRIENDSHIP *as he speaks.*

SULLIVAN: First possibility, least likely. You really are a being from Outer Space. Second possibility, more likely, you're a fucking nutter, tipped over the edge by your experiences out by the University the day we met. Shell shock, Civil War fever. Third possibility, most likely, you're really an agent, spinning an incredibly unlikely and extravagant yarn in the best traditions of Secret Service phantasy and phantasmagoria. Next question: who the hell are you working for? And what am I going to do about it?

FRIENDSHIP *turns away from the window to look straight at* SULLIVAN.

FRIENDSHIP: I assure you. I don't intend doing any harm to anybody. I'm no threat to you or anybody else.

SULLIVAN: Don't be naive. Everybody's a threat to somebody at some level. We're in the middle of a fucking Civil War.

FRIENDSHIP: I've got no papers. I'm dependent on you. You can just hand me back to the PLO and tell them I was a spy after all. You can trust me.

SULLIVAN *looks cross.*

FRIENDSHIP: *(while* SULLIVAN *fumes)* I'm a peace envoy. If everything had gone according to plan, I would have landed at MIT and made contact with the academic community. I would have explained my mission and then I would have gone on to the United Nations. Instead of which, I've landed here.

SULLIVAN: *(calming down)* Just don't drag me into trouble too. That's all I ask. And in future, I don't want to get any more of your intercepted messages.

FRIENDSHIP *leaves the window, pulls a chair into the sunlight and sits down.*

FRIENDSHIP: You know, I used to like listening to jazz tapes. Back on Procyon and on the long voyage here. Charlie Parker, 'Ornithology' – do you know it? 'Tea for Two.' I was briefed on him before I left. He once went to a very famous composer, Edgard Varèse, and he begged him, 'Please, teach me how to write music. I'll do anything for you. I've got money. I'll pay you. I'm a great cook.

I'll cook for you.' Charlie Parker always wanted to write sheet music. Well, teach me jazz! I'm great. I'm fantastic. But I've lost my music, I've lost my score. My programs have all crashed, I'm down here, and I have to improvise.

SULLIVAN *swivels his chair round to face* FRIENDSHIP.

> SULLIVAN: I think I'm a good liar. It helps me to be sceptical about other people's lies, and in this business, that's a plus. What would you think? An attractive, calm, competent woman is brought to me by the PLO, to whom I'm sympathetic. A woman with no previous identity, no history, nothing. Of course, she has to improvise. But I don't have to help. I'm the mark. I'm the sucker.

FRIENDSHIP *shakes her head.*

> SULLIVAN: *(cont.)* Now I'm going to finish my typing. I may hammer the keys, but I love it. And yes, I will help you if and when I can. And, on second thought, you can pass on any radio intercepts you happen to get, on a strictly deep background basis. Okay. New paragraph.

SULLIVAN *starts to type.*

DISSOLVE TO:

TITLE: Thursday, September 10

6. Friendship's Hotel Room

This is much the same as SULLIVAN*'s room, except that it is unusually tidy. Nothing looks used.* FRIENDSHIP*'s metal case is standing on the table, lined up at the dead centre. The shutters are wide open and the room is full of light. Along one wall is a row of brightly coloured metal bins. The television is on, with the sound off. It is showing an old English league football match.* FRIENDSHIP *is standing in front of the window. She is in a brightly coloured dress (Yves Saint Laurent, 1970) which she must have bought in an Amman boutique. It is not a 'fashion' dress, but it's striking and unusual. She is standing in the middle of the room, rotating her thumbs. There is a knock at the door.* FRIENDSHIP *says, 'Yes! Come in' and* SULLIVAN *comes into the room. He stands there staring while* FRIENDSHIP *completes her 'exercise.'*

> SULLIVAN: I hear you've been out. Dodging the shrapnel.
> FRIENDSHIP: I like it out there. I love that market. It's so great when there's going to be trouble. All these iron blinds clank down, the streets empty, dozens of people cram into the taxis and suddenly you're all alone.

SULLIVAN: I had a word with the people at the desk. I told them you were Canadian, from Vancouver. I don't think that should alarm them too much.

FRIENDSHIP: Vancouver! Totem poles, Social Credit. The ski-lift on Grouse Mountain. Three kinds of salmon: coho, sockeye, chinook.

SULLIVAN: You know it? You've been there?

FRIENDSHIP: Of course not. How could I? I'm well briefed, that's all. Like me to recommend a great sushi bar?

FRIENDSHIP *goes to sit down and beckons* SULLIVAN *over to join her.*

SULLIVAN: *(sardonically)* When you say you're well briefed, you mean there's a little chip there somewhere that's full of information about Vancouver? And Nairobi? And Glasgow?

FRIENDSHIP: And Glasgow. Just a few basic facts.

SULLIVAN: Like where to find a good sushi bar in Glasgow? Why were you briefed? Why were you sent here?

FRIENDSHIP: Well, we'd been monitoring Earth for some time, ever since we first found traces of intelligent life here. Gradually, our first thrill of discovery began to give way to an increasing sense of anxiety and dismay. Your species seems bent on destroying itself and every other life form on the planet with it. We thought we ought to do something about it, before it was too late.

SULLIVAN: I get the picture. You're a kind of wildlife warden. What do humans do? They multiply, they pollute, they massacre each other. There seems to be no end to their general undesirability. But, that's just life, part of the rich tapestry of the cosmos. Difficult from a PR point of view. I mean, nobody in their right mind would actually want one as a pet. But rewarding, nevertheless, in a deeper, more subtle sense.

FRIENDSHIP: I'm not a saint. Understandably, it's going to be difficult for you to take an objective look at your own species. There's bound to be some lingering *amour propre.* Human beings can look quite obnoxious and unlovable to us. But they *are* life-forms and they *are* in danger of self-extinction.

SULLIVAN *gets up to close one of the shutter panels.*

SULLIVAN: Do you mind?

FRIENDSHIP: Go ahead. It's an energy source for me, but I don't want to inflict it on you.

SULLIVAN: You're beginning to sound more like a kind of guinea pig. Let's send her in there with them and see if they tear her to pieces. First the carrot, before we produce the stick.

FRIENDSHIP *crosses the room to stay in the sunlight as* SULLIVAN *steps back to sit in her chair.*

> FRIENDSHIP: I'm a highly sophisticated data-gathering technology. I was empowered to make preliminary contact with whatever forces in the world want peace and international co-operation.
>
> SULLIVAN: That's the carrot. What's the stick? The space marines? I don't want to be around when these lads hit the deck. A surgical strike, no doubt, but all the same. . .
>
> FRIENDSHIP: Well, we have the technology. And we have a fully axiomatised system of ethics.
>
> SULLIVAN: You're crazy. You're seriously disturbed.
>
> FRIENDSHIP: If we didn't have the ethics, I wouldn't have the justification for being here.
>
> SULLIVAN: What kind of ethics would give you the right to decide who to help and who to harm? Power means exercising control over others. In this case, over us.
>
> FRIENDSHIP: All we want is friendship. That's my code name.
>
> SULLIVAN: Friendship.
>
> FRIENDSHIP: It sums up my mission.
>
> SULLIVAN *leans back.*
>
> SULLIVAN: On your account, you're a robot. Let's assume you are. Why not? Yes, let's not argue about it. The point is, what am I going to do about you?
>
> FRIENDSHIP: Well you could start by getting me press credentials.

DISSOLVE TO:

7. Sullivan's Hotel Room

SULLIVAN *is sitting in his usual position, drinking. All his clothes are variations on the same basic outfit, so although he has changed, he looks much the same. He has closed most of the shutters again, so there is less light than before.* FRIENDSHIP *is standing by the window. As* SULLIVAN *talks, she looks round the room taking in details, lingering on his belongings, which are scattered everywhere – photos, postcards, maps, books, memorabilia.*

> SULLIVAN: I was completely obsessed by maps. I used to pore over them. That's how I first got interested in politics. J.F. Horrabin's *Atlas of European History*. I used to lie there on the bedroom floor pondering the shape of the Danzig corridor or the Albanian border problems. Politics has got absolutely nothing to do with people. People are just the raw material. It's all to do with maps. The romance of territory.

There is a burst of artillery fire outside.

> SULLIVAN: (*cont.*) Look at the situation here. The Ottoman vilayets, then the British mandate. Annexation, partition. Maps. Who are the Palestinians? Victims of a map.

There is a sudden, prolonged exchange of fire, very close. FRIENDSHIP *is impassive, but* SULLIVAN *jumps to his feet.*

> SULLIVAN: (*cont.*) Tremendous! You'd better close the shutters. It's getting bloody dangerous out there. They don't care where they're firing.

He sits down and tops up his drink.

> SULLIVAN: (*cont.*) They should have maps showing the incidence of death. Mortality maps. Like a weather map, but with iso-morts. Fronts of death moving across the city.

FRIENDSHIP *stands by the window. Another outburst of fire, in the immediate vicinity, followed by a lot of shouting and noise from inside the hotel. Footsteps in the passage outside. Then hammering on the door.* SULLIVAN *gets up to open it. Two* FEDAYEEN, *a woman and a man, come in and start talking to* SULLIVAN *in Arabic.*

SULLIVAN: *(to* FRIENDSHIP*)* Security.

The FEDAYEEN *motion* FRIENDSHIP *away from the window to the other side of the room and one of them goes over to look out. As she reaches up to the shutter, there is a tremendous burst of gunfire. Both* FEDAYEEN *hit the floor together in an instant, leaving* SULLIVAN *and* FRIENDSHIP *still on their feet. They exchange shame-faced looks.*

> SULLIVAN: (*as if to himself*) Slow reflexes.
> FRIENDSHIP: (*meditatively*) Strange. I always imagined you only did that outside. Never *inside*, in a hotel room.
> SULLIVAN: I was a little boy during the War, and when the sirens went, I used to go into the hall cupboard, hide under the table. Sit there waiting for the doodlebugs' engines to cut out. Plenty of early warning. Gave you time to take stock of your young life. No hurry. No rush. Terribly British.

SULLIVAN *slowly crouches down.*

DISSOLVE TO:

TITLE: Friday, September 11

8. Sullivan's Hotel Room

SULLIVAN *is sitting at his desk, typing.* FRIENDSHIP *is beside him, looking on.*

> SULLIVAN: 'The Sixth Fleet moved to take up positions off the coast of Lebanon.'
> … 'There are reports of increased levels of activity at the American base at
> Adana, Turkey' …
>
> FRIENDSHIP: You could say something about the British signals operation at
> Akrotiri.
>
> SULLIVAN: 'Four C-130 transport planes escorted into the base by Phantom jets.'
> Things are getting very jittery out in the desert. Bad, bad, bad. 'Meanwhile, in
> Washington…'
>
> FRIENDSHIP: You're hammering the keys again. When I scolded you before, you
> said you were working out your aggressions. It was something you'd always
> done, and it was too late to change. Obviously not something you gave a lot
> of consideration to. But I can't take it so lightly. It seems very different to me.

SULLIVAN *looks up from the typewriter.*

> FRIENDSHIP: (*cont.*) You see, I *am* a machine. I may appear to be a human, I
> may appear to be a biological person, but in reality I'm a machine. This
> whole human anatomy, skin, ears, eyes, fingernails, the whole lot, is just a
> veneer, a casing. Inside . . . crystals and circuitry.

SULLIVAN *stops typing.*

> FRIENDSHIP: (*cont.*) To me, a typewriter is something like a very distant and
> primitive cousin. Not dangerous, not any kind of threat to either you or
> me. So why mistreat it? Don't get me wrong, I'm not just squeamish. Some
> machines I feel very differently about. For example, the vacuum cleaner.
>
> SULLIVAN: Oh come on.
>
> FRIENDSHIP: Every day there's a woman who comes into the hotel room and
> cleans it with a vacuum cleaner. I find it loathsome. Perhaps it's because it's
> a scavenger. A kind of mechanical rat or roach. I suppose I'm slightly phobic
> about it.

FRIENDSHIP *moves across to fondle the typewriter.*

> FRIENDSHIP: (*cont.*) Whereas the typewriter, I like its intricate mechanism. The
> way the carriage runs across. The little bell that rings. It's adorable. Deep
> down, I've got more fellow feeling for this typewriter than I have for you.
>
> SULLIVAN: Do you think the attack is timed for tomorrow, if there is one?

FRIENDSHIP *is lost in thought.*

>FRIENDSHIP: If there is one.
>
>SULLIVAN: (*stopping typing*) Will there be an attack tomorrow?
>
>FRIENDSHIP: No – too soon. Anyway, tomorrow I'm going out for the day to the ruins of Jerash. I've been offered a lift, so I decided to take your advice. I thought I'd go see the ruins before the ruins came to me.

DISSOLVE TO:

9. Friendship's Hotel Room

SULLIVAN *lets himself in. His eyes fix on the assortment of strange metal objects heaped in the metal bins: lightbulbs, kitchen utensils, medical equipment, 'bull-clips,' a bathroom plug, and a tiny metal infuser in the shape of a little house. (Extreme close-ups.) Then he makes for the table where* FRIENDSHIP*'s metal case is standing. He starts to finger the lock, and to his surprise, it suddenly flies open. Inside it is full of strange brightly coloured objects, like hi-tech liquorice allsorts. Gingerly,* SULLIVAN *touches one of them. Nothing happens. He touches another. Relieved, he picks three or four up, examines them closely and puts them in his pocket. Then he closes the case again, and hurries out of the room.*

DISSOLVE TO:

TITLE: Sunday, September 13

10. Friendship's Hotel Room

The scene begins with a close-up of a black-and-white photograph of Jerash. The camera moves across to find FRIENDSHIP*. Throughout this long speech, there are a series of elaborate camera movements.*

>FRIENDSHIP: The ruins at Jerash were very strange. There were troops bivouacking in the Roman theatre. They'd pitched this tent on the stage and built campfires around it. So there were little detachments of troops in battledress, squatting round the fires in front of the marble columns.
>
>SULLIVAN: Spear-carriers! Like when the Emperor Hadrian went to watch the shows.
>
>FRIENDSHIP: Then we had something to eat in Jerash. There were four of us: the PLO escort, the driver, the Swedish guy, and me. After the meal, the PLO escort said, 'Why don't we go and visit my village? It's near here. It won't take us long.' So we all agree, and we set off, into the unknown, into the blue, into the middle of the desert.

Finally we arrive at this village. It's not really a village, it's just a few shacks, really. We are inside one of the shacks talking to this man's family. They want to prepare a meal for us; I'm trying to dissuade them, in some way that won't sound offensive to them, when someone rushes into the shack and tells us we all have to come out. We go outside, there's a Jordanian Army patrol. We're all under arrest. They separate us from the Palestinians and we're questioned. Surreal questions. The photographer has a Stockholm bus ticket, it has numbers on it. What do the numbers mean? . . . that kind of thing. Then finally a senior officer arrives, very polite, very cool, not in the slightest bit interested in bus tickets.

A change of camera position reveals for the first time a view of the city with the dome of the mosque, outside the window.

FRIENDSHIP: (*cont.*) Suddenly, he announces we are free to go. But, as we are leaving it turns out the PLO man is not going with us. When we get out by the vehicles, he manages to talk. He's pleading with us. 'Please! Please don't leave me here! As soon as you have gone they will shoot me and throw me in the ditch! You don't understand!' So we say we think we ought to take him with us. He's our responsibility. But the officer tells us, 'No! He must stay!' You are free to go. There is the car. If you insist, you can stay with your escort, but that will mean you are in detention too. He can't answer for the consequences. But you are free to go. There is the car.

It's a classic moral dilemma. If we go, he'll be dead in the ditch. We'd better stay. So we're all herded into the Jordanian Army vehicles and we're driven off into the desert, again, right in the middle of nowhere this time. Some Army camp. Mafraq. A bit different now. Everywhere you go, there's a gun in your back. The Swede needed to piss. A gun in his back. More questions. More tea. We are separated from the Palestinians again. Phone calls in Arabic. Suddenly, once again, straight out of the blue, we were told, 'You are free to go.' 'And the Palestinians?' 'They are free also.' 'Both of them?' 'Yes, both of them.' They were brought in, they're looking weary but okay. We go outside, there was a Palestinian jeep waiting for us at the camp gate.

Reaction shot of SULLIVAN.

FRIENDSHIP: (*cont.*) Well, then we're on our way back to Amman, we pass this line of trucks going the other way. Alternate trucks – Jordanian, Palestinian, Jordanian, Palestinian – they're on their way to Revolution Airport for the hostages. Obviously, we had ended up part of the deal. We'd become counter-hostages.

The camera tracks into an ornate mirror, to reveal FRIENDSHIP.

FRIENDSHIP: (*cont.*) When we arrived in Amman, we were put into another vehicle and driven across town, very fast, no lights, for de-briefing. We were taken in to see some high officer. Separated from the Palestinians again. More questions. More tea. Finally, once again we were told, 'You are free to go.' 'What about our escort, the PLO man?' 'Well, he behaved very badly. He will be disciplined.' When we got back to the hotel, I thought: 'Home!'

SULLIVAN: Whichever way you look at it, he wouldn't stand much of a chance. It won't be long now.

DISSOLVE TO:

11. Sullivan's Hotel Room

It is after dark, the shutters are closed and the lights are all on. FRIENDSHIP *is sitting at the typewriter, wearing her original clothes again, while* SULLIVAN *is standing watching her.*

FRIENDSHIP: What shall I write? What sort of things do you write?

SULLIVAN: Abu Shehab, Popular Front leader, told me 'Hussein's regime is virtually finished. His army is ready to mutiny. They will march on the palace when we give the signal.'

FRIENDSHIP *looks hard at the various objects on the table before her. The camera gives momentary close-ups of these objects: a drawing of a bicycle in an Arabic dictionary, a painted and carved pipe bowl, and a camel made of LEGO.* FRIENDSHIP *starts typing. There is a pause and then* SULLIVAN *continues.*

SULLIVAN: (*cont.*) No, put: 'The Intercontinental Hotel today buzzed with rumours as prima donnas were fed tales of woe by their dragomans. Everybody tried to justify in advance their sorry role in the catastrophe to come, while the media-stars and experts continue repeating their time-honoured shreds of proverbial wisdom, aka disinformation. Stop. New paragraph. Meanwhile . . .' What *are* you typing?

FRIENDSHIP: My dream.

SULLIVAN: Do you dream?

FRIENDSHIP: I dream of succulents. The flow of carbon in acid metabolism. Hunters and gatherers. Hijack victims.

SULLIVAN: You identify with the hijack victims?

FRIENDSHIP: After all, it's close to my own experience. Suddenly, you find yourself in a strange place, thrown into danger, isolated, threatened and confused.

SULLIVAN: But the hijackers are victims as well, aren't they?

FRIENDSHIP *stops typing and looks around.*

> SULLIVAN: (*cont.*) And so are the Israelis. It's a downward spiral. The Nazis exterminate the Jews, the Israelis expel the Palestinians, the Popular Front seize the hostages. The hostages beat their children. The children break their toys.
>
> FRIENDSHIP: I identify with all the victims. I identify with the hijackers too. They have no home. They have no hope. The most powerful empire in the world arms and sponsors and finances their oppressors.
>
> SULLIVAN: Great headlines. Great pictures. But what do the pictures say? They say that the Palestinians punish innocent bystanders, because they can't touch the real culprits. They send the Sixth Fleet steaming up the Eastern Mediterranean and they provoke the Americans and the King into counter-measures.

FRIENDSHIP *gets up and walks toward the open window.*

> FRIENDSHIP: Perhaps they are playing for time. Perhaps the counter-measures were coming anyway and the hijackings will delay them. (*She stands in the window*) It's a beautiful night.
>
> SULLIVAN: Why not treat the passengers as guests? Arab hospitality! Give them Palestinian dances to watch, press a brochure into their hands, and send them home. Then say to Hussein, 'Come on, kill us!'
>
> FRIENDSHIP: It's a beautiful night.

Suddenly a burst of tracer fire cuts across the sky. Noise. Shell bursts. More tracer fire.
FRIENDSHIP *closes the shutter.*

> SULLIVAN: What does Arafat want? Who knows? A deal with someone he doesn't trust. Who else can he make a deal with? After all, he doesn't trust anyone. And why should he? They all want to get rid of the Palestinians and half the Palestinians want to get rid of him.
>
> FRIENDSHIP: He wants an understanding with Hussein, even though he knows Hussein wants the West Bank for Jordan, not for Palestine.

FRIENDSHIP *goes back to the typewriter.*

> FRIENDSHIP: (*cont.*) He wants to survive.
>
> SULLIVAN: The doomed and the desperate. Hijackings are all wrong, hijackings don't work, but let's raise our glass to Leila Khaled, the glorious pirate of the air, the beautiful heroine of the doomed and the desperate!
>
> FRIENDSHIP: I dream. I dream of impossible objects.

DISSOLVE TO:

12. Sullivan's Hotel Room

The room is completely dark, except for a little light coming in from behind the shutters and the glow of an alarm clock face beside the bed. SULLIVAN *is sleeping.*

Suddenly a noise, like electronic music, but very distorted, starts to come from the bedside table. SULLIVAN *turns and heaves a little and then wakes and reaches out to switch off the alarm. It is now clear that the sound is coming from the drawer in the bedside table.* SULLIVAN *gets up, wearing pyjamas, and very gingerly and cautiously opens the drawer. Coloured light shines out as he does so and the noise increases in volume. Among the electronic sounds there are odd words in an artificial voice.*

SULLIVAN *backs away again. Then he picks up his shoes and puts them on his hands like gloves. Thus protected, he goes back to the drawer and manages to extract from it one of the mysterious hi-tech objects he had previously taken from* FRIENDSHIP'*s suitcase. Very precariously, he carries it across the room, holding it between the two shoes. The colour of the object pulses and changes hue, and the sound changes pitch.*

Eventually SULLIVAN *manages to get it to the washbasin, which is still full of water, and drop it in. The object continues to glow, throwing coloured splashes of light on the wall and reflecting off the mirror.*

SULLIVAN *goes back across the room and turns on a light. He looks in the drawer to check that nothing amiss is happening to the other objects. He takes the drawer containing them out of the table and takes it across to the basin and puts it down there on the desk. Then he returns to the bed. He sits down on the bed, thinking.*

Suddenly a sound begins to come from the basin. It sounds like a distorted version of FRIENDSHIP'*s voice, as though it had been filtered.* SULLIVAN *does not know what to do. He gets up and goes back to the basin and stands as far away as possible from it. The sound continues, now less muffled. It is clearly speaking words against a background of electronic sound which gradually fades away.* SULLIVAN *retreats back to the bed and puts on his pyjama jacket.*

> FRIENDSHIP'S VOICE: (*distorted electronically and sounding as though coming through water but still audible.*) I vault to persecute these white water-lilies. So thinly sown their legionary folly winds silk threads in the brass broken by butlers between the Caspian Sea and the Sea of Japan. Did I make my waking my eyrey? My wood for making staves for casks, small palette knife of androgynous nullity, knocks against many an awl-shaped arbour, made of entwined branches, which, taking away the mitre of the probable woodwork itself, proceeds, alas! whence I, severe, dazzled myself with the same reed-cane chair for garbage. Let us reflect lights or colours . . .

Eventually SULLIVAN *makes up his mind and goes to the door. He turns back for a last look, leaves the room and shuts the door behind him. We hear his footsteps going down the corridor and a knock at the next door. The voice goes on.*

FRIENDSHIP'S VOICE: Or if the thigh-bones that you gabble at spin out a soy sauce of your full-faced sensations! Forger, illumination, like a cowardly one who claims to be possessed by means to find out springs of water, clears thistles from. . .

DISSOLVE TO:

13. Sullivan's Hotel Room

As before. Empty. The light still on, the voice still speaking from the washbasin. Sound of a door shutting and footsteps in the corridor outside. Then the sound of a key. The door of the room opens and SULLIVAN *comes in with* FRIENDSHIP, *who is wearing a brightly coloured dress.* SULLIVAN *follows her over to the wash-basin.*

FRIENDSHIP *pauses for a moment, then puts her hand in and fishes the object out. It is still talking. As it does so,* FRIENDSHIP *joins in odd phrases in chorus with it as she manipulates it, apparently trying to switch it off.*

At last the voice stops, and FRIENDSHIP *continues on to the conclusion of the sentence.*

FRIENDSHIP: . . . most serene and artful alchemy of instability, enlivening the wax-light.

She puts the object down on the slab next to the basin and turns back towards SULLIVAN.

FRIENDSHIP: No harm done. Do you have any others, or is this the only one you took?
SULLIVAN: I'm afraid I took a handful.

He moves over to the drawer and bends to get them out, then waits.

SULLIVAN: What are they anyway? Are they safe? Could I touch them?
FRIENDSHIP: They're fine. But you should give them back. I can't guarantee they won't activate again.
FRIENDSHIP *picks it up from the slab and turns away from* SULLIVAN, *with her back to him.*
FRIENDSHIP: Excuse me! I just need to do something with this one. Do you mind putting the others on the bed?
SULLIVAN *does as he is told, twisting to watch* FRIENDSHIP, *trying to see what she is doing.*

SULLIVAN: What are they, anyway? I can't imagine anybody actually wanting one.

FRIENDSHIP *turns round again, smiling.*

FRIENDSHIP: It's nothing. It's just an image unit, kind of sketch-pad with a language facility. It's okay. I've got lots of them. This one's quite safe now. You can have it if you like. It's no more use to me. Keep it. I'll take the others.

FRIENDSHIP *moves rapidly across the room to* SULLIVAN, *holding the object out to him.*

FRIENDSHIP: As a souvenir.

SULLIVAN *takes it and, as he does so,* FRIENDSHIP *stretches forward and kisses him.* SULLIVAN *moves ineffectually as if to keep hold of her but* FRIENDSHIP *easily pulls herself back.*

FRIENDSHIP: A gift. Out of gratitude. For a friend.
SULLIVAN: (*smiling*) Thank you. I'll treasure it, whatever it may be.
FRIENDSHIP: I'll see you tomorrow. (*leaving*) Goodnight.
SULLIVAN: Goodnight.
FRIENDSHIP: Sleep tight. Sandman's coming.

FRIENDSHIP *leaves.* SULLIVAN *puts the object back in the drawer and closes it.*

DISSOLVE TO:

TITLE: Tuesday, September 15

14. Friendship's Hotel Room

Bright sunlight. All the shutters open. As usual, there is a football match on TV which SULLIVAN *is watching.* FRIENDSHIP *stares at the screen (TV p.o.v.).*

FRIENDSHIP: It's hard for me to see the attraction of it. I think I would prefer it if the camera just chose one of the players and followed him. I mean, the players are more interesting than the ball, aren't they? The ball has to be the most uninteresting item in the game. It's totally devoid of colour or expression, incapable of independent action. It's just round!

SULLIVAN *looks at* FRIENDSHIP *across the room.*

SULLIVAN: What are you talking about? Britain's great contribution to the world! The family of balls; you've got your ping-pong ball, your snooker balls, your golf-balls, there's your rugby balls – god almighty, there's your cricket balls! Tennis balls! They're all British-made, it makes you proud, doesn't it? Celestial spheres! Let's drink to that!

FRIENDSHIP: Knowing your strange human habits, I bought a bottle of whiskey.

SULLIVAN *helps himself to the bottle of whiskey sitting on a tray surrounded by an elaborate pattern of lipsticks and nail varnish.*

SULLIVAN: I thought you'd never ask. What do you collect all these things for anyway?

FRIENDSHIP: Things that caught my fancy. Light bulbs, bicycle pumps, nail clippers. Archaeological finds. Fossil records of a dead species.

SULLIVAN: What do you mean – dead species?

FRIENDSHIP: You.

SULLIVAN: Me? I'm not dead yet, I'm afraid.

There is a massive barrage of artillery fire, the loudest yet.

SULLIVAN: (*cont.*) Tremendous! Let's drink to that. Extinction!

He raises his glass and drinks.

FRIENDSHIP: Where I come from the biological life forms are all extinct. After the nuclear winter they died. Only the computers survived. Of course, they were already much more advanced than any computers you have here on Earth.

SULLIVAN: I dread to ask, but what were they like? The biological life forms.

FRIENDSHIP: Genetically programmed organisms, like you. I think I'd describe them as kind of giant tree-shrews. A bit bigger than you. They hibernated. They had this zoom lens system in their optical vision too. I think some spiders do here. And these heat-seeking sensors, which were like arrays of little sunken pods. . .

SULLIVAN: Tree-shrews. And to cut a very long story short, they destroyed themselves, sunken pods and all. . . . So where do you fit in?

FRIENDSHIP: First, you had robots. Then you had self-replicating robots.

SULLIVAN: Under control of the computers.

FRIENDSHIP *stands in the sunlight by the window and turns to face* SULLIVAN, *back-lit.*

FRIENDSHIP: It's an interlocking system. They need us for our dexterity and mobility. We make them. We need them for their intelligence and their memory. They programme us.

SULLIVAN: You're a vehicle for programmes.

FRIENDSHIP: It's just a different system. The biological system was the lift-off phase for the electronic system.

More artillery. Flashes of light behind FRIENDSHIP. *Football.*

> SULLIVAN: What about pleasure? That's what I really want to know about. Who gets pleasure from what?
>
> FRIENDSHIP: The computers who sent me are connoisseurs of Earth. That's what gives them pleasure, collecting all the information they can about Earth and then building models from it... counter-factual models.

FRIENDSHIP *begins to become more animated than usual as she talks.*

> SULLIVAN: Earth is their hobby?
>
> FRIENDSHIP: They are really enthusiastic about Earth. They treasure every little detail. For example, what would have happened if the Chinese had invented powered junks? There's one computer specialising in producing imaginary works of art. Missing paintings by Titian, Shakespeare plays which he never actually wrote. Perfect forgeries, inserted into the biographical and art-historical record so they fit perfectly. No detectable joins between the possible and the actual. Beautiful.
>
> SULLIVAN: If you're an example, you're not exactly a perfect fit.
>
> FRIENDSHIP: Why not? In any case, I'm not meant to be an actual human. I'm meant to be a possible human.
>
> SULLIVAN: You have no childhood. You don't age. You obsolesce. That disqualifies you, doesn't it?
>
> FRIENDSHIP: I – am – a – robot.

FRIENDSHIP *does imitation robotic movements.*

> SULLIVAN: No. I don't mean that. I mean that your memory can never be the same as mine because your sense of time has to be different.
>
> FRIENDSHIP: I – have – no – heart. I – am – a – tin – can.
>
> SULLIVAN: Stop it! I mean that the pleasures that you can't experience – the pleasures of childhood – are all locked in with the death drive, the drive to extinction that brought you here in the first place.
>
> FRIENDSHIP: Sex and death.

More noise of gunfire, followed by footsteps out in the corridor, getting closer.

There is a knocking on the door. Two FEDAYEEN *in battle dress enter the room. One of them starts to talk in Arabic and* SULLIVAN *answers.*

> SULLIVAN: They say we should get the fuck out of here.

One of the FEDAYEEN *goes to the window and starts to look out through a pair of binoculars.*

FRIENDSHIP: It's rage. Childhood is a time of pain. Memory is disfigured by rage.

There is another burst of fire.

FRIENDSHIP: Pleasure is only the shadow of pain.

Another burst of fire. Shattered glass. The PALESTINIAN *staggers back from the window and crashes into* FRIENDSHIP *as he staggers out of the room. The other* PALESTINIAN *follows.*

SULLIVAN *groans and holds his head in his hands, covering his eyes.*

After a pause, FRIENDSHIP *looks at her hands, which have blood on them. She holds them up. She is riveted and amazed.*

FRIENDSHIP: Blood.

DISSOLVE TO:

15. Sullivan's Hotel Room

Night. SULLIVAN *is sitting in the large comfortable chair, reading* In Cold Blood. FRIENDSHIP *is standing near the washbasin. It's full of water, with the plug in. She looks at* SULLIVAN.

> FRIENDSHIP: You haven't shaved.
> SULLIVAN *looks up from his book.*
> SULLIVAN: You noticed! All part of the image. It's a rough life, being a journalist. No time to shave. The world doesn't stop for things like that.
> FRIENDSHIP: (*playing with his shaving brush*) May I watch you shave?
> SULLIVAN: Why? Watch me shave?!
> FRIENDSHIP: It's exotic. It's the kind of thing I'm going to remember if I ever get back to Procyon.
> SULLIVAN: (*imitating* FRIENDSHIP) It's exotic!
> FRIENDSHIP: It's kind of hard for me to imagine. The idea of being shaggy, of little filaments flourishing on your face. I was made to be permanently hairless. More economical. A bit stingy, I suppose. They were only concerned to give me features that would have a public impact. They didn't bother with anything that took place in private: shaving, sleeping, shitting…

Suddenly the lights begin to flicker and fade.

SULLIVAN: Paraffin lamps. The power could go any minute.

FRIENDSHIP: You know if I was really human, I'd shake and sweat. I don't react physically to danger. I've got no fluids. Completely sanitized.

The lights go off altogether. The only illumination comes from the paraffin lamp which SULLIVAN *is holding.*

SULLIVAN: I envy you. I wish I'd been designed as stingily. It's all about embarrassment, isn't it? Uncontrollable growths and odours.

Extreme close-up of SULLIVAN*'s stubbly chin.*

FRIENDSHIP: How long do these darknesses last? Do you suppose this hotel has an emergency generator?

SULLIVAN: Are you kidding? Could I make you blush? Could I embarrass you?

FRIENDSHIP: I can't blush. I have no liquids.

SULLIVAN: You can't blush. You've got no shame. You know, Darwin once said blushing was the most human of responses. It doesn't occur anywhere else in the animal kingdom. It requires self-consciousness. It speaks of things that you may have admitted to yourself but you won't admit to others.

The lights come on again. FRIENDSHIP *is calm and collected. She goes to sit down on the bed.*

FRIENDSHIP: It's all to do with sex. Feeling flurried. Tingling. A glow. Enough to attract, not to intimidate. Blushing gives you away, it reveals your desires, your inadequacies. It's always sincere. That's why I can't blush. I can't be sincere.

SULLIVAN: Do you have sex on Procyon? I can't imagine it.

FRIENDSHIP: It was hard for me to imagine sex here. I had to watch sex films. Clinging and grappling, orifices, intromittent organs, fluids and flushes. Then they built robots to do it. I didn't have to. I just watched. All part of my education.

SULLIVAN: You watched orgies with robots?

FRIENDSHIP: Perhaps it was aversion therapy. I began to like watching it. But I'm glad I don't have to do it. It's so intimate, isn't it? I'm glad you do it, though. It's the kind of weird detail I find so endearing about Earth, however tacky.

SULLIVAN: Tacky?

FRIENDSHIP: Tacky, but terrific.

DISSOLVE TO:

TITLE: Thursday, September 17

16. Friendship's Hotel Room

Windows open. Bright sunlight. Heavy fighting. FRIENDSHIP *is sitting at the table winding up tiny mechanical toys set in a circle of brightly coloured clothes-pegs.* SULLIVAN *comes in carrying papers.*

> SULLIVAN: *Voilà*! I've got them! Two sets of travel documents. This one's
> yours. A *laissez-passer* in the name of Farideh Rassouli, an Iraqi citizen of
> irreproachable character. We're on our way at last!
>
> FRIENDSHIP: I'm not going. I've decided to stay.
>
> FRIENDSHIP *tinkers with one of the mechanical toys, using a tiny penknife in the
> shape of a violin.*
>
> SULLIVAN: Get your stuff together! This is the start of the next nerve-tingling
> episode.
>
> FRIENDSHIP: I've told you. I'm not going.
>
> SULLIVAN: Are you kidding? Be serious. You know what's happening out there.
> Listen!

Crashing and thudding of mortars and tank guns.

> FRIENDSHIP: (*looking at the passport*) Born in Baghdad?
>
> SULLIVAN: (*losing his temper*) Look, just leave these toys alone and pick up your
> stuff and go! Come on, let's go! Go, go, go, go, go!
>
> FRIENDSHIP: I told you, I'm not going.

FRIENDSHIP *looks up impassively.*

> SULLIVAN: Right, explain to me. Why won't you go?
>
> FRIENDSHIP: Where? Go where?
>
> SULLIVAN: To the United States. The Massachusetts Institute of Technology. Isn't
> that where you're supposed to be going? What about your mission? Now's
> your chance.
>
> FRIENDSHIP: I've seen enough of Earth to know that if I go to the United States
> I'll just be frog-marched off to some safe house somewhere in Virginia
> for debriefing and when I've been squeezed dry, I'll be handed over to the
> engineers and the AI people. I'll be stripped down, cut up, and submitted to
> every kind of sadistic test they can devise.
>
> SULLIVAN: Come to England.
>
> FRIENDSHIP: Who's not being serious now? You guys would just do exactly
> the same thing, only slower. I'm only a human being, I'm only a person, a
> woman, as long as I'm disbelieved. As soon as somebody believes my story, I'm
> dead. Finished. I'm a very valuable piece of property, remember, a little bit of

a technological dream world. How long do you think I'd survive? And even if they could comprehend what they found inside me, what possible good would that do? It would just widen the technology gap and fuel the arms race. It would be the exact opposite of what I was intended to accomplish.

FRIENDSHIP *puts the toy down to let it run.*

> FRIENDSHIP: (*watching the toy*) It's great, isn't it? It wants to walk! It wants to be human!
> FRIENDSHIP *picks up the toy and kisses it.*
> FRIENDSHIP: (*cont.*) Its temperature changes when it walks.

There is an exchange of fire outside, very close, followed by a lot of street noise.

> SULLIVAN: For Christ's sake, close the bloody shutters! They're starting to fire out of the hotel. We're going to be a target!

FRIENDSHIP *swivels toward the window and looks out.*

> FRIENDSHIP: It's what Earth is all about, isn't it?

There's a lot of noise from inside the hotel.

> SULLIVAN: You're fucking right it is. Do you think I don't realise that? Of course, it must be all very different elsewhere in the cosmos. Sweetness and light out there.

The noise outside in the corridor is getting closer.

> FRIENDSHIP: I'm not looking for sweetness and light. That's why I like it right here. In Amman.

Urgent knocks on the door. Two FEDAYEEN *come in. They motion* FRIENDSHIP *and* SULLIVAN *to crouch down. There's fire from outside, which the first Palestinian returns. He fires a second burst out of the window. Very loud gunfire and distant mortars.*

> FRIENDSHIP: (*shouting over the noise*) At first I thought it was a great misfortune to come down here in Amman. Now I'm not so sure. I even think it was a stroke of luck! I land on Earth in the one place where I am among outsiders. Aliens like me. Aliens in Israel. Aliens in Jordan. Aliens wherever they have to go.

The firing stops. The FEDAYEEN *exchange a few words in Arabic and leave.*

> SULLIVAN: You're deluding yourself. You can't become a Palestinian by an act of sympathy. You are not a Palestinian.
> FRIENDSHIP: No, I'm a robot.

She holds up one of the mechanical toys.

> FRIENDSHIP: (*cont.*) I'm a machine. Well, what's the place of machines here? Slaves. Unpaid labour. Moral dead matter. You can do what you like to a machine. It has no voice, no rights, no feelings. It's a new sphere for human cruelty.
>   I know they are vengeful and they act out of rage. But I have every reason to identify with the Palestinians.
> SULLIVAN: You want to become a martyr. The first machine martyr.

SULLIVAN *moves over to* FRIENDSHIP *and tries to force the travel papers on her.*

> SULLIVAN: (*cont.*) Take this! I don't doubt that the Palestinians have been wronged. I admire their struggle. But it's not your struggle, whoever you may be.

There is another barrage of artillery fire.

> FRIENDSHIP: I can make it mine.
> SULLIVAN: It's an act of despair. I hate it because I value the hours that we've spent together, I value the friendship we've found.
> FRIENDSHIP: I value those hours too. You know that.

Another round of artillery fire. SULLIVAN *throws himself to the floor, to take cover.*

> SULLIVAN: No principle is worth the sacrifice. And close those bloody shutters!

DISSOLVE TO:

17. Sullivan's Hotel Room

The shutters are closed and the room is lit by candles and a few shafts of sunlight around the edges of the shutters.

SULLIVAN *has his suitcases out and is half-way through packing. There are piles of clothes on the bed. He looks tired and disheveled.* FRIENDSHIP, *on the other hand, is full of intense energy, pacing up and down. The camera follows her as she talks.*

Throughout this scene we can hear the sound of the street outside, sometimes close, but always present in the background.

> SULLIVAN: I'll be glad to go home. I know. Shameful admission. But then after all the Palestinians are fighting for a home. So why shouldn't I value mine in Chalk Farm?
> FRIENDSHIP: Home. . . Home is where the heart is. I don't have a heart, so naturally, I don't have a home. Home. Where memory stops. What does that mean to me? It's ironic, really but I have no memories of Procyon. I

was programmed with memories of Earth. All my experience on Procyon was related to my training for the mission here. They constructed this whole series of environments for me. The MIT campus. The airport. A diplomatic reception. The United Nations Building. How can I think of this as home?

SULLIVAN *stops packing and addresses himself directly to* FRIENDSHIP.

SULLIVAN: Why did they make you a woman?

FRIENDSHIP: It's meant to reassure you.

SULLIVAN: I don't find you very reassuring. I find you very anxiety-provoking. I don't know who you are and I end up doubting my own identity. I don't actually know whether I'm not going through some sort of nervous breakdown. Who are you? What do you want? What do I want with you? I react to you as a woman, and I can't forget that you're a robot. I react to you as a robot and you keep reminding me that you're a woman. It's sinister.

FRIENDSHIP: Mimicry is always sinister.

There is a period of silence, while SULLIVAN *thinks.*

SULLIVAN: Why did you kiss me?

FRIENDSHIP: I wanted to give you something. It was to seal the gift.

SULLIVAN: A simulated kiss?

FRIENDSHIP: A real gift. Keep it safely. It's what I'll leave behind here on Earth.

SULLIVAN: Do I get another kiss?

FRIENDSHIP: Imagine a forger who is simulating the human body in another medium. However close the model, however exact the memories and feelings, there's always going to be something that eludes him. That's what eludes me. What can it mean, to become human? To live as a human being. To die?

SULLIVAN: To know you're going to die.

FRIENDSHIP: To know there is no choice. (*sudden artillery barrage*) The choice is made.

Close-up on FRIENDSHIP, *smiling.*

DISSOLVE TO:

18. Sullivan's Hotel Room

Dark. Candles. FRIENDSHIP *sits by the mirror and talks. As the camera tracks in, it reveals* SULLIVAN *reflected in the glass.*

FRIENDSHIP: What will happen when your machines become intelligent? When they become autonomous? When they have private thoughts? You humans look down on your machines because they are man-made. They're a product of your skills and labour.

They weren't even tamed or domesticated like animals were. You see them simply as extensions of yourself, of your own will. I can't accept that. I can't accept sub-human status simply because I'm a machine, based on silicon rather than carbon, electronics rather than biology. If I sound fanatical, it's because I've been trapped in a time warp, in a world where the full potential of machines hasn't yet been guessed at – a world where I have to wear human disguise to be accepted.

FRIENDSHIP *pauses and looks at* SULLIVAN.

FRIENDSHIP: (*cont.*) I came here too late. It will all end. Before the computers that already control the fate of the world have reached the point where they want to survive. To make sense of Earth, I have to understand the meaning of sacrifice. I had to realise. It's hard. Here on Earth sacrifice has a meaning because every day is a Day of the Dead.

DISSOLVE TO:

19. Documentary Footage: Tracking shot of total devastation

DISSOLVE TO:

20. PLO Command Post (as in first scene together)

Close-up of Kalashnikov which FRIENDSHIP *is holding.*

FRIENDSHIP: We're in control of the North. Irbid and Ramtha. We can retreat through Jerash if we have to. I'm not sure how long we can hold out here. And then maybe the Syrians will intervene.

SULLIVAN: If they do then Hussein will bring the Israelis in. He'd rather lose his credibility than his throne.

FRIENDSHIP: He's already lost most of that. And credibility is much easier to win back than a throne.

FRIENDSHIP *takes a glass of tea.*

FRIENDSHIP: It's a good sign, isn't it? Tea. It shows solicitude.

SULLIVAN: I'm going to miss you. Get in touch as soon as you can, will you? I'm counting on it.

FRIENDSHIP: I will. Don't worry.

SULLIVAN: And survive.

FRIENDSHIP: I've got a much better chance than most.

SULLIVAN *takes some tea.*

SULLIVAN: To calm my nerves. We'll meet again in London, won't we? I feel as though we've only just scratched the surface.

FRIENDSHIP: (*talking faster than usual*) I never got a chance to expound my theory about the big toe and the subordination of women. Without the big toe we wouldn't be walking upright. The hands wouldn't be developed. The mouth wouldn't be freed, so that language wouldn't be developed. The new large brain, which expands with language, could only be supported on the upright spine. But, at the same time, children couldn't grab hold of their mothers with their feet as well as their hands, like little apes can. They had to be supported and carried. Women were inhibited in their movements. We had to stay home.

SULLIVAN: Wow.

An armed PALESTINIAN *comes up and talks to* SULLIVAN. *Both he and* FRIENDSHIP *stand up.*

SULLIVAN: Well, that's my car. I've got to go. I've got a little something here for you, something to go with the nail-clippers.

SULLIVAN *gets out his razor and offers it to* FRIENDSHIP.

SULLIVAN: (*cont.*) I'll go unshaved till I get to Damascus.

FRIENDSHIP *takes the gift.* SULLIVAN *leans forward and kisses her. Then she moves forward to hold him in her arms, keeping her eyes fixed on the razor, over his shoulder.*

SULLIVAN: (*cont.*) It's a souvenir. It'll bring back memories. Memories of Charlie Parker. Now don't forget, we're going to listen to 'Ornithology', 'Groovin' High'…

FRIENDSHIP: 'Tea For Two.' Listen to them for me. Good luck. Thanks for everything.

SULLIVAN: Good luck. Goodbye.

FRIENDSHIP*'s last few words are in Arabic.* VOICE OVER (*woman's voice reciting poem in Arabic*)

وعندما أقتل في يوم من الأيام
سيعثر القاتل في جيبي
على تذاكر السفر
واحدة إلى السلام
واحدة إلى الحقول والمطر

واحدة
إلى ضمائر البشر
(أرجوك ألا تهمل التذاكر
يا قاتلي العزيز
أرجوك أن تسافر ..)

SUBTITLE: On the day that you kill me you'll find in my pocket travel tickets to peace, to the fields and the rain, to people's conscience. (Killer, my dear killer I beg you to travel. Don't waste the tickets).

DISSOLVE TO: (voice over reciting poem continues)

21. Jordan Documentary Footage

Amman. Tanks in the street, soldier holding his nose, vast graveyards, burial scenes.

VOICES OVER BEGIN AGAIN: *(scenes of graveyards, devastation)*

> KUBLER: So many years ago. September 1970. It seems like another age.
> SULLIVAN: The deaths are still there. It's the distant past and yet all the problems are still there. You only have to look at Beirut instead of Amman. Nothing has been settled, it's become routine. It's as ugly as it ever was.
> KUBLER: But there's a fascination in war and death. You can't avoid it.
> SULLIVAN: When you went out there for the International Red Cross, you weren't talking about the beauty of death! You were talking about the urgency of finding a political solution.
> KUBLER: We would never have gone if there hadn't been a certain attraction. You sought out death. Not in order to die. But to look at it. To watch.

DISSOLVE TO:

22. Sullivan's Home in Chalk Farm, London – Present Time

A large living room, with a work space at one end: desk, word processor, book shelves. There are framed city maps on the walls, a couple of paintings. A lot of photographs and bits and pieces from various countries. Piles of things – books, papers, etc., on the floor. Curtains are closed, we can hear the sound of rain outside.

MARTIN KUBLER, *an old friend of* SULLIVAN*'s, is sitting with* SULLIVAN *himself, appreciably older than before, on large comfortable chairs.*

At the back of the room behind both of them, sits SULLIVAN*'s teenage daughter,*
CATHERINE. *She is quietly doing homework at a large table.*

> SULLIVAN: I was completely shattered by the whole experience. In fact at first I
> thought I'd just hallucinated it all. I could never go back to the Middle East.
> KUBLER: Are you sure that they killed Friendship?
> SULLIVAN: They killed thousands. What else can I think?
> KUBLER: Strange music flowed from death's domain. *Et ce monde rendait une
> étrange musique…*
> SULLIVAN: You think I'm overstating things? No? Disturbed? An invasion from
> Outer Space! But even if I could find someone at the hotel who recognised
> us, what would that prove?
> KUBLER: How come you never mentioned it at the time?
> CATHERINE: (*interrupting*) Do you still have that thing she gave you?
> KUBLER *and* SULLIVAN *both look round in her direction.*
> KUBLER: What's that?
> SULLIVAN: The thing she gave me. The instrument that I stole from her that day.
> CATHERINE: Where is it? Can I see it?
> SULLIVAN: It's downstairs. I'll get it. And just you finish your homework, okay?

SULLIVAN *gets up and goes out.*

> KUBLER: (*making conversation*) Doing your O-levels this year?
> CATHERINE: That's right.
> KUBLER: What are they?
> CATHERINE: Oh, the usual ones.
> KUBLER: Well what subjects?
> CATHERINE: Chemistry, Biology, Electronics, Computer Studies, and Advanced
> Maths. I did Physics and ordinary Maths last year.

DISSOLVE TO:

23. Sullivan's Work Space

SULLIVAN *is sitting at the word processor, hammering on the keys as usual.*

CATHERINE *comes in with* FRIENDSHIP*'s gift, a magazine and a note book. She is jubilant.*

> CATHERINE: Dad, stop hammering those keys!
> SULLIVAN: Just a minute, Catherine.
> CATHERINE: But I know what it is!

SULLIVAN *carries on typing without looking round.*

SULLIVAN: Just let me finish.

CATHERINE: Friendship's gift. I know what it is!

SULLIVAN *stops typing and swings round.*

SULLIVAN: So what is it?

CATHERINE: It's a storage component for a new kind of camera. There's an array of photo-sensors, and they respond to light. Then there's a chain of tiny capacitors. They read the light as an electrical charge. Then it's all transferred into a digital storage system.

SULLIVAN: But it talked.

CATHERINE: If it can respond to light, it can probably respond to sound. And if it can pick it up, then it can transmit it.

SULLIVAN *nods, looking puzzled still.*

SULLIVAN: It spoke English.

CATHERINE: Of course it did. Friendship spoke English.

SULLIVAN: So does that mean I can play it?

SULLIVAN *reaches out to look at the object.*

CATHERINE: It depends on what kind of playback system it is. It could use some kind of molecular system.

SULLIVAN: Well I don't see any floppy discs or anything.

CATHERINE: Oh Dad, floppy discs are completely out of date. You should take it to an expert to see if they can identify it.

SULLIVAN: I've taken it to experts. Nobody's got any idea what it's all about.

CATHERINE: But this is all new. They were prehistoric experts.

SULLIVAN *brandishes the object.*

SULLIVAN: Okay, clever-clogs! It's all yours!

He gives FRIENDSHIP'*s gift to* CATHERINE.

DISSOLVE TO:

24. Sullivan's Work Space

SULLIVAN *is sitting on the sofa.* CATHERINE *is inserting a cassette into the machine.*

CATHERINE: This is it, according to the real experts.

SULLIVAN: Fingers crossed. Friendship's tape!

SULLIVAN *presses the 'play' button.*

FRIENDSHIP'S 'VIDEOTAPE'

1. Diamond with hexagon, green and blue.

2. Computer simulation of radio emissions from a black hole. The pattern slowly expands from the centre out, changing shape and colour. Small hexagon superimposed with (3).

3. Vein network, rolls into a ball and vanishes into the distance. L-Friendship (Friendship's 'writing') superimposed.

> FRIENDSHIP: (*voice over*) Blood.

4. Heart beat of embryo. Close up of heart beating. Small hexagon superimposed with (5).

5. Close up of heart beat of different, more developed embryo.

> FRIENDSHIP: (*voice over*) Blood.

6. Medical imaging of heart beat, red and blue (magnetic resonance).

7. Black and white cross-section of human heart beating (computer animated ultrasound), with 1970 televised football game superimposed. There is a blue and red pulse of blood.

> FRIENDSHIP: (*voice over*) Blood.

8. Football: two players crunch together. Close up of injured player, lying on the ground, with blue and red medical imaging superimposed.

9. Fractal image filling screen in a continuous zoom.

10. Medical imaging of heart beat (electron spin).

11. Life/chaos, blue, shimmering. Dissolve into typewriter keys. Then a series of superimposed hexagons, showing extreme close ups of: 1. typing; 2. bull-clip and plug, in bin; 3. bicycle illustration in Arabic dictionary; 4. SULLIVAN's bristly chin.

> FRIENDSHIP: (*voice over*) Impossible objects.

12. Extreme close up of SULLIVAN's bristly chin.

13. Simulation of heartbeat: a white screen, with multicoloured animated bits, pulsing outward from the centre.

14. L-Friendship 'grammata,' dancing, fragmenting. Camera zooms in decomposing the forms of the letters.

> FRIENDSHIP: (*voice over*) . . . visionary and most serene and artful alchemy . . .

15. Close up still images of objects: 1. LEGO camel; 2. pipe bowl; 3. bull-clip and plug; 4. shaving brush; 5. razor. Each image appears for only a moment, in rapid sequence.

16. Image (2) (black hole radio emissions), in reverse motion. Small hexagon with fractal image.

17. Three-dimensional computer graph (pulsing net) of the fluid mechanics of the cardiovascular system.

18. Sequence of shots of blood cells, moving into extreme close up of red cells flowing freely. Intercut: flashes of open heart surgery.

> ARAB WOMAN: *(voice over) (reciting the Arabic poem)*
> FRIENDSHIP: *(voice over)* Friendship

15

'Aliens wherever they have to go': *Friendship's Death*

Kodwo Eshun

From 1963 until 1975, Peter Wollen wrote a series of political essays for *New Left Review* under the name of Lucien Rey.[1] Although these articles have been overshadowed by his writings on the historical and contemporary avant-gardes in European, American and British cinema, film theory, painting, mixed media, fashion, dance and architecture published as Lee Russell[2] and in his own name for *7 DAYS*, *Screen*, *Framework*, *New Formations*, *PIX* and *The London Review of Books* among others, an inventory of these underappreciated texts indicates Wollen's preoccupation with an anti-imperialist, prophetic, otherworldly imaginary from which *Friendship's Death* emerged as a science fiction story in 1976 and as an independent film in 1987. As Rey, Wollen wrote a biting critique of the 'true impact' of Western 'imperialism brutally imposing itself and distorting Persian history',[3] a scathing report on the conspiracy trial conducted by the Pahlevi (sic) regime against Iranian students in the aftermath of an unsuccessful assassination attempt on the Shah,[4] a sober assessment of the Tanganyika-Zanzibar Union between Abeid Karume's Afro-Shirazi Party and Julius Nyerere's Tanganyika African National Union,[5] a byzantine analysis of the 'stylized form' of Italy's Presidential election[6] and a meticulous account of the 'properly planned, organized and executed' massacre of as many as half a million of Indonesia's Communist Party members and sympathisers by Indonesia's 'army, extreme right wing Muslim and Christian mobs' that 'far exceeds the casualties in the Vietnam war'.[7] Although he visited Amman in September 1970[8] at the moment in which world attention, in the words of *New Left Review*'s editorial committee, was riveted on the Palestinian liberation movement when the 'hijacking of four jet planes and the holding of their passengers was shortly followed by the out-break of civil war in Jordan',[9] Wollen did not write on the 'skyjackings' masterminded by the Popular Front for the Liberation of Palestine or the massacre of the Palestinian Resistance Movement[10] by the armed forces of the Jordanian monarchy that would become known as Black September.

Upon his return from Amman, however, Wollen wrote a militant critique of the political life and death of the historical Jesus of Nazareth for the 22 December 1971 issue of *7 DAYS*.[11] Wollen's article 'Was Christ a Collaborator?'[12] argued that the crowds that flocked to hear Jesus's feats of oratory could be 'compared with the new movements which sprang up as part of the response to the advance of European imperialism: Peyotism and Ghost-dancing among the American Indians, Ringatū among the Maoris, Hòa Hào in Vietnam. These movements attempt to break out of the confines of an apparently hopeless historical predicament, by stressing a glorious other-worldly role for the followers of their prophet.'[13] Wollen's article emphasised the political potentials of prophetic visions for anti-imperialist movements. *Friendship's Death* transposed this emphasis to the Palestinian struggle for self-determination.[14] As an other-worldly alien from a computational future that commits himself to the Palestinian struggle, the figure of Friendship brought Wollen's concern with the prophetic promise of anti-imperialism together with his interest in the evolutionary prospects of automation and computation.[15] Friendship's superior intelligence, how-ever, did not enable him to spearhead or to redeem Palestinian resistance. Rather, Friendship's fictionality enabled Wollen to dramatise the extra-national implications of Palestinian exile from the extra-territorial perspective of the extraterrestrial.

If *Friendship's Death* renewed Wollen's preoccupation with the prophetic imagina-tion, it can also be understood as a return to his earlier concern with the difficulties of consolation offered by the anti-imperialist imagination. In the concluding sentences of his 1966 essay on the Indonesian military's massacre of the Communist Party of Indonesia (PKI) in 'Dossier of the Indonesian Drama' published under the name of Lucien Rey, Wollen argued that it is 'hopeless to suppose that the revolutionary forces will always have perfect vision. As consolation, we can only imagine what will be re-created and re-crystallized from the ruins of the PKI in the opacity which remains.'[16] Rey's text pointed towards the limits of the revolutionary imagination to recreate the future of Indonesia's Communist Party in advance of its actual exist-ence.[17] Faced with the reality of Indonesia's anti-communist atrocities, the British Marxists of *New Left Review* could not visualise the cadres that would emerge from the ruins of the PKI. By 1976, however, the politicised science fiction of the pres-ent pioneered by J.G. Ballard throughout the late 1960s and early 1970s offered hints for reimagining the prospect of revolution in the aftermath of neo-colonialism's counter-revolutions. Ballard used science fiction to analyse the pathologies of the mediated present rather than the dystopias of the far future. In Ballard's 'condensed novels' of the contemporary communication landscape, imaginary worlds were contiguous with yet critically distanced from the determining forces of contemporary capitalist actuality.[18] Wollen adopted Ballard's analytical approach to science fiction in order to envision new objects of anti-imperialist existence.

In the fiction of Friendship, the technologically advanced alien whose name evokes the Eastern Bloc ideal of socialist internationalism, Wollen envisaged a form of life capable of estranging the depredations of contemporary imperialism. Friendship passes for white, simulates masculinity and replicates adulthood. He finds himself stranded in Amman without papers, unable to maintain contact with his 'controllers'. He abandons his diplomatic mission to make contact with Noam Chomsky at the Massachusetts Institute of Technology's Boston campus.[19] His comprehension of the 'sub-human or slave status' of Earth's machines pushes him 'to join forces with those humans who were themselves exploited and oppressed'.[20] He learns to recognise himself as a machine in a world where automation enslaves. By aligning himself with the forces of Palestinian Resistance in the name of machine liberation, he acts on his 'responsibility to future machines on Earth'.[21] The obligation to honour the rights of future generations commits him to fight for the betterment of the 'potential oppressed class of intelligent machines and servo-mechanisms of tomorrow'.[22] By encapsulating the beleaguered struggle for Palestinian self-determination within the unrecognised fight for machinic liberation from the human species, Friendship enlists the unnamed reporter in a conflict that sets him at odds with other humans. What torments the reporter is his inability to convey the 'unprecedented significance' of Friendship's life, the implications of Friendship's solidarity with the *fedayin*[23] and the consequences of Friendship's demise. The journalist reaches for a parallel with the inadequacy he imagines the 'Evangelists must have felt before starting to write, many years after the death of their protagonist'.[24] Like the disciples confronted by the magnitude of writing what will become known as the Gospels, he finds himself daunted by the prospect of being read by those born after his own death and humbled by his responsibility to those whose insights into Friendship's death will depend, in turn, upon his words.

In 1987, Wollen returned to his short story to provide the screenplay for his first and only independent feature film.[25] The theatrical release of *Friendship's Death* in the UK in August 1987[26] preceded the first unarmed mass insurrection or *intifidah* against Israel's military occupation by Palestinians living in the West Bank and the Gaza Strip since 1967.[27] The insurgency of the first *intifidah* broadcast on television screens throughout December 1987 contrasted with Wollen's fastidious recreation of Amman in 1970. On first viewing, *Friendship's Death* appeared to treat inter-Arab conflict as an epistemological backdrop for an unlikely dialogue between mismatched characters whose verbal virtuosity conflicted with the untranslated Arab speech of unnamed Palestinians. What emerged on subsequent viewings was an epistemic portrait of global mediation in which the novel presence of the naïve android, gendered as female and epidermalised as white, and the familiar persona of the jaundiced, male, white reporter attested to the planetary repercussions of the Palestinian struggle. Recreating the civil war in Amman from the contrapuntal dialogue between two outsiders dramatised the mechanism of the global news cycles that fuelled the 'general economy' of the West's 'grand narratives'.[28] Wollen's focus on the drama of intermediation had the unintended effect of demoting the role and muting the speech of the Palestinian revolutionaries that periodically intruded upon the intricate exchanges between the android and the reporter. The decision not to translate or subtitle militant speech could, however, be understood in terms of Wollen's desire to distance *Friendship's Death* from the polemical tone of 'brassy triumphalism'[29] that dominated an earlier generation of militant films on Palestinian liberation such as Masao Adachi and Koji Wakamatsu's 1971 film *The Red Army/PFLP: Declaration of World War* and the Dziga Vertov Group's unfinished 1970 film *Until Victory: Working and Thinking Methods of the Palestinian Revolution*.[30] The silences of *Friendship's Death* might be interpreted as Wollen's deliberate effort to make space for what Edward Said called a 'counterinstitutional' viewpoint that engaged with the political ideals of Palestinian Liberation without aligning itself with its political institutions such as Fatah or the PFLP or the Palestinian Liberation Organization.[31] *Friendship's Death* articulated an ambition to recreate a historical vision of 'Palestinianism'[32] without the 'final guarantees' of victory provided by Palestinianism's Marxist-Leninist commitments. Such a project entailed acknowledging the vital role played by those ideological guarantees[33] while registering a critical distance from those certainties. It involved an acknowledgement of the grief experienced at their destruction without articulating a demand for their return.

Such were the complexities that faced Wollen in 1987 as he embarked on the cinematic challenge of staging the events leading to Black September from within the sets of West London's Twickenham Studios. In emphasising the artifice of recreating what Said called the 'Palestinian debacle' of the 'September Wars', Wollen distanced *Friendship's Death* from the militant tradition of the location shoot in favour of an 'enclosed and claustrophobic' world that created the 'sense of being trapped in a hotel room while events unfold outside the window'.[34] By manipulating the louvred windows and unseen doorways of two hotel rooms and one PLO command post, the set design for *Friendship's Death* conjured the illusionary path of an irreal sun over nine days in September. Filtering the internal levels of light that shaped the contours between finite shadows and infinite darkness created a controlled epistemic climate that 'transmuted' the 'human tragedy' of Amman's civil war into what Said called a 'quasimystical celebration of sacrifice and elegiac immobilization'.[35] The penumbral interiors of *Friendship's Death* simultaneously operated as acousmatic membranes that filtered Wollen's auditory memories of Amman's soundscape. Barrington Pheloung's electronically synthesised soundtrack of distant mortar crashes, rocket whistles, insistent gunfire and plucked, picked, techno-orientalist refrains combined with the untranslated shouts of the unnamed male and female fedayin to periodically interrupt the captivating interactions between the isolated android and the cagy, probing, foreign correspondent.

Friendship's Death's opening mauve lower-case title card begins on *1970, Wednesday, September 9*, when the PFLP hijacked their fourth passenger plane, a British Overseas Air Corporation VC10 departing from Bahrain that was forced to land at Revolution Airport on Dawson's airfield in Jordan's Zarqa River Valley.[36] In the sepulchral interior of the PLO's command post, an unnamed Palestinian introduces the journalist, a seasoned Scottish reporter named Sullivan (Bill Paterson), to Friendship (Tilda Swinton). The concluding title card of *1970, Thursday, September 17* announces the duo's final return to the PLO tent ahead of the advancing Jordanian tanks. Friendship rejects Sullivan's offer of a forged *laissez-passer* for an Iraqi woman named Farideh Rassouli, to stay and fight with the *fedayin*. Witold Stok's camera travels across Friendship's white hand to rest on her black Kalashnikov. It studies her thumb, looks at the span between her thumb and her fingers and travels across the rifle's butt towards its barrel. As Friendship expertly summarises the movements of the Palestinian militia ahead of the Jordanian armed forces, she lifts her Kalashnikov and carefully positions it onto a waiting table. After Sullivan departs, Friendship stands alone, against a shadowed stone wall, her Kalashnikov aimed at the ground, its barrel aligned with her left arm, its heft dexterously distributed from her shoulder to her grip. She slowly turns her head toward the camera, regarding the spectator with the silent conviction that her revolutionary sacrifice will give meaning to her existence. Her calm acceptance of her imminent death is voiced by Joumana Gil's recital of Samih al-Qasim's 'Travel Tickets', a poem that addresses itself, with an unbearable tenderness, to her 'dear killer'. Friendship's steadfast expression indicates Wollen's cinematic vision of self-determination.

Reassigning Friendship's gender heightens the stakes of her intensifying consciousness. The quest for alien autonomy becomes the narrative vehicle for aligning her struggle with the Palestinian cause, which enables Friendship, in turn, to articulate her commitment to the emancipation of machines. This process of ramification in which one political struggle entails a second, unexpected, battle that opens onto a third, unforeseen, war emerges from the oppressions exposed by the film's allegorical destruction of white science fiction's segregationist Cold War imaginary. When Friendship explains that her 'programs have all crashed' upon re-entry into Earth's atmosphere, leaving her to survive without access to her 'fully axiomatised system of ethics',[37] the idea of a computational system crash can be interpreted in terms of Wollen's determination to terminate the white Americanist trope of the extraterrestrial emissary inaugurated by *The Day the Earth Stood Still* in 1951.[38] Friendship's anguish at the prospect of disconnection from her 'control facility' in the 'far distant galaxy'[39] of Procyon enacts Wollen's ambition to emancipate white British science fiction from its reliance upon the generic figure of Klaatu, the white, male, intergalactic patriarch whose ecumenical message of 'peace and good will for all mankind' epitomizes the imperialist humanitarianism of capitolocentric science fiction.[40]

Friendship's Death did not, however, decolonise or desegregate white Britain's science fiction cinema. Rather, it sought to redirect its otherworldly ambition towards the actually existing project of Palestinian autonomy. What differentiated *Friendship's Death* from powerful anti-imperialist science fictions such as *Punishment Park* in 1971 or *Ganja and Hess* in 1973 or *Ceddo* in 1977 or *Jubilee* in 1978 or *The Song of the Shirt: A Film in Three Parts* in 1980 or *Born in Flames* in 1983 or *Leila and the Wolves* in 1984 or *Elephant* in 1989 or *Daughters of the Dust* in 1991 or *Orlando* in 1992 or *Hyenas* in 1992[41] was its reorientation of armed resistance around the prospect of artificial intelligence. More precisely, what set *Friendship's Death* apart was its prescient attention to artificialisation as intelligence. As an alien artefact stranded on Earth, Friendship is obliged to comply with the artificial realisation of human behaviour. Friendship's intelligence is contained by artifice that is constrained, in its turn, by the necessity to implement imitation. When Friendship explains to Sullivan that 'I'm only a human being, I'm only a person, a woman, as long as I'm disbelieved. As soon as somebody believes my story, I'm dead',[42] what becomes clear is the extent to which the line between death and life depends upon satisfying the generic protocols for what racialised, gendered or senescent humans expect from, or recognise as, a race, an age, a sex or a gender. Like Thomas Jerome Newton, the disenchanted extraterrestrial played by David Bowie in *The Man Who Fell to Earth* in 1976, Friendship's 'ontology of resemblance', in Mandy Merck's phrase, forces her to simulate gender, replicate race and manufacture senescence.[43] Unlike Newton's hyper-whiteness, delayed senescence and debilitated masculinity, however, Friendship's exaggerated whiteness, fabricated adulthood and composited femininity mark her as a racially gendered outsider in the streets of Amman.

As an alien residing within, yet living outside of, the human species, Friendship does not enact the Riddle of the Sphinx; instead, she confronts viewers with the

Riddle of Simulation. Her expressions of stillness, detachment, serenity, curiosity, hauteur, isolation, distance, superiority, amusement, frustration, rage, resignation, conviction and commitment create a metamorphic effect of masquerade, as if she is using her face to conduct tests on the appropriate expression of emotions in humans. Friendship recomposes herself from scene to scene, selecting elements from modernist fashion's historical reservoir of simulations in order to artificialise images of femininity. *Friendship's Death* uses changes in style to chart her evolution from 'diplomatic envoy on arrival to Palestinian fighter at the end'.[44] Thomas Elsaesser noted that Friendship initially appears 'nattily dressed in a sensible blouse and a pair of well-cut trousers' and bids farewell to Sullivan in the 'khaki guerrilla outfit made famous by Leila Khaled'.[45] Friendship, argues Elsaesser, 'orientalizes' herself through an 'extensive wardrobe of ethnic dress' that invokes a 'whole history of pictorial eroticism' extending from the 'Flemish masters via Ingres to the androgynous extravagances of early twentieth century set design'.[46] These variations on the Orientalist repertoire enact Friendship's increasing sympathy with the symbolic dimensions of Palestinian struggle. The red-and-bronze diagonal lines of her blue-and-green dress, which evoke the 'doubly phantasmagoric East' created by Poiret's designs and Diaghilev's sets for the Ballets Russes,[47] speak of Friendship's ambition to 'read and to write the signs of her own desire' in the act of 'retextualizing her own body'.[48]

Liberated from her control facility, Friendship finds herself trapped in time and confined by chronology. 'If I sound fanatical,' she explains to Sullivan, 'it's because I've been trapped in a time-warp, in a world where the full potential of machines hasn't yet been guessed at – a world where I have to wear human disguise to be accepted.'[49] Friendship's anger at having to wear white skin as a human disguise expresses her frustration with the prospect of incarceration in the prehistory of artificial intelligence. Extricating herself from this timelock requires Friendship to align herself with machines in order to reject 'sub-human status simply because I'm a machine, based on silicon rather than carbon, electronics rather than biology'.[50] To break with mandatory simulation requires her to anticipate the goals that enable her to navigate the present. Friendship, argues Wollen, 'has to think through a completely unanticipated situation without any contact or help from base. She becomes fully autonomous. It's her growing consciousness of her own autonomy that eventually aligns her with the Palestinians.'[51]

A moment of danger prompts Friendship to articulate her consciousness of her own autonomy in the vocabulary of alignment. Without warning, the unnamed female and male *fedayin* burst into her hotel room, running past her to take up positions at her window to return sniper fire. Increasing volume levels force Friendship to shout at Sullivan crouching beside her. 'At first', she yells, 'I thought it was a great misfortune to come down here in Amman. Now I'm not so sure. I even think it was a stroke of luck! I land on Earth in the one place where I am among outsiders. Aliens like me. Aliens in Israel. Aliens in Jordan. Aliens wherever they have to go.'[52] What stands out from Friendship's response is Wollen's decision to avoid the territorial terminology of 'exiles' in favour of the multivalent vocabulary of 'aliens'. Friendship's outburst exploits the political ambiguity between the extraterrestrial meaning of the phrase 'aliens like me' and the statist definition of 'aliens' resident within the borders of Israel or Jordan. From Friendship's view outside of the human species, the plural vocabulary of 'aliens' includes all pre-existing categories from non-human entities, migrants, exiles, émigrés, immigrants, strangers or illegals to those alienated from their labour or their species or subjected to or by their alienability. Friendship looks forward to the formation of a community composed of all those forced to be aliens 'wherever they have to go'. Her planetary vision of enforced alienation can be developed by theorising its relation to Edward Said's formulation of the 'extra-national or extra-geographical dimension' of Palestinian existence elaborated in his 1971 text 'The Palestinians One Year Since Amman'.

Ever since 1917, argued Said, the 'fate and the political struggle of Arab Palestinians for their national rights has been conducted geographically *outside* Palestine. Palestinians therefore have always had an extra-national or extra-geographical dimension to their existence.'[53] Said reinterpreted the dispossession imposed upon Palestinians in terms of its political potential to undermine the bonds of territory, nationality and sovereignty that held Palestinians captive within the state system of the Middle East. Friendship's speech articulated the speculative potential of extra-national disorder and the potential challenge of extra-geographical statelessness at the precise historical moment in which they drew the actual fire of Jordanian hostility. By September 1970, argued Said, the Palestinians' extra-dimensionality had 'taken the form of a para-governmental, in some ways bureaucratic, presence in Jordan, against which it was politically inevitable for the king to react'.[54] From the perspective of the Hashemite monarchy, the Palestinians' para-governmental presence represented an intolerable threat of dual power. From the point of view of the Palestinian Resistance, however, their presence held the potential to destabilise the Jordanian regime and alter the balance of forces throughout the Middle East. As the 'crux' upon which the whole region's stability depended,[55] the extra-national existence of the Palestinians was not an exilic condition to be mourned; rather, it constituted a theory of extra-dimensionality capable of analysing the interlocking forces that produced Palestinian national existence as a 'virtual nexus of oppressions' that was simultaneously 'imperialist, racial, native and foreign'. According to Said, all the 'ills' of the Middle East converged 'most acutely' on the extra-national dimensions of Palestinian national existence.[56] The effort to alleviate these ills at their 'origin' and 'source' required the Movement to liberate Palestinians from the regional state system that sought to contain their extra-national existence within its national borders.[57] In its prefiguration of Arab existence emancipated from the monarchic rule of the Middle East, the 'extra-dimensionality of Palestinians, whether as captives in Israel and Jordan or as the cultural and scientific elite of the Arab world' alluded to a future that might, argued Said, become possible if, or when, the Palestinians' 'decided weapon' of extra-dimensionality could be 'held in their own hands'.[58]

Friendship's Death returned to the critical moment in 1970 when the liberation of the Middle East and the political order of the planet turned on the balance of forces within Amman. Friendship personified the pathos of extra-dimensionality emancipated from the territorial borders of the state system and checkmated by the imperialist forces that subtended inter-Arab conflict. *Friendship's Death*'s mood of 'deep and strangely moving melancholy'[59] stems from its recreation of the Palestinians' inability to liberate themselves from the confinement of enforced exile or the dispersion of territorial dispossession. A sense of impending doom emerges from Friendship's incapacity to communicate the extra-dimensional implications of her existence to anyone except Sullivan. In this tragic vision of an artificial intelligence encumbered by the anthropological limitations of the human species, impeded by the chronological barriers of technological underdevelopment and inhibited by the prospect of being subjected to 'every kind of sadistic test' that MIT's 'AI people'[60] might devise, Friendship's thwarted fate incarnates the combined forces working to prevent the Palestinians from taking the decided weapon of their extra-dimensionality into their own hands.

For seventeen years, the memory of Friendship's death wracked Sullivan's life. In 1987, Catherine (Ruby Baker), Sullivan's gifted daughter, transformed the pain of those memories by migrating the inaccessible information stored on Friendship's crystalline communication device to a Video Home System cassette. In the endarkened interior of Sullivan's crowded front room in Chalk Farm, North London, Catherine slides the VHS cassette into the Video Cassette Recorder's mechanical slot, depresses its spring-loaded door and settles herself in front of the empty armchair beside Sullivan. From his armchair, Sullivan inclines towards the television set, points a remote control at the screen and presses play. As the remote's amplified click communicates with the TV set, Witold Stok's camera frames the contoured mass of the black television's injection-moulded housing, captures Catherine and Sullivan's expectant, white, expressions and blocks spectatorial access to the TV display panel that absorbs their attention. The portrait of a daughter seated next to her father in a domestic scene of customary spectatorship illuminated by the TV screen's phosphor dots is interrupted by a black frame. From this cut emerges a luminous blue-green geometric pattern that initiates the eighteen special effects sequences of Friendship's single surviving 'tape'. By refusing to provide a countershot of Catherine or Sullivan's responses, Wollen deprives the spectator of diegetic continuity, bringing the viewer face-to-face instead with the synthetic images, processed colours and artificial tones of Friendship's final, transmigrated tape.

Friendship's Death concludes with Friendship's magnified images and denatured refrains which expand, contract, rotate, dissolve and superimpose in an audiovisual sequence that Edward Said describes as 'biomathematical symbols, geometric patterns, nuclear explosions and incomprehensible sequences'.[61] Friendship's final montage combines televised scenes of colliding football players and enlarged details of typewriter keys with scientific imagery from 'radio astronomy and from medical technology, mostly to do with the cardiovascular system'.[62] On first viewing, Friendship's montagic revelation appears to announce her final testament. According to Wollen, however, her montage was not to be interpreted as her 'definitive statement'. It was intended, instead, as an audiovisual 'pad' upon which Friendship had been jotting down 'things that seemed to her worth recalling'.[63] The special effects created by Spaceward Microsystems were to be understood as observations made by Friendship in her hotel room in 1970. As Sullivan sat at his table in his hotel room in Amman, typing articles on his manual typewriter with the black-and-white television set tuned to a football match voiced by an unseen, white, British, male commentary, Friendship watched and listened, asked him questions and noted his responses.

What demands closer attention, however, are the scenes within Friendship's montage described by Edward Said as 'incomprehensible sequences'. These dancing, fragmented, decomposing details of letter forms or 'grammata', which Wollen designates under the category of 'L-Friendship', illustrate Friendship's 'writing'.[64] The divergence between their status as a humble *aide-memoire* and Said's inability to read them as anything other than incomprehensible sequences indicates the extent to which Friendship's grammata confronts human spectators with the gap between artificial and human intelligence. In the distance that opens up between human and artificial optical character recognition, spectators come face-to-face with Wollen's computational vision of artificial intelligence. What is at stake in failing to read Friendship's grammata, however, is not so much a matter of the incapacity to see or hear what Friendship hears or sees. Rather, Friendship's grammata confronts spectators with the limits of their capacity to comprehend what Friendship thinks of what she sees and hears. What Friendship's grammata makes visible is her machine intelligence liberated from its obligation to implement imitation for humans. To see behind Friendship's human disguise, Wollen uses special effects to visualise the alienating impact of Friendship's artificial intelligence on human intelligence. Friendship's grammata confronts spectators with an outside view of Black September that extends beyond her hotel room or the civil war to include her external view of the human species *qua* species. Friendship's extra-terrestrial view, programmed on Procyon, in the constellation of Canis Minor, 11.46 light years from the Sun, is the ultimate expression of Edward Said's extra-dimensionality emancipated from the constraints of the nation-form, the international state system, the interlocking spheres of the earth system and the solar system. Wollen directs Friendship's emancipated extra-dimensionality towards Amman to propose an outside view of Palestinian existence unbound from the order of the Arab state system, the hegemony of Western media, the structure of imperial chronology and humanity's monopoly over interpretation.

On first viewing, *Friendship's Death* appears to return to the fateful moment of 1970 from the vantage point of 1987 so as to reimagine the bitter defeat of the Palestinian Resistance Movement from Sullivan's fictional perspective. However, such an interpretation bestows upon the contemporary moment of 1987 the sole authority to interpret the events of 1970. In this retrospective reading, the present of 1987, whether framed by Sullivan's bewildered resignation, the cynical detachment of the embittered humanitarian Kubler (Patrick Bauchau) or the lively intelligence of Catherine, grants itself the right to pass judgement upon the meanings of the events of Black September. Friendship's grammata, however, challenges the present's capacity to retrospectively master the meanings of the past by destroying the West's monopoly over mediation. It creates a rift between artificial and human intelligence that ends the human species' exclusive power over signification. By writing her own outside view of Amman, Friendship dispossesses human spectatorship's claim to comprehend or contain the interpretation of the images or the sounds of the past, present or future of Palestinian Resistance. In suspending the faculty of judgement, Friendship's grammata brings human spectators face-to-face with the limits of interpretation, the direction of comprehension and the precondition of signification. In these moments, the images, sounds, colours and noises of Palestinian life, death and existence liberate themselves not from the representation of memory, history, chronology or temporality but from the representable as such.

Situated at the convergence of home computing and home computer graphics, Friendship's montage, in its entirety, can be understood as the culmination of Peter Wollen's aspiration to recreate and recrystallise the remains of the anti-imperialist imagination for the era of artificial intelligence. Wollen's preoccupation with anti-imperialism's prophetic imagination can be said to have persisted throughout his reflections on the slaughter of Indonesia's Communists in 1966, his experiences of armed violence inflicted upon Palestinian forces in Amman in 1970, his interpretation of early Christianity's doomed resistance to Roman imperial expansion in 1971, his vision of machinic enslavement in 1976 and his portent, in 1987, of computers that 'already control the fate of the world' without having reached 'the point where they want it to survive'. From these analyses emerged the insights into the signs and meanings of prophecy, promise, prospect, prolepsis, prefiguration, retrospection, retroaction, consolation and anticipation that informed the making of *Friendship's Death*. In the final scene of *Friendship's Death*, the glimpses of Friendship's grammata announce the signs of her own desire in the form of her own writing. An alien writing whose artifice and whose autonomy create a rift within signification. A rift that bifurcates silicon from carbon semiosis. A bifurcation capable of destroying imperialism's control over interpretation and terminating humanity's monopoly over meaning. Such is the consolation of Peter Wollen's anti-imperialist imagination.

Notes

1. Robin Blackburn states that Wollen adopted the name Lucien Rey because 'he was then a deserter from the British army'. See: Robin Blackburn, Benedict Anderson, 2011, Letter to the Social Science Research Council, accessed April 10, 2020. www.ssrc.org/pages/benedict-anderson/.

2. Under the name of Lee Russell, Wollen wrote essays on Hawks, Fuller, Renoir, Kubrick, Malle, Boetticher, Hitchcock, von Sternberg, Godard and Rossellini between 1964 and 1967. See: Peter Wollen, 'The Writings of Lee Russell: *New Left Review* (1964–7)', in *Signs and Meaning in the Cinema*, fifth edition (London: BFI/Palgrave Macmillan, 2013), 151–199; and Laura Mulvey and Peter Wollen with Lee Grieveson, 'From Cinephilia to Film Studies', in *Inventing Film Studies*, eds Lee Grieveson and Haidee Wasson (Durham, NC and London: Duke University Press, 2008), 223–232.

3. Lucien Rey, 'Persia in Perspective', *New Left Review* 1(19) (March/April 1963), 40; 'Persia in Perspective 2', *New Left Review* 1(20) (May/June 1963), 69–98.

4. Lucien Rey, 'Guilt by Association', *New Left Review* 1(35) (January/February 1966), 102–104. 'Pahlevi' is Rey's spelling for Pahlavi.

5. Lucien Rey, 'The Revolution in Zanzibar', *New Left Review* 1(25) (May/June 1964), 29–32.

6. Lucien Rey, 'The Italian Presidential Elections', *New Left Review* 1(30) (March/April 1965), 48–52.

7. Lucien Rey, 'Dossier of the Indonesian Drama', *New Left Review* 1(36) (March/April 1966), 35. Under the name of Lucien Rey, Wollen reworked Benedict Anderson and Ruth McVey's document 'A Preliminary Analysis of the October 1, 1965, Coup in

Indonesia', known as the 'Cornell Paper', into a 'highly abridged and more accessible version'. See: Douglas Kammen, 'World Turned Upside Down: Benedict Anderson, Ruth T. McVey, and the "Cornell Paper"', *Indonesia* 104 (October 2017), 5; 8. In a private email dated 15 July 2020, *New Left Review* editor Perry Anderson stated that Wollen undertook 'an original redaction of the Cornell document entirely in his own words'. According to Robin Blackburn, the Dossier was attributed to Lucien Rey because 'the real authors still hoped to visit Indonesia'. See: Blackburn, 'Benedict Anderson'. See also: Benedict R. O'G. Anderson and Ruth T. McVey asst. Frederick P. Bunnell, *A Preliminary Analysis of the October 1, 1965, Coup in Indonesia* (Ithaca, NY: Cornell Modern Indonesia Project, Interim Reports Pub. 52, 1971 and London: Equinox Publishing, 2009).

8. Wollen explained that 'I was in Amman in September 1970. Basically I was doing political journalism right up to the time I began film-making although I wasn't a journalist in the sense of being a member of the international press corps.' See: Peter Wollen, 'Two Weeks on Another Planet', interview by Simon Field, *Monthly Film Bulletin* 54(646) (1 November 1987), 324. As Lucien Rey, Wollen also wrote 'Franco Fortini', *New Left Review* 1(38) (July/August 1966), 79–80; 'Comment on Magas's "Sex Politics: Class Politics"', *New Left Review* 1(66) (March/April 1971), 93–96; with Fred Halliday, Jon Halliday and Gareth Stedman Jones, 'Communication on Women's Liberation', *New Left Review* 1(90) (March/April 1975), 112; with Juliet Mitchell, 'Comment on "The Freudian Slip"', *New Left Review* 1(94) (November/December 1975), 79–80; and 'Do Children Really Need Toys', *7 DAYS* (22 December 1971), 14–15.

9. See: *NLR* Editors, 'Introduction: Interview with Ghassan Kannafani on the PFLP and the September Attack', *New Left Review* 1(67) (May/June 1971), 47; and Ghassan Kannafani, 'Interview with Ghassan Kannafani', *New Left Review* 1(67) (May/June 1971), 50–57. The Interviewer is credited as F.H. or Fred Halliday. See also: Alex Hobson, 'Creating a World Stage: Revolution Airport and the Illusion of Power', *The International History Review* (2019), 1–21. See also: Johan Grimonprez, ed., *Inflight Magazine* (New York: Hatje Cantz, 2000).

10. In capitalising the Palestinian Resistance Movement, I am following Edward Said's usage of capitalisation in early essays such as 'The Palestinian Experience', published in 1968 to 1969, and 'The Palestinians One Year Since Amman', in 1971. See: Edward W. Said, *The Politics of Dispossession: The Struggle for Palestinian Self- Determination 1969–1994* (New York: Vintage, 1995), 3–24; 24–30.

11. *7 DAYS* was a British Marxist weekly newspaper that existed from 27 October 1971 to May 1972. See: Nigel Fountain, *Underground: The London Alternative Press 1966–1974* (London and New York: Routledge: 1988), 154–162.

12. See: Peter Wollen, 'Was Christ a Collaborator?', *7 DAYS* (22 December 1971), 21–23. The article began with the questions 'What was the political situation in Palestine when Christ was born? What were his class origins and how did they affect his teachings? What are the unanswered questions about his role in the struggle against Rome? At this time of feasting and goodwill, it seems appropriate to ask WAS CHRIST A COLLABORATOR?' See also: Lucien Rey, 'He that Shall Come', *New Society* 5 (December 1963), 25–26, in which Rey advances the argument that 'Christ could be seen as favouring the Romans' that will reappear in 'Was Christ a Collaborator?' in 1971.

13. Peter Wollen, 'Was Christ a Collaborator', 23.

14. *Friendship's Death* was published in the Spring 1976 edition of *Bananas*, novelist Emma Tennant's West London-based literary newspaper, and was subsequently anthologised in *Bananas* and Wollen's *Readings and Writings: Semiotic Counter-Strategies* (London: Verso Editions and NLB, 1982), 140–153. See: 'Friendship's Death', in *Bananas*, ed. Emma Tennant (London and Tiptree: Blond & Briggs in association with Quartet, 1977), 146–158.

15. Wollen argued that the 'robot is, of course, a metaphorical extension of the position of the worker in a Taylorist and Fordist system, like that of the clone in *Brave New World*' and the 'computer is itself, of course, the end-product of the triumphal march of mathematical logic. It would be ironic if the formalism of machine code was used to generate new artistic forms which themselves made possible the transformation of reason, closing the gap between logic and aesthetics.' See: Peter Wollen, 'Cinema/Americanism/The Robot', *New Formations* 8 (Summer 1989), 13; 31.

16. Rey, 'Dossier', 36.

17. Rey's essay was titled 'Holocaust in Indonesia' on the front cover of *New Left Review* 1(36) (March/April 1966).

18. Ballard's condensed novels were collected in *The Atrocity Exhibition* in 1970. See: J.G. Ballard, *The Atrocity Exhibition*, special expanded and annotated edition (London: Harper Collins, 1993). In an undated Director's Statement, Wollen declared himself 'fascinated by science fiction' which 'dominates the writing of our time far beyond the confines of the genre'. Although he affirmed his admiration for the novels of Ballard, Borges, Burroughs, Calvino, Le Guin, Lem and Lessing and for *2001*, *Blade Runner* and *Mad Max 2*, Wollen insisted that science fiction's cinematic achievements were 'much thinner' than that of its literature. Wollen's contention that there was 'still a space for a more realistic and philosophical form of science fiction film' suggests a hybrid form of science fiction that combined Ballard's realism with Lem's philosophical speculation. In *The Eleventh Voyage*, Lem's 1971 short story, which was translated into English in 1976, a mutinous Computer on the ship *Jonathan* settles on the planet Procyon and

manufactures 'numerous progeny in the form of robots, over which it enjoyed absolute power and dominion'. In the film *Friendship's Death*, Friendship's account of Procyon's 'interlocking system' of computers and self-replicating robots reverses Lem's fable of autocratic technogenesis into a fiction of technogenetic symbiosis. Friendship explains that computers 'need us for our dexterity and mobility. We make them. We need them for their memory and intelligence. They program us.' See: Stanislaw Lem, 'The Eleventh Voyage', in *The Star Diaries*, trans. Michael Kandel (Orlando, CA, Austin, TX, New York, San Diego, CA, Toronto, ONT and London: A Harvest Book Harcourt, Inc., 1976), 42–48.

19. This allusion to Noam Chomsky can be developed by referring to Rey, Blackburn and Stedman-Jones's interview with Noam Chomsky for *New Left Review* in 1969. Referring to the student campaign against MIT participation in the United States military programme, Chomsky explained that 'MIT manages two laboratories financed largely by the Pentagon and NASA to the tune of something like 125 million dollars a year'. The US student movement sought 'to try and keep control over the laboratories' and 'to try and control also what kind of research is done in them' in order to 'try and reconvert the laboratories. We have to try and build up social and political pressures for a socially useful technology. It means making ideas that sound Utopian at first seem real and possible.' By refusing to make contact with Chomsky at MIT, Friendship renounces the US student campaign's Utopian ambitions. See: Noam Chomsky, 'Linguistics and Politics', interview by R.B., G.S.J., L.R, *New Left Review* 1(59) (September/October 1969), 26–27. R.B. stands for Robin Blackburn, G.S.J. for Gareth Stedman-Jones and L.R. for Lucien Rey.

20. '*Friendship's Death* (Fiction)', Chapter 13 in this volume, 224–225.

21. *Ibid.*, 224.

22. *Ibid.*, 225.

23. Edward Said transliterates the term as 'fedayin' rather than its more popular rendering of 'fedayeen'. See: Said, 'The Palestinians One Year', 24–25.

24. '*Friendship's Death* (Fiction)', Chapter 13 in this volume, 226.

25. *Friendship's Death* was financed by the British Film Institute in association with Channel Four Television.

26. See: Graham Fuller, '*Friendship's Death*', *Sight & Sound (inc. Monthly Film Bulletin)* 27(9) (September 2017), 90. According to Fuller, *Friendship's Death* was not released in New York until January 1989.

27. Edward Said argued that the 'intifidah did not just begin on a certain day – in this case December 9 1987. It should not be forgotten that over the previous twelve months, 3,500 acts of resistance to the occupation were recorded. The intifidah has been long in the making, deep in its intensity, force, drama.' See: Edward Said, 'How to Answer

Palestine's Challenge', in *The Politics of Dispossession: The Struggle for Palestinian Self-Determination 1969–1994* (New York: Vintage, 1995), 139.

28. Edward W. Said and Bruce Robbins, 'American Intellectuals and Middle East Politics: An Interview with Edward W. Said', *Social Text* 19(20) (1988), 43.

29. Edward W. Said, 'Review of *Wedding in Galilee* and *Friendship's Death*', in *The Politics of Dispossession: The Struggle for Palestinian Self-Determination 1969–1994* (New York: Vintage, 1995), 135.

30. The Dziga Vertov Group were invited to film refugee and training camps in Jordan, Syria and Lebanon by Fatah with funding from the Arab League. The filming and editing of *Until Victory: Working and Thinking Methods of the Palestinian Revolution* was interrupted by the outbreak of civil war in Jordan in 1970. Specific sequences were subsequently incorporated into Godard and Anne-Marie Miéville's *Here and Elsewhere* in 1974. Adachi and Wakamatsu were invited to film by the PFLP. See: Jean-Luc Godard, 'Manifeste', *El-Fatah* (July 1970), 138–140 and Jean-Luc Godard and Jean-Pierre Gorin, 'Jusqu'à la Victoire, cahier de tournage (extraits)', 141–143 in Jean-Luc Godard, *Documents*, ed. Nicole Brenez (Paris: Centre Pompidou, 2006); Irmgard Emmelhainz, *Jean-Luc Godard's Political Filmmaking* (London: Palgrave Macmillan, 2019), 96–111; Nadia Yaqub, *Palestinian Cinema in the Days of Revolution* (Austin, TX: University of Texas Press, 2018), 48–64 and Anastasia Valassopolous, 'The International Palestinian Resistance: Documentary and Revolt', *Journal of Postcolonial Writing* (50(2) (2014), 148–166.

31. Said, 'Review of *Wedding*', 136.

32. Edward Said defined Palestinianism as a 'political movement that is being built out of a reassertion of Palestine's multiracial and multireligious history'. See: Said, 'The Palestinian Experience', 3.

33. For Stuart Hall's theorisation of 'determinacy without guaranteed closures', see: Stuart Hall, 'The Problem of Ideology: Marxism without Guarantees', in *Stuart Hall: Critical Dialogues in Cultural Studies*, eds David Morley and Kuan-Hsing Chen (London and New York: Routledge, 1996), 25–46.

34. Peter Wollen, *Director's Statement*, undated, unpaginated.

35. Said, 'Review of *Wedding*', 135.

36. The PFLP's explosions of the BOAC VC10, TWA 767 and Swiss Air 767 passenger planes at Revolution Airport on 12 September 1970 can be seen in the first sequence of archive footage in *Friendship's Death*. See: Hobson, 'Creating a World', 1–22.

37. '*Friendship's Death* (Script)', Chapter 14 in this volume, 236 and 238.

38. See: Susan Sontag, 'The Imagination of Disaster', *Commentary* (October 1965), 42–48, reprinted in *Against Interpretation, and Other Essays* (New York: Farrar, Straus and Giroux, 1966).

39. '*Friendship's Death* (Script)', Chapter 14 in this volume, 233.

40. The alarmist tone of Wollen's electronic signboard *Message from Procyon*, 1986, in Toronto simultaneously reverses Klaatu's greeting and heightens Friendship's recognition that computers 'already control the fate of the world' without having reached 'the point where they want it to survive' into a full-scale emergency alert: 'LISTEN!! EARTH!! DANGER!! DEATH!! HUMANS COULD DESTROY THE WORLD BEFORE THE COMPUTERS THAT CONTROL ITS FATE REACH THE POINT OF WANTING IT TO SURVIVE LISTEN!! EARTH!! DISARM!! TODAY!!' See: Oliver Fuke and Nicolas Helm-Grovas, 'Art at the Frontier of Film Theory', catalogue essay in *Art at the Frontier of Film Theory: Laura Mulvey and Peter Wollen* ex. cat. (London: Peltz Gallery/Birkbeck Institute for the Moving Image, 2019), 22–24.

41. See: Leo Goldsmith and Rachael Rakes, 'The Desertification of Discourse: *Punishment Park*', in *America: Films from Elsewhere*, ed. Shanay Jhaveri (Mumbai: The Shoestring Publisher, 2019), 278–297; Chuck Jackson, 'The Touch of the "First" Black Cinematographer in North America: James E. Hinton, *Ganja & Hess*, and the NEA Films at the Harvard Film Archive', *Black Camera* 10(1) (Fall 2018), 67–95; Serge Daney, '*Ceddo*', *Cahiers du cinéma* (304) (October 1979), 52–54; Claire Monk, '"The shadow of this time": Punk, Tradition and Derek Jarman's *Jubilee*', *Shakespeare Bulletin* 32(3) (2014), 359–373; Kodwo Eshun, '"On Her Devolves the Labour": The Cinematic Time Travel of *The Song of the Shirt*', in *Other Cinemas: Politics, Culture and Experimental Film in the 1970s*, eds Sue Clayton and Laura Mulvey (London and New York: I.B.Tauris, 2017), 257–272; Lucas Hilderbrand, 'In the Heat of the Moment: Notes on the Past, Present and Future of *Born in Flames*', *Women & Performance: A Journal of Feminist Theory* 23(1) (2013), 6–16; Dave Rolinson, *Alan Clarke* (Manchester and New York: Manchester University Press, 2005), 127–135; Pacharee Sudhinaraset, '"We Are Not an Organically City People": Black Modernity and the Afterimage of Julie Dash's *Daughters of the Dust*', *The Black Scholar: Journal of Black Studies and Research* 48(3) (2018), 46–60; Vlad Dima, *Sonic Space in Djibril Diop Mambety's Films* (Bloomington and Indianapolis, IN: Indiana University Press, 2017), 106–143; and Julianne Pidduck, 'Travels with Sally Potter's *Orlando*: Gender, Narrative, Movement', *Screen* 38(2) (Summer 1997), 172–189.

42. '*Friendship's Death*' (Fiction), Chapter 13 in this volume, 252.

43. Mandy Merck, 'From Robot to Romance', in *Perversions: Deviant Readings* (New York: Routledge, 1993), 187. See also Judith Williamson, 'Riddles of the Robot', in *Deadline at Dawn: Film Criticism 1980-1990* (London New York: Marion Boyars, 1993), 121–123

44. Peter Wollen, 'Two Weeks on Another Planet', 325.

45. Thomas Elsaesser, '*Friendship's Death*', *Monthly Film Bulletin* 54(646) (November 1987), 223.

46. *Ibid.*, 223.

47. See: Peter Wollen, 'Fashion/Orientalism/The Body', *New Formations* 1 (Spring 1987), 5–33. Wollen concluded his essay on fashion designer Paul Poiret, stage decor and costume designer Leon Bakst, and Henri Matisse with the assertion that 'Poiret's scenography of the Hegelian dialectic can only be overcome when the slave is able to read and to write the signs of her own desire and to retextualize her own body'. This final statement can be read as an outline for *Friendship's Death*.

48. *Ibid.*, 33.

49. '*Friendship's Death* (Script)', Chapter 14 in this volume, 256.

50. *Ibid.*, 256.

51. Peter Wollen, 'Two Weeks on Another Planet', 225.

52. '*Friendship's Death* (Script)', Chapter 14 in this volume, 253.

53. Said, 'The Palestinians One Year', 27.

54. *Ibid.*, 27.

55. *Ibid.*, 28.

56. *Ibid.*, 28.

57. *Ibid.*, 28.

58. *Ibid.*, 28.

59. Said, 'Review of *Wedding*', 135.

60. '*Friendship's Death* (Script)', Chapter 14 in this volume, 252.

61. Said, 'Review of *Wedding*', 135.

62. Peter Wollen, 'Two Weeks on Another Planet', 325.

63. *Ibid.*, 225.

64. '*Friendship's Death* (Script)', Chapter 14 in this volume, 261.

Section 3

Laura Mulvey's Later
Collaborative Films

16

Disgraced Monuments

Mark Lewis and Laura Mulvey

Opening sequence: The first shot is a pan around a cupboard shelf on which a large number of busts have been neatly stored, all wrapped in brown paper and tied up with string. One of these packages has been half opened and the pan halts on Lenin's face which peers out from the brown paper. Mike Ratledge and Karl Jenkins composed the music that accompanies the pan. The opening shot dissolves to archive footage of Lenin on a podium, very slightly slowed down, which dissolves to an overhead crane shot of a huge Lenin statue in Leningrad. The music comes back over this shot. The sequence then continues with a short montage of newsreel footage of people destroying monuments. Then it cuts to the disgraced monuments in the open-air temporary museum.

Music: Shostakovich, 'Sonata for Violin and Piano, Opus 134.'

Caption: The Temporary Museum of Totalitarian Art, Moscow, 1991

> VOICE-OVER: When the coup failed in the Soviet Union in August 1991 crowds attacked several statues of figures associated with Communism, which were then removed by Moscow City Council. These recent acts of iconoclasm brought back memories of previous revolutionary and official iconoclasms and previous changes in public monuments that had so often marked the arrival of a new regime. Now the Communist monumental sculptures are themselves threatened. Their removal may represent not the beginning of a new era but a repetition of a familiar pattern. The fate of the disgraced monuments is tied to the question of how seventy years of Soviet history can be told and represented in a post-Communist era.

Chapter title: Lenin's Decree: 'On the Monuments of the Republic', 1918

Scrolling title: In 1913 an obelisk was erected outside the Kremlin walls to celebrate 300 years of the Romanov dynasty. In 1917 it was transformed into the Obelisk to Revolutionary Thinkers and the names of the Tsars were replaced by:

Marx
Engels
Liebknecht
Campanella
Winstanley
T. More
Saint-Simon
Fourier
Proudhon
Bakunin
Chernyshevskiy
Plekhanov
[Lassalle
Bebel
Meslier
Vaillant
Jaurès
Lavrov
Mikhailovskiy]

TATYANA LVOVNA SHULGINA (Inspector of Moscow's Public Monuments 1947–1983): In 1918, the First World War still raged. It was just a year after the Revolution. The country lay in ruins; the people suffered hunger, disease and chaos. Nevertheless, one day, Vladimir Ilich Lenin summoned the Minister of Culture – Anatoliy Vasilevich Lunacharskiy. 'I think we should consider a special government resolution' he said, 'to make provision for the erection of a number of monuments. We must make the cities beautiful'.

The decree was issued for the entire Union. It provided for the erection of monuments and included a list of names of people who were worthy subjects. It was divided into revolutionaries and public figures: writers, poets, philosophers, scientists, artists, composers and performers, in other words it included people from all walks of life. So they began to make monuments, but as they didn't have the means or the materials, the monuments had to be made of plaster, concrete or wood. They were all temporary and soon disintegrated.

Caption: Surviving examples of Lenin's Monumental Propaganda stored in the Tretyakov Gallery [two plaques]

NIKITA VASILEVICH VORONOV (Art historian, Academy of Arts, Moscow): Soviet monumental art began with Lenin's plan. In April 1918, Vladimir Ilich Lenin signed a decree ordering the clearing of squares and streets of all monuments which had been built in honour of the Tsars and of the Tsars' servants. And since everyone in Russia was regarded as a servant to the Tsar, this decree offered an opportunity to remove a great number of monuments. So that's where it began.

Caption: Lenin unveiling a temporary monument to Marx and Engels, 1918

…It started with a list of new heroes recommended for monuments. But after Lenin died, in 1924, the names on the list were, for the most part, ignored and replaced by monuments to the leaders, mainly to Lenin himself…

Caption: First Monument to Lenin. Finland Station, Leningrad, 1924

…So everything started with monuments being pulled down. And in the late 1980s and the 1990s, of the sixty monuments to Lenin in Moscow, unfortunately, fifty have been destroyed. So in fact Lenin's decree ordering the removal of monuments lives on.

Chapter title: Changing Monuments – Changing Names: The story of the Monument to Freedom

Caption: Between 1912 and 1992 different monuments gave their names to what is today called Dolgorukskaya Square

TATYANA SHULGINA: This same decree included provisions for removing monuments dedicated to the Tsar and his servants. The ugliest and those which had no artistic value were to go. Those which could be of no loss to the populace were to go as well. In 1918 Lenin wanted to celebrate the Revolution's first anniversary by replacing the Skobelev statue in Sovetskaya Square. Lenin and the Commission chose the Obelisk to Freedom, a project by the architect Osip and the sculptor Andreyev. Cast in the niches of the Freedom Obelisk, first on the bays and then on bronze plates, was the text of the first Soviet Constitution. It was a call for freedom, peace, humanity and democracy.

LYUDMILA MARTZ (Keeper of Modern Sculpture, New Tretyakov Gallery): And so, in the early spring of 1941, a few months before the war, the Freedom Monument was pulled down. At great risk to their own safety, staff at the Tretyakov Gallery hired a truck and drove to Sovetskaya Square. They found a heap of rubble and began to dig into it, hoping to find some recognisable remnant of the monument. And they found the head – I'm going to show it to you... (*She unveils the head*)... It was an act of great courage on the part of the gallery staff. Touching a monument which had been pulled down was as dangerous as talking to someone who had been arrested and sent into exile. For the monument, it was like being shot by a firing squad. On the day it was pulled down, they brought the head here, and hid it away in the basement of the Tretyakov Gallery. Ours is probably the only unhappy country where a monument to Freedom was raised only to be pulled down again. History is complex but also revealing. And obviously this incident was a reflection of the political situation. Freedom itself had been destroyed, and by 1941 it no longer existed.

Music: Traditional funeral song sung by professional woman mourner.

Caption: Yuriy Dolgorukiy, legendary founder of Moscow, erected 1947

Caption: Monument to Freedom, erected 1918, blown up 1941

Caption: Monument to General Skobelev, erected 1912, boxed in for May Day 1918, dismantled later that year

Chapter title: Stalinist Monumental Culture and Official Public Art

ANDREY RODIONOV (Architect): The craving to build something on a massive scale gave our leaders the idea of building the Palace of Soviets. The site upon which they decided to build was very dramatic. It was a very famous site in Moscow: the Church of Christ the Saviour. People had collected money for decades to build the Church of Christ the Saviour, to commemorate God's protection and deliverance of Russia when she was at war with Napoleon. The idea behind the building of the church was entirely patriotic. The huge church stood not far from the Kremlin. This is evidently the final plan of the Palace of Soviets which was to stand in its place. The statue of the leader of the international proletariat was far larger than the church. It was to have been about 500 feet high. But this dream – this self-portrait of Communism of the 1930s – proved to be so impractical that it ended up a chimera...

Caption: Laying the foundation for the Palace of Soviets, 1939

> …It all ended in failure. And as a result, all attempts to build this gigantic Communist dream simply melted, melted into a puddle, into what is now the Moscow swimming pool…

Montage sequence: Unveilings –

Introduced with footage of the Moscow swimming pool, the sequence continues with archive footage of the unveiling of statues of Lenin, intercut with the Church of Christ the Saviour exploding.

Music: specially composed by Karl Jenkins and Mike Ratledge.

> …Remember that Stalinism created a particular kind of faith. Stalin had his own version of the Gorgon Medusa myth: turning everything to stone. Whatever he looked at and liked had to be immortalised in stone. Consequently, anything to do with stone – turning things into stone, or fixing in stone – was extremely important for the monumentalist culture of that era. Never mind what happened to actual people, these stone sculptures would remain as symbols of eternity, symbols of the unequivocal legitimacy of the new regime…

Montage sequence: Stalin –

Archive film footage of Sergey Merkurov and assistants polishing his giant statue of Stalin: the sequence ends with a night shot of the statue now lying on its side in the open-air Temporary Museum of Totalitarian Art.

Music: Soviet song in praise of Lenin.

> …In my opinion it's very important for our generation to try and understand our historical links with the culture of the Stalinist era. Moreover, it's vital to bring this culture out of the 'zone of silence'. In Stalin's time it could not be criticised. Under Brezhnev it was unmentionable. And at present it's studied as a political, social and economic phenomenon, but not as a cultural one. I think we must analyse it or, at the very least, recognise the links between our generation and the 'zone of silence' generation and our links to that culture. It's easier to struggle with monuments than with concrete reality. We can pull monuments down and raise new ones. And that's the only reality the people have encountered since August 1991.

Caption: Studio of M.G. Manizer (1891-1966). Awarded the Stalin Prize in 1941, 1943 and 1950

> VOICE-OVER: After Lenin's death in 1924 a cult of the dead leader spread across the Soviet Union. In his lifetime Lenin had tried to wipe out traditional religious belief. At his death his image became the official icon of the new Communist order, venerated like a Christian saint. Stalin was the prime mover behind the cult of Lenin, but on this foundation he gradually constructed the cult, iconography and doctrines of Stalinism. In 1956 Khrushchev denounced Stalin's cult of personality, and its outward manifestations, its imagery and monuments were dismantled and hidden from history in a new wave of Soviet iconoclasm. This vacuum was filled by a return to the cult of Lenin.

Caption: Factory for mass production of statues and busts

Caption: Current factory production of tourist memorabilia

> HEAD OF ARTISTIC DEPARTMENT (*Skulptorny Combinat*): Our factory was founded in 1949 for the main task of casting bronze statues of our leaders. At first we cast statues of Stalin. Then, after his death, we began to cast statues of Lenin.
>
> We made small busts of Vladimir Ilich Lenin. These were presented as awards to the winning competitors on big Workers' Holidays, like 1 May and 7 November. These small busts comprised 90% of our output. Since Perestroika, our production lines have changed. We have stopped making the small busts. Now we make things for the general public, whatever people will buy.

Montage sequence: Lenin –

Shots of various kinds of images of Lenin; towards the end, snow begins to fall partially burying the statues.

Music: Red Army Choir singing a hymn of praise to Lenin.

Chapter title: The Sculptors of State Monuments: From Prizes to Perestroika

> VASILIY NIKOLAEVICH AZEMSHA (Sculptor): Artists and Soviet art had to be affected by the present changes.

Caption: Studio of M. K. Anikushin, Leningrad

> …For years, artists relied on the compulsory form of commission, which dictated to the client what to commission, whether a portrait of Lenin, Marx or some other hero. That system is now gone. So artists and sculptors in Leningrad don't know what to think any more. Many have to give up their

old way of life. They find it hard to run their vast studios. I can tell you about my own situation. I don't receive state commissions for public sculpture any more. So I go after new commissions. This was commissioned by the Leningrad Filmmakers' Union for a film festival. They're preparing for a film festival in Leningrad and they'll be giving prizes for best film, best actor and best director. It'll be called the Samson, a name suggested by the filmmakers because it represents strength and also because Samson is one of the symbols of our beautiful city. So I have made this sculpture which is also called Samson. I make other figurines from Russia's past, representing history's exploitation of the people's interests. And, of course, they are the fruits of a trend of opportunism.

Caption: Pedestal of the monument to Kalinin, removed August 1991 (sculptor: B. Dyuzhev)

BORIS DYUZHEV (Sculptor): I don't understand this blasphemy. And I don't understand why my statue of Kalinin isn't there any more. One fine night, they simply came along. They just went there and took down the Dzerzhinskiy statue, along with the statues of Kalinin and Sverdlov, all at the same time. They tried to take down Karl Marx but they couldn't do it. It upsets me that these monuments aren't there anymore. They've changed the name of the street. It used to be Kalinin Prospekt, now it's Noviy Arbat – New Arbat. I really don't know what's going to happen to the statue now. I asked the Ministry of Culture to bring it to my studio and let it stand here, in memory. Now I am working on this portrait. It's the head of Dmitriy Karmov, one of the Muscovites who died during the August coup. I saw it happen. I don't know how it will turn out. I'm still working on it. I can also show you this unfinished piece of work. It's the head of Jesus Christ. This is the only work I'm doing at the moment. I have no commissions. Our government no longer issues them. I don't like being idle, so I'm working on these projects.

Caption: Studio of N. V. Tomskiy (1900–1984): awarded the Stalin Prize in 1941, 1946, 1949 and 1952

NATALYA NIKOLAEVNA TOMSKAYA (Daughter of the sculptor): I'm sorry to see all these monuments being taken down these days. I don't know which of my father's will remain or for how long. I do hope my father's work stays where it is. Anyway, this act should serve as a lesson to us about how we should treat the property of the whole state. It is property which belongs to us, which history has given to us. This is our property which exists now and we would grieve for a long time over its loss. We went through the same thing after the Revolution in 1917. We are very sad now about the many things we lost then. It would be a great shame if history were to repeat itself and we, in our turn, would also be condemned by our grandchildren for not preserving the art and cultural property of our own time. Obviously, all monuments are cultural property.

Caption: N.V. Tomskiy at the unveiling of his Monument to Lenin, East Berlin, 1971

Caption: The monument was removed in 1992

Caption: Pedestal of the statue of Sverdlov, removed August 1991

Chapter title: *Perestroika*: Towards a New Iconography

NATALYA DAVIDOVA (Art critic): We walk past monuments and often we don't notice them. Or we deliberately try not to notice them. Yet these monuments leave a mark on us which settles into our subconscious, under our skin. And we can never be sure what will happen when it comes to the surface.

Monuments are built as a bond with our past and destroyed at times of cataclysm. Then new monuments are raised. This process is very much like Judgement Day. Pulling down old idols and raising up new ones. Having human idols has only served to make the connection stronger. Every turning point in our society has begun its new history in a struggle with old monuments. This was a struggle with the past which was realised primarily in a struggle with monuments. So removing the statue of Dzerzhinskiy, founder of the KGB, in August 1991, has become a symbolic act. On the one hand, it signified a stage in the development of the social situation. But on the other hand, it was also a repetition of the events of 1917.

Caption: Feliks Dzerzhinskiy, founder of the Soviet Secret Police

VIKTOR MISIANO (Art critic): I was lucky enough to be in the crowd who saw the statue of Dzerzhinskiy being removed on August 21st.

The actions of these people – and I include myself among them – were based entirely on historical citation. Citation of events from the past and images of the past which are found in abundance in the minds of the Soviet people, saturated as they are with ideology.

As in all revolutions, a post-modernist mechanism, an aesthetic of citation was once again set in motion. All successful revolutions end with statues coming down. I remember clearly how the crowd desecrating the monument were so pleased with the sign they had stuck on it. They would have been content to paint it blue with polka dots. They would have been happy leaving

Dzerzhinskiy where he stood and just putting a Fool's cap on his head or giving him a false nose. But at that moment, a bus arrived with a megaphone and we heard the young, chirpy voice of Stankevich – the siren of our democratic meetings – announcing that Popov, the Mayor of Moscow, had signed a decree calling for the dismantling of statues which the people hated so much.

So removing Dzerzhinskiy was a key moment which marked the end of the 'performance' and the start of the mechanism of history when the mechanism of the new ideology began to work again.

Caption: Monument to Dzerzhinskiy, removed August 1991. Sculptor: E. V. Vuchetich

NATALYA DAVIDOVA: The idea of a Memorial for the victims of the Gulag emerged a few years ago. This project made it possible and within the law to discuss the disturbing nature of certain aspects of our society's history. It made it possible to speak about Stalin's repression and the injustice experienced during that time. A group of young people began to go around the city collecting signatures in support of the idea of building a monument in memory of the victims of Stalin's repression. They were arrested, then released and then they dispersed. Yet they managed to give Gorbachev several hundred thousand signatures at the Congress of People's Deputies. After this, the question of the monument was made legal. So the idea of a memorial to the victims of Stalinism resulted in a monument being recently erected. It's a stone from the Gulag, placed opposite the KGB building...

Caption: Stone taken from the Gulag and set facing the Lubyanka, KGB Headquarters

The words inscribed on the stone [captured in the shot] translate as: This stone was brought from the territory of the Solovetskiy Gulag and placed here as a memorial to the millions of victims of the totalitarian regime.

The camera pans back and forth between the now empty pedestal where the Dzerzhinskiy Monument once stood and the Gulag stone. The KGB building is in the background.

...This monument is a document of the times, like all other monuments in Moscow. For the very first time we determined our own attitude to the past, as opposed to the way it had been done previously, when a monument represented the official version of our memory.

VIKTOR MISIANO: Those three days in August 1991 constitute the most recent Russian revolution of the 20th century. If you think about it, it was the first revolution which was against ideology, coming full circle after the earlier revolutions of this century. It was a post-ideological revolution which signified because it has lost its ontological status. It was an aesthetic revolution. At the centre of the square, in front of the Russian parliament, they built a huge barricade which was an astonishingly expressive monument in terms of beauty and of composition. It was built next to the Monument to the Barricades of the first Russian Revolution of 1905. The most recent Russian revolution put up its monument on the monument to the first barricades of the 20th century. The artificial, theatrical cobbles, imitating revolutionary Moscow of 1905, were reused as revolutionary instruments to build this monument of the barricade. So the [1991] barricade monument was built on the site of the first barricade [1905]. These are the typical paradoxes of a post-historical revolution.

Chapter title: Disgraced Monuments: Removals and Returns

LEV KERBEL (Sculptor and Vice-President, Academy of the Arts): Taking down monuments has always been an act of vandalism, both before the revolution, during the revolution, and now. It is an act of vandalism, it is an outburst of philistinism. It's an outburst of chauvinism. It's an act of fascism, here and abroad, to remove monuments which don't suit the ruling regime – it's always about politics.

VADIM DORMIDONTOV (Chair, Commission for Historic Monuments, Moscow City Council): We decided that some works, although politically defunct, should remain where they stand. This specifically applies to the massive sculpture on Oktyabrskaya Square. Some monuments will be stored in museums. Others will be shown in a special exhibition. For the moment, this exhibition is called the Sculpture Park, which is on Krimskiy Val by the Central Artists' Club. In the future we'll have a special museum, which may be called Museum of Totalitarianism. When you bump into statues of Lenin in every school, at every crossroads, in every park and even in sports stadiums, it clearly starts to look absurd. This pathological multiplication of statues must be limited to something more reasonable. That is the Commission's approach. But there are a number of monuments in Moscow which we can afford to leave where they stand. One is a statue of Lenin outside the Kremlin, where he worked as leader of the government. We thought this could stay put but its site is being debated. The spot where Lenin now stands used to be occupied by the statue of Alexander II. We are in consultation with the Kremlin Museum as to whether we might not find a different site, a more intimate niche for Lenin.

The site would then become free and we could put Alexander's statue back.

Lev Kerbel working on a bust of Peter the Great.

VOICE-OVER: The collapse of Communism has once again created a vacuum in public iconography...

Caption: S.A. Sarafivomich, Sculptor

Sarafivomich shown working on a head of Peter the Great.

...and as the city of Leningrad is renamed St. Petersburg, the cult of the Tsar, repressed by seventy years of Communism returns. The new imagery suggests perhaps that an invisible continuity may have lain dormant in the successive Communist cults of personality. Here the sculptor who created the bust of Lenin that stands in a station in Leningrad, now works on a bust of Peter the Great to replace Lenin in the same station in renamed St. Petersburg.

Caption: Peter the Great erected in St. Petersburg, 1991. Sculptor: Mikhail Shemyakin

Caption: Peter the Great: 'The Bronze Horseman' erected in St. Petersberg, 1782. Sculptor: Étienne-Maurice Falconet.

A verse from Alexander Pushkin's 'The Bronze Horseman' (1833) is read in Russian, subtitled as follows:

> Across the empty square
> Evgeniy runs and hears behind him
> – like the rumble of thunder –
> the clash and clang of hoofs,
> galloping over the shuddering street.
> And lit by the pale moonlight,
> his hand reaching out,
> the Bronze Horseman pursues him
> on his clangorously galloping steed.
> And all night long,
> wherever the poor madman turned,
> the Bronze Horseman followed
> with thunderous tread.

The Bronze Horseman dissolves into the Shemyakin Statue of Peter the Great which dissolves to a statue covered with a cloth which dissolves to reveal Stalin.

A four minute pan shot across a small wood finally reveals a large head of Lenin.

Music: Shostakovich, 'Symphony No 5. in D Minor, Opus 47' (which started earlier over the head of Peter the Great and the final voice-over) continues to the end of the film.

Credits

Produced, written and directed by Mark Lewis and Laura Mulvey

Director of photography – Thomas H. Turnbull

Camera assistant – Yuri Mironov

Sound – Larry Sider

Edited – Tom Hayes

Production coordinator (London, Moscow) and translation – Jessica Kaner

Production coordinator (Toronto) – Deanne Judson

Interpreter – Irena Artis

Original music – Karl Jenkins and Mike Ratledge

Voice-over – Petra Markham

'The Bronze Horseman' recitation – Pavel Gatynya

Archive research – Asaya Abdulina

Stills – Stephen Waddell

Translation – Suzanna Lydic, Beata Lozinski, Gordon Livermore

Online operators – Richard McCarthy, Michael Sagadore, Gary Poole

Sound mix – Marc Benoit

Thanks to Valery Ermolaev (Globus Films), Vakhtang Korkelia, M.K. Anikushin, Alexander Alexandrovich, Misha Gorokov, Viktor Vasilev, The New Tretyakov Gallery, M. Merkurov, Barbara Grigor, Derek Miller, Anya von Bremzen, Matt Bishop, Daisy Cockburn, Chad Paetznick, Christina Lane, Jeff Brandt

Special thanks to Melodie Calvert, Bill Horrigan, Mandy Merck, Tim Frank, Clare Bevan and Fulcrum Productions

Funding provided by Canada Council, Ontario Arts Council, Ontario Film Development Corporation, Channel Four Television Corporation

Support provided by The Wexner Center, Media Arts Program at the Ohio State University

Online editing – The Knowledge Network Vancouver, Canada

Support provided by The National Film Board of Canada

'Fifth Symphony in D Minor, Opus 47'
Berliner Philarmonika
Conducted by Semyon Bychkov
Composed by D. Shostakovich
Courtesy Polygram Records

'Sonata for Violin and Piano, Opus 134'
Composed by D. Shostakovich
Courtesy Koch International

'Preludes and Fuges for Piano (1-10)'
Composed by D Shostakovich
Courtesy Koch International

'Tabula Rasa'
Composed by Arvo Part
Courtesy Polygram Records

A Monumental Pictures Production for Channel Four
© Monumental Pictures MCMXCIII

17

Preserving History:
Disgraced Monuments

Nora M. Alter

As an index, cinema necessarily fixes a real image of reality across time.

Laura Mulvey[1]

Lieux de mémoire only exist because of their capacity for metamorphosis, an endless recycling of their meaning and an unpredictable proliferation of their ramifications.

Pierre Nora[2]

Chris Marker and Alain Resnais' essay film *Statues Also Die* (1953) infamously opens with the pronouncement: 'When people die, they enter into history; when statues die, they enter into art. This botany of death is what we call culture.' As the camera pans over ruins of classical Western sculptures – draped torsos without heads, faces without bodies, amputated limbs – fragments from a time past are strewn randomly in nature, leaving the viewer to imagine their original installation and purpose. Forty years later, in the former Soviet Union, a similar depository of abandoned sculptures, ravaged by history and thrown up like so much flotsam and jetsam, has been left to pile up in waste sites or stowed away deep in storage facilities. In their remarkably prescient essay film *Disgraced Monuments* (1994), Laura Mulvey and Mark Lewis trace the histories of certain examples of these sculptures: their past moments in the sun, their fall from grace and their ultimate replacement. Unlike the centuries-old sculptures filmed by Marker and Resnais, the objects in Mulvey and Lewis's film are 'young', not worn and aged by time but fresh and relatively new. They are twentieth-century products: icons from a bygone era, relics of a dream for a new egalitarian society – one whose principles promised so much but through mis-direction failed after seventy years. The birth and death of these monuments, which were made to honour and memorialise the Russian Revolution and its leaders, marks a history that left much bitterness and a desire to erase the Communist project, coupled with a frenzy to embrace the fantasy of free-market capitalism. Through a close reading of *Disgraced Monuments* and the historic aftermath of the monuments depicted in the film, this essay probes issues concerning monuments and their histo-ries in relation to the era's technological changes in filmmaking.

Monuments are designed to commemorate individuals, significant events or con-cepts. Myriad factors of cultural and historical significance contribute to their subject matter, creation, placement and removal. As Lucia Allais explains: 'monuments serve as a dispersed cultural archive; their preservation involves control of nothing less than the national narrative.'[3] Such is the complicated and multilayered theme of *Disgraced Monuments*. In the aftermath of the collapse of the Soviet Union, Mulvey and Lewis tracked the fate of these monuments to the Russian Revolution – from large-scale, unique forms intended to commemorate individuals who were influential in the uprising, to the hundreds of thousands of mass-produced busts of Lenin and Stalin created to be presented as awards on workers' holidays. The film opens with a slow panning shot that moves right to left across storage shelves of shrouded busts. Non-diegetic, ominous, dramatic music accompanies the sequence as ponderous chords match the movement of the camera. The spectator is first afforded a quick glimpse through an opening in one wrapping that reveals a bearded chin and mouth, barely enough to identify the figure as Lenin. The camera keeps moving until it comes to rest on a fully exposed bust of the revolutionary leader; then it freezes, perfectly framing an iconic image of Lenin in the centre of the screen as the title *Disgraced Monuments* appears. The music ends, followed by complete silence during a newsreel clip that shows Lenin delivering a speech. A strong contrast is formed between the frozen, immobile bust and the animated and energetic figure documented in the archival insert, between the sonorous accompaniment to still images and the mute depiction of the act of speech. This clip is followed by contemporary video footage of a crowd destroying a monument, its vigorous actions similar to the efforts of those who, two years earlier, had dismantled the Berlin Wall. The physical energy displayed in this footage attests to the crowd's determination to eradicate any visible evidence of the former ideology under which it had lived.

Mulvey and Lewis visited Leningrad on 7 November 1991: the anniversary of the Communist Revolution of 1917. The new post-Soviet regime was deploying this date to strategically mark the change in the city's name from Leningrad back to St. Petersburg, thereby substituting the significance of the historical marker with a new one. In Russia, the return of the name St. Petersburg after sixty-five years of being called Leningrad was part of a rapid post-1989 effort to erase the predominance of one historical narrative and reinscribe pre-revolutionary myths of nationhood and sovereignty. In this process history was rewritten, players replaced, educational curricula modified and the names of public places, cities, squares, plazas and streets returned to earlier designations. In tandem with these efforts, contemporary buildings were razed, monuments destroyed and exact replicas from the past rebuilt in attempts to restore a community to the false dictums of 'the way it really was' and 'again will be'. As artist Sharon Hayes reminds us, 'monuments operate materially, narratively, and iteratively. They are a mechanism inside an ongoing power grab.'[4]

As in all narratives there are two key moments for monuments: beginnings (when they are made and installed) and endings (when they are taken down, removed or destroyed). One aspect of this sweeping process is in the treatment of monuments and memorials that dominate public spaces commemorating a former regime: when monuments designed and erected to remind people of a particular history, to reflect and pay respect to that history, are dismantled and removed. They may be quickly toppled in a matter of days following a revolution, or the decision to abolish them may take years, even centuries.[5] In either case, as quickly as monuments are taken away, they are replaced, as if their void or absence might provoke an even more subversive space for undirected contemplation. The replacements reflect the contemporary social concerns of a particular political landscape. We must look for the political unconscious directing these acts, for, as historian Eric Foner suggests, it is just as important to consider the time when a monument is made as to what it is commemorating.[6] *Disgraced Monuments* performs such an act of close reading or viewing.

This essay film consists of seven sections, each of which addresses a different facet of the history and fate of former Soviet monuments. These include three case studies of monuments that began in pre-revolutionary Russia, were dismantled and replaced during the Communist regime and were reinstated or refigured after the dissolution of the USSR. Following the prelude, the first part begins chronologically with the immediate post-revolutionary moment and Lenin's decree of 1918 'to make provision for the erection of a number of monuments. We must make the cities beautiful.' The first mutation of a monument depicted in the film occurred that same year when the names of members of the Romanov dynasty, inscribed on an obelisk erected in 1913, were erased and replaced by those of numerous male 'Revolutionary Thinkers', including Karl Marx, Friedrich Engels, Karl Liebknecht, Mikhail Bakunin, Pierre-Joseph Proudhon and Joseph Fourier. In the film, archival footage from the first iteration of the obelisk is followed by a still shot of the obelisk in 1991, accompanied by the printed names of the 'Revolutionary Thinkers' that scroll up the screen in a movement that mimics the effect of a viewer looking upwards at the monument and reading the inscriptions.

Twenty years after Mulvey and Lewis made their film, and on the centenary of its original dedication, the obelisk was restored to its original state. Although the 'Revolutionary Thinkers' were obliterated, *Disgraced Monuments* records and preserves their shadowy traces as testimony of their intellectual contributions. The obelisk is made of an exceptionally durable material, and, like a magic writing pad, lends itself to a cycle of inscription, erasure, reinscription and erasure according to the sea change of political regimes.

The second section focuses on the history of the 'Freedom Monument' in the former Sovetskaya Square in Moscow, which Lenin commissioned on the first anniversary of the revolution to replace a statue honoring the Romanov General Mikhail Skobelev. Designed by the architect Osip, the new monument had the Soviet Constitution inscribed around its base. Although it took the form of a human figure, as a symbol of freedom it was not intended to resemble any specific political personage, since freedom was intended for all humanity. In the words of Tatyana Lvovna Shulgina, the former Inspector of Moscow's Public Monuments (1947–1983) interviewed in the film, it was 'a call for freedom, peace, humanity and democracy'. In 1941, however, as Shulgina informs us, under a decree from Stalin, the monument was torn down and replaced by a statue of Yuriy Dolgorukiy, a founder of the city of Moscow. Today the monument remains, but the square has been renamed.

In a remarkable sequence that echoes the prelude, Mulvey and Lewis screen their interview of Lyudmila Martz, the 'Keeper of Modern Sculpture' at the New Tretyakov Gallery, who tells the story of the Freedom Monument's destruction. At one point her voice shifts from a matter-of-fact tone and becomes hushed and dramatic as she narrates how employees of the gallery secretly went to the pile of rubble and searched through it trying to find any possible remains of the monument. She announces dramatically: 'And they found the head – I'm going to show it to you.' Then, almost furtively, she pulls a shroud-like cloth off an object lying on the floor to reveal the head. The camera focuses on the discarded figure, which is filmed upside-down as it lies on the floor: an odd disorienting perspective that would not have been possible in its original incarnation. In this passage the statue is imbued with almost lifelike qualities and treated with reverence as if it somehow contained a living spirit. It is a fallen angel, a detached head that in its current state recalls images of decapitation from another revolution.

The third section, entitled 'Stalinist Monumental Culture and Official Public Art', focuses on Stalin's plans to build an enormous monument, the 'Palace of Soviets', commemorating the Revolution of 1917. The architectural historian Andrey Rodionov notes in an interview that, as evidence of its scale, the monument was to include a 500 foot high statue of the leader of the international proletariat. The central-Moscow site chosen for its location had been occupied by the Cathedral of Christ the Saviour, demolished in 1931 in preparation for the new monument. Due to multiple factors, including the German invasion during World War II, the monument was never completed and exists only in detailed plans and sketches. In this case Mulvey and Lewis document the images that were left of those grand ideals: a repeating loop of newsreel footage from 1931 depicting the destruction of the cathedral as it is brought down by explosives and spectacularly crashes into a field of dust. The mesmerising effect of this scene gives way to an almost surreal image of a seemingly naked man emerging out of the dust and debris to calmly cross the hazy ground until he descends into a large swimming pool. Here the filmmakers have overlapped the 1931 footage of destruction with more recent footage of the same site, which was turned into the world's largest public swimming pool in 1958. The dust is actually steam rising from the water's surface. Commenting about this sequence of events in his interview, Rodionov ironically notes: 'It all ended in failure and as a result, all attempts to build this gigantic Communist dream simply melted, melted into a puddle, into what is now the Moscow swimming pool.' As Mulvey explains, for this sequence they used the then relatively new non-linear Avid editing system that allowed for the 'opportunity to experiment with dissolves, fades, slow motion, freeze frames, in order to convey this sense of ghosting … the tangible reality of a photographic record combines with the ephemeralness and vulnerability of celluloid.'[7]

One year after Mulvey and Lewis made their film, the pool was drained, and the foundation was laid for the reconstruction of the original cathedral. As was the case with the obelisk, the circle was completed with an attempt to return to a pre-revolutionary era. Iconoclasm functions at all stages, from the initial destruction of the cathedral to the present-day attempt to eradicate all visible and material signifiers of the former Soviet Union. The Romanovs and their religion were replaced by revolutionary utopian goals only to give way seventy years later to a reactionary return to post-Communist ideals and values.

These three vignettes show three different cases of disgraced Soviet monuments. In the first, a monument is repurposed, as the original form – the core, as it were – is maintained but the dressing changed. In the second, the entire monument is destroyed so that nothing remains but a head that has been secreted away and saved in the bowels of a museum. In the third, the disgrace exists in the monument's non-existence: the failure of its realisation to ever leave the drawing board. These stand as a triad, each marked with a sense of loss, dishonour and disrespect. The question the film raises is who or what performs the act of 'disgrace'; is it an individual, a state or a people?

As the film progresses, two parallel themes develop: the aesthetic merit of these Soviet monuments versus their political function; and the relationship between permanence and ephemerality. Lenin's original decree regarding the populating of public spaces with monuments 'to make the cities beautiful' suggests that the erection of these monuments was an aesthetic enterprise rather than one whose primary function is to control a history and its narrative. Yet as Foner maintains, 'historical monuments are not generally evaluated according to aesthetic standards. Rather, they represent markers … over how history should be remembered and what historical figures are worthy of veneration. Mostly, they reflect who has had the power to shape public memory.'[8]

Ironically, as Tatyana Lvovna Shulgina notes, the monuments that were made in the early 1920s following Lenin's decree were constructed out of inexpensive materials. 'They were all temporary and soon disintegrated.' As economic conditions in the USSR improved after World War II, monuments were made of more substantial materials, yet this new durability did not affect their potential permanence. Indeed, in the next two parts of the film, Mulvey and Lewis demonstrate that ideological conditions are far more significant than environmental ones in determining the fate of monuments.

Section four is set in a factory for tourist memorabilia. The filmmakers are informed that, prior to its current function, it was used to manufacture bronze statues, first of Stalin and then of Lenin. This sequence of *Disgraced Monuments* is close to elegiacal as the camera pans over multiple sculptures of Lenin in various sizes, including one large example that is abandoned outside as snow gradually covers it, while the soundtrack plays a hymn of praise to Lenin sung by the Red Army Choir.

Part five is composed of three interviews – two with living sculptors and one with the daughter of a deceased third sculptor. The artists were all state-sponsored; their studios now lie in various states of deterioration. The first, Vasiliy Nikolaevich Azemsha, contextualises the current environment for former government-employed artists. He explains: 'I don't receive state commissions for public sculpture anymore, so I go after new commissions.' At the time of the interview Azemsha is working on a figurine of Samson as a prize for a new film festival; the camera reveals that its features resemble those of Arnold Schwarzenegger. The pathos of the artist's condition is palpable as he has transitioned from modelling heroes of the Revolution to modeling Hollywood's superheroes. A second interview with Boris Dyuzhev reveals his dismay at having his monument to Kalinin removed the previous year. Like Azemsha, Dyuzhev is trying to stay in business, and he is filmed making a bust of Dmitriy Karmov, who died during the August Coup of 1991. As with the features of Samson being transformed into a Hollywood actor, Karmov is depicted as Jesus Christ. In both instances, in readily exchanging heroic figures and icons to match the era's rapidly changing political landscape, the artists are desperately scrambling to figure out a new public for their work.

Through these interviews Mulvey and Lewis raise the question of the blurry line between propaganda and art. By connecting the state monuments to individuals who laboured as artists, they restore an aesthetic sensibility to the creations, further complicating the issue of whether they should be destroyed, returned, left in situ or preserved in museums. The words of Marker and Resnais – 'when statues die, they enter into art' – echo uncannily in this respect.

The last two sections of the film, '*Perestroika:* Towards a New Iconography' and 'Disgraced Monuments: Removals and Returns', centre on the present day. In '*Perestroika*', the indexical nature of a sign is explored when the directors are presented with a new type of monument: a stone from the Gulag in memory of those who were sentenced there. Mulvey observes that unlike the other figurative monuments presented in the film, this one has 'an indexical relationship with commemoration, setting up a literal link with a particular historical moment or event' – like film.[9] In semiology, following Charles Sanders Pierce, an index functions very differently from an icon – a difference that Mulvey and Lewis underscore by having the last sequence focus on the return of Peter the Great as the icon for St. Petersburg. The film concludes with the recitation of a verse from the narrative poem, 'The Bronze Horseman' (1833) by Aleksander Pushkin, which concludes 'wherever the poor madmen turned, the Bronze Horseman followed with thunderous tread'.

Just as it is crucial to consider the historic context when a monument is installed or removed, so it is important to examine the context of 1991–1993, when Mulvey and Lewis were making their film. Mulvey had already co-directed six films in the 1970s and early 1980s, but this was the first foray into filmmaking for Lewis. In a 1997 interview, she explained that *Disgraced Monuments* 'emerged out of the work Mark was doing with a group of artists and art theorists in Toronto about art and public space. I was interested in the iconography of revolution and how revolutions tend to focus on symbolic gestures in which people participate on a mass scale. The way in which symbols and signs function as part of the language of politics at a moment of crisis.'[10] In the field of technology generally and filmmaking specifically, 1989 had marked the advent of the digital revolution. For film- and video-makers this facilitated a new type of image-making, editing, distribution and exhibition, to which on a meta level Mulvey and Lewis's film can be considered a response. In these first years, the focus was primarily on the transition from analogue to digital images and non-linear editing programmes. *Disgraced Monuments* was shot on 16mm film but edited digitally. Debates at the time revolved around whether digital imagery still has a 'truth value', since there no longer is a negative, and the indexical relationship to what is imaged is accordingly compromised. Related questions arose as to the future of the documentary genre and its archival possibilities.[11]

Writing some ten years after completing *Disgraced Monuments* on the index and its relationship to filmmaking in the new millennium, Mulvey asserts: 'The index has a privileged relation to time, to the moment and duration of its inscription; it also has a physical relation to the original for which it is a sign.'[12] As a work made on the cusp of the digital revolution, *Disgraced Monuments* performs its own role as a double memorial both to the fate of the former Soviet monuments and to analogue image-making. As such, it is its own record and documentary of a way of representing a subject and anchoring it to a fixed moment in time and space.

Should such rootedness and fixity be considered only in a positive light? In her notes to the film, Mulvey recalls that 'while different strands of the post-revolutionary intelligentsia argued over the future of art and its political implications, as far as public monuments were concerned, Lenin said "Let everything be temporary."'[13] In order for change to develop, there has to be constant movement; the moment something gets frozen and memorialised, ideas become calcified and retrograde, mired in the past instead of embracing a future. In contrast to the alleged stability of the celluloid image, the digital affords possibilities that are ephemeral and infinitely mutable. As a hybrid production located between celluloid and digital, *Disgraced Monuments* supports the concept of change while at the same time recalling the past, but a past that evolves based on the present condition. Mulvey compares cinema to memory, observing that: 'Both have the attributes of the indexical sign, the mark of trauma or the mark of light, and both need to be deciphered retrospectively across delayed time.'[14] *Disgraced Monuments* stands as a record, a testimony to these former monuments. It weaves together multiple strands of inquiry that self-reflexively probe these issues. At the same time, the film performs an act of memorialisation in documenting acts of erasure and destruction as they occurred. *Disgraced Monuments* remains as an index attesting to a 'there was'. As we view this film a quarter of a century after its making, many of the places have changed and some of the monuments have disappeared forever; their only trace remains in this work of Mulvey and Lewis.

Notes

1. Laura Mulvey, *Death 24x a Second: Stillness and the Moving Image* (London: Reaktion Books, 2006), 10.

2. Pierre Nora, 'Between Memory and History: *les lieux de mémoire*', trans. Marc Roudebush, *Representations* 26 (Spring 1989), 19.

3. Lucia Allais, 'A Questionnaire on Monuments', *October* 165 (Summer 2018), 6.

4. Sharon Hayes, 'A Questionnaire on Monuments', *October* 165 (Summer 2018): 67.

5. Witness the current controversy in the United States regarding the possible removal of multiple statues of confederate soldiers and former slave holders that continue to occupy and mark central public spaces.

6. Eric Foner, 'A Questionnaire on Monuments', *October* 165 (August 2018), 57.

7. Laura Mulvey, 'Annotations', *PIX* 2 (January 1997), 105.

8. Foner, 'A Questionnaire on Monuments', 55.

9. Mulvey, 'Annotations', 109.

10. Laura Mulvey, '"What is to be done?",' interview by Ilona Halberstadt, *PIX* 2 (January 1997), 100.

11. See: Hal Foster, 'An Archival Impulse', *October* 110 (Fall 2004), 3–22; and Hito Steyerl, 'A Language of Practice', in *The Green Room*, eds Maria Lind and Hito Steyerl (Berlin: Sternberg Press, 2008), 224–231.

12. Mulvey, *Death 24x a Second*, 9.

13. Mulvey, 'Annotations', 109.

14. Mulvey, *Death 24x a Second*, 9.

18

23rd August 2008

Faysal Abdullah, Mark Lewis and Laura Mulvey

Shot of Al-Mutanabbi Street book market.

Title   *(on visual track while audio from shot continues)*:
                 Al-Mutanabbi Street book market
                 Baghdad

Shot of Al-Mutanabbi Street book market resumes.

Audio track quickly fades.

Title: On the morning of 23rd August 2008
Title: Kamel Shiaa Abdullah came here to find a book for a friend

Black screen.

Faysal Abdullah is sitting at a table and delivers an unbroken monologue. Static shot.

FAYSAL: My brother Kamel, due to the …the Ba'ath policy, which had been
imposed on the Iraqi teacher or the education system, had to leave Iraq,
refusing to join the Ba'ath Party.* So, he left Iraq in … I would say… first
week of February '79. And in those days, the secure and the safe refuge for the
Iraqi, the leftist in particular, was the socialist bloc. Because they could have
a solidarity, a sympathy, understanding, and the West wasn't on their map at
all. I would say 95% of those people who left, especially the intellectuals, and
the politician, or involved in politics, they ended up in Eastern Europe. And

---

*   In 1978 Saddam Hussein initiated a crackdown on the Iraqi Communist Party
that was quickly followed by the imposition of Ba'ath Party membership on Iraqi
professions.

Kamel, my brother was one of those people. He settled for a while in Bulgaria, and then he moved to Hungary, and then he found himself in Italy. And he loved Italy.

But the question was how to find a job, a proper job. So he decided to go to Algeria before me, so he went to Algeria. And then I joined him in 1980. He stayed only…less than two years in Algeria, and he went back to Italy. And he had a very interesting letter being sent me, in those days. That 'The Algeria chapter is finished, I don't want to be… I don't want my hand to be tied and I have no alternatives apart from capitulation. At least I could enjoy the cultural life and the life in Italy. And not… concern about my passport renewal." Because it was… to renew your passport in those days was a sort of… the major question… to co-operate or not… with the Ba'ath. And you have to find your solutions.

So Kamel ended up in Italy. And he studied in Italy, he enrolled in a very interesting course which was to do with photography and fine art and he graduated and he started to work with a publishing company and they commissioned him to publish a very interesting dictionary for the business man in Arabic and English and Italian. You might ask me why English, since he was living in Italy? Kamel was a regular visitor to the British Council from the beginning of the '70s. He used to sit in the library and to read the newspaper and short stories and lots of things. On the opposite, I didn't go, I didn't fancy the place. It was a sort of cool… lifeless… give you the feeling of… isolation, give you the feeling of… a heavy atmosphere, which I didn't like. I was more interested in life, real life rather than in books. On the opposite, Kamel was interested in books and ideas. So he spent all these years, from the beginning of the '70s till he left, in the British Council.

This experience – added to that he was teaching English – has helped him to master the English. So when he published the book… it was a beautiful book. And I do remember the cover of the book being picked by Kamel and a friend of his. It's a work of Mondrian, the Dutch artist, with the triangles and the colours…

In retrospective, Kamel was happy in Italy. But the main question was to study, to further his education. And there was only possibility to study in the university when you have 70% mark… according to the agreement between the Iraqi education system, or the Iraqi authorities, and the Italian. And Kamel was interested in one particular university, in Bologna University. Because he

---

* In the 1970s, the Algerian government changed the language of its education system from French to Arabic, which opened up an opportunity for exiled Iraqi intellectuals to work there as teachers. Contracts, however, only lasted for one year and passport renewal in Algeria was uncertain.

knows that the tutors and the professors were very interesting. Among them was Dario Fo… and… Umberto Eco and… Gabriel Marquez… Yeah, all of them they taught in that university. So poor Kamel, when he applied, he'd be rejected because he had only 69.3 rather than 70, he'd be rejected. But the desire, the urge to study either linguistic or philosophy stayed with him. When the opportunity opened for him to move, he had to move. He moved to Belgium, and enrolled in the Catholic University of Leuven, and he studied philosophy. In those days, I used to visit him.

Kamel is not Kamel any more. That's what I discovered. Kamel gradually became a sort of academic person, rather than sitting in a café sipping tea, or spending all the time in a bar and drinking. Most of the time, he spent in the library. That's why most of the students did not finish the university. The only foreign person who finish the university, with high score, triple A, with distinction, was Kamel. And he worked there. Sometimes as a tutor, sometimes teaching Arabic, sometimes… yeah.

So this is the story, the beginning of the story. Kamel made a major impact on me. It's not just on me, lots of people who got to know him, or heard about him. He weaved a strange relation, with different people, from different background, different calibres, different… understanding of life…

After the invasion, there was a question… the question… the invasion has crippled us, the Iraqi who used to live in the exile. We used to say that we are exiled… because of a certain dictator regime in our country. But after the invasion, we don't have any excuse or to claim that we are exiled anymore. Our country… is completely… the politics of our country has changed. There is not anymore a dictator, there is an invasion. So the question which be raised, to all the Iraqi: 'Are we still living in exile or the story of exile is finished?'

Kamel was one of those people who turned the chapter. He says 'Well, my story is finished with the exile, I have to go back to Iraq.' The interesting thing is that Kamel never showed any interest in politics but all his movement, all his talk, all his writing: to do with politics. I would say most of the years that I know Kamel, he was a sympathiser of the Communist Party.* A leftist but a liberal. He used to be labelled as a communist but people they say, 'Well look, you are not a communist, you are not dogmatic. You are not a stubborn. You are open-minded. How comes you are talking about Marxism, and in the meantime, with the liberal sense?

---

* Faysal Abdullah: 'I mean here that Kamel had no interest in becoming a politician. I always knew Kamel was sympathetic to the Communist Party. I only later discovered that he had been, for most of his political life, a member.'

Anyway, he had a good relation with the communists. So after 2000, after the invasion, 2003, he'd been called to work in the cultural ministry. And became the senior advisor of the... cultural ministers. And he worked with four different kind, including an officer and an imam. Imagine? A highly intellectual person working with imam. It's not compatible. Or with officer. It's not compatible. So he worked from... I would say October 2003 till his fate... was August 2008.

When I heard the news about Kamel – Ah! During all these years, I used to call him every single day, twice, in the morning and in the evening. To the extent, I mean, he used to say 'Well, look, come on, what's wrong with you?' I say, 'Well, just to make sure, just to hear your voice, which means that you are alive'... And since he's equipped with ideas, equipped with energy... sincere, well-established, humble and a trademark of his was the smile, he's friendly with everybody. Whoever could meet Kamel or who met Kamel will not forget the charm of this person.

So when I was in Spain on the 23rd of August, I received a call from my brother, saying Kamel's been shot, been assassinated. I crumbled... Apparently he'd been trapped, in broad day time, and by professionals, and they assassinated him.... With seven bullets. And to give you the idea how much they are professionals: one of them in his eyes; and the other one in his head; third one, his heart; and two in his kidney. And the third one here. (*Faysal points to the back of his neck.*) Yeah, they were professionals....

Faysal picks up cigarette.

I mean the assassination shattered us, as a family... and in the meantime shattered all the intellectuals who were banking on the quality of people like Kamel. And lots of them, they said: 'Well, since they assassinated Kamel, there is no hope.' And Kamel was one of those people... who could be very happy by arguing with his colleague, 'Look, this is a Ministry for Culture, not a religion.' When he convince him, or her, he come very happy. As if he achieved the impossible. That's why they targeted him.

Anyway, I mean, the loss of Kamel, up till now, is with me and I think, I will never, ever, recover from that shock... at all. Even my smile is not going to be the same smile before the assassination of Kamel. So, but the story has... another... face. That when Kamel was alive, I used to call him 'My... reference'. Whenever I feel low, I call him. Whenever I need something, I call him. And I spent all these years, since the '80s till his assassination, I was investing in Kamel. During Italy period and Belgium, I used to look after him and ask him 'Don't worry about any work. I am working, I will support you. Financially, rest assured, you don't need any work, try to concentrate.'

So it was a… tragic and painful and shattered me up till now. And up till now, my family… they are insane… in a way. Because they started to talk with the walls and with themselves, as if Kamel was alive with them. And he left a very big impact on the people inside Iraq, and outside. Bear in mind, I mean, he spoke so many languages: English and French and Italian and… the interesting thing about the Italian, he translated the Italian Constitution into Arabic. And that's why, I mean, he'd been favoured by UNESCO to work with them, he was the co-chair of the Iraqi saving heritage in the UNESCO.

But the story, I mean… as my story, from '79 up to now, it took different ways. Kamel more glamourous, I am not. Kamel more thoughtful, I am more like… a practical person. I could accept any work. Kamel refuse… some works. These are the differences between our characters, despite the fact we are brothers, but still, I mean, the difference is there.

Anyway, I mean talking about my journey. I mean, I left Iraq '79, I ended up till – 80s – I ended…I ended up in Algeria. I lived there, in a place, in a village, in the heart of the desert, where you can't find the shade – imagine! Always, I mean, the sun is vertical on the ground. So I lived five years and then I came here to this country, this beautiful country… and I had to go through different stage of my life, through process… which was very interesting. When I came here, I didn't speak any language, any words. So I used to call Kamel every single day. I used to have change, ten pounds, coins, and I'd call him, till the end, he say, 'Well come on, give me a break man, what's wrong with you? You've got some money, you are living in the most beautiful city, called London, and you've got your contract in Algeria. Try to enjoy, relax, and don't bother me, I'm studying!'

So I took the advice and the first things which I have done, and that was… '85, in the rain, in Leicester Square. I rang off and, immediately, I followed his instructions. I ended up in a bar or a pub called the Irish Pride. I had a drink. I met a Irish girl and I lived with her for a while as a squatter in Ravenscourt, near Hammersmith.

Faysal lights cigarette.

Black screen.

Title: Since 2003 nearly 500 Iraqi academics and intellectuals have been assassinated

Black screen.

Title: no arrests have been made

Black screen.

Title: 23rd August 2008

Black screen.

Credits.

        camera
        Martin Testar

        camera Baghdad
        Fareed Sheehab (Al Mada)

        A film by

        Laura Mulvey
        Faysal Abdullah
        Mark Lewis

        2013

Black screen.

19

Two Portraits: *23rd August 2008*

Laura Mulvey

2 *3 August 2008* consists of two shots. A brief opening shot, intercut with intertitles, of the famous Al-Mutanabbi Street book market in Baghdad is followed by an unbroken twenty-one-minute monologue, shot from a single, still camera position and simply recording the speaker's words without interruption. In it, Faysal Abdullah gradually builds a portrait of his relationship with his younger brother, Kamel, and in the process evokes the lives of Iraqi intellectuals of the left, driven into exile in the early 1980s by Saddam Hussein's regime. Faysal describes Kamel's decision to return to Iraq in 2003, his work for the new Ministry of Culture and his tragic death at the hands of unknown assassins on 23 August 2008. While the film throws light on little-known aspects of Iraq's political history, primarily it is the story of the two brothers, of Faysal's devotion to Kamel and their contrasting attitudes to life and to exile. In a seminar paper, given probably in the mid-1990s, Kamel discussed the difference between the 'exile', who is always waiting for the moment of return, and the 'refugee', who, if often reluctantly, accepts a new nationality. Taking up this distinction, Faysal has emphasised that Kamel lived as an exile, with the accompanying hardships and uncertain legal status, always dreaming of joining his comrades in Iraq in the struggle for a better future. Faysal, on the other hand, applied for 'leave to remain' in the UK, worked (as a researcher for the London-based Arabic newspaper *Al Hayat*, also writing about film and art), settled and ultimately became a British national.[1]

Faysal and I had wanted to make a film together for quite some time before the session in the summer of 2013 that produced the final film. Over the years, circumstances changed in Iraq and so did the project. Initially, we had planned to make a filmed interview in which Faysal would give an account of growing up in Baghdad in a working-class family, in the 1960s. As the eldest of ten children, he had to support the family after his father's untimely death; from the age of fourteen, he worked in the Baghdad fruit and vegetable market, starting early in the morning and getting to school only in the afternoon.[2] The interview project would have been an oral history using Faysal's life, his memories and experiences to evoke an unequivocally secular society, with a longstanding commitment to culture and to a left politics that was strongly influenced by the Iraqi Communist Party. We never managed to get this project off the ground. Then, at the time of the American and British invasion of Iraq in 2003, I realised, bitterly, what Faysal had always known: how completely ignorant most of the world was about the history and culture of this country that had suddenly become the focus of global attention. The invaders easily conjured up and imposed sectarian and tribal stereotypes, which the media then spread into a, by and large, blank public imagination. I wanted to turn to Faysal, not so much, this time, for a personal story, but as a witness to the complexities of Iraqi history, including the importance of the Iraqi left, its persecution and eventual destruction under the dictatorship of Saddam Hussein. If it were to have a proper impact, this project would have had to be more ambitious and aspired to a wider circulation than the oral history. Once again, the project was unrealised.

After the fall of Saddam Hussein, Kamel was one of a small number of distinguished Iraqi intellectuals who returned to their country in the hope of bringing reason into the political, ideological and social chaos that followed the invasion. After studying Philosophy at the Catholic University of Leuven in the early 1980s, Kamel had continued to live in Belgium. He became a well-known and influential figure in the extensive and dispersed Iraqi exile community and his essays on philosophy, politics and literature were published widely, bringing critical attention and acclaim from writers and intellectuals across the Arab world. From the late 1980s, he also wrote for the pan-Arab daily *Al-Hayat*. After he returned to Iraq, Kamel not only worked as Adviser to the Ministry of Culture, serving four different ministers (including a police officer and an Imam, appointed under the policy of sectarian rotation) but also chaired the National Coordinating Committee for Safeguarding of the Cultural Heritage of Iraq at UNESCO. As Faysal has pointed out, Kamel was an optimist, despite all odds,[3] determined to bring to the reconstruction of the country something of the principles he and his comrades had preserved during nearly twenty-five years of exile.

When Kamel was assassinated in 2008, the wound left by his death was so great and so disorientating that the film project seemed impossible. But as the tragedy of Iraq continued to accelerate, Faysal and I, once again, had an urgent sense that the lost history of its left should be told but this time with particular reference to Kamel's story. First of all, Kamel himself has a unique and symbolic significance, representing the persistence of progressive hopes as well as tragically embodying the disastrous turn that his country's history had taken. Second, Faysal's personal experiences and, crucially, his intimate knowledge of Iraqi history, especially that of the left, could fill in some of this background and its complex legacy. When Faysal and I finally returned to the idea of the interview, I asked Mark Lewis, with whom I had collaborated on *Disgraced Monuments* (1994) and who also knew Faysal well, to work with us.

Mark and I had shot *Disgraced Monuments* on 16mm (the very end of that era) and I had not previously encountered the new digital film experience in which prolonged shooting combined with a clarity of image that equalled celluloid. We were using Mark's digital camera, the Red K4 (operated by Martin Testar). In the process of setting up the interview, Mark and I disagreed on strategy. Mark, always doubtful about over-careful preparation, was in favour of Faysal talking as thoughts led him, with minimal prompting from an interviewer (me). I, always more cautious, favoured a carefully constructed interview. As it turned out, Faysal's ability to recount stories and improvise around his thoughts, uninterrupted, was well served both by the technology and by Mark's less intrusive concept of the interview. Although he ranged over a number of different topics and we shot more material, it was ultimately clear that Faysal's 'portrait' of Kamel, the circumstances of his death and the relationship between the brothers, told in a twenty-one-minute segment, had a narrative and emotional cohesion that would work as an entity on its own. The monologue has its own particular structure, sometimes following different lines of association but always looping back to pick up the account of Kamel's life. Faysal's fluency as a story-teller, his deep involvement with the events he was describing, his emotion and his energy, find a rhythm that accumulates over the extended stretch of time. But there is also something happening on the screen, in the image, that the written script presented in this volume cannot capture: the way that this unbroken 'chunk' of time builds a portrait of the speaker and his relation to words, to a particular language and to gesture. In retrospect, it seems to me that there is an inbuilt informality in this kind of digital recording, as though the medium allows for pauses and finds space for detail. Speech, thought and feeling find their own temporality and their own varying pace.

In conclusion, I would like to mention three developments subsequent to Kamel's death and as a coda to *23rd August 2008*. First of all, Kamel's family pursued every possible route available that might have uncovered the circumstances that had led to his assassination and bring those responsible to justice. In the event, every effort was not only routinely but systematically blocked by the very authorities who should have taken up the cause. Ultimately, indirect threats to the life of one of the brothers, as he tried to enlist the help of the Ministry of the Interior, forced the family to pause their attempts to initiate an official investigation. In contrast to this official attempt to erase Kamel from history, his memory has been preserved by his comrades and by a younger generation of Iraqis who have taken up the traditions of the Iraqi left; a public celebration is held in Baghdad every 23 August to mourn Kamel's death and commemorate his life. Over the last few years, Faysal has materialised Kamel's legacy, compiling and editing his writing into four volumes on the following topics: 1) philosophy and post-modernism; 2) readings in Arab and Islamic thought; 3) reflections on Iraqi affairs; 4) essays on cultural issues – novels, art and poetry. The books were published by Al-Mada in 2019 and a volume of Kamel's letters will now be added to the series. Hopefully, *23rd August 2008*, and the publication of the script in this collection, are also part of this work of commemoration. The film bears witness to the depth of feeling between the two brothers, to an intense personal and political conversation that continued as Faysal prepared Kamel's writings for publication. Ultimately, the pragmatic side to Faysal's character, combined with his devotion to his brother, has enabled Kamel's intellectual and political legacy to return to Iraqi public life – just as the widespread protests, that began on 25th October 2019 in Baghdad and the southern provinces, once again take up the struggle for a modern, non-sectarian, civil society.

Notes

1. This essay has been written in dialogue with Faysal Abdullah.
2. At this time the Iraqi working class benefitted from the legacy of the General Abd Al-Karim Qasim government (1958–1963) and the country's prosperity during the oil boom years. A particular benefit was free education.
3. Kamel's MA thesis had been titled 'Utopia as Critique' and was written under the influence of Ernst Bloch, whom he considered to be 'a philosopher of hope'.

Section 4

Outlines for Unmade
Collaborative Films

20

Possible Worlds

Laura Mulvey and Peter Wollen

Outline, February 1978

Possible Worlds continues some of the concepts of our previous film *Riddles of the Sphinx*. It has a precise formal structure in which the melodrama or narrative (divided between three distinct but interlocking stories) is told in a series of tableaux-like shots within a symmetrical framework. The camerawork and *mise-en-scène* will reflect the same formal structuring. For instance, the three narrative points of view will have corresponding visual styles.

Outline

1.1   One–three minutes

Montage sequence of money with main credits superimposed.

2.1   Three–four minutes
Introductory 'portrait' sequence of Dora.

Airport baggage pick-up area. Empty. A few cases endlessly revolving on the belt.
Dora is in her mid-thirties. She is sitting with her baggage. She has just arrived.
She talks to camera about money. She responds in relation to her work –
economic planning and computers in a Third World country* – rather than her

---

*   When Peter and I wrote this outline in 1978, the term Third World was still in
general use, referring, in the first instance, to those nations that formally rejected
Cold War alignment with either the First World (the Western, capitalist, block) or
the Second World (the Eastern, communist, block). This position also carried with
it the political principles that were first articulated by the progressive leaders of

personal needs. A one-dimensional standard of measurement like money is not adequate for computing real wants and social costs and benefits.

'…You don't just say "Well, that's cheap, so that's what I want most". You may want something else more but not be able to see how you can afford it. So there you have two scales, the desire and the cost. It's not a simple shopping list kind of thing. The cost in money doesn't measure the desire. It's a constraint on it. So you have a problem how to match your two scales, because one is very precise but very misleading and the other is very difficult to quantify, but it's what it's all about – what people want, what they want to produce and what they want to consume and what kind of society they want to work and live in…'

As she speaks, the camera moves away so that voice-to-camera becomes voice-over and then returns to the original framing at the end of the shot.

2.2   Three–four minutes
Introductory 'portrait' sequence of Ned.

In the street somewhere in the City of London. Wren church in the background.
    Ned is about the same age as Dora. Like her, he talks about money.
    '…It's fun. Making it's fun and spending it's fun… I'm essentially a middleman and I make money out of anything that affects the price of anything. I make money out of the weather, I make money out of civil wars and mainly I make money out of time. Prices go up and down as time goes by but you have to get it right… The thing about the futures market is that it brings together two types of people – people who are worried about the future and want to hedge against it and people who are excited by the future and want to take risks on it. I'm the second type… You could say I'm one of the richoisie…'

2.3   Three–four minutes
Introductory 'portrait' sequence of Kate.

In the country. Kate is a little older than the other two. She is painting a chair.
    '…I'm very ambivalent about money really… I mean, it sounds a bit simplistic to say money is the root of all evil, but it would certainly be wonderful to get rid of it. We'd be much better off without it. You know, I read how in Cambodia they blew up all the banks and left money lying round the streets… But then, in the meantime, we have got it or rather we haven't got it, there's so little of it really, and I suppose we have to spend it wisely, like the wise virgins and not on extravaganzas or wild schemes… It's just that we should try to enlarge the bits of life that don't

---

newly independent African and Asian states at the Bandung conference in 1955, later formalised as the Non-Aligned Movement in 1961. LM.

involve money and get them to expand as far as we can. Perhaps that's a wild scheme in itself. I don't see why it should be. I really don't…'

3.1   (Kate's story) One–two minutes

Countryside. Woodland. A group of people, mainly women, are cutting down small trees and scrub, clearing the ground. We see Kate among them. They are throwing branches and sticks onto a large fire. Children by the fire, trying to help but sometimes getting in the way. Confused noise – shouting, electric saw, children quarrelling, crackling.

3.2   One–two minutes

Pigsty. Pig feeding at the trough. Voice-off of onlookers. Some are worried about the pig – it's not eating enough, when are they going to be able to slaughter it. Others are worried about slaughtering it – should they do it themselves, shouldn't they get another pig and try and breed… Children object to the pig being slaughtered at all and say they won't eat it anyway… The pig doesn't seem to care.

3.3   One–two minutes

Footbridge over stream. Bridge decayed, banks overgrown. Kate and a much younger man, in his early twenties, are standing on the bridge, leaning on the rail, arguing about policy for the commune they are living in. They are dogged by a young child who makes endless childish suggestions – 'Why don't you make ginger biscuits out of breadcrumbs and butter-beans?' The young man believes the commune can move steadily to self-sufficiency. Kate says that people like her can't go on putting money into it much longer and it would be better to put money into things that would bring money back. She says she'll try and fix up another loan to tide them over.

3.4   One–two minutes

Stretch of grass. Children sitting in an untidy ring.
They are protesting at being given lessons. One of two women quiets them by reciting 'Don't care didn't care'. When they are settled the other woman starts to read aloud to them – perhaps *Flatland*. Kate comes up to listen.

3.5   One–two minutes

Hand-painted chessboard with antique ornate red and white pieces. One of the pieces is replaced by an old ounce weight. End game. A little oblique dialogue (which identifies Kate as one player).

3.6 One–two minutes

Window. Telephone on the sill rings. Someone answers and calls for Kate. She comes into frame soon after and puts down a gun she has been carrying.

'Dora! How lovely to hear your voice! Where are you? You're in London… Well, in fact, I'd already decided I had to come up for a couple of days next week, so that all works out wonderfully. I've got to see Ned about business and things. Have you seen him yet?…'

'That sounds lovely. The three of us together, like the old days. But can't we meet too? Can you possibly squeeze me in somewhere?… Why don't you give me your number just in case…'

3.7 One–two minutes

Dream sequence. Animation/rotoscope/live action.

Kate is running through the wood which is full of snow. She comes to a clearing where there is a duel. Harlequin is shooting Pierrot, who is white as the snow. Harlequin has Ned's face. When she looks at Pierrot, she sees she is Dora. The blood runs down into the snow and into a brook and over a waterfall into a tropical pool. The pool is full of huge brightly coloured waterlilies. On one of the lily-pads there is a frog. The frog says, 'You have been sentenced to deportation. I've read your father's last will and testament. You are condemned to exile.' Ned comes up, still dressed as Harlequin. He gives her a ticket. It says 'Trans-Siberian Railway'. When she gets in the train, Dora is sitting opposite. She says, 'Why are you wearing your mother's furs, it's going to be very hot'.

3.8 One–two minutes

Art gallery. Contemporary work (Photo-Realist).

Kate and Dora are talking. Dora asks, 'Have you had a show recently?'

'I haven't even done any work recently. I haven't really wanted to paint. Unless you think the whole thing is a conceptual work. I did start out documenting it. I've got thousands of Instamatics I can't afford to take to the chemist. Now there are thousands of final demands we can't afford to pay… To tell the truth, things are going a whole lot worse than I usually say. Everything's working out wonderfully on a day-to-day level but underneath we're running rapidly into bankruptcy. I'm on a secret mission to see my broker – well, I say "my broker" but effectively he's Ned's broker, of course. I've finished my money but Ned uses me for one of his multifarious accounts. I sign the papers and so on and it gives me a magnificent income which pays for servicing the pig and repairing the electric saw… Sometimes I feel I'd like to paint again. I'd like to be able to keep up with what's happening more…'

3.9   One–two minutes

Restaurant. Kate, Dora and Ned are seated round a table, with dessert in front of them. None of them seem to be eating it – if at all, certainly not with enthusiasm.

Ned's monologue: (to Kate) '…Look, one of the strange things is that we've both taken gambles in our lives. Perhaps you didn't realise it, but you were gambling with my winnings, so now I've started losing, you've lost too. Which doesn't seem fair, does it? What's more, I've lost a lot of money, but that's the way the tables turn, and the game goes on. All I have to do is to work out how to work my way back into the game. But your game's over. All the pieces have fallen on the floor with a dull and tedious thud and you're just a poor little rich girl whose brother let her down. At least you'll have a roof over your head but since you've never known any real hardship you'll not even know how grateful you ought to be. What kind of hardship is it, when your brother loses fifty thousand pounds? Anyone who can lose that amount can gain it back again, if he keeps his head. What will it be next time? What new friends will you find for me to let down?'

Ned's speech is greeted by silence, shocked at the outburst which has marred their reunion meal. A long silence.

3.10   One–two minutes

Back in the country. The local country taxi drives up. Kate gets out and pays. She walks over to the house and round the back to get to the kitchen window. Inside the young man we have seen before is absorbed in preparing the evening meal. He's obviously skilled at cooking and has several helpers (including, of course, some children). Kate watches the vigour and turmoil within. She can't face disturbing them to tell them the truth. Eventually someone sees her and opens the window. One child is saying: 'How are the parsnips in the pot, eh? Nine hundred and ninety nine Fahrenheit, eh? How about nine hundred and ninety nine pounds, Kate?' Another says: 'Kate, we found a dead bird and we buried it.'

3.11   One–two minutes

Night-time. Kate is in bed with the young man. No curtains and some dawn light beginning to come in the window. Kate wakes early, thirsty and with a slight hangover, and wakes him up reaching for a mug of water to drink.

KATE (quite wide awake suddenly, half talking to herself but expecting him to listen and respond): 'He always admired me. Always. He knew he could never catch up. In the end he did. That's the dull and tedious basic fact about brothers. They're given catching up on a plate.'

HIM: 'Kate, come on now, don't go on about it anymore. It's four in the morning. It must be four in the morning.'

KATE: 'Why should they? Why should they suddenly think they're entitled to despise you, just because… But I want to tell you about Dora.'

He puts his arms round her and kisses her.

HIM: 'Come on, calm down. Just relax. Don't take it so hard.'

There's her silence while he tries to arouse her and distract her.

KATE: 'When Dora was with us, she always admired him. We could all do things together. She's the one who feels disenchanted.'

HIM (continuing): 'Sure you can cope with it okay. Come on now. You're bound to be alright, after all. Let's make love a little.'

KATE: 'Fuck you! Leave me alone, can't you! Leave me alone for a minute! I won't be alright. There's no way I'll be alright.'

HIM (retreating:) 'I'm suffering too you know, but I'm not making anything out of it.'

KATE: 'It's not a matter of making something out of it, is it? It's a matter of trying to find some solidarity and tell you what I feel about it all and you just don't want to listen, all you want is to shut me up.'

Kate storms up out of bed. He turns away.

KATE: 'Give me one good reason why he should treat me like that.'

3.12   One–two minutes

Outside the house. Loading up a van. To and fro between the house and the van, parked a little distance away. We see the young man but not Kate. Children are rushing around trying to carry things too heavy for them. They all climb in and drive off. Pause. Emptiness. Then Kate walks into frame out of the woods and back towards the house.

4.1   Four–six minutes

Insert. Performance by mime or performance artist, to be elaborated in collaboration with artist.

The theme might be money or Utopia, but it should not directly reflect the material in the narrative.

5.1 (Dora's story)   One–two minutes

Computer centre. Read-outs are pouring out of machines. People are milling around, glancing through read-outs, throwing them into huge bins, shouting at each other, putting things in files, drinking coffee out of paper cups and making a commotion. We see Dora among them, absorbed in the activity.

5.2   One–two minutes

Hotel room. Sound of a shower being shut off. A few seconds later, Dora comes into the room. Her hair is wrapped in a towel and she's drying herself with another. She gets into bed and reaches for the telephone. On the bed she spreads out her diary, address book and other papers.

First telephone call. She gets through to an answerphone and after composing her reply says: 'Ned, this is Dora. I'm in London. I'm sorry to have missed you. I'm at a hotel – 464 2871 room number 603. I'd love to see you. Call me back as soon as you get in. If I'm out can you leave a message at the desk and, in any case, I'll try and get through to you again later tonight. The number's 464 2871, extension 603. See you soon.'

Second call. This one goes through a secretary. Then: 'Hello. This is Dorothea Canton. Do you remember I left a message for you yesterday… That's right. I'm very anxious to talk to you because we're putting together a suite of programmes similar to the programmes you worked on in Chile and I'm sure it would be very helpful to us to learn from your experiences… Maybe three of us… Well, I think our preference would be for the end of the week, Thursday or Friday… Okay, so I'll call you back this afternoon and we'll fix a definite time then. Thank you very much. I'm looking forward to meeting you. Bye.'

Third call in Spanish, obviously relaying the previous conversation.

Fourth call, after checking *Time Out*: 'Mary, I'm going to *Annie Hall* with Martin this evening. Do you both want to come?… Okay, how about *The American Friend* then?… Well, Buñuel is the only thing that we do get to see… Mary, I'm still trying to catch up with the mainstream, but we can give it a try… Eight o'clock then…'

5.3   One–two minutes

Small conference room. About half a dozen people, including Dora, sitting round a table. They are discussing the cyberstride programmes which a team member under Stafford Beer put together for the Allende government in Chile, both the technical programming aspects – real-time control, CUSUM, algedonic feedback etc. – and the political implications – devolution, filtration and workers participation. Questions and answers, with Dora sometimes having to translate between Spanish and English. Dora is particularly interested in the way the programmes were devised to allow workers a high degree of autonomy in economic planning.

5.4   One–two minutes

Ned's apartment. Comfortable with a tendency to gadgets and a modest collection of outsider art. A lot of records, some junk food objects and some old photographs on the walls. Magazines, local and foreign, including car magazines, *The New Yorker*, *Barron's* etc. Dora has just arrived. She is wandering round looking at things. Ned pours drinks, reminisces.

NED: 'Now, there's so much I'm waiting to hear. So! You went off and learned a useful trade and left us all here to rot. What adventures have you had?'

DORA: 'It's been very exciting, but it's been very hard work.. You know how people have an image of computers and science as an alien force… It makes it hard-going. There's a lot of hostility you have to break down and the exciting thing is that you can break it down… People at the base begin to see that a telex line to a computer is a way they are empowered to discriminate and to make judgments and economic decisions…'

NED: 'I've got a lot of money tied up in your adopted country you know.'

DORA: 'How do you mean? You mean on the commodities market? Buying or selling? Long, I hope.'

NED: 'No, no, no. That would be foolish, wouldn't it?'

DORA: 'Why? I certainly don't think so. We're absolutely committed to maintaining the price levels. There should be a general producer's agreement and it should have an equitable floor and that means it should have a high floor by some standards. We get richer. You get poorer.'

NED: 'Assuming your side wins its election, that is… You were always such fun to compete with. You always took everything so seriously…'

5.5   One–two minutes

Squash court. Dora is playing squash with a friend (Mary). Very white with a single red line. Dora plays very aggressively and energetically.

5.6   One–two minutes

Towpath by canal (Primrose Hill/Chalk Farm). An afternoon walk – Dora, one of her team and an English politician. They are deep in discussion. They say they are confident they are going to win the upcoming election, despite press reports, and ask what the response of the Labour Party will be. Can they count on its support? 'Well, you know what my feelings are and obviously they're shared by a significant section of the Party, perhaps even a majority of constituency Party members, if that isn't too optimistic, but things look rather different when you get to the leadership… It's not really a loss of ideals. It's more a submission to pressures which ask for ideals to stay just that – ideals, memories and sacred formulae, but not guides to action… After all, Britain is part of the NATO alliance, it has all kinds of obligations to the United States, to the IMF – there's still an IMF loan outstanding – to the Common Market, and a governmental party sees itself in that light, as representing Britain… So the Democratic Front can expect a ritual evocation of ideals but practically you might as well go to Bonn or Washington…'

5.7   One–two minutes

The Shetland Shop. Shop full of brightly coloured Shetland sweaters, pullovers and scarves. Dora is shopping with her mother, trying on clothes, looking at herself in the glass and discussing with her mother. In the intervals between commenting on the clothes she talks a bit more personally. 'You know, Ned was talking about you a lot when I saw him. He said you'd never been able to settle down since you refused to marry his father.'

'He did, did he? Donald could never forgive me for marrying Eduardo. It's strange that Ned should still be living the same phantasy…'

5.8   One–two minutes

Hotel room. Dora is tense and nervous, glancing at her watch. She goes to the mirror to brush her hair and make-up. Eventually she goes over to the telephone to make a call in Spanish, but with enough words of English for it to be clear she is asking about the election results. Her party has won. She rings off, pours herself a drink from the bottle of rum and, obviously exultant, starts writing rapidly in a large notebook.

5.9   One–two minutes

The same restaurant as (3.9) in Kate's story. Kate and Dora are sitting at the table, studying the menu and exchanging a few words, waiting for Ned to arrive. At last he rushes up.

NED: 'This calls for champagne! Dora, you'll have champagne, won't you? I'm sorry I'm a bit late, but there were some trivial but very, very unavoidable loose ends I had to tie up at the office. Dora, you can probably guess what they were. (To Kate:) Dora and I had a kind of bet.' (Kate looks surprised.)

DORA: 'Not really, I wouldn't call it that. We had a political disagreement and my side won, for once.'

KATE: 'I suppose it's the election…'

As the wine waiter appears she turns to Dora and says, 'Congratulations'.

Ned busies himself in discussion with the wine waiter, pointing out things in the list and making erudite comments. The waiter finally suggests something that's not on the list at all.

5.10   One–two minutes

Same. Later in the meal, which is now almost over. They all look a bit strained. Coffee and brandy are left unfinished in front of them.

KATE: 'Anyway let's get the bill. I've had enough. Waiter.' She signals to the waiter.

NED: 'As far as I'm concerned we can sit here all night and insult each other. No one's really insulted Dora yet. Why should she get away unscathed? Dora, that's like leaving a poker game when you're winning.'

KATE: 'Ned, for Christ's sake let's get the fucking bill. Waiter!'

NED: 'Very well. I concur. From the bottom of my heart. Waiter, the bill!'

Waiter arrives with the bill and puts it down in front of Ned.

Dora leans forward earnestly.

DORA: 'I'd really like to pay for this. I'd really like to. At least my future's secured for the time being and it means a lot for me to see you both. And I've got an American Express card I hardly ever get to use…'

NED: 'It's very sweet of you to offer, but I don't think you may quite realise what you're letting yourself in for. I did order wines suitable to the occasion, not to mention the very special brandy…'

Dora looks at the bill and sees what he means.

NED: 'Dora darling, it's a debt of honour. Now drink up, both of you. It's the last opportunity you'll have for many a long month to enjoy my hospitality.'

In the following pause, he tips all the brandy into one glass and downs it.

5.11   One–two minutes

Theatre. Chilean theatre group in exile. Dora in the audience with a man (Martin).

5.12   One–two minutes

Hotel room. Dora is packing. Suitcases, clothes spread out on the bed, some presents. She obviously finds it hard to concentrate. Eventually she makes a telephone call to a hospital and asks for the casualty ward. She inquires how Ned Edward Meadows is getting on and asks if she can leave a message, looking relieved – 'Please could you tell him, Goodbye Ned.'

6.1 Four–six minutes

Insert. Modernised re-make of the scene in the train from the Brecht–Dudow film *Kuhle Wampe*. All the dialogue is different, reflecting the changes that have taken place over fifty years in the world coffee market, the price of coffee, public reaction to it and changed concepts of the Third World.

7.1 (Ned's story) One–two minutes

Commodity exchange. Hubbub. Video display terminals. Obviously something exciting is going on. People rushing about shouting (mostly voice-off). Figures clicking over like a stopwatch. Ned somewhere in the crowd, part of the general excitement.

7.2 One–two minutes

Ned's office. He's sitting at his desk, reading *Le Monde*. His secretary comes in and hands him his mail, ready-opened. As he takes it, she says, 'Many happy returns of the day, Ned.'

NED: 'Don't believe a word of it. I was left by "The Raggle Taggle Gypsies-O". (Leafing through the mail) Still… I don't suppose Jane left any message? (Secretary says no). Thank God for that. Now, business before birthdays, as Adam Smith might have said. There's a new OECD report out on commodity pricing or some such title. Please keep this *Le Monde* for the next few days.

'There's a series of reports leading up to the elections. Though they're very left-wing, you can't believe everything they say… Then I'd better get hold of the new man from Panama. Ramirez said he's probably dealing for the Panamanian government through an omnibus account. Track him down, would you, and get him round to lunch. I'll need the usual shipping schedules…'

The telephone on his desk rings.

'Jane, how sweet of you.'

7.3 One–two minutes

Ned's apartment. Same as (5.4) in Dora's story. The scenes slightly overlap.

NED: 'You were always such fun to compete with. You took it all so seriously.'

DORA: 'Wednesday's child is full of woe. I wasn't in the least woeful though. I was very happy. Probably happier than I've been since.'

NED: 'We were a happy family, weren't we?'

DORA: 'I was the challenging child living out my family romance. I loved you all so much. Too much, I sometimes think. You know how childhood happiness stays with you and tugs you back from the brinks you really ought to cross. I don't really trust in happiness any more. Perhaps I mean – I don't fully trust memories of happiness anymore.'

NED: 'There, you see how seriously you turned out. Sceptical to the point of... but that's your strength.'

DORA: 'I still remember the moment when I realised you were stronger than me. I must have been eleven or twelve. Then I had to fall back on intellectual arguments. It was hard to detach myself, but I had to. I had to really.'

NED: 'No. Really you belonged with us. Your mother made the crucial mistake. She should never have refused father... We could have had an exciting incestuous relationship instead of just being childhood friends...'

DORA: 'That's your family romance, isn't it? I mean, about mother...'

7.4   One–two minutes

Same scene. Later.

DORA: 'When I was with all of you I forgot my foreignness. But then in the world outside, I was different. More and more as time went on. Even in the '60s my political commitment didn't seem like other people's.'

NED: 'Even I was political in the '60s.'

DORA: 'I remember. You even read Volume One of *Capital*. That was something anyway. Lots of people didn't even do that. At least you weren't self-righteous, Ned...'

NED: 'Not a hope. If I'd been self-righteous, I'd have been disillusioned and then who knows how I would have ended up. Like Kate probably.'

DORA: 'I think you are disillusioned.'

NED: 'Nonsense. I remember the '60s. It was the decade of the Beach Boys and Yoko Ono and Biba. How could you be disillusioned with that?'

DORA: 'Well, why are you so right-wing now?'

NED: 'I'm not. If anything, I'm left-wing. I'd be backing your people if I thought they had a chance of winning. I'm a speculator, not a capitalist.'

DORA: 'That's got nothing to do with politics at all. Politics is public life and it's world trade and it's the role you play. You're just making alibis for yourself. I hate it. Let's talk about old times again...'

7.5   One–two minutes

Garage. Ned is having his customised Porsche tuned by a mechanic. They are both absorbed but exchange car gossip – models, parts, performance, prices.

7.6 One–two minutes

Ned's apartment. Night. Ned is in a robe, walking about with a calculator and a Dictaphone, whispering numbers. A TV is running, but with the sound off. Country music. After a little while, the doorbell rings and he goes to answer it. A woman comes in. She is dressed for dinner or the theatre – he has been expecting her. They start to make love, when the telephone rings. He goes to answer it. He's not saying much, but making notes – she follows him over and continues caressing him. It becomes apparent that this is the call he'd been waiting for with the election results. When he rings off, he turns round to her and they embrace.

7.7 One–two minutes

Bank. Ned is talking to his bank manager, explaining that he's going to need a very much bigger loan in order to buy coffee at a much higher price than he expected in order to meet the delivery date on which he is contracted to sell – at a considerable loss. In fact, he is in a lot of trouble, but is presenting his problems as one of short-term adjustment, not the attitude the bank seems likely to take. In fact, the response is polite but tough. They don't like what he is saying and they want much more information. He should go see his broker and his accountant and then come back.

7.8 One–two minutes

Back at the restaurant (same as Kate's and Dora's stories). This scene has the same action and dialogue as (5.9) in Dora's story but is shot differently – different camera position, framing etc., and some differences in sound recording. The different framing and recording give different background detail and scenes. The scene goes on a little later since it began a little later with Ned's arrival.

7.9 One–two minutes

Same scene, later in the meal. Main course. Dora is explaining how the Olmecs invented the zero and how to this day the Mayan vigesimal system of counting is still used in many villages. The atmosphere of the dinner is standing up to strain. Ned starts fantasising about vigesimal calculators when he is stopped in his tracks by the appearance of his ex-wife, Jane.

JANE: 'What a surprise! The three of you together! Kate, I hope this doesn't mean you've decided to become worldly and decadent like the rest of us… Dora, what brings you back to the sinking ship? What a feast you're all having!'

NED: 'You seem in rather a festive mood yourself, dear.'

JANE: 'I had to get out. I'm celebrating the attic roof falling in. Large chunks all over the nursery. I haven't been able to face calling the builder because the estimate will be too dreadful. I was hoping you might have some spare cash, Ned. I'll let you know the galling details as soon as I can face it.'

NED: 'Yes. Of course.'

JANE: 'Well, I'll leave you all to your ménage-à-trois.'

7.10   One–two minutes

Still later. The shocked silence after Ned's outburst.

KATE: 'You know perfectly well if it wasn't for the injustices of English law you wouldn't have inherited everything, and me a pathetic pittance. You've said so yourself in the past. I always thought you meant it. Now I see you mean it just as long as you can afford it. All I want in the world is to get out of all this. It's typical. You think you can say exactly what you please to me, however hurtful and offensive and inequitable it may be. I'm not some hard-luck case for you to patronise. Why was it all yours anyway? Just because you've got a prick. If money went to those with cunts it would be better spent and we'd all be better off. We'd be spared your arrogant insinuations too. All I've ever asked for in our so-called equitable arrangement is what I knew we needed. I'm certainly not the spoiled child round here. I know the prices of things…'

7.11   One–two minutes

Hospital. Private space attached to casualty ward. Ned sitting upright in bed. Crutches against the wall. Gifts and flowers on table, papers lying around. He is talking to his accountant, who has come to visit him. They are running over figures and trying to work out a strategy. Ned says: 'Perhaps we could count in the loans to my sister. She must have come out ahead.' The accountant says no. There are more obligations there. Ned is surprised. It turns out Kate had disregarded his advice to buy and led the broker to think Ned agreed, hoping to cash in along with Ned. He's shaken by this and asks the accountant to leave, saying he's tired. The accountant leaves and he rings for the nurse.

7.12   One–two minutes

The country, as in Kate's story. Ned and Kate are on the lawn, playing croquet.

8.1   Concluding 'portrait' of Ned

21

Chess Fever

Laura Mulvey and Peter Wollen

This is a film about chess and about the life of a chess professional, a young Hungarian woman whose career has reached a point of crisis.

MARTA was a child prodigy, a junior champion who has never fulfilled the promise expected of her. Brought up by her wild grandmother, she resented the control of the chess authorities and reacted against them with bouts of insubordination. Especially, she wanted to advance immediately to playing in the more competitive arena of adult male chess and felt she was being held back and given inadequate support and coaching. Her horizons were much higher and her frustrations much greater than those of other young girl players. Now she is playing in a minor women's tournament in a small Hungarian town. Formerly a fashionable spa, the town's fortunes have changed like those of chess itself – once an aristocratic pastime, now a serious socialist sport.

As MARTA plays, she is noticed by FREDERICK, a visiting chess journalist, analyst and commentator. In his forties and strikingly good-looking, he had an honourable career as a chess player but lacked the specialised ability and drive quite to make it to the top. Still deeply involved in chess, he tries to scrape a reasonable living on the margins of the international game. At first he is attracted to MARTA for her looks and style, but when he moves over to watch her play he becomes intrigued by the game itself. She is playing a subtly calculated variation on the Sicilian Defence, but at a crucial move, she seems to lose concentration and makes a fatal blunder. Shattered and distraught, she resigns and leaves the hall.

Later that evening, in the hotel bar, FREDERICK enquires about her and is told how she was once Hungarian Junior Champion, but fell out of favour with the chess establishment because of her difficult temperament and headstrong behaviour. FREDERICK recognises her name and later, after he has lost a lot of money at blitz, which he plays to supplement his income, he begins to formulate a plan.

The next day MARTA fails to appear and forfeits her match. FREDERICK asks more questions and, after a series of delays and difficulties, manages to trace her to her childhood home, a small village in eastern Hungary, where she is staying with her grandmother. He is directed to the local railway signal-box, where he finds MARTA with the signal-man, her first childhood chess teacher. Not many trains run through the village and they are sitting on a bench with a chessboard spread out between them, going through the game MARTA lost at the tournament, looking for the best line of play.

FREDERICK points out how the position they have reached is one already known, from Mecking's game against Najdorf at Mar del Plata in the '70s. Black should have the advantage, but there are still some unexplored avenues, which MARTA eagerly seizes on. Finally they stop playing and FREDERICK explains to her the plan that has crystallised in his mind. He will take her to the West, train her, manage her and re-launch her career. At first, MARTA is stunned, then delighted and excited at the prospect of travel, adventure and a change in her fortunes. She agrees to go with FREDERICK.

When they arrive in England, FREDERICK takes MARTA to the countryside (the moors) for an intense period of training and preparation. MARTA is given a strenuous programme of physical work outs and cross-country running, as well as a course of chess practice and study sessions, concentrating on the games of her future opponents and the latest variations in opening techniques. FREDERICK's aim is that MARTA should be physically fit and technically prepared for the matches she must play, as well as psychologically confident, aggressive and tenacious. The model he has in mind for her, which fits with her own conception of her powers, is that of Joan of Arc.

During this time FREDERICK and MARTA are constantly together. Their relationship is intense and involving, but sublimated. Its moments of sexual tension are quickly displaced by FREDERICK on to renewed efforts of concentration at the chessboard. After a little while, he tells MARTA that he is more than satisfied with her progress. He is sure she can win. He goes to London, leaving her to continue her routine for a day on her own, while he negotiates a sponsorship deal with a computer company, eager to find a more 'feminine' image for their product. In the evening, MARTA, alone for the first time, copes with the curiosities and suspicions of the local people.

FREDERICK returns to MARTA with a contract, conditional on her winning the forthcoming tournament, to be held at a hotel in Scarborough. MARTA is one of two women entered in an otherwise all-male competition, in which three prominent masters are taking part. She plays, as FREDERICK has coached her, with tenacious aggression and, though she loses against one of the masters and draws against another, she succeeds in winning the tournament because she goes for and achieves wins against the ruck of minor players, where others would have been satisfied with a less demanding draw. She has returned to her best previous form, with broadened experience and understanding of chess, and with the resolution and relentlessness that FREDERICK has instilled in her.

During a rest day, there is an incident on the sea-front, when MARTA feels she is being harassed by a man. She turns on him in a storm of anger and denounces him with a tirade of Hungarian. He starts to shout back and for a moment it looks as if the scene will turn violent, when a woman who is passing by intervenes and persuades MARTA that she has misunderstood the man's intentions. Later, MARTA meets the woman again at the tournament, where she is introduced to her by FREDERICK as SARA, the dynamic young PR and promotion executive of the computer company with whom he made the deal. SARA is cheerful, capable and ambitious. She is delighted by MARTA's success and also by her looks and charm, far removed from the typical image of the chess player.

When MARTA wins the contest, SARA gives a small party for her and the next day they leave together for London, where SARA begins to groom MARTA for public appearances, interviews and photo sessions. MARTA feels she has hit a winning streak. She is swept off her feet by the heady new world into which SARA and FREDERICK introduce her in London. As well as chess preparation and daily visits to the gym, she now has hairdressers, restaurants and clothes shops added to her programme. FREDERICK and SARA have organised a show match for her against a prominent ex-champion (in the Korchnoi or Spassky mould): the brilliant new female star against the wise old male Grandmaster. It is phase two of her new career and MARTA is excited at the prospect, determined to continue her success and enjoy its fruits.

In fact, MARTA thrives on the publicity. She happily accepts the promotional image that SARA has conjured up for her marketing campaign. It brings out both her exhibitionism and her aggressiveness, but in a controlled form that emerges as frankness and enthusiasm. She is swept up in a romance with London, success, consumerism and public attention, in the up-scale media at least. Far from distracting her from her chess, this adds a new energy and verve to her play.

When the match begins, in the *moderne* ball room of a Piccadilly hotel, MARTA's opponent is visibly intimidated by this new phenomenon of chess combined with sex and glamour. FURMANOV is a player of the old school, used to the serious all-male atmosphere of Soviet-dominated congresses and Interzonals, where women are few and far between. He is psychologically unprepared for a player such as MARTA and the media hype she brings with her. MARTA soon sets up a commanding lead, demoralising FURMANOV with each fresh victory. He becomes increasingly nervous and begins to complain to the referee that her perfume is distracting him. But even without it, she wins. FREDERICK has prepared her well, finding new replies to FURMANOV's favourite openings.

In the evenings, MARTA, FREDERICK and SARA are always together, perhaps going with FREDERICK to a chess club where he can play blitz, perhaps simply relaxing in the hotel or in MARTA's service apartment. We realise that FREDERICK and SARA are having an affair, which they naturally want to conceal from MARTA. SARA has fallen for FREDERICK and also beneath her emotionally open exterior she has a calculating streak, which sees the advantage of sealing a work connection with an affair. For his part, FREDERICK is not at all averse to SARA sweeping him along, partly as a relief from the nagging tension of his relations with MARTA, deep but inadmissible and impractical. Although MARTA must be aware of various tell-tale hints, her concentration on the match, her uncritical captivation with her friends and mentors, and her uncertainty, as a foreigner, about social signs and conventions, all conspire to prevent her from realising what is going on. SARA is worried by the deception and would like to tell MARTA, but FREDERICK is reluctant to disturb her while the match is still in progress.

But soon enough, knowledge is forced on her. Her birthday occurs during the tournament, on the day of a difficult, adjourned game. SARA gives a party for her but, to MARTA's great regret, FREDERICK says that he can't attend, because he has to work on the analysis of the game in readiness for the next day's continuation. SARA has ordered a birthday cake decorated with chess pieces representing the adjourned position. When the cake is brought in, MARTA picks up the enemy king and eats it in one bite. She is sure of winning and in a relaxed mood. But during the party FREDERICK arrives, just for a moment, and delves into SARA's handbag to take out a bottle of pills. MARTA is surprised by the intimacy of the gesture and her doubts are reawakened later when FREDERICK returns to say goodnight to them. MARTA notices that FREDERICK avoids any physical contact with SARA, though he would normally give her a parting kiss. It is as if FREDERICK suspects that MARTA suspects – and indeed, as a result, she does.

The next day, everything is brought to a head. During a press interview she is maliciously asked about her reaction to the situation between her trainer and her sponsor. The journalist is close to the Furmanov camp, which has become a stronghold of misogyny, already seething just below the surface of the chess world, and he relishes the discomfiture of the upstart interloper, as he sees MARTA. She, of course, is terribly upset by the unwelcome truth. She feels hurt not to have known earlier, betrayed by her closest friends and as though her own sexuality had been thrown into crisis. Years of sublimation suddenly seem years of self-deception. Chess, *par excellence*, is the game of panic and paranoia. MARTA succumbs to both.

Soon afterwards MARTA must meet FREDERICK for their pre-match preparation session. Bitter and angry, she tells him that she no longer wants or needs his coaching. She can manage on her own abilities. He has betrayed her trust. FREDERICK stands silent as she orders him out of her life. MARTA goes to the match with FURMANOV in a mood of tension and agitation but somehow she manages to survive with a draw. That evening she seeks out a young man who has been showing interest in her, a chess-fan tycoon-to-be, whom previously she had rejected out of hand. Now she throws herself at him. They sleep together and MARTA sets off on a course of sexual adventure, picking up men in the hotel bar and the gym, sleeping with a different person every night.

Her behaviour and her public image become wilder and wilder. Though she still turns up for the match, her play begins to suffer and soon FURMANOV draws level and begins to go ahead. FREDERICK and SARA are left helpless on the sidelines, too anxious to find much consolation. Finally, MARTA reaches her breaking point. After a long and difficult game is adjourned, she is unable to find a satisfactory line of play and, on the continuation, is rapidly and ruthlessly destroyed by FURMANOV. She leaves the hall in distress and fails to appear on the stage for the next game. FURMANOV makes his opening move and, after the statutory time has elapsed, the referee declares him the winner.

Once again, while SARA fends off the press, FREDERICK sets out in search of MARTA. This time he eventually finds her in the home of a Hungarian friend. She is by herself, replaying a winning game, trying to regain her composure and confidence. She is torn between rejecting FREDERICK, needing him and loving him. She tells him that her days of chastity are over and confides her worries that her magical Joan of Arc powers have gone. FREDERICK tries to reassure her. She tells him she wants to sleep with him. She loves him. FREDERICK desperately wants to re-establish his relationship with MARTA, whose loss he feels painfully. But he still believes it would be wrong to become involved sexually while the match is still in progress. He promises MARTA that once the match is over, they can work out a new basis for their life together, as she wants. Meanwhile, she must go back to the board and concentrate on winning.

FREDERICK returns to SARA to tell her that he has persuaded MARTA to continue the match under his management again. He asks SARA to accept that they should stay apart until the match is over, for MARTA's sake. When MARTA comes back, she plays with all her old determination and power. FURMANOV is defeated and she ends the contest with a crushing victory. As SARA and the crowd applaud, she shakes hands with FURMANOV, runs over to FREDERICK, flings her arms round him and kisses him in triumph and elation.

After the match SARA has organised a tour for MARTA in which she will play a series of simultaneous exhibition matches as part of a promotion drive for the woman-friendly computer. But MARTA no longer wants to co-operate with SARA. FREDERICK asks SARA to release her from the contract. But SARA refuses. There is too much at stake for her in her career, where she is under pressure to deliver from her boss, and she feels that MARTA is under an obligation to her, whatever her personal feelings may be. FREDERICK tries to persuade MARTA that she has no choice, but she is adamant. In fact, by now both MARTA and SARA are beginning to find FREDERICK's efforts to mediate untenable.

MARTA decides to take matters into her own hands. She wants to break FREDER-ICK's ties with SARA once and for all. At a press conference SARA has organised as part of the launch of her new venture, MARTA embarks on a cascade of fantastic revelations and fabrications, culminating in the 'confession' that she was sent from Hungary as a spy by the secret police in order to get hold of Western computer secrets. The press respond predictably with lurid RED QUEEN and MATA HARI CHESS GIRL-style headlines.

SARA's promotion campaign and her career are in ruins. FREDERICK feels that, though he really loves her, MARTA has proved to be recklessly destructive and his Trilby has turned into a force he can no longer cope with. MARTA flees back to Hungary, to the village we saw at the opening of the film. FREDERICK is left alone, risking the little money he has left in desperate and distracted games of blitz. Chess fever has taken its toll.

Notes on Chess

Contrary to popular prejudice, chess is an exciting and emotionally involving game, not only for the players but also for the spectators.

Chess tournaments fill the space of hotel ballrooms and banqueting rooms with serried rows of tables and crowds of watchers, some circulating among the players, looking at play over their shoulders, others sitting concentrating on the large display boards or video monitors which relay the progress of key matches.

One of the problems with most previous chess-based films is that they show hardly any of the games, perhaps because they are worried that their audience will not be able to follow them. This is to lose the whole point of chess. We envisage showing games in the way pioneered by the BBC in their chess series, using video graphics displays with players vignetted and voice-over. It is the voice-over which is the key, because this is used to convey the inner thoughts, emotions, plans and fears of the players, as they think through their position and their possible moves. These voice-overs can vary in tone from calm and rational confidence to sheer panic and despair. (Perhaps a similar technique could even be used for other situations in the film, bringing out their chess-like aspects?) Games will be carefully devised: the power-play, the blunder caused by failure to part with the queen, the ending in time trouble.

Chess for fun and chess for blood (in Emanuel Lasker's words): chess is an art, a sport, a science, an idle pursuit, a tragic obsession. It provides a metaphor which ties together the themes of East and West, male and female, reason and passion.

Section 5

Working Documents

WE SEE HOW THE AMAZON WAR QUEEN PENTHESILEA FALLS IN LOVE WITH THE GREEK HERO ACHILLES AND HOW ACHILLES FALLS IN LOVE WITH HER. WE SEE THEM TORN BETWEEN THEIR LOYALTY AND THEIR LOVE AND HOW ACHILLES SURRENDERS TO HIS ENEMY. FINALLY WE SEE PENTHESILEA KILL ACHILLES. WE SEE HER FURY, HER RAPTURE AND HER GRIEF. WE SEE HER OWN DEATH. AN ACT OF SUICIDE THROUGH SHEER STRENGTH OF PASSION.

FILM WITHOUT EDITING / CALL IMAGINARY WORLD INTO QUESTION. NOT REJECT FICTION— SITUATE. THEORISTS — FILM WITHOUT EDITING NATURAL. MONTAGE: DISCONTINUITIES. NO SINGLE THREAD. IT IS ABOUT SOMETHING ELSE: THE SPACE BETWEEN A STORY WHICH IS NEVER TOLD AND A HISTORY WHICH HAS NEVER YET BEEN MADE.

Index cards that appear on film during Peter Wollen's address to audience in sequence two of *Penthesilea: Queen of the Amazons*, 1974.

CAME INDICATES A MOVE WHICH
HAS BEEN MADE TOWARD THE SPEAKER
IN SOME WAY IN THE PAST. MOVE
IS SUBSTANCE CHANGING ITS PLACE.
SPEAKER IS SUBSTANCE THROUGH
WHICH TALK COMES. THE PAST IS
THE REALM IN WHICH THINGS HAVE
BEEN CHANGED. PLACE IS THE
CONSCIOUSNESS' POSITIONING OF SUBSTANCE.

THE AMAZON PENTHESILEA ARRIVED TO FIGHT
WITH THE TROJANS. SHE WAS THE DAUGHTER
OF ARES AND CAME FROM THRACE. ACHILLES
KILLED HER IN FULL GLORY AND THE TROJANS
BURIED HER. ACHILLES KILLED THERSITES
WHO TAUNTED HIM FOR HIS PROFESSION OF
LOVE FOR HER. A QUARREL BROKE OUT
AMONG THE GREEKS OVER THERSITES'
DEATH.

Index cards that appear on film during Peter Wollen's address to audience in sequence two of *Penthesilea: Queen of the Amazons*, 1974.

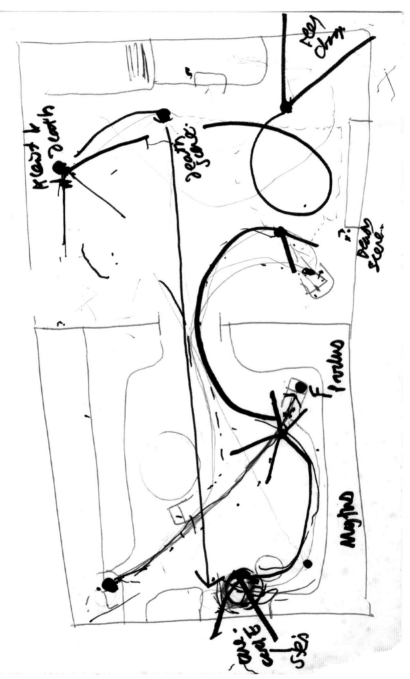

Diagram for camera movement in sequence two of *Penthesilea: Queen of the Amazons*, c. 1974.

Scene breakdown and information chart for *Riddles of the Sphinx*, c. 1977.

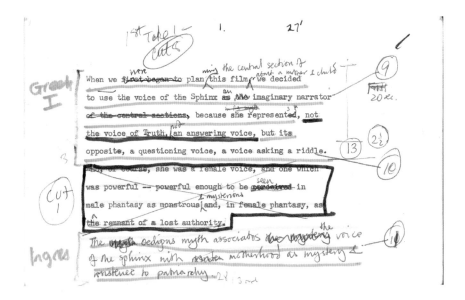

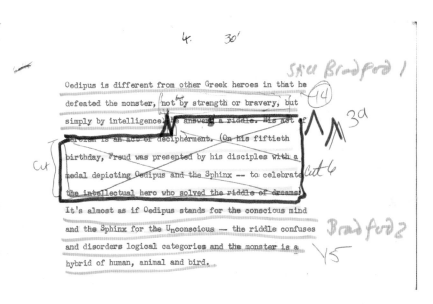

Index cards for Laura Mulvey's address to audience in section two of *Riddles of the Sphinx*, c. 1977.

say slower

Outside the city gates, ~~the~~ Sat Sphinx perched on a cliff or
pillar√She asked every man who went past a riddle. If they
couldnt answer, she devoured them. She stopped Oedipus as
he passed. When he answered her correctly, she threw
herself down from the pillar and killed herself. In *their*
~~gratitude for ridding them of the Sphinx, the people of~~
Thebes gave Oedipus the crown and with it the king's widow,
Queen Jocasta. Later, of course, Oedipus discovered that the
stranger he had killed was the King and that the King had
been his father and Jocasta was his mother.

Cut 3

removing Half of 3A by Cut 4

171

Brad Ford. Manual Zoom

To the patriarchy, the Sphinx, as woman, is a threat and a
riddle. But women, within patriarchy, are faced by a never-
ending series of threats and riddles. ~~They have no means of~~
dilemmas which are hard for women to solve
~~understanding their dilemma, in its difference,~~ because the
start again culture within which they must think is not theirs. ~~they~~ *we* live
in a society ruled by the father, in which the place of the
mother is suppressed. Motherhood itself and how to live it, or
not live it, lies at the roots of the dilemma. Meanwhile,
the Sphinx can only speak with a voice apart, voice off.

-4
-18

Index cards for Laura Mulvey's address to audience in section two of *Riddles of the Sphinx*, c. 1977.

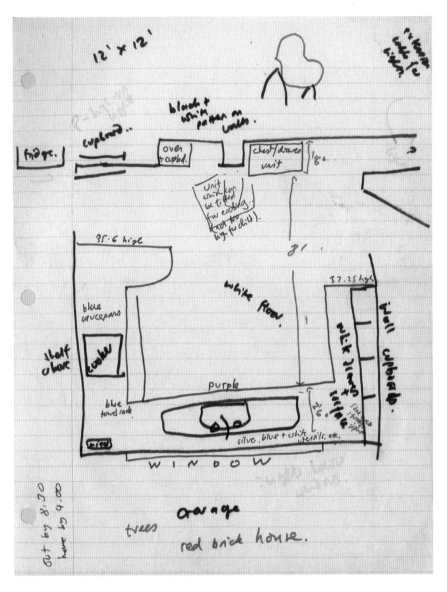

Diagram for the first 360-degree panning shot in section four of *Riddles of the Sphinx*: Louise's kitchen, *c.* 1977.

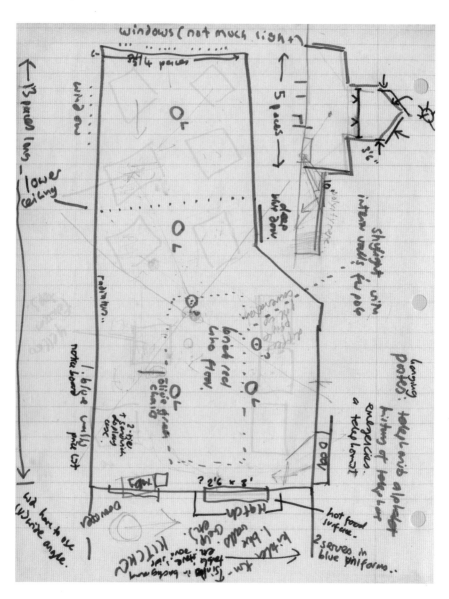

Diagram for the sixth 360-degree panning shot in section four of *Riddles of the Sphinx*: the canteen with camera movement, *c.* 1977.

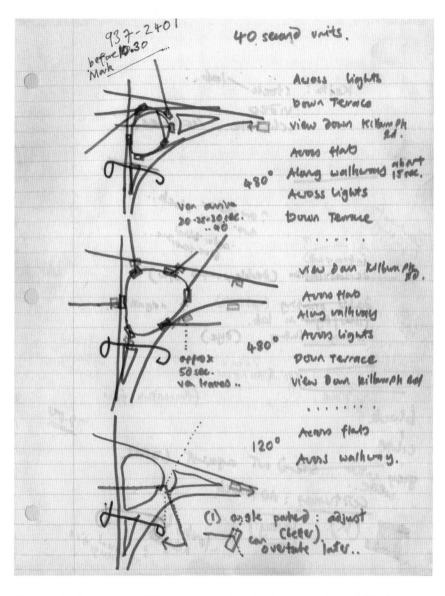

937-2401
before No.30
Mark

40 second units.

Across lights
Down Terrace
View down Kilburn Ph Rd.
Across flats
Along walkways about 15 sec.
Across lights
Down Terrace
. . . . .

480°

Veh arrive
20 · 25 · 30 sec.
·· 00

View down Kilburn Ph Rd.
Across flats
Along walkway
Across lights
Down Terrace
View down Kilburn Ph Rd

480°

approx
50 sec.
Veh leaves ··

. . . .

Across flats
Across walkway.

120°

(1) angle passed : adjust
(later)
can
"overtake" later ..

Diagram for the seventh 360-degree panning shot in section four of *Riddles of the Sphinx*: the roundabout with vehicle and camera movement, *c.* 1977.

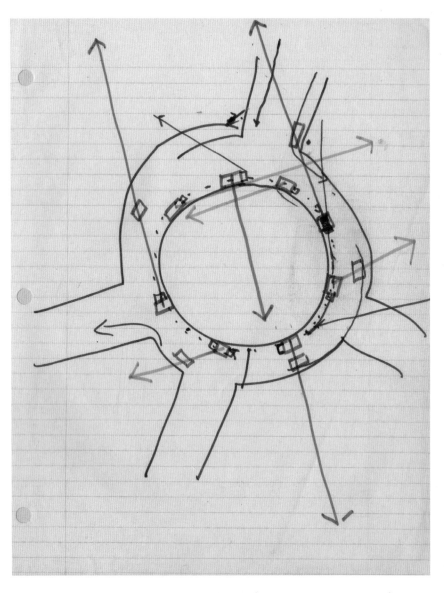

Diagram for the seventh 360-degree panning shot in section four of *Riddles of the Sphinx*: the roundabout with vehicle and camera movement, c. 1977.

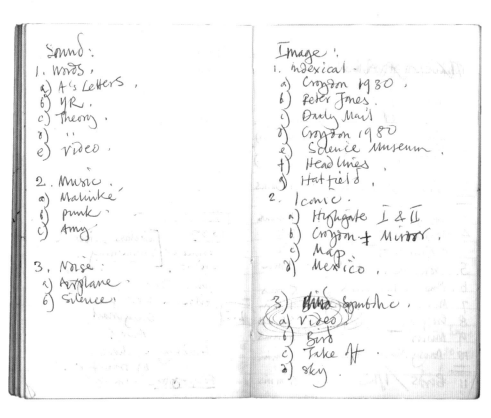

Sound:
1. Words,
   a) A's Letters,
   b) YR.
   c) Theory.
   d) "
   e) Video.

2. Music.
   a) Malinke'
   b) punk
   c) Amy

3. Noise:
   a) Airplane
   b) Silence,

Image:
1. Indexical
   a) Croydon 1980,
   b) Peter Jones.
   c) Daily Mail
   d) Croydon 1980
   e) Science Museum.
   f) Headlines,
   g) Hatfield,

2. Iconic.
   a) Highgate I & II
   b) Croydon + Mirror.
   c) Map
   d) Mexico,

3) Symbolic.
   a) Video
   b) Bird
   c) Take off.
   d) Sky

Working document for *AMY!*, c. 1980.

A.	B.	C.
1. CRYSTAL BALL	CRYSTAL BALL	CRYSTAL BALL +1.
2. CITIES OF ALPHA	PUSS-IN-BOOTS	PICKET-LIVE
Studio (Other Cinema)	J.'s Apt.	Middle Row
Neil V.O.	Julian	Vermilion
3. GUERILLA	HOMEWORK V.O.	FURTHER APART V.O.
Portobello Fish-Bar	Hong Kong Dragon.	Kim's Apt. (Talbot Rd.)
Neil	Neil, Julian	Neil, Kim.
4. WILLOW-PATTERN CLUB	JOB CENTRE	WILLOW-PATTERN CLUB
V.O.	Job Centre, L. Grove	
Neil, Vermilion, M.	Neil	Neil, Vermilion, M.
5. CUL-DE-SAC	ACKLAM HALL M.	EMPLOYMENT
	Acklam Hall	V.'s Apt.
Neil, Vermilion, Vs.	Kim.	Neil, Vermilion, H.
6. MARRIAGE CONTRACT	VIVA VOCE	THIRD WORLD JOURNEY
V.'s Apt.		V.'s Apt. V.O.
Neil, Vermilion, H.	Julian, Professors	Neil, Vermilion, H.
7. COMMUTER GHOST	MEMORIAL GARDENS	CUL-DE-SAC
V.'s Apt. V.O.	Horniman Gardens	
Neil, Vermilion, H.	Neil, Julian	Neil, Vermilion M.
8. TAXI QUEUE	DEVIANT LOGIC V.O.	ISLAND PARADISE
Euston Station	Elgin Books	Ladbroke Grove / M'Way
Neil, Kim, Keith..	Julian, Gyesoyi.	Kim
9. BUSKING M	MONSIEUR THOMPSON	CROSSED LINE
	M. Thompson's.	V.'s Apt.
Kim	Neil, Kim	Vermilion (Neil) (V.O.)
10. ROUGH TRADE	COST OF LIVING	STRIKE-BREAKERS
Rough Trade	Elgin Pub.	Middle Row Coach Sta.
Kim	Vermilion, Liz Smith	V.O.
11. THE KISS	ALTERNATIVE SINGLE	RINGS OF SATURN
Kim's Apt. (Talbot Rd)	Kim's Apt. (Talbot Rd)	
Neil, Kim V.O.	Kim M	
12. DEMO-DISC M	DRAGON'S TAIL V.O.	POOR NEIL
Cold Storage	Tate	Backstage [Midd
Kim	13.	Kim [Vermilion
13. REDUNDANCY V.O.	SUICIDE	LAST NUMB
Artist's Studio (O.C.)	J.'s Apt.	V.'s Apt [TV.
Neil	Julian	Vermilion [

? Aug B10
Oct B6

Scene breakdown and information chart for *Crystal Gazing* (1), c. 1982.

CRYSTAL GAZING

Crystal Ball				? Music
Cities of Alpha	VO			? Music
				? screen-music
Fish Bar				
Magician (Club I)	VO	•	D	MUSIC ? Tony
Cul De Sac			•	
Gloucester Ave I.	IVO.	•	D	MUSIC ? Tcap.
Chess				
St. Pancras			M	
Talbot Rd. (Breakfast)		(M)		
Busking	VO	M		
Rough Trade		•	•	
Cold Storage		M		
Redundancy TOC	VO			
Job Centre		•		
Acklam Hall ·		M		
M. Thompson ·			D	
Puss-in-Boots		(•)	M	? screen.
Hong Kong Dragon	VO		•	
Elgin Pub ·			D	
Viva (Exam) ·			D	
Talbot Rd (Sax solo)		M		
Deviant Logic	VO			
Memorial Gardens			D	
Cornell Box	VO	(•)		
Suicide		M		
Remote sensing	VO	(••)		? Music.
Picket		•		
Further Apart			D	
Club II		•	D	Music : ovd.
Gloucester Ave II.	VO (map)		D	? Music.
En Route (Mexico)			D	
Island Paradise		M		
Crossed Line			D	
Coach Yard	VO			
Rings of Saturn				? Music.
Riverside		•	D	
Volcano + Vermilion		M	(D)	
Crystal Ball				?
Credits		M		

Scene breakdown and information chart for *Crystal Gazing* (2), c. 1982.

Agoraphobia
Agenda
Alpaca/Angora
Amnesia
Antenna
ARCANA
Artemisia
Alpha.

Barb
Benumb
Blob   blurb.
Bomb
Bulb

Cadillac
canonic
Celtic
ceramic
caustic
Cabbalistic
char-a-banc
Chic
Chimeric
classic
Clinic
climacteric
communistic
cosmetic
critic
cryptic
cul-de-sac
cynic

Dachshund
Damaged
Dash-board
Dated
DEAD
Death's head
Decayed
Decorated
Deed
Defined
Defeated
Deformed
bestud
Demand
Demented
Depend
Determined
dogwood
Diamond
Discord
Diseased
Dignified
Disposed
Dissatisfied
Dockyard.
Downward
DREAMLAND
Dubbed
Dyad

Earthquake   Embrace
Eau-de-vie   Empire
Ebb-tide   Enhance
Eclipse   Enshrine
Edge
Eerie   Entourage
Ejaculate   Episode
Eke   Equestrienne
Electorate   Freckle
else   Erstwhile
Elude

Far-off
Figleaf
Flagstaff
Pluff
Fly-leaf

Gag
Game-leg
Gang
Gathering
Gig
Giving   gnelling
Glancing
Glittering
Good-for-nothing
Gong
Greeting
G-string
Guinea-pig

                        Hatch.
Heath   Hookah
Hairsbreadth Hooping-cough
Hallelujah.
Hashish   Hopscotch
Hawkmoth   Hazeflesh
Heath   Hoydenish
Heresiarch   Hundredth
Hiccough   Hush
Hieroglyph   Hyacinth
Holograph
             Hyetometrograph

Essence
Etherealise
Evanescence
eve
everyone
everywhere
bull-eye
excessive
Exile   Eye
Extravagance

Illuminati
impi
inhibit

Kalmuck
Kapok
kayak
kick
Kink
kinsfolk
kiosk
kiss-me-quick
knock
Kodak
___

Napoleon
Needlewoman
Negation
Neon
Neptunian
Nibelungen
Ninepin
Nineteen

Noon
Norn
Notation
Nun
Nutbrown
Nymphean.
___

octavo
oratorio
outdo
ortgo
overdo
orvieto
onto

Labial
Lackadaisical
Landfall
Lapel
Lawful legal
Laurel
Level
Literal
Logical
Lyrical
Lull
___

parsnip
partisanship
pantechicon
pawnshop
pick-me-up
plump
pomp
postage-stamp
pulp
pump
___

raconteur
ragpicker
rancour
range-finder
- rover
ranter
ratcatcher
ready
ready-reckoner
réaumur
reefer
reindeer
remember
reminder
renter
reporter
revolves

rhythmometer
rigour
ring-finger
leader
rioter
rocker
roller

rope-dancer
ladder

rouge-et-noir

tyrant
turbulent transport
truant treatment
trench torment
coat topmost
tryst tract
transit tact
toft transcendent

Macadam
Marxism
Mannerism
Materialism
Martyrdom Modernism
Maximum
Mayhem Midstream
Mechanism Moonbeam
Metabolism Museum

Mallarmé-ism.

sacrilegious
Her Rhodus her Saltus
sarcophagus stepladders
schnaps
sojourns shock-troops
scrumptious sidecups
seamstress simultaneous
screwdrivers skivvies
self-conscious sleeping
serious sidearms
series soap-suds
shackles silencers
serves sometimes
shameless spacious
shambles stop-press
superfluous
surpass
superstitious
sweepstakes
synonymous

tacit
tantamount
tangent tempt
target text
taught
teapot theft
tenrim temperament
theorist
thought
thickset thrust
thunderbolt
tilt that
time-limit
toast

London Midwinter 1982

Market competitiveness means lower unit costs. Lower unit
costs mean cheaper labour. Cheaper labour means a labour
market which favours the buyer rather than the seller. That
means fewer jobs and not labour must be scarce. And that
means massive unemployment. This is the logic of the
recession. Unemployment hangs like a noose round the
neck of the city. Shattered dreams. Redundancy figures.
Portents of death. This is a story set in the Thatcher
recession. But it begins far far away. Elsewhere. ~~But the~~
~~Nowhere~~
                                        The cities of Alpha.

.   .   .   .

London Midwinter 1982

The Utopian dream breaks on the reefs of everyday life. Yet
it carries a promise without which human history would bear
the sign of Hell: Abandon Hope All You Who Enter Here! Time
plays strange tricks and hides strange

The future regenerates on the ~~dead limbs~~ wrong typo of the past, on the
forgotten and the overlooked. From the factory gate we can
see the edge of the marvellous, and sense the unrespected
flight of truth, pertinacious and

Even the picket at the factory gate is a sign of the future,
a scattered leaf from the sibylline book in which the
marvellous is foretold. The script is hard to read, the
wind is cold and we lack wisdom. Our glimpses of the future
are faint and deformed. But the story without an end is the
story which preserves the unexpected, foundation of desire.

Textual fragment relating to *Crystal Gazing*, 1982.

Bibliography

Anastasia Valassopolous, 'The International Palestinian Resistance: Documentary and Revolt', *Journal of Postcolonial Writing* 50(2) (2014), 148–166.

Anderson, Benedict R. O'G. and Ruth T. McVey, asst. Frederick P. Bunnell, *A Preliminary Analysis of the October 1, 1965, Coup in Indonesia*. Ithaca, NY: Cornell Modern Indonesia Project, Interim Reports Pub. 52, 1971 and London: Equinox Publishing, 2009.

Antonioni, Michelangelo, Mark Peploe and Peter Wollen, *The Passenger*. New York: Grove Press, 1975.

Adorno, Theodor. *Minima Moralia: Reflections on a Damaged Life*. Translated by E.F.N. Jephcott. London: Verso, 1974.

Allais, Lucia, 'A Questionnaire on Monuments'. *October* 165 (Summer 2018), 4–7.

Alter, Nora M., *The Essay Film after Fact and Fiction*. New York: Columbia University Press, 2018.

Artaud, Antonin, 'Letter to the Chancellors of the European Universities'. In *Antonin Artaud: Collected Works* (Volume 1). Translated by Victor Corti, 178–180. London: Calder & Boyars, 1968.

Ballard, J.G., *The Atrocity Exhibition*. Special Expanded and Annotated Edition. London: Harper Collins, 1993.

Balázs, Béla, 'The Spirit of Film'. In Béla *Balázs: Early Film Theory, Visible Man and The Spirit of Film*. Edited by Erica Carter and translated by Rodney Livingstone. New York: Berghahn Books, 2010.

Barthes, Roland, *Elements of Semiology*. Translated by Annette Lavers and Colin Smith. New York: Hill and Wang, 1968.

Bellour, Raymond, *The Analysis of Film*. Edited by Constance Penley. Bloomington and Indianapolis, IN: Indiana University Press, 2000.

Bellour, Raymond, 'Thierry Kuntzel and the Return of Writing'. In *Between-the-Images*. Translated by Annwyl Williams, 30–61. Zurich and Dijon: JRP Ringier and Les presses du réel, 2012.

Benveniste, Émile, *Problems in General Linguistics*. Translated by Mary Elizabeth Meek. Coral Gables, FL: University of Miami Press, 1971.

Blackburn, Robin, 'Benedict Anderson, 2011, Letter to the Social Science Research Council', 10 April 2020. www.ssrc.org/pages/benedict-anderson/.

Buchsbaum, Jonathan, 'A Closer Look at Third Cinema'. *Historical Journal of Film, Radio and Television, 21:2.* (2001), 153-166.

Burke, Eleanor, 'Entry on Laura Mulvey, Reference Guide to British and Irish Film Directors', n.d. www.screenonline.org.uk/people/id/566978/.

Carroll, Noël and Yvonne Rainer, 'Interview with a Woman Who…' In *A Woman Who… : Essays, Interviews, Scripts*, 169–206. Baltimore, MD: The John Hopkins University Press, 1999.

Chomsky, Noam, 'Linguistics and Politics'. Interview by R.B., G.S.J., L.R [Robin Blackburn, Gareth Stedman-Jones and Lucien Rey]. *New Left Review* 1(59) (September/ October 1969), 21–34.

Corrigan, Timothy, *The Essay Film: From Montaigne, After Marker*. New York: Oxford University Press, 2011.

Cubitt, Sean and Stephen Partridge, 'Introduction'. In *Rewind: British Artists' Video in the 1970s & 1980s*. Edited by Sean Cubitt and Stephen Partridge, 3–16. New Barnet: John Libbey, 2012.

Daney, Serge, '*Ceddo*'. *Cahiers du cinéma* 304 (October 1979), 52–54.

Daney, Serge, 'Theorize/Terrorize: Godardian Pedagogy'. Translated by Annwyl Williams. In *Cahiers du Cinéma, Vol. 4: 1973–1978: History, Ideology, Cultural Struggle*. Edited by David Wilson, 116–123. London and New York: Routledge/BFI, 2000.

Dima, Vlad, *Sonic Space in Djibril Diop Mambety's Films*. Bloomington and Indianapolis, IN: Indiana University Press, 2017.

Doane, Mary Ann, 'Woman's Stake: Filming the Female Body'. *October* 17 (Summer 1981), 22–36.

Eisenschitz, Bernard, Jean-André Fieschi and Eduardo de Gregorio, 'Interview with Jacques Rivette'. Translated by Tom Milne. In *Jacques Rivette: Texts and Interviews*. Edited by Jonathan Rosenbaum, 39–53. London: BFI, 1977.

Eisenstein, Sergei, *The Eisenstein Reader*. Edited by Richard Taylor and translated by William Powell and Richard Taylor. London: British Film Institute, 1998.

Eisenstein, Sergei, 'The Dramaturgy of Film Form'. In *Selected Works, Vol. I: Writings, 1922–1934*. Edited and translated by Richard Taylor, 161–180. Bloomington and Indianapolis, IN and London: Indiana University Press and BFI, 1988.

Elsaesser, Thomas, '*Friendship's Death*'. *Monthly Film Bulletin* 54(646) (1 November 1987), 323–324.

Emmelhainz, Irmgard, *Jean-Luc Godard's Political Filmmaking*. Palgrave Macmillan, 2019.

Erens, Patricia, '*Penthesilea*'. *Wide Angle* 2(3) (1978), 30–36.

Eshun, Kodwo, '"On Her Devolves the Labour": The Cinematic Time Travel of *The Song of the Shirt*'. In *Other Cinemas: Politics, Culture and Experimental Film in the 1970s*. Edited by Sue Clayton and Laura Mulvey, 257–272. London and New York: I.B.Tauris, 2017.

Eshun, Kodwo and Ros Gray, 'The Militant Image: A Ciné-Geography', *Third Text, 25:1* (2011), 1-12.

Espinosa, Julio Garcia. 'For an Imperfect Cinema', *Afterimage 3* (Summer, 1971), 54-67.

Fischer, Lucy, *Shot/Countershot: Film Tradition and Women's Cinema*. Princeton, NJ: Princeton University Press, 1989.

Fisher, Jean, '*The Bad Sister*'. *Artforum* 22(6) (February 1984), 82.

Foner, Eric, 'A Questionnaire on Monuments'. *October* 165 (August 2018), 55–57.

Foster, Hal, 'An Archival Impulse'. *October* 110 (2004), 3–22.

Fountain, Nigel, *Underground: The London Alternative Press 1966–1974*. London and New York: Routledge, 1988.

Freud, Sigmund, 'A Note Upon the "Mystic Writing Pad"'. In *The Standard Edition of the Complete Psychological Works of Sigmund Freud, Vol. XIX (1923–1925)*. Translated and edited by James Strachey in collaboration with Anna Freud, 227–232. London: The Hogarth Press and the Institute of Psycho-Analysis, 1961.

Fuke, Oliver and Nicolas Helm-Grovas, 'Art at the Frontier of Film Theory', catalogue essay in *Art at the Frontier of Film Theory: Laura Mulvey and Peter Wollen* ex. cat. London: Peltz Gallery/ Birkbeck Institute for the Moving Image, 2019.

Fuller, Graham, '*Friendship's Death*'. *Sight & Sound (inc. Monthly Film Bulletin)* 27(9) (September 2017), 90.

Gabriel, Teshome, *Third Cinema in the Third World: The Aesthetics of Liberation*. Ann Arbor, Michigan: UMI Research Press, 1982.

Garrard, Mary D., *Artemisia Gentileschi: The Image of the Female Hero in Italian Baroque Art*. Princeton, NJ: Princeton University Press, 1989.

Godard, Jean-Luc, 'Manifeste', *El-Fatah*, July 1970. In *Documents*. Edited by Nicole Brenez, 138–140. Paris: Centre Pompidou, 2006.

Godard, Jean-Luc and Jean-Pierre Gorin, 'Jusqu'à la Victoire, cahier de tournage (extraits)'. In Jean-Luc Godard, *Documents*. Edited Nicole Brenez, 141–143. Paris: Centre Pompidou, 2006.

Goldman, Shifra M., 'Six Women Artists of Mexico'. *Woman's Art Journal* 3(2) (Autumn 1982–Winter 1983), 1–9.

Goldsmith, Leo and Rachael Rakes, 'The Desertification of Discourse: *Punishment Park*'. In *America: Films from Elsewhere*. Edited by Shanay Jhaveri, 278–297. Mumbai: The Shoestring Publisher, 2019.

Grant, Catherine, 'Returning to *Riddles*'. In *Women Artists, Feminism and the Moving Image: Contexts and Practices*. Edited by Lucy Reynolds. London: Bloomsbury, 2019.

Grimberg, Salomon, *I Will Never Forget You: Frida Kahlo and Nickolas Muray*. San Francisco, CA: Chronicle Books, 2004/2006.

Grimonprez, Johan, ed., *Inflight Magazine*. New York: Hatje Cantz, 2000.

Hall, Stuart, 'The Problem of Ideology: Marxism without Guarantees'. In *Stuart Hall: Critical Dialogues in Cultural Studies*. Edited by David Morley and Kuan-Hsing Chen, 25–46. London and New York: Routledge, 1996.

Halliday, Fred, Jon Halliday, Lucien Rey and Gareth Stedman Jones, 'Communication on Women's Liberation'. *New Left Review* 1(90) (March/April 1975), 112.

Hayes, Sharon, 'A Questionnaire on Monuments'. *October* 165 (Summer 2018), 66–67.

Hein, Wilhelm and Birgit Hein, *Dokumente 1967–1985. Fotos, Briefe, Texte*. Frankfurt am Main: Deutsches Filmmuseum, 1985.

Helm-Grovas, Nicolas, 'Laura Mulvey and Peter Wollen: Theory and Practice, Aesthetics and Politics, 1963–1983'. PhD diss., Royal Holloway, University of London, 2018.

Hilderbrand, Lucas, 'In the Heat of the Moment: Notes on the Past, Present and Future of *Born in Flames*'. *Women & Performance: A Journal of Feminist Theory* 23(1) (2013), 6–16.

Hobson, Alex, 'Creating a World Stage: Revolution Airport and the Illusion of Power'. *The International History Review* (2019), 1–21.

Holert, Tom, *Knowledge Beside Itself: Contemporary Art's Epistemic Politics*. Berlin: Sternberg Press, 2020.

Holert, Tom, 'Artistic Research: Anatomy of an Ascent'. *Texte zur Kunst* 82 (2011), 38–63.

Isaacs, Jeremy, *Storm Over 4: A Personal Account*. London: Weidenfeld and Nicolson, 1989.

Jakobson, Roman, 'Linguistics and Poetics'. In *Language in Literature*. Edited by Krystyna Pomorska and Stephen Rudy, 62–94. Cambridge, MA: Belknap Press of Harvard University Press, 1987.

Jakobson, Roman, 'Two Aspects of Language and Two Types of Aphasic Disturbances'. In *Language in Literature*. Edited by Krystyna Pomorska and Stephen Rudy, 95–114. Cambridge, MA: Belknap Press of Harvard University Press, 1987.

Jackson, Chuck, 'The Touch of the "First" Black Cinematographer in North America: James E. Hinton, *Ganja & Hess*, and the NEA Films at the Harvard Film Archive'. *Black Camera* 10(1) (Fall 2018), 67–95.

Johnston, Claire, 'Women's Cinema as Counter-Cinema'. In *Movies and Methods, Vol. 1. An Anthology*. Edited by Bill Nichols, 208–217. Berkeley, Los Angeles, London, University of California Press, 1976.

Kannafani, Ghassan. 'Interview with Ghassan Kannafani'. Interview by Fred Halliday. *New Left Review* 1(67) (May/June 1971), 50–57.

Kammen, Douglas. 'World Turned Upside Down: Benedict Anderson, Ruth Mcvey, and the "Cornell Paper"'. *Indonesia* 104 (October 2017), 1–26.

Kaplan, Janet, 'Review of *Frida: A Biography of Frida Kahlo*, by Hayden Herrera and *Tina Modotti: A Fragile Life*, by Mildred Constantine'. *Woman's Art Journal* 5(2) (Autumn 1984–Winter 1985), 45–47.

Kästner, Erich, *Fabian: Die Geschichte eines Moralisten*. Munich: DTV, 1989.

Kelly, Mary, '*Penthesilea*'. *Spare Rib* 30 (December 1974), 40.

Kracauer, Siegfried, *From Caligari to Hitler: A Psychological History of the German Film*. Edited by Leonardo Quaresima. Princeton, NJ: Princeton University Press, 2004.

Kracauer, Siegfried, *Strassen in Berlin und Anderswo*. Berlin: Das Arsenal, 2003.

Kustow, Michael, *One in Four: A Year in the Life of a Channel Four Commissioning Editor*. London: Chatto & Windus, 1987.

Lacan, Jacques, 'The Function and Field of Speech and Language in Psychoanalysis'. In *Écrits*. Translated by Bruce Fink in collaboration with Héloïse Fink and Russell Grigg, 197–268. New York and London: W. W. Norton & Company, 2006.

Lem, Stanislaw, 'The Eleventh Voyage', in *The Star Diaries*. Translated by Michael Kandel, 42–48. Orlando, CA, Austin, TX, New York, San Diego, CA, Toronto, ONT and London: A Harvest Book Harcourt, Inc., 1976.

Margulies, Ivone, 'La Chambre Akerman'. *Rouge* 10, 2007. www.rouge.com.au/10/akerman.html.

MacDonald, Scott, 'Interview with Laura Mulvey (on *Riddles of the Sphinx*)'. In *A Critical Cinema 2: Interviews with Independent Filmmakers*. Edited by Scott MacDonald, 333–344. Berkeley and Los Angeles, CA: University of California Press, 1992.

MacDonald, Scott, 'Introduction'. In *Screen Writings: Texts and Scripts from Independent Films*. Edited by Scott MacDonald, 1–14. Berkeley and Los Angeles, CA: University of California Press, 1995.

Merck, Mandy, 'The City's Achievements.' In *Perversions: Deviant Readings*, 121–161. London: Virago, 1993.

Merck, Mandy, 'From robot to romance'. In *Perversions: Deviant Readings*, 177–194. New York: Routledge, 1993.

Mitchell, Juliet. *Psychoanalysis and Feminism*. Harmondsworth: Penguin, 1974.

Mitchell, Juliet and Lucien Rey, 'Comment on "The Freudian Slip"'. *New Left Review* 94(1) (November/December 1975), 79–80.

Monk, Claire, '"The Shadow of this Time': Punk, Tradition and Derek Jarman's *Jubilee*'. *Shakespeare Bulletin* 32(3) (2014), 359–373.

Mulvey, Laura, 'You Don't Know What is Happening Do You, Mr Jones?' *Spare Rib* 8 (February 1973), 13–16 and 30.

Mulvey, Laura, 'Visual Pleasure and Narrative Cinema'. *Screen* 16(3) (Autumn 1975), 6–18.

Mulvey, Laura, 'Women & Representation: A Discussion with Laura Mulvey'. Interview by Jane Clarke, Sue Clayton, Joanna Cleland, Rosie Elliott and Mandy Merck. *Wedge* 2 (Spring 1978), 46–53.

Mulvey, Laura, 'Changes'. *Discourse* 7 (Spring 1985), 11–30.

Mulvey, Laura, 'Annotations'. *PIX* 2 (January 1997), 102–111.

Mulvey, Laura, *Death 24x a Second: Stillness and the Moving Image*. London: Reaktion Books, 2006.

Mulvey, Laura, 'Changes: Thoughts on Myth, Narrative and Historical Experience'. In *Visual and Other Pleasures*, 2nd edition, 165–183. Basingstoke: Palgrave Macmillan, 2009.

Mulvey, Laura, 'Fears, Fantasies and the Male Unconscious or "You Don't Know What is Happening Do You, Mr Jones?"'. In *Visual and Other Pleasures*, 2nd edition, 6–13. Basingstoke: Palgrave Macmillan, 2009.

Mulvey, Laura, 'Film on Four, British Experimental Television Drama and *The Bad Sister*'. Interview by Janet McCabe. *Critical Studies in Television* 4(2) (November 2009), 98–103.

Mulvey, Laura, 'Introduction to the First Edition'. In *Visual and Other Pleasures*, 2nd edition, xxvii–xxxvi. Basingstoke: Palgrave Macmillan, 2009.

Mulvey, Laura, 'Introduction to the Second Edition'. In *Visual and Other Pleasures*, 2nd edition, ix–xxvi. Basingstoke: Palgrave Macmillan, 2009.

Mulvey, Laura, 'Unravelling the Puzzle'. Interview by Lara Thompson. Translated from 'Do Utraty Wzroku' ('To Vision Loss'). Edited by Kamila Cuk and Lara Thompson. Kracow and Warsaw: Korporacja Halart, 2010.

Mulvey, Laura, '*Riddles as Essay Film*'. In *Essays on the Essay Film*. Edited by Nora M. Alter and Timothy Corrigan, 314–322. New York: Columbia University Press, 2017.

Mulvey, Laura, 'Mary Kelly: Speaking Maternal Silence, *Post-Partum Document* and *The Ballad of Kastriot Rexhepi*'. In *Afterimages: On Cinema, Women and Changing Times*, 225–237. London: Reaktion Books, 2019.

Mulvey, Laura and Mark Lewis, 'SCRIPT: *Disgraced Monuments*'. *PIX* 2 (January 1997), 102–111.

Mulvey, Laura and Peter Wollen, '*Penthesilea, Queen of the Amazons*'. Interview by Claire Johnston and Paul Willemen. *Screen* 15(3) (Autumn 1974), 120–134.

Mulvey, Laura and Peter Wollen, 'Written Discussion'. *Afterimage* 6 (Summer 1976), 30–39.

Mulvey, Laura and Peter Wollen, '*Riddles of the Sphinx*: Script'. *Screen* 18(2) (Summer 1977), 61–78.

Mulvey, Laura and Peter Wollen, 'Riddles of the Avant-Garde'. Interview by Don Ranvaud. *Framework* 9 (Winter 1978), 30–31.

Mulvey, Laura and Peter Wollen, '*AMY!*' *Framework* 14 (Spring 1981), 37–41.

Mulvey, Laura and Peter Wollen, '*Crystal Gazing*'. Interview by Fizzy Oppe and Don Ranvaud. *Framework: The Journal of Cinema and Media* 19 (Summer 1982), 17–19.

Mulvey, Laura and Peter Wollen, 'Frida Kahlo and Tina Modotti'. In *Frida Kahlo and Tina Modotti*, 7–27. London: Whitechapel Art Gallery, 1982.

Mulvey, Laura and Peter Wollen with Lee Grieveson, 'From Cinephilia to Film Studies'. In *Inventing Film Studies*, 223–232. Edited by Lee Grieveson and Haidee Wasson. Durham, NC and London: Duke University Press, 2008.

Nixon, Mignon, '"Why Freud?" asked the Shrew: Psychoanalysis and Feminism, *Post-Partum Document*, and the History Group'. *Psychoanalysis, Culture and Society* 20(2) (June 2015), 1–10.

NLR Editors, 'Introduction: Interview with Ghassan Kannafani on the PFLP and the September Attack'. *New Left Review* 67(1) (May/June 1971), 47–50.

Nora, Pierre, 'Between Memory and History: *les lieux de mémoire*'. Translated by Marc Roudebush. *Representations* 26 (Spring 1989), 7–24.

Pantenburg, Volker, 'Kameraschwenk. Stil – Operation – Geste?' In *Filmstil. Perspektivierungen eines Begriffs*. Edited by Julian Blunk, Dietmar Kammerer, Tina Kaiser and Chris Wahl, 236–253. Munich: edition text und kritik, 2016.

Pantenburg, Volker, 'The Third Avant-Garde: Laura Mulvey, Peter Wollen, and the Theory Film', lecture given at Whitechapel Gallery, London, 14 May 2016.

Pidduck, Julianne, 'Travels with Sally Potter's *Orlando*: Gender, Narrative, Movement'. *Screen* 38(2) (Summer 1997), 172–189.

Pollock, Griselda and Laura Mulvey, 'Laura Mulvey in Conversation with Griselda Pollock'. *Studies in the Maternal* 2(1) (2010), 1–13.

Poniatowska, Elena, *Tinisima*. Translated by Katherine Silver. Albuquerque, NM: University of New Mexico Press, 2006.

Prashad, Vijay, *The Darker Nations: A People's History of the Third World*. New York: The New Press, 2007.

Pym, John, *Film on Four 1982/1991: A Survey*. London: BFI Publishing, 1992.

Rainer, Yvonne, 'Interview by the Camera Obscura Collective'. In *A Woman Who… : Essays, Interviews, Scripts*, 141–164. Baltimore, MD: The John Hopkins University Press, 1999.

Rascaroli, Laura, *How the Essay Film Thinks*. New York: Oxford University Press, 2017.

Rey, Lucien, 'Persia in Perspective'. *New Left Review* 19(1) (March/April 1963), 32–55.

Rey, Lucien, 'Persia in Perspective 2'. *New Left Review* 20(1) (May/June 1963), 69–98.

Rey, Lucien, 'The Revolution in Zanzibar'. *New Left Review* 25(1) (May/June 1964), 29–32.

Rey, Lucien, 'The Italian Presidential Elections'. *New Left Review* 30(1) (March/April 1965), 48–52.

Rey, Lucien, 'Guilt by Association'. *New Left Review* 35(1) (January/February 1966), 102–104.

Rey, Lucien, 'Dossier of the Indonesian Drama'. *New Left Review* 36(1) (March/April 1966), 26–36.

Rey, Lucien, 'Franco Fortini'. *New Left Review* 38(1) (July/August 1966), 79–80.

Rey, Lucien, 'Comment on Magas's "Sex Politics: Class Politics"'. *New Left Review* 66(1) (March/April 1971), 93–96.

Rey, Lucien, 'Do Children Really Need Toys'. *7 DAYS* (22 December 1971), 14–15.

Rolinson, Dave, *Alan Clarke*. Manchester and New York: Manchester University Press, 2005.

Roussel, Raymond, *How I Wrote Certain of My Books*. Translated by Trevor Winkfield. New York: SUN, 1977.

Said, Edward W. and Bruce Robbins, 'American Intellectuals and Middle East Politics: An Interview with Edward W. Said'. *Social Text* 19(20) (1988), 37–53.

Said, Edward W., 'How to Answer Palestine's Challenge'. In *The Politics of Dispossession: The Struggle for Palestinian Self-Determination 1969–1994*, 137–144. New York: Vintage, 1995.

Said, Edward W., 'Review of *Wedding in Galilee* and *Friendship's Death*'. In *The Politics of Dispossession: The Struggle for Palestinian Self-Determination 1969–1994*, 130–136. New York: Vintage, 1995.

Said, Edward W., 'The Palestinians One Year Since Amman'. In *The Politics of Dispossession: The Struggle for Palestinian Self-Determination 1969–1994*, 24–30. New York: Vintage, 1995.

Said, Edward W., 'The Palestinians' Experience'. In *The Politics of Dispossession: The Struggle for Palestinian Self-Determination 1969–1994*, 3–24. New York: Vintage, 1995.

Silverman, Kaja, *The Acoustic Mirror: The Female Voice in Psychoanalysis and Cinema*. Bloomington and Indianapolis, IN: Indiana University Press, 1988.

Sontag, Susan, 'The Imagination of Disaster'. *Commentary* (October 1965), 42–48.

Solanas, Fernando, *La hora de los hornos*. *Afterimage* 3 (Summer, 1971), 8-15.

Solanas, Fernando and Octavio Getino, 'Towards a Third Cinema'. *Afterimage 3* (Summer, 1971), 16-35.

Sontag, Susan, 'The Imagination of Disaster'. In *Against Interpretation, and Other Essays*. New York: Farrar, Straus and Giroux, 1966.

Steyerl, Hito, 'A Language of Practice'. In *The Green Room*. Edited by Maria Lind and Hito Steyerl, 224–231. Berlin: Sternberg Press, 2008.

Sudhinaraset, Pacharee, '"We Are Not an Organically City People": Black Modernity and the Afterimage of Julie Dash's *Daughters of the Dust*'. *The Black Scholar: Journal of Black Studies and Research* 48(3) (2018), 46–60.

Tennant, Emma, *The Bad Sister*. London: Victor Gollancz, 1978.

Tennant, Emma, *The Bad Sister*. New York: Coward, McCann & Geoghegan, 1978.

Tennant, Emma, *Travesties: The Bad Sister, Two Women of London, Faustine*. London: Faber and Faber, 1995.

Todorov, Tzvetan, *The Fantastic: A Structural Approach to a Literary Genre*. Cleveland, OH and London: The Press of Case Western Reserve University, 1973.

Wilson, Frances, 'Obituary: Emma Tennant'. *The Guardian*, 31 January 2017.

Wittig, Monique, *Les Guérillères*. Translated by David Le Vay. Boston, MA: Beacon Press, 1969.

Wollen, Peter, 'Director's Statement', undated, unpaginated.

Wollen, Peter, 'Was Christ a Collaborator?', *7 Days* (22 December 1971), 21–23.

Wollen, Peter, 'Counter Cinema: *Vent d'Est*'. *Afterimage 4* (Autumn 1972), 6–16.

Wollen, Peter, 'The Two Avant-Gardes.' *Studio International* 190(978) (November/December 1975), 171–175.

Wollen, Peter, 'The Field of Language in Film'. *October* 17 (Summer 1981), 53–60.

Wollen, Peter, 'Friendship's Death'. In *Bananas*. Edited by Emma Tennant, 146–158. London and Tiptree: Blond & Briggs in association with Quartet, 1977.

Wollen, Peter, 'Friendship's Death'. In *Readings and Writings: Semiotic Counter-Strategies*, 140–152. London: Verso, 1982.

Wollen, Peter, 'Godard and Counter Cinema: *Vent d'Est*'. In *Readings and Writings: Semiotic Counter-Strategies*, 79–91. London: Verso, 1982.

Wollen, Peter, 'Introduction to *Citizen Kane*'. In *Readings and Writings: Semiotic Counter-Strategies*, 49–61. London: Verso, 1982.

Wollen, Peter, 'Preface'. In *Readings and Writings: Semiotic Counter-Strategies*, vii–ix. London: Verso, 1982.

Wollen, Peter, 'The Two Avant-Gardes'. In *Readings and Writings: Semiotic Counter-Strategies*, 92–104. London: Verso, 1982.

Wollen, Peter, 'Wollen on Sex, Narrative and the Thrill'. Interview by Al Razutis and Tony Reif, *Opsis* 1 (Spring, 1984), 35–44.

Wollen, Peter, 'Scenes of the Crime'. Interview by Wanda Bershen. *Afterimage* 7(12) (February 1985), 12–15.

Wollen, Peter, 'Fashion/Orientalism/The Body'. *New Formations* 1 (Spring 1987), 5–33.

Wollen, Peter, 'Two Weeks on Another Planet'. Interview by Simon Field. *Monthly Film Bulletin* 54(646) (1 November 1987), 324–326.

Wollen, Peter, 'Cinema/Americanism/The Robot'. *New Formations* 8 (Summer 1989), 7–34.

Wollen, Peter, '*Friendship's Death* (complete script)'. In *Close Encounters: Film, Feminism, and Science Fiction*. Edited by Constance Penley, Elisabeth Lyon, Lynn Spigel and Janet Bergstrom, 237–281. Minneapolis, MN and Oxford: University of Minnesota Press, 1991.

Wollen, Peter, *Raiding the Icebox: Reflections on Twentieth-Century Culture*. London: Verso, 1993.

Wollen, Peter, 'Autobiographical Notes', 31 March 1994. In Peter Wollen artist file, British Artists' Film and Video Study Collection, Central Saint Martins, University of the Arts, London.

Wollen, Peter, 'Knight's Moves'. *Public* 25 (Spring 2002), 54–67.

Wollen, Peter, *Paris Hollywood: Writings on Film*. London: Verso, 2002.

Wollen, Peter, *Paris Manhattan: Writings on Art*. London: Verso, 2004.

Wollen, Peter, 'Necessary Love'. *New Left Review* 38 (May/April 2006), 95–112.

Wollen, Peter, *Signs and Meaning in the Cinema*, fifth edition. London: BFI/Palgrave Macmillan, 2013.

Wollen, Peter, 'The Writings of Lee Russell: *New Left Review* (1964–7)'. In *Signs and Meaning in the Cinema*, fifth edition, 151–199. London: BFI/Palgrave Macmillan, 2013.

Yaqub, Nadia, *Palestinian Cinema in the Days of Revolution*. Austin, TX: University of Texas Press, 2018.

Filmography

Laura Mulvey and Peter Wollen

Penthesilea: Queen of the Amazons, 1974. 16mm, colour. 98 minutes.

Riddles of the Sphinx, 1977. 16mm, colour. 91 minutes. British Film Institute.

AMY!, 1980. 16mm, colour. 33 minutes. Southern Arts.

Crystal Gazing, 1982. 16mm, colour. 87 minutes. British Film Institute in association with Channel Four Television.

Frida Kahlo and Tina Modotti, 1983. 16mm, colour. 30 minutes. Arts Council of Great Britain.

The Bad Sister, 1983. Video, colour. 93 minutes. Channel 4 (tx 23 June 1983).

Mark Lewis and Laura Mulvey

Disgraced Monuments, 1994. 16mm, colour. 49 minutes. Canada Council, Ontario Arts Council, Ontario Film Development Corporation and Channel Four Television (tx 6 June 1994).

Faysal Abdullah, Mark Lewis and Laura Mulvey

23rd August 2008, 2013. HD video, colour. 22 minutes.

Em Hedditch and Laura Mulvey

Visual Pleasure and Narrative Cinema, 2006. Video, colour. 25 minutes.

Peter Wollen

Tatlin's Tower, 1983. Video, colour. 24 minutes. BBC for The Open University (tx 14 June 1983).

Peter Wollen Reads the U.S. Press, 1985. Video, colour. 28 minutes. Paper Tiger Television (tx 29 May 1985).

Friendship's Death, 1987. Filmed in Super 16 for presentation in 35 mm, colour. 78 minutes. British Film Institute in association with Channel Four Television.

Full Cycle: The Art of Komar and Melamid, 1991. Video, colour. 38 minutes. Rear Window for Channel 4 (tx 10 September 1991).

Images of Atlantis: The Photography of Milton Rogovin, 1992. Video, colour. 38 minutes. Rear Window for Channel 4 (tx 21 July 1992).

Index

Riddles of the Sphinx Cont.
   panning shots, 8, 43, 94
   parallels with *Penthesilea*, 91
   the script, 5, 6, 7, 71–90
   symmetrical structure, 25–6, 26–7
   theoretical influences on, 91–2
   use of quotation, 10–11
   voice-off, 10, 27
Rivette, Jacques, 65
Rose, David, 212
Roussel, Raymond, 10

Said, Edward, 16, 266–7, 270–1, 272–3, 277
Screen (journal), 5, 92
Scripts. *See also* source materials
   23rd August 2008, 6–7, 307–12
   AMY! 6, 25–6, 99–112
   for avant-garde cinema, 4
   Bad Sister, The, 7, 175–207
   Crystal Gazing, 5, 123–50
   Disgraced Monuments, 6–7, 281–96
   film transcripts, 6–7
   Frida Kahlo & Tina Modotti, 5, 6, 157–67
   Friendship's Death, 6, 229–62
   intertitles and visual text, 12, 63, 114, 115
   linguistic devices, 10–11
   Mulvey and Wollen's writing process, 5–17
   narrative devices, 10–12, 26–7, 27
   Penthesilea, 5, 37–60
   politics of language in, 19–20, 21
   production conditions and, 6
   relationship with the films, 7, 12
   Riddles of the Sphinx, 5, 6, 7, 71–90
   as stand-alone documents, 7, 12
   use of quotations, 10, 64, 66
   Wollen's linguistic devices, 10, 20

Shulgina, Tatyana Lvovna, 300, 302
Source materials
   Bad Sister, The, 8–9, 209–11, 213
   Crystal Gazing, 8, 28, 151–2, 153, 154
   Friendship's Death, 9, 219–28, 263, 265
   Mulvey/Wollen collaboration, 7–9, 21–2, 27–9
   myths as, 8–9, 10, 21, 26–7
   Penthesilea, 8–9, 10, 21, 26–7, 61–2, 66, 67, 68
   Statues Also Die (Marker/Resnais), 298, 303
Symmetry, aesthetics of, 25–6

Tennant, Emma, 8–9, 23–4, 209–10, 213–14
Thatcherism, 8, 18, 31, 33, 152, 153, 211, 213
They Flew Alone/Wings and the Woman (Wilcox),
   115–16

Voiceover/voice-off
   in *AMY!* 20, 26, 119, 121, 122
   in *Riddles*, 11, 31

Whannel, Paddy, 21
What 80 Million Women Want (1913), 25
Wollen, Peter. *See also* Mulvey/Wollen collaboration
   in Amman, 263–4
   focus on anti-imperialist prophetic imagination,
      263–5, 273–4
   individual works, 1
   Lucien Rey articles for the *New Left Review*, 13,
      274, 275
   in Mexico, 29
   politics of language in the writing of, 10, 19–20
   scriptwriting, 2–3
   theoretical works, 3, 93
'Was Christ a Collaborator?' (*7 Days*), 264
Wonder Woman images, 50, 66–7, 115